Piety, Fraternity and Power

RELIGIOUS GILDS IN LATE MEDIEVAL YORKSHIRE
1389–1547

The religious gild was central to the structure of late medieval society, providing lay people with a focus for public expressions of orthodox piety that accorded with the doctrinal views of government between 1399 and 1531. Using evidence from the county of Yorkshire, this book argues that beyond their devotional and ceremonial roles, the influence of these basically pious institutions permeated all aspects of late medieval political, social and economic activity.

The author begins by discussing the evidence for Yorkshire gilds in the late fourteenth century, moving on to survey the changing distribution, development and membership of fraternities throughout the county over the next century and a half. Special attention is given to the ways in which the religious gilds of York interacted with the city government, with clerical bodies, with occupational organisations and with one another illustrated with detailed case-studies of the gilds of Corpus Christi, York, and St Mary in Holy Trinity, Hull, which are particularly well-documented. The final section of the book deals with the decline and disappearance of religious gilds during the Reformation, showing how their devotional purposes were eroded by the new policies of central government and how many gilds anticipated their official dissolution.

DAVID J. F. CROUCH is a Research Associate of the Centre for Medieval Studies, University of York.

YORK MEDIEVAL PRESS

York Medieval Press is published by the University of York's Centre for Medieval Studies in association with Boydell & Brewer Ltd. Our objective is the promotion of innovative scholarship and fresh criticism on medieval culture. We have a special commitment to interdisciplinary study, in line with the Centre's belief that the future of Medieval Studies lies in those areas in which its major constituent disciplines at once inform and challenge each other.

Editorial Board (1998–2001):

Prof. W. M. Ormrod (Chair; Dept of History)
Dr P. P. A. Biller (Dept of History)
Dr J. W. Binns (Dept of English & Related Literature)
Dr E. C. Norton (Art History)
Dr N. F. McDonald (Dept of English & Related Literature)
Dr J. D. Richards (Dept of Archaeology)

All inquiries of an editorial kind, including suggestions for monographs and essay collections, should be addressed to: The Director, University of York, Centre for Medieval Studies, The King's Manor, York YO1 7EP (E-mail: lah1@york.ac.uk).

Previous publications in York Studies in Medieval Theology:

Medieval Theology and the Natural Body, ed. Peter Biller and A. J. Minnis (1997)

Handling Sin: Confession in the Middle Ages, ed. Peter Biller and A. J. Minnis (1998)

Other publications of York Medieval Press:

God's Words, Women's Voices: The Discernment of Spirits in the Writing of Late-Medieval Women Visionaries, Rosalynn Voaden (1999)

Pilgrimage Explored, ed. J. Stopford (1999)

Previous publications of The Centre for Medieval Studies:

Latin and Vernacular: Studies in Late-Medieval Texts and Manuscripts, ed. A. J. Minnis (1989) [Proceedings of the 1987 York Manuscripts Conference]

Regionalism in Late-Medieval Manuscripts and Texts: Essays celebrating the publication of 'A Linguistic Atlas of Late Mediaeval English', ed. Felicity Riddy (1991) [Proceedings of the 1989 York Manuscripts Conference]

Late-Medieval Religious Texts and their Transmission: Essays in Honour of A. I. Doyle, ed. A. J. Minnis (1994) [Proceedings of the 1991 York Manuscripts Conference]

Piety
Fraternity and Power

RELIGIOUS GILDS IN
LATE MEDIEVAL YORKSHIRE
1389–1547

David J. F. Crouch

THE UNIVERSITY *of York*

YORK MEDIEVAL PRESS

© David J. F. Crouch 2000

All Rights Reserved. Except as permitted under current legislation
no part of this work may be photocopied, stored in a retrieval system,
published, performed in public, adapted, broadcast,
transmitted, recorded or reproduced in any form or by any means,
without the prior permission of the copyright owner

BX
808.5
.Y67
C76
2000

First published 2000

A York Medieval Press publication
in association with The Boydell Press
an imprint of Boydell & Brewer Ltd
PO Box 9   Woodbridge   Suffolk IP12 3DF   UK
and of Boydell & Brewer Inc.
PO Box 41026   Rochester   NY 14604–4126   USA
website: http://www.boydell.co.uk
and with the
Centre for Medieval Studies, University of York

ISBN 0 9529734 4 8

A catalogue record for this book is available
from the British Library

Library of Congress Cataloging-in-Publication Data
Crouch, David J. F., 1934–
    Piety, fraternity, and power : religious gilds in late Medieval Yorkshire,
1389–1547 / David J.F. Crouch.
        p.   cm.
    Includes bibliographical references and index.
    ISBN 0–9529734–4–8 (alk. paper)
    1. Confraternities – England – Yorkshire – History.   2. Corpus Christi
Gild of York (York, England) – History.   3. Gild of St. Mary Trinity (Hull,
England) – History.   4. Yorkshire (England) – Church history.   5. Yorkshire
(England) – Religious life and customs.   6. Yorkshire (England) – Social
life and customs.   I. Title.
BX808.5.Y67 C76 2000
267'.2424281 – dc21   99–046618

This publication is printed on acid-free paper

Printed in Great Britain by
St Edmundsbury Press Ltd, Bury St Edmunds, Suffolk

CONTENTS

MAPS

TABLES AND GRAPHS

Chapter One: English Gilds in 1389

Chapter Two: Geographical Distribution and Chronological Development in Yorkshire

Chapter Three: The Membership and Activities of Yorkshire Gilds

Chapter Four: Religious Gilds of Medieval York

Chapter Five: Corpus Christi Gild of York

Chapter Six: Gild of St Mary in Holy Trinity

ABBREVIATIONS

BL	London, British Library.
BIHR	York, Borthwick Institute of Historical Research.
Cal. Pat.	*Calendar of Patent Rolls.*
Cal. Close	*Calendar of Close Rolls.*
Certificates	Ed. W. Page, *The Certificates of the Commissioners Appointed to Survey the Chantries, Guilds, Hospitals etc. in the County of York*, 2 vols., Surtees Society 91–2 (1894–95).
FR	Ed. F. Collins, *Register of the Freemen of the City of York*, 2 vols., Surtees Society 96–7 (1897).
HCRO	Beverley, Humberside County Record Office.
KHRO	Kingston upon Hull, Record Office.
PRO	London, Public Record Office.
RCHM York	Royal Commission on Historical Monuments (England), *City of York*. 6 vols. (London, 1972–81).
REED York	A. F. Johnston and M. Rogerson, *Records of Early English Drama: York* (Manchester, 1979).
Sellers, *YMA*	Ed. M. Sellers, *The York Mercers and Merchant Adventurers 1356–1917*, Surtees Society 129 (1918).
Test. Ebor.	*Testamenta Eboracensia*, 6 vols., Surtees Society 4, 30, 45, 53, 79 and 106 (1836–1906).
VCH	Ed. W. Page, *Victoria History of the County of York*, 3 vols. (London, 1907–13)
VCH ER:	Ed. K. J. Allison, *Victoria History of the County of York: East Riding*, 6 vols. (Oxford, 1969–89).
VCH NR:	Ed. W. Page, *Victoria History of the County of York: North Riding*, 2 vols. (London, 1914–23).
VCH York:	Ed. P. M. Tillot, *Victoria History of the County of York: The City of York* (Oxford, 1961).
YAJ	Yorkshire Archaeological Journal.
YAS	Yorkshire Archaeological Society, Record Series.
YCA	York City Archive.
YCR	A. Raine, *York Civic Records*, vols. 1–5 (Yorkshire Archaeological Society Record Series 98, 103, 106, 108, 110 (1939–1946)).
YMA	York, Merchant Adventurers' Hall, Archives of the Company of Merchant Adventurers.
YMB A/Y	Ed. M. Sellers, *York Memorandum Book*, 2 vols., Surtees Society 120, 125 (1912–15).
YMB B/Y	Ed. J. W. Percy, *York Memorandum Book*, Surtees Society 186 (1969).
YML	York, Minster Library.

ACKNOWLEDGEMENTS

I wish to thank all the people who have assisted me in so many ways in researching and writing this book and the thesis on which it is based. In particular, I must acknowledge my debt to Dr Sarah Rees Jones, the supervisor of my thesis, for her patience, wisdom and encouragement. I am also grateful for the supervision I received from Dr Jeremy Goldberg during a long period when Dr Rees Jones was on leave, and for the advice and support offered by Professor Claire Cross, the chairperson of my advisory panel. I am indebted to Professor Mark Ormrod for information on Lincolnshire gilds and for advice on presentation and layout, to Professor Richard Marks for references on glass and iconography, to Louise Wheatley of the Merchant Adventurers' Hall for information on the Holy Trinity Gild, Fossgate, to Dr Eileen White for permission to use her index of York bequests to gilds, to Richard Smith for supplying me with his unpublished list of Yorkshire 1377 Poll Tax values, to John Lunn for material on gilds in Luton and Dunstable and to Anne Rycraft for assistance with occasional problems of palaeography and Latin and Middle English vocabulary. My research was greatly aided by the help and advice offered by David Smith and the staff of the Borthwick Institute of Historical Research, by Bernard Barr and the staff and volunteers of York Minster Library, by Rita Freedman and the staff and volunteers of York City Archive, by Mr Oxley and the staff of Kingston-upon-Hull Record Office and the staffs of other libraries and archives, including the Humberside County Record Office, the City of York Reference Library, the Public Record Office and the British Library. In conclusion, the completion of this work would have been impossible without the forbearance, support and proof-reading skills of my wife Barbara.

INTRODUCTION

An HABERDASSHERE and a CARPENTER,
A WEBBE, a DYERE, and a TAPYCER, –
And they were clothed alle in o lyveree
Of a solempne and a greet fraternitee.
Full fresshe and newe hir geere apiked was;
Hir knyves were chaped noght with bras
But al with silver; wroght ful clene and weel
Hire girdles and her pouches everydeel.
Wel semed ech of hem a fair burgeys
To sitten in a yeldhalle on a deys.
Everich, for the wisdom that he kan,
Was shaply for to been an alderman.
For catel hadde they ynogh and rente,
And eek hir wyves wolde it wel assente;
And elles certeyne were they to blame.
It is ful fair to been ycleped 'madame',
And goon to vigilies al before,
And have a mantel roialliche ybore.[1]

Chaucer's craftsmen, en route to Canterbury, give us a rarely-drawn picture of gild members through contemporary eyes. Their pride in their fraternity is displayed for the world to see in its livery, which they all wear. Their equipment, newly trimmed in silver, displays their wealth and status. These are substantial citizens with ample means, whose political ambitions are reinforced by the social aspirations of their wives. Although they are on a major pilgrimage and are members of a religious gild, Chaucer's description does not hint at the piety which should have been basic to both activities. This should not surprise us. *The Canterbury Tales* is a satirical work, in which many characters, with greater devotional responsibilities, are much more roughly treated. Compared with the venal Friar or the mountebank Pardoner, the gildsmen and their wives are figures of mild fun in their pride, ambition and display of wealth, but their faults are relatively harmless.

This view, contemporary with the gild returns of 1389, is, even allowing for Chaucer's intention to entertain rather than record, an interesting one. Whilst the activities of the five gildsmen do not impose a moral threat to society, they are, nevertheless, by implication, using pious institutions for worldly ends. Their fraternity is seen as a route by which these wealthy craftsmen can realize their

---

[1] Geoffrey Chaucer, *The Canterbury Tales: 'General Prologue'*, ll. 361–78.

1

political ambitions within the urban society in which they live. It is a means by which they can achieve power within their local community.

The developing relationship of religious gilds with secular power, of different kinds and at many levels, in the society of late medieval Yorkshire, will be a major theme of this book.[2] This was a complex and changing phenomenon. Each gild was a unique institution, with its own particular structures and functions, many of which altered throughout the period. They varied in scale from village-based, rural, parish gilds to immensely influential civic fraternities in large centres of population. How far they were subject to the control of local authority, whether of local lords, aristocrats, gentry, ecclesiastics wielding secular power, mayors and corporations, or representatives of the king, and the extent to which membership provided a conduit for influence and promotion with these power bases, will be addressed. This can be done most fully in the case of urban gilds, where the evidence is more plentiful.

Beyond local politics, I hope to show that gilds were also subject to national trends, to the actions of government and to the vicissitudes of dynastic power struggles. At the outset of the period under consideration, they were under parliamentary threat of suppression. Subsequently, it will be demonstrated that they followed the doctrinally orthodox religious policies of the Lancastrian kings. Time and again, however, gild popularity will be shown to have wavered, in Yorkshire, in the face of the political and military crises of internecine conflicts, such as that between York and Lancaster, and to have been re-established in times of stability. Examination of the long-drawn-out process of their final dissolution will involve a discussion of how far their suppression was the result of an inherent inability to adjust to the radical doctrines of the Reformation, imposed by a government that was now out of tune with orthodox beliefs and practices. They will emerge as profoundly conservative institutions, whose political role, within the local area, was to manipulate the current regime rather than to promote innovation. These attitudes were demonstrated and furthered by increasingly elaborate ceremonial, driven by traditional forms of piety.

Not all power, however, is political. Gilds were also economic entities. Their expenditure on feasting and on ceremonial objects, for example, might have contributed to local economies and their methods of generating income, through trade, agriculture or rents, imply that many fraternities wielded considerable economic influence. This topic will lead to an examination of the complicated relationships between religious fraternities and craft or merchant organizations. Questions such as to what extent all gilds were religious, how far craft associations were gilds at all and to what degree rural gilds were agricultural combines will be considered. Most gilds that were substantial enough to have left records were landlords and property-owners, some of them on a very large scale. In a

---

2 This book is based on D. J. F. Crouch, 'Piety, Fraternity and Power: Religious Gilds in Late Medieval Yorkshire 1389–1547' (unpublished D.Phil. Thesis, University of York, 1995). Material from the thesis has also been used in a chapter on Yorkshire gilds in *English Gilds*, ed. Ken Farnhill (in preparation).

number of cases, the only proof of their existence lies in post-Reformation land transactions.[3] Their ownership of land and property will be examined. Basic to these questions is their geographical distribution and the extent to which they were found in economically successful communities.

Gilds were also local employers. Large gilds had professional beadles and offered fees for casual tasks of a ceremonial, secretarial or menial character.[4] Perhaps the most important employees, however, were priests. It will be argued that 'services', commonly found in the West Riding, were types of gild whose principal function was to maintain a priest. The employment of gild chaplains raises the question of the relationship between gilds and ecclesiastical power. A body of laymen employing a priest within the structure of a parish, or of a religious house, implies a conflict of allegiance on the part of the priest himself. As a cleric he was subject to the authority of his bishop but, as the employee of a body that might be closely associated with lay powers, he might also have a special relationship with local government. Although the gild priest's position was technically similar to that of the private chaplain of a magnate, it posed a potential threat to the organization of the parishes within which most religious gilds operated. How far this threat was realized will be considered, especially in the case of York, where relevant evidence survives.

The need of fraternities to employ priests underlines their basis in traditional medieval piety. The fundamental devotional purpose of a gild was the celebration of the cult of its dedication. It will be seen that this was fulfilled in a public and corporate way through its fraternal activities, such as feasting, ceremonial, the maintenance of images and lights and, above all, through common acts of worship, for which a priest, whether fully employed by the gild or paid a fee for the occasion, was essential. The charitable actions that it performed on behalf of its members and, particularly, its conducting of funerals and obits will be shown to have arisen from an acceptance of the orthodox doctrines of purgatory and justification by works. The whole ethos of the religious gild as an institution can be seen as largely supportive of those aspects of the 'official' church which were most vulnerable to the attacks of its critics, including the use of indulgences, the purchase of masses for the dead, the worship of saints and the promotion of elaborate and costly ceremonial.

Much of the research relating to religious gilds has concentrated upon their devotional role. However, doctrine and politics in the Late Middle Ages are so intertwined that it is difficult, and probably profitless, to attempt to disentangle

---

3 E.g. St Michael Gild, Bempton: *Cal. Pat. 1569–1572*, p. 38: gild house granted to Robert Sharp and gild lands to Hugh Counsell and Robert Pistor. St Margaret Gild, Flamborough: *VCH ER*, II, p. 161 quotes let of former property to Stephen Leckenby in 1566 including a cottage called the gild house. PRO E 310/32/192 no. 54. Holy Cross Gild, Sedburgh: *Cal. Pat. 1550–1553*, pp. 97–8: Grant of a Grammar School to Sedburgh: '. . . the messuage called Depmyre in tenure of Brian Huddelston within the parish of Mellyng Lancashire which belonged to the late gild called the Rood Gild in Sedburgh and all other possessions of that gild . . .'.

4 E.g. Corpus Christi, York, see Chapter 5, pp. 191–92.

them. The veneration of images and the doctrine of purgatory, for example, were political as well as doctrinal issues in both the late fourteenth and the mid-sixteenth centuries. Furthermore, whilst the economic activities of gilds were intended to finance their pious objectives, the wealth of the most successful fraternities permitted increasingly lavish displays, which were often used for worldly as well as devotional ends. It seems likely that, in his account of the social and political aspirations of five affluent gildsmen, Chaucer conveyed a basically accurate picture.

Historiography

The place of the religious gild, or fraternity, in late medieval society, has, until very recently, either been ignored or underestimated by most twentieth century historians. The reason for this lies in the nature of the evidence. It seems certain that the vast majority of gild records were deliberately and covertly destroyed, during the lengthy and confused period of their dissolution, by the gilds themselves. Those documents that survived did so because of luck, or particularly effective concealment, or because the gild itself changed its nature at that time. Toulmin Smith's collection of those 1389 gild returns that were written in English, together with abstracts and translations of other documents, published posthumously in 1870 and edited by his daughter, was one of the first books to draw attention to the importance of religious or 'social' fraternities, although Lujo Brentano's introductory essay tells us more about nineteenth century perceptions of social development than about medieval gilds.[5] In this century, H. F. Westlake's *The Parish Gilds of Mediæval England* remains the standard critical work.[6] No major volume had been published, since 1919, that was solely devoted to religious gilds as a general topic, until the publication of Virginia Bainbridge's study of Cambridgeshire gilds in 1996.[7] This important contribution, although focused on one particular geographical area, leads the author to general conclusions on the nature, development and functions of gilds. Whilst the emphasis of her work is on rural fraternities, it is inevitable that gilds in townships such as Cambridge and Wisbech also receive some detailed attention.

Other recent work appearing in learned articles and in books, where gild history is a relevant but not a principal concern, relies heavily on two areas of research. Some historians, like Westlake himself, have made extensive use of the 1389 gild returns.[8] This quarry of detailed information on gilds gives an apparently comprehensive account of late fourteenth century fraternities. However,

---

5 Ed. T. Smith, *English Gilds*, Early English Texts OS 40 (Oxford, 1870).
6 H. F. Westlake, *The Parish Gilds of Mediæval England* (London, 1919). This book will be considered in some detail in Chapter 1.
7 V. R. Bainbridge, *Gilds in the Medieval Countryside: Social and Religious Change in Cambridgeshire c.1350–1558*, Studies in the History of Medieval Religion 10 (Woodbridge, 1996).
8 PRO C 47/46.

the returns are extant for a limited area of the country, principally East Anglia, Lincolnshire and London, giving only a partial picture of gild geography. Furthermore, the circumstances of the survey, and the questions that it asked, coloured some of the responses. Both the nature of the evidence and the interests of Westlake, their principal summarist, place some emphasis on the devotional purposes of gilds. Whilst this was undoubtedly an important aspect of their function, secular factors have often been underestimated.

Other commentators have approached gilds through the perspective of the Reformation. Whilst the contribution of fraternities to late medieval lay piety, in the sixteenth century, was largely ignored until the late 1970s, historians such as Scarisbrick, Bossy, Haigh and Duffy have since recognized their importance and have given them a place in pre-reformation society.[9] However, the reformation context, within which these historians have written, dictates that gilds be seen largely as pious institutions. They concentrate on funerary practices, on the holding of obits and on the maintenance of shrines and images, using them to illustrate a widespread lay acceptance of the doctrine of purgatory and the penitential cycle. Duffy's book, in particular, provides valuable insights into the place of the gild within the parish and into the processes that led to their dissolution. However, the focus of these studies generally is on gilds as the victims of changing government attitudes at the time of their suppression rather than as allies, whether by intent or coincidence, of authority during their heyday.

Miri Rubin's recent book also treats gilds from a particular viewpoint that is mainly devotional.[10] She examines Corpus Christi fraternities as part of her study of the liturgy and development of the cult. Its proliferation was part of a series of trends in eucharistic doctrine which led to the foundation of new gilds and the development of processional ceremonial throughout late medieval Europe. Her analysis of iconography and her descriptions of ritual are of great assistance in interpreting Yorkshire evidence, especially the documentation of the York Corpus Christi Gild. Her purposes, here, do not include the wider social, economic and political dimensions of gilds. However, her recent articles, analysing the political role of elite gilds and of Corpus Christi processions and calling into question the distinction commonly made between urban and rural gilds, are important contributions to current thought in these areas.[11]

Rubin's book also contributes to the large body of literature on the history of

---

[9] J. J. Scarisbrick, *The Reformation and the English People* (Oxford, 1984), J. Bossy, *Christianity in the West* (Oxford, 1985), E. Duffy, *The Stripping of the Altars* (Yale, 1992), C. Haigh, *English Reformations* (Oxford, 1993).

[10] M. Rubin, *Corpus Christi: The Eucharist in Late Medieval Culture* (Cambridge, 1991); M. Rubin, 'Corpus Christi Fraternities and Late Medieval Piety', in *Voluntary Religion*, eds. W. J. Shields and D. Wood, Studies in Church History 23 (Oxford, 1986), pp. 97–109.

[11] M. Rubin, 'Small Groups: Identity and Solidarity in the Late Middle Ages', in *Enterprise and Individuals in Fifteenth-Century England*, ed. J. Kermode (Stroud, 1991), pp. 132–48. M. Rubin, 'Religious Culture in Town and Country: Reflections on a Great Divide', in *Church and City 1000–1500: Essays in honour of Christopher Brooke*, eds. D. Abulafia, M. Franklin and M. Rubin (Cambridge, 1992), pp. 3–22.

drama and civic ceremonial, in which gilds figure. In England, however, much of the surviving evidence in this sphere relates to Corpus Christi plays and the other dramatic activities of mercantile and craft organizations rather than those of religious fraternities. This is particularly true of the northern English cycle plays whose surviving texts have generated a vast quantity of research, both historical and literary, overshadowing the activities of the religious gilds. This uneven survival of sources is directly related to the exemption of occupational associations from dissolution, in the mid-sixteenth century, and the survival of performances of the cycles into the Elizabethan era. Detailed discussion of the York, Beverley and Wakefield cycles is outside the remit of this volume, although passing reference may be made to them.

In contrast to those historians that approach gilds through a study of their devotional functions are those who are interested principally in their social and political roles. A major pioneer in this field is Charles Phythian-Adams, whose work on Coventry is an important contribution to our understanding of religious gilds in an urban context.[12] His account of their contribution to the ceremonial year has provoked an ongoing debate concerning the social and political functions of processions and rituals in this period and, especially, how far civic display involving gilds was an agent of harmony within a community and to what extent it was a vehicle for strife and sedition.[13] Equally influential is his analysis of the close relationship of the Corpus Christi and Holy Trinity Gilds with the town authorities, showing that the latter was, in effect, a manifestation of the local government itself.

This important theme, too, has since been pursued by others. Gervase Rosser's study of medieval Westminster, for example, shows that the gild of the Assumption of the Virgin Mary also acted as a 'surrogate town council'.[14] Emphasizing the social, economic and political aspects of gilds within the parish, he demonstrates that they wielded a powerful influence in local affairs. In other articles, less locally focused, Rosser examines further the relationship between gild and parish, arguing that gild influence frequently crossed parish boundaries, implying that the two institutions could be in opposition to each other.[15] In a more recent article he has continued to pursue the social importance of gilds

---

[12] C. Phythian-Adams, 'Ceremony and the Citizen: The Communal Year at Coventry 1450–1550', in *Crisis and Order in English Towns*, eds. P. Clark and P. Slack (London, 1972), pp. 57–85. C. Phythian-Adams, *Desolation of a City: Coventry and the Urban Crisis of the Late Middle Ages* (Cambridge, 1979).

[13] E.g. M. R. James, 'Ritual, Drama and Social Body in the Late Medieval English Town', *Past and Present* 98 (1983), 3–29. B. R. McRee, 'Unity or Division? The Social Meaning of Guild Ceremony in Urban Communities', in *City and Spectacle in Medieval Europe*, eds. B. A. Hanawalt and K. L. Reyerson (Minneapolis, 1994), pp. 189–207.

[14] G. Rosser, *Medieval Westminster 1200–1540* (Oxford, 1989), pp. 281–93.

[15] G. Rosser, 'Communities of Parish and Guild in the Late Middle Ages', in *Parish, Church and People: Local Studies in Lay Religion 1350–1750*, ed. S. J. Wright (London 1988), pp. 29–55. G. Rosser, 'Parochial Conformity and Voluntary Religion in Late-Medieval England', *Transactions of the Royal Historical Society*, 6th series 1 (1991), 173–89.

through a detailed examination of feasting, demonstrating that gild feasts had both social and eucharistic significance.[16]

As is clear from some of the above examples, much of the secondary literature relating to religious gilds is a mosaic of local studies. The work of antiquarians has been vastly supplemented by learned articles, pamphlets, introductions to printed editions of documents and sections of local and regional histories. Here each historian is examining aspects of medieval life within a particular community. Fraternities are seen as a part of a local picture which is often, in turn, related to the larger canvas of the country as a whole. Such work is vital to our understanding of the nature of gilds and their importance in wider context. This work is intended to contribute to this literature through a study of the gilds of the largest English county.

Historians of other regions, or who have worked on localities within Yorkshire, including those who address themes that are tangential to gild history, have, through their writing, provided ideas and material that have been of great assistance. Whilst it would be impossible to catalogue all of them in this introduction, it is appropriate to mention just a few of those whose ideas and information have proved particularly useful. Peter Heath's article on Hull, for example, provided a useful starting point for an examination of Yorkshire gilds through testamentary evidence, reinforced by Clive Burgess's use of wills in his studies of Bristol parishes.[17] Burgess's work on chantries and anniversaries has also formed vital context for Barrie Dobson's articles on chantries in York and to interpretations of the Yorkshire chantry certificates by Kitching and Rosenthal, all of which were of great value in assessing the relationship of gilds to chantries in the county.[18] Vital to my chapter on York has been Heather Swanson's studies of

---

[16] G. Rosser, 'Going to the Fraternity Feast: Commensiality and Social Relations in Late Medieval England', *Journal of British Studies* 33 (October 1994), 430–46.

[17] P. Heath, 'Urban Piety in the later Middle Ages: the Evidence of Hull Wills', in *The Church, Politics and Patronage in the Fifteenth Century*, ed. B. Dobson (Gloucester, 1984). C. Burgess, ' "By Quick and by Dead": wills and pious provision in medieval Bristol', *English Historical Review* 102 (1987), 56–84. C. Burgess, 'Late Medieval Wills and Pious Convention: Testamentary Evidence Reconsidered', in *Profit, Piety and the Professions in Later Medieval England*, ed. M. Hicks (Gloucester, 1990), pp. 14–33.

[18] C. Burgess, ' "For the Increase of Divine Service": Chantries in the Parish in Late Medieval Bristol' *Journal of Ecclesiastical History* 36:1 (January 1985), 46–65. C. Burgess, 'A Service for the Dead: The Form and Function of the Anniversary in Late Medieval Bristol', *Transactions of the Bristol and Gloucestershire Archaeological Society* 105 (1987), 183–211. C. Burgess, ' "A fond thing vainly invented": an essay on Purgatory and pious motive in later medieval England', in *Parish, Church and People: Local Studies in Lay Religion 1350–1750*, ed. S. J. Wright (London, 1988), pp. 56–84. C. Burgess and B. Kumin, 'Penitential Bequests and Parish Regimes in Late Medieval England', *Journal of Ecclesiastical History* 44 (October 1993), 610–30. R. B. Dobson, 'The Foundation of Perpetual Chantries by the Citizens of Medieval York', in *The Province of York*, Studies in Church History 4 (Leiden, 1967), pp. 22–38. R. B. Dobson, 'Citizens and Chantries in Late Medieval York', in *Church and City 1000–1500: Essays in honour of Christopher Brooke*, ed. D. Abulafia, M. Franklin, M. Rubin (Cambridge, 1992), pp. 3–22. C. J. Kitching, 'The Chantries of the East Riding of Yorkshire at the Dissolution in 1548', *YAJ* 44 (Wakefield,

medieval artisans and their relationship with the city government, and Jeremy Goldberg's work, especially his recent book which, although written from the perspective of women's history, was essential to my understanding of the world of work in general in late medieval York and Yorkshire.[19] These were of great value, especially in stimulating my analysis of the overlapping functions of gilds and craft associations. Important background to the dissolution of the gilds in Yorkshire included work by Claire Cross and David Palliser.[20] Useful comparative material from other areas included Caroline Barron's article on London gilds, Dorothy Owen's work on medieval Lincolnshire and King's Lynn and N. P. Tanner's study of Norwich.[21] Recent work specifically devoted to religious gilds in Yorkshire is, however, with the exception of Eileen White's pamphlet, extremely sparse, and any thesis that deals with them must inevitably rely principally on primary sources.[22]

Sources

The primary sources used in this volume fall into three main categories: national records, local gild and civic documents and testamentary evidence. Parish records are not included in these classifications because there are almost none surviving in Yorkshire for this period. Most of the sources that are briefly described here are analysed in more detail at relevant points in the book.

National records concerning gilds are, on the face of it, unsatisfactory for this county. Only thirteen returns are extant from the survey of 1389 and only a

1972) 178–194. J. T. Rosenthal, 'The Yorkshire Chantry Certificates of 1546: An Analysis', *Northern History* 9 (1974), 26–47.

[19] H. Swanson, 'The Illusion of Economic Structure: Craft Guilds in Late Medieval English Towns, *Past and Present* 121 (November 1988), 29–48. H. Swanson, *Medieval Artisans* (Oxford, 1989). P. J. P. Goldberg, *Women, Work and Life Cycle in a Medieval Economy: Women in York and Yorkshire c.1300–1520* (Oxford, 1992).

[20] M. C. Cross, 'The Economic Problems of the See of York: Decline and Recovery in the Sixteenth Century' in *Land Church and People*, ed. J. Thirsk, British Agricultural History Society 18 Supplement (Reading, 1970), pp. 64–83; M. C. Cross, 'Parochial Structure and the Dissemination of Protestantism in Sixteenth Century England: A Tale of Two Cities', in *The Church in Town and Countryside*, Studies in Church History 16, ed. D. Baker (Oxford, 1979), pp. 269–78. D. M. Palliser, *The Reformation in York 1534–1553*, Borthwick Paper 40 (York, 1971); D. M. Palliser, *Tudor York* (Oxford, 1979).

[21] C. M. Barron, 'The Parish Fraternities of Medieval London', in *The Church in Pre-Reformation Society*, ed. C. M. Barron and C. Harper-Bill (Woodbridge, 1985), pp. 13–37. D. M. Owen, *Church and Society in Medieval Lincolnshire*, History of Lincolnshire 5 (Lincoln, 1981, repr. 1990); D. M. Owen, *The Making of King's Lynn: a Documentary Survey*, The British Academy, Records of Social and Economic History NS 9 (London, 1984). N. P. Tanner, 'The Reformation and Regionalism: Further Reflections on the Church in Late Medieval Norwich', in *Towns and People in the Fifteenth Century*, ed. J. A. F. Thomson (Gloucester, 1988) pp. 129–47. Bainbridge, *Gilds in the Medieval Countryside*, was published after the submission of the thesis on which the present work was based but has been used in its revision for publication.

[22] E. White, *The St Christopher and St George Guild of York*, Borthwick Paper 72 (York, 1987).

handful of institutions were described as gilds in the commissioners' certificates of 1546 and 1548.[23] However, the surviving county writs for the 1389 returns provide useful information and the extant returns are, individually, often very informative.[24] Furthermore, a close examination of the commissioners' certificates reveals that more gilds survived to the eve of the Reformation than appears to be the case from first impressions.[25]

Gild documents survive only in the larger centres of population. The best recorded fraternity is probably the Corpus Christi Gild of York, whose extant documentation includes a complete membership book and a broken series of account rolls.[26] There is also a body of information concerning the Holy Trinity Gild in Fossgate, York, which was related to the mistery of mercers in the city.[27] Civic records contain many passing references to York gilds as well as the ordinances of a large number of crafts. Beverley records, too, contain gild references and the ordinances of a few gilds and many craft organizations are written into its 'Great Gild Book'.[28] In Hull, besides the town records, there are extant accounts of the gilds of Holy Trinity and of St Mary, both in the parish of Holy Trinity, the latter comprising an uninterrupted sequence covering the period 1463–1536, and a small rental book of the Corpus Christi Gild.[29] The choice of Corpus Christi, York, and St Mary in Holy Trinity, Hull, as gilds on which to base special case studies, was made taking into consideration the availability and quality of the sources and the absence of recent research.

Clearly, national and local gild records were unable to offer a general picture of gilds in late medieval Yorkshire. Some indication of their spread throughout the country and of changes over the 150 years of the period can, however, be gleaned from the wills of those individuals who made bequests to them and were, therefore, almost certainly members. This survey of wills was a large undertaking. I am grateful for permission to use an index, compiled by Eileen White, of bequests made in York to York gilds.[30] Whilst it may not be wholly complete, omitting, as it does, some suburban bequests, it enabled me to find and read the majority of wills relating to gilds within the city. The huge quantity of wills made, over the period, in the rest of the county, could only be sampled in the time available to me. The sources of the sample were limited to wills recorded

---

23 PRO C 47/46/444–455.

24 PRO C 47/46/482 28, 30.

25 PRO E 301 65–69.

26 London, British Library, MS Lansdowne 304, YCA G C99:1–8, C100:1–6, C101:1–4, C102:1–3, C103:1–2.

27 D. M. Smith, *A Guide to the Archives of the Company of Merchant Adventurers of York*, Borthwick Texts and Calendars 16 (York, 1990), lists the gild records, which are housed in the Merchant Adventurers' Hall York.

28 Ed. A. F. Leach, *Beverley Town Documents*, Selden Society 14 (1900). HCRO BC II3.

29 D. Woodward, 'The Accounts of the Building of Trinity House, Hull, 1465–1476', *YAJ* 62 (Leeds, 1990), 153–70. A. J. Mill, 'The Hull Noah Play', *Modern Language Review* 33 (October 1938), 489–505. KHRO BRA 87/8, BRA 88.

30 The MS index is lodged in the BIHR.

in the probate registers of the Diocesan Exchequer Court, the Dean and Chapter's Court and the archbishops' registers, making use of the standard will indices.[31] The total number of available wills relating to the historic county of Yorkshire, excluding York, for this period from these sources is approximately fifteen thousand. The method of sampling chosen, of four years in every twelve throughout the period, yielded a total of 5,261 wills read. This total also included all extant fourteenth century wills and those for 1547, the year of dissolution. The actual dates of all the sample periods are shown in Figure 2.1. Wills from peculiar jurisdictions in the county were investigated only through such printed sources as were available.[32] They yielded little information. A much more useful exercise was an analysis of printed Lincolnshire wills, which was undertaken for comparative purposes.[33] The limitations of testamentary evidence are discussed elsewhere but the task enabled the locations of known gilds to be mapped and the existence of what were, clearly, large and important fraternities, such as the Corpus Christi Gild of Pontefract and the St Mary Gild of Swine, to be recognized.[34] It also allowed a number of the more affluent gild members to be identified.

All these sources provide a body of evidence for gilds in Yorkshire, the bulk of which is too great to be cited within the argument of this work. The gilds that have been identified are listed in Appendix 1, in alphabetical order according to the location in which they were found, together with an indication of the nature of the evidence for their existence. Space does not permit the inclusion of a detailed listing of all the references to every gild. This information can, however, be found in the gazetteer to the thesis on which this work is based.[35]

The structure of this volume itself has been, to some degree, dictated by the nature of the sources. The starting point of 1389 was chosen, not only because the gild survey provides an impression of the spread of fraternities in the county, but also because there is little testamentary or other evidence relating to gilds in Yorkshire before this date. The sample of county wills offers a broad general impression of gild history over the next century and a half, permitting an analysis of trends and geographical variations in both the distribution of gilds and of their memberships. The York material offers the opportunity of examining the functions of gilds in more depth, in a specific urban context. The two case

---

31 F. Collins, *Index of Wills in the York Registry 1389–1514*, YAS 6 (1889). F. Collins, *Index of Wills in the York Registry 1514–1553*, YAS 11 (1891). F. Collins, *Index of Wills etc. from the Dean and Chapter's Court at York 1321–1636*, YAS 38 (1907). J. Charlesworth and A. V. Hudson, *Index of Wills and Administrations entered in the Registers of the Archbishops at York: The Archbishops' Wills*, YAS 93 (1937).

32 Ed. E. J. Raine, *Wills and Inventories from the Registry of the Archdeaconry of Richmond*, Surtees Society 26 (1853), ed. F. Collins, *Wills and Administrations from the Knaresborough Court Rolls*, Surtees Society 104 (1902).

33 Ed. C. W. Foster, *Lincoln Wills*, The Lincoln Record Society, 3 vols. (1914–1930).

34 The limitations of testamentary evidence are discussed in Chapter 2, pp. 46–50.

35 Crouch, 'Piety, Fraternity and Power', pp. 412–510.

studies, based on particular collections of documents, are used to illustrate and reinforce general impressions by studying two gilds in greater detail. The final chapter is not solely an account of the dissolution of the gilds. The process itself, through its documentation, reveals much about the nature of gilds themselves against a background of doctrinal and political change.

CHAPTER ONE

English Gilds in 1389

In 1388, the Cambridge Parliament of Richard II's government viewed gilds with such suspicion that it contemplated the suppression of large numbers of them. It also believed that they were so wealthy that their confiscated funds could finance the king's French wars.[1] These suspicions and beliefs clearly show that the government at this time saw gilds as important political and economic entities whose purposes were not necessarily compatible with their own. The survey that was conducted during the following year produced a series of returns that provide a benchmark against which to measure the subsequent development of gilds. An examination of the context of the survey, including the motives of the petitioners to the Cambridge Parliament in initiating it and those of the king in implementing it, will help to explain how the gilds were seen by the authorities. The mechanisms by which information was elicited from the gilds, the questions that the gild officers were asked and the manner of their replies are also essential background to an understanding of their relationships with authority.

The surviving returns paint a picture of a common purpose but wide variation in practice and organization, over a large range of fraternities of differing sizes and in a variety of environments, at a fixed point in time. Using a general examination of the material as a basis, the chapter will go on to explore the nature and function of religious gilds in England, during the second half of the fourteenth century. In particular, a more detailed assessment of the returns from Yorkshire will form a useful background to themes to be pursued in subsequent chapters. A general analysis of the material will also be used to address the question of how far gilds were proliferating during the late fourteenth century, providing a starting point for the study of their distribution and development which will be undertaken in Chapter 2.

The Context of the 1389 Gild Returns

The returns were called for as a result of a petition to the Cambridge Parliament of 10 September to 17 October 1388. It proposed that almost all gilds and fraternities be suppressed. The motivation for the petition was ostensibly financial. The

---

[1] J. A. Tuck, 'The Cambridge Parliament, 1388', *English Historical Review* 231 (1969), 225–43 (pp. 236–8), provides the basis for this discussion.

Commons asked that the possessions of the dissolved gilds be sold to finance the war in France. This was clearly an attractive proposition for Richard II, or rather for the Lords Appellant under whose control he was at this time, and a device to reduce the burden of taxation upon those whose interests were represented in the Commons. There is no doubt that gilds were perceived as wealthy institutions that might be expected to provide the crown with a considerable sum. That many such fraternities were, indeed, affluent institutions was further recognized in 1391, when Parliament made them subject to mortmain legislation.[2] The proposal was made against a background of agitation and parliamentary lobbying by Lollards in favour of a general disendowment of the institutions of the Church.[3] Whilst the possessions of gilds do not seem to have been directly attacked by this, ultimately unsuccessful, reforming movement, its attitudes may have been part of the motivation for the initiative.

Other purposes, however, lay behind the proposal. These are evident in part of its wording. The Commons did not wish to suppress all gilds. Their proposal included certain significant exceptions. In addition to excluding 'ancient chantries' from the general dissolution, it also excepted 'other things ordained to the honour of Holy Church and the increase of divine service without livery, confederacy, maintenance or riots in breach of the law'.[4] The wording of this exclusion reveals that the Commons saw certain gilds and fraternities as possible focuses for sedition and public unrest. The land-owning representatives were still influenced by the events of the Peasants' Revolt, seven years previously, and by its violent aftermath in certain areas of the country. Although there is a view that gilds were institutions that promoted harmony in society, Parliament clearly took a contrary position.[5] This perception may have had some justification.

It has been suggested that parish gilds, at this time, might have been used to foment action against local lords, both lay and spiritual.[6] In a near-contemporary case, the Holy Trinity Gild of York was accused, before Chancery, of occupying a tenement in the city by force of arms.[7] Gilds also could be used for more subtle political purposes, later exemplified by the involvement of the Duke of Suffolk in the processions of the St George Gild in Norwich during the 1430s.[8] Abroad, gilds were sometimes involved in political violence of an extreme kind.[9] Two

2   *Statutes of the Realm*, 11 vols. (London, 1810–24), II, p. 80.
3   M. Aston, ' "Caim's Castles" ': Poverty, Politics and Disendowment', in *The Church, Politics and Patronage in the Fifteenth Century*, ed. B. Dobson (Gloucester, 1984), pp. 49–54.
4   . . . *autres choses ordenez al honour de sient esglise et encres de divine service sanz liverie, confederacie, meintenaunce, ou riotes en arrerissement du ley*. Quoted in Tuck, 'The Cambridge Parliament', p. 237.
5   E.g. James, 'Ritual, Drama and the Social Body', p. 10.
6   M. M. Postan, *The Medieval Economy and Society* (London, 1972), p. 120. Bainbridge, *Gilds in the Medieval Countryside*, p. 130.
7   W. Baildon, *Select Cases in Chancery*, Selden Society 10 (London, 1896), pp. 75–6, case 79, *circa* 1396.
8   McRee, 'Unity or Division?', pp. 198–9.
9   G. Brucker, *The Society of Renaissance Florence: A Documentary Study* (New York, 1971), pp.

recently-formed fraternities were suppressed in Florence, in 1382, for supporting the Ghibellines against the Guelfs in street battles. In 1419, the Florentine city priors dissolved all confraternities for their scandals and divisions, confiscating their property and permitting only those that they had newly licensed to survive, although the ban did not prove to be permanent. It is, therefore, understandable that, in England, there was a history of a royal suspicion of unchartered gilds. An inquiry by Henry II, in 1179, had found eighteen illegal gilds in London and, in 1306, Edward I had suppressed a Holy Trinity Gild in York that had been established without royal charter.[10] Furthermore, recent research suggests that the timing of central events of the Peasants Revolt, on Corpus Christi Day, 1381, was directly related to feasts and processions in which the gilds were involved and which offered an ideal opportunity for insurrection.[11]

The petition was expressing the Commons' fears against a background of royal disquiet. However, the Lords Appellant, in their domination of the Cambridge Parliament, may have had more mistrust of gilds than the king himself, whose traditional piety was well known and who issued letters patent to the St Christopher Gild of York on his visit to the city in 1396.[12] There seems to have been a change of attitude by government towards gilds after the defeat of the Oldcastle revolt, culminating in a measure taken by Henry VI's administration, in 1436, confirming that local authorities must license all new gilds whose ordinances were 'reasonable'.[13]

The petition's provision excepting gilds of ancient foundation from dissolution was probably not entirely a matter of reverence for traditional and hallowed institutions. There must also have been anxiety on the part of burgesses, who would wish to ensure that grants of gild merchant, enshrining the freedoms of their boroughs, were not threatened. Similar concerns were also reflected in the subsequent decision of the crown to issue a separate writ, calling for returns from occupational gilds. The suppression of officially recognized craft organizations would be detrimental to the economic survival and prosperity of cities and boroughs. The charter granted by Henry II to the York weavers, for example, granted them the exclusive right of making dyed and striped cloth throughout most of Yorkshire.[14] The city would be anxious to retain such privileges.

The Commons' initiative was directed at fraternities of recent foundation.

78–81, 83–4. R. F. E. Weissman, *Ritual Brotherhood in Renaissance Florence* (New York, 1982), pp. 165–6.

[10] N. Fryde, 'Gilds in England Before the Black Death', *Vorträge und Forschungen* 29 (1985), 215–29 (p. 223). G. O. Sayles, 'The Dissolution of a Gild at York in 1306', *English Historical Review* 55 (1940), 83–97.

[11] M. Aston, 'Corpus Christi and *Corpus Regni*: Heresy and the Peasants' Revolt', *Past and Present* 143 (May 1994), 3–47 (pp. 3–13).

[12] N. Saul, 'Richard II and the City of York', in *The Government of Medieval York – Essays in commemoration of the 1396 Royal Charter*, ed. S. Rees Jones, Borthwick Studies in History 3 (York, 1997), pp. 1–13 (p. 11). White, *The St Christopher and St George Guild of York*, p. 2.

[13] *Statutes of the Realm*, II, pp. 298–9. See below p. 44.

[14] *YMB A/Y*, I, pp. xxvii, 240.

This suggests that they thought that there had been a proliferation of gilds in recent years, and that some of the new fraternities were potential agents of sedition. An organization that allowed groups to assemble, to wear liveries and to threaten the king's peace by holding processions and meetings, which could easily become riots, was a threat to local authority. A newly-formed gild might even have been instituted by persons involved in the recent troubles. The Cambridge Parliament was clearly unhappy about the level of social unrest in general terms. Other petitions to the Parliament demanded the abolition of all recent liveries and for powers to prevent maintenance and the intimidation of juries.[15] Against this background, the move against gilds can be seen as a series of measures promoting law and order and, at the same time, offering the crown a financial opportunity. The government lost no time in investigating the gilds in the light of this petition.

The Yorkshire Writs[16]

Writs were sent to sheriffs on 1 November 1388, commanding that they issue proclamations instructing gild officers to make returns by the Feast of the Purification of the Virgin in the following February. The Sheriffs of London were to make public proclamation in the city and suburbs. The sheriffs of all shires were to do the same in the full shire moot and in all cities, boroughs, market towns and other places within their bailiwicks, ordering all gild officials to make full written returns by the appointed date.

The information that was required was comprehensive and the instructions were precise. The masters and wardens of all gilds and brotherhoods were to report on the circumstances of the foundation of their fraternities, presumably to discover if they were recent or not. They were to supply information concerning the gilds' oaths, meetings, feasts and practices of all kinds. Their privileges, ordinances and customs were to be described. This would provide information as to the nature of the gild, perhaps to enable the government to assess whether it constituted a threat to law and order. All the gilds' lands and property, whether held in mortmain or not, and all their other possessions were to be listed and their annual value assessed and stated. Persons who held gild property or real estate were to be identified in order to help the authorities to estimate whether a significant financial return would result from the dissolution. In a general catch-all provision, all other matters concerning each gild were to be revealed. All these questions were to be answered fully. The failure of any gild to comply with these instructions would lead to the withdrawal of any charters and letters patent and the sequestration of all its property.

A separate series of writs required the wardens and searchers of all misteries

---

[15] Tuck, 'The Cambridge Parliament', pp. 234–35.
[16] PRO C 47/46/482. Smith, *English Gilds*, pp. 127–31.

and crafts to produce charters and letters patent by the octave of St Hilary (20 January). This shows that a clear distinction was being made, by the government, between craft organizations and the rest. It also implies that the only occupational bodies recognized by the government were those in possession of charters or letters patent. Misteries and crafts failing to reply were threatened with the annulment of their royal charters and privileges. Significantly, there was no provision for penalizing unchartered misteries, which were probably regarded as illegal. Opposition by previous administrations to the unauthorized foundation of craft gilds supports this impression. The bailiffs of Norwich, for example, evidently felt that the king's authority was threatened by the formation of prohibited gilds of tanners, shoemakers, fullers and saddlers in the late thirteenth century.[17] The earlier date of return required of occupational bodies might suggest that fewer replies were expected from them.

The sheriffs executed the writs by organizing proclamations at strategic places in their territories. Some of the surviving writs are indorsed with a description of the way in which this was carried out. In London, for example, Sheriffs Karlille and Austyn reported that the proclamation had been made, on 4 January, in Fleet Street, Westcheap, Cornhill, Bridge Street, the Vintry and Southwark by William Averey, clerk, and William Popiltone, sergeant.[18] The process was inevitably more complicated in Worcestershire where, to deal with the greater distances involved, the process began on 12 December and lasted until Christmas Eve. Five officials made proclamation in nine towns as well as the shire moot.[19]

The writ sent to John Godard, sheriff of Yorkshire, although very faded in places, seems to be identical to that received by the sheriffs of London, apart from the address.[20] On its dorse, written in a minuscule hand, are recorded the dates and locations of the reading of the proclamation throughout the county, giving the names of the persons entrusted with the task. Here the process was even more complicated, reflecting the administrative difficulties involved in covering the largest county in the land.[21] The indorsement begins with a brief preamble in which John Godard stated that public proclamation had been made in all the cities, boroughs, towns and other places within his bailiwick to the effect that each and every master and keeper of gilds and fraternities must carry out the wishes of the king and his council. The replies, in the form commanded, were to reach Chancery by the Feast of the Purification of the Virgin. There then follows the timetable of the proclamations, which is reproduced in tabular form in Figure 1.1.

---

[17] W. Hudson, *Leet Jurisdiction in the City of Norwich during the Thirteenth and Fourteenth Centuries*, Selden Society 5 (London, 1822), pp. 13, 42–3.

[18] Smith, *English Gilds*, p. 129.

[19] *Ibid.*, p. 131.

[20] PRO C 47/46/482 28, Smith, *English Gilds*, p. 127.

[21] *Ibid.*, p. 129.

Figure 1.1: Proclamations of the Writ for the 1389 Gild Returns in Yorkshire

Based on the reply made by Sheriff John Godard of York on the dorse of the writ and attached copy: PRO C 47/46/482 28 and 30, but also including the wapentakes, poll tax populations and the presence of gilds in the places of proclamation.

Date	Location	Wapentake	Proclaimed by	Population	Gild Date
Tue. 15	York	County	John de Hamerton and		
Dec. 1388			John de Otryngton	7248	1306
(Tue.					
following					
St Lucy)					
Thu. 17	Otley WR	Skyrack	William de Craven	68	1518
Dec. 1388	Wetherby WR	Claro	Thomas Chaloner	90	none
(Thu.	Ripon WR	Liberty	William de Cawod	280	1379
following)					
Fri. 18	Sherburn in Elmet WR	Barkston Ash	Robert Warde	170	1484
Dec. 1388	Wakefield WR	Agbrigg	Ralph Yong	482	1521
(Fri.	Hull ER	Borough	Thomas de Wandefford	1557	1358
following)					
Sun. 20	Beverley ER	Borough	John Voynour	2663	1355
Dec. 1388	Doncaster WR	Strafforth	Robert Kyng	800	1398
(Sun.	Pontefract WR	Osgoldcross	Richard Talcok	1085	1387
following)	Pocklington ER	Harthill	Robert de Fenton	341	1396
	Kilham ER	Dickering	William Stabler	368	1493
	Hornsea ER	Holderness	John de Kyrkby	535	1504
	Malton NR	Ryedale	Edmund Tanner	354	1399
	Skipton WR	Staincliffe	Alan Catterall	176	1548
	Stokesley NR	Langbargh	Richard de Preston	nr	none
	Allerton NR	Liberty	John Halbarne	312	1485
	Richmond NR	Gilling West	William Wawayne	568	1446
	Helmsley NR	Ryedale	Edmund Tanner	348	1461
	Howden ER	Liberty	Stephen Cecill	407	1549
Mon. 21	Thirsk NR	Birdforth	William Stedeman	nr	1431
Dec. 1388	Rotherham WR	Strafforth	Robert Kyng	321	1356
(Mon. in	Leeds WR	Skyrack	William de Craven	160	1515
St Thomas	Selby WR	Barkston Ash	Robert Warde	586	1441
Apostle)	Guisborough NR	Langbargh	Richard de Preston	nr	1478
	Settle WR	Staincliffe	Alan Catterall	87	none
	South Cave ER	Harthill	Robert de Fenton	19	none
	Pickering NR	Liberty	John de Rouceby	420	1496
Tue. 22	Scarborough NR	Borough	William de Stapilton	2873	1349
Dec. 1388	Whitby NR	Liberty	John Gower	640	1349

Date	Location	Wapentake	Proclaimed by	Population	Gild Date
(Tue.	Hedon ER	Holderness	William de Lyndewod	482	1392
following)	Easingwold NR	Bulmer	Robert Grymshagh	206	1430
	Sherburn ER	Buckrose	Thomas Foxholes	133	1505

Wapentake: wapentake, liberty, or borough etc.
Population: poll tax population in 1377. Figures in brackets taken from poll tax values of 1379 or 1381. nr: no return.
Gild Date: earliest known date of a recorded gild in the location.

On Tuesday 5 and Wednesday 6 January 1389 (Tuesday before Epiphany and days following) the proclamation was repeated in the County of York by John Whitburn.

Wednesday 20 January 1389 (Octave of St Hilary) was the deadline for occupational returns to reach Chancery.

Tuesday 2 February 1389 (Purification) was the deadline for other returns to reach Chancery.

Analysis of the locations mentioned in the timetable suggests that it was largely based on the normal administrative structure of wapentakes, boroughs and liberties. However, seven of the county's wapentakes were not covered. If we assume that the Ainsty was included in the York proclamations and that that in Richmond took in Gilling East as well as Gilling West, the wapentakes of Halikeld and Hang, in the North Riding, and of Morley, Staincross and Tickhill in the West were not visited by the sheriff's agents. By contrast the proclamations were made in two centres in each of Holderness, Harthill and Langbargh.

Below the timetable, across the bottom of the parchment, written in a series of highly contracted figures, is a list of Yorkshire wapentakes and liberties.

Ebor, Hull, Staincliffe, Claro, Skyrack, Beverley, Holderness, Hang, Whitby, Harthill, Scarborough, Howden, Birdforth, Pickering, Allerton, Richmond, Tickhill, Gilling, Osgoldcross, Langbargh, Bulmer, Buckrose, Strafforth, Ripon, Morley.

It is far from being a complete list, although it includes three of the wapentakes missing from the timetable: Hang, Morley and Tickhill. Whilst its purpose remains a mystery, a tentative suggestion might be that it was a check-list of some kind, perhaps for the use of John Whitburn, who made a second series of proclamations in January 1389, or possibly to aid Sheriff Godard in collating the returns. On the dorse of a second copy of the writ is the same timetable, word for word, with one minor exception, but neither the preamble nor the list of wapentakes is present.[22] Toulmin Smith implies that this second writ applies to craft gilds in the county but this does not seem to be the case.[23] Such a writ for Yorkshire was not found.

---

[22] PRO C 47/46/482 30.
[23] Smith, *English Gilds*, p. 132.

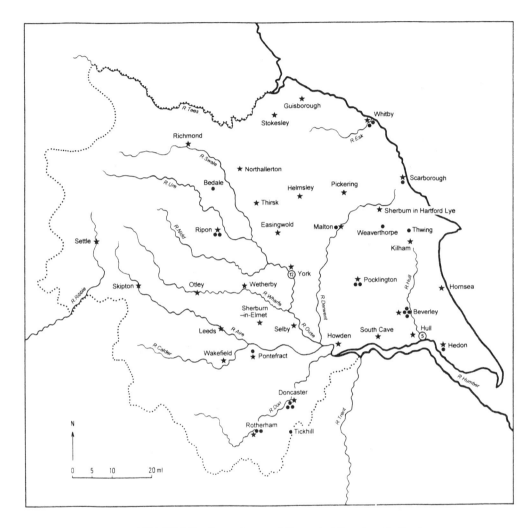

Map 1: 1389 Gild Proclamations and Recorded Fourteenth Century
Gilds in Yorkshire

Each small black disk indicates the presence of a gild recorded before 1400 within
the named location. Places where more than four gilds were recorded before this
date are indicated by a larger disk with a number indicating the number of gilds
found there.
Each star indicates a place where the gild return was proclaimed.

The system used by the sheriff of proclaiming the writ in most, but not all, of the county's administrative units ensured that a majority of the larger centres of population were included. Only three locations with a poll tax population of over 400 in 1377, Kirkbymoorside, Sheffield and Tickhill, were not visited by his officers.[24] Of these, Kirkbymoorside was the only large location in the county where no evidence for gilds was found.[25] There is, however, testamentary evidence for the existence of a gild of the Assumption in Tickhill as early as 1395, only six years after the return was made.[26] Using many of the county's administrative centres also had the effect of including, on the timetable, a number of places with very small poll tax populations. Wetherby, with ninety, Settle, with eighty seven, and South Cave with only nineteen all fall into this category. A glance at Map 1, however, demonstrates that the sheriff, in his choice of locations for publishing the writ, attempted to ensure that most of the well-populated areas of the county were covered.

Evidence of gilds in fourteenth century Yorkshire is not plentiful. Only forty recorded bequests were made to fraternities in the county, including York, before 1400.[27] Furthermore, only thirteen gilds were named in the return, most of which do not appear in testamentary evidence. However, the majority of the forty fourteenth century gilds that were identified in the county were found in locations where the proclamation was read. The only exceptions were those in Bedale, Thwing, Weaverthorpe and Tickhill. At least twelve of the locations to which Godard's emissaries were being dispatched were places where gilds are known to have been active. It seems likely that he was aware that gilds were flourishing in these places. According to the preamble to his indorsement of the writ, the returns were to be made by the masters and stewards of the gilds and fraternities.[28] The inference is that most major population centres sustained gilds at this time. That they also existed in four towns where the writ was not read but which made returns, and in other places, where bequests to gilds were made, implies that they also flourished, unrecorded, elsewhere.

The proclamations were made over a period of eight days between 15 and 22 December. It was evidently thought wise to complete them before Christmas. There is no particular geographical pattern to the days on which each was made. The proclamation was made in York on the first day, probably in a number of locations, as the city was the only place to have two officials assigned to read the writ. The timetable was arranged in such a way as to provide travelling time for those officials who proclaimed in more than one place. Thus, William de Craven

---

[24] I am grateful to Richard Smith for the use of his unpublished list of 1377 poll tax values in Yorkshire.

[25] See below, Chapter 2, p. 54.

[26] BIHR PR 1 93v–94r 1395 John de Derfeld, vicar of Darfield.

[27] See below, Figure 2.1. That there were forty bequests made to gilds and forty gilds identified in fourteenth century Yorkshire is coincidental.

[28] *Magistri & Custodes Gildaii & fraternitati.*

was in Otley on the 17th and in Leeds on the 21st, Richard de Preston in Stokesley on the 20th and in Guisborough on the 21st, Robert de Fenton in Pocklington on the 20th and in South Cave on the 21st, Alan Catterall in Skipton on the 20th and in Settle on the 21st and Robert Kyng in Rotherham on the 21st and in Doncaster on the 22nd. Edmund Tanner managed to proclaim in Helmsley and Malton on the same day.

That some of the agents were assigned two locations, which were, in each case, relatively close to one other, suggests that Sheriff Godard chose local men. What we know of a few of them seems to bear this out. John de Hamerton, who read the writ in York, was described as a clerk in a lawsuit of 1388.[29] He was probably the John Hamerton who appears as the son of Alan de Hamerton, merchant, who was city chamberlain in 1405, in the latter's will.[30] His companion, John de Otryngton, was a lawyer who was made free as a serjeant in 1363 and may have been a son of William de Ottrington, another merchant, who was chamberlain in 1355 and bailiff in 1360–1.[31] William de Stapilton of Scarborough was a burgess and a former bailiff of the town. That he may have been remiss in levying a fine from a fellow burgess in 1385 did not prevent him from being employed by the sheriff on this occasion.[32] William Wawayne, who proclaimed in Richmond, was a commissioner of oyer and terminer there in 1386.[33] John de Kyrkby, who read the writ in Hornsea, was active in the South East of the county. He figured in a legal dispute with John de Cotyngham of Beverley in 1385.[34] Master William de Cawod, clerk, who proclaimed in Ripon, was also involved in contemporary lawsuits.[35] He cannot, however, be placed geographically and it is not known whether he was a local man. Robert Warde, who did so in Sherburn in Elmet and Selby, was possibly a York merchant. A man of that name was recorded as trading between Hull and Prussia, during legal proceedings that took place in 1388.[36] If Godard's agent was not some other Robert Warde, he was a clear exception to the practice of employing men with local contacts for this purpose. Unfortunately the other nineteen names cannot be identified, including John Whitburn, who made the general proclamation in January. The eight identifiable men were all clerks, lawyers or men with legal experience. Some of them at least, and especially those designated clerks, were probably on the sheriff's permanent staff and his local agents in the places where they proclaimed.[37]

After Christmas, on 5 January and the days following, the proclamation was made a second time throughout the county. The other copy of the itinerary, in its

---

[29] *Cal. Pat. 1385–1389*, p. 488.

[30] BIHR PR 3 244.

[31] *FR*, I, p. 57. R. L. Skaife, 'City Officials of York' 3 vols., MSS in York City Reference Library.

[32] *Cal. Close 1385–1389*, p. 15.

[33] *Cal. Pat. 1385–1389*, p. 257.

[34] *Cal. Close 1385–89*, pp. 86–7, *Cal. Pat. 1385–1389*, p. 257.

[35] *Ibid.*, pp. 86–7.

[36] *Ibid. 1386*, p. 268, *1389*, p. 674.

[37] H. M. Jewell, *English Local Administration in the Middle Ages* (Newton Abbot, 1972), p. 198.

only deviation from the text of that on the dorse of the second copy of the writ, says it was proclaimed in the 'whole county of York' (. . . *pleno Comitate Ebor*).[38] This was carried out by John Whitburn. As the completed returns were due in London on 2 February, it seems likely that Whitburn's mission included collecting the completed documents. The map indicates that he must have followed a long and complicated itinerary in covering all the proclamation places, if he discharged these duties personally. It seems likely that returns from a place such as Bedale, where the writ was not read, although its return is extant, were collected from the nearest proclamation point. After collection, the returns would have been collated by Godard and his staff before dispatch to Chancery in time for the deadline.

The returns from all the county sheriffs were due to be submitted to Chancery on 10 February. We do not know whether they all arrived on time, how many of them were accompanied by indorsed copies of the writs, or indeed how many returns there originally were. Nor do we know who, if anyone, read them. What is certain is that no gilds were suppressed as a result of the survey. The information might have been used later, perhaps in connection with the statute which extended the provisions of mortmain legislation to include gilds, in 1391, but the likelihood is that the documents simply gathered dust for several centuries.[39]

The Yorkshire Returns

Whilst the process of serving the writ, receiving the returns and sending them to Chancery was firmly in the hands of the county sheriff and his agents, the actual composition of the returns themselves was officially in the hands of the gild officers. However, interference in the process seems to have taken place in some towns on the part of other local agencies. All four extant returns from Beverley were scrutinized by the same lawyer. Each ends with a note that Robert de Garton is the attorney (*Robertus de Garton est Attornatus*).[40] Unless he was employed by all four gilds to supervise their returns, it suggests that the town authorities appointed him to ensure that the king's writ was obeyed. His role may have been to verify lists of the gilds' possessions, which were added to each return in a different hand that might be his. There is evidence of a different kind from Ripon which indicates that this return, too, was not exclusively the work of gild officials. The return is for two gilds, both on the same parchment.[41] The second gild is introduced by the phrase 'the certification of another fraternity'.[42] That the compiler of the return placed the description of a second gild, that he was unable to name, on the same page as that of the gild of St Mary, St Wilfrid and All Saints, suggests that the involvement of the master of the 'other gild'

---

[38] PRO C 47/46/482 30.
[39] Tuck, 'The Cambridge Parliament', p. 238.
[40] PRO C 47/46/445–8.
[41] PRO C 47/46/452.
[42] *La certification dune Autre fraternite.*

must have been minimal. The two York returns both bore the seal of the Vicar General of the Archbishop of York, explaining that their wardens' seals would not be generally recognized.[43] The presence of these seals, however, suggests that both gilds' returns were scrutinised by the archiepiscopal authorities. In Hull, the Dean of Harthill similarly used his seal to confirm the identities of the men, wives and unmarried women who were members of the gild of St Mary in St Mary's Chapel.[44] The returns of the gilds of Corpus Christi and St John the Baptist both included the seals of the mayor and bailiff, who were first among the witnesses.[45] The brief return from Bedale is particularly revealing.[46] This gild was clearly the concern of the Nevilles. Although it was sustained by the good men of the town and the mesne, and by *plusours persons & vicairs du parosse*, the short list of founders is headed by the name of *le Sieur Nevill qui dieu assoil*. Here we have an example of a gild founded, supported and probably controlled by local government in the shape of an aristocratic family. It seems likely that the Nevilles or their agents were instrumental in drawing up the reply, which was written in legal French, rather than the more usual Latin. It is certain, then, that at least some of the Yorkshire returns were not solely the work of gild officers and were, at the very least, subject to scrutiny by other powerful agencies with which the gilds sustained relationships.

Gilds responded to the writ in at least three different ways. Some reproduced their ordinances, thus emphasizing the privileges and duties of membership, some transcribed their charters of incorporation, which concentrated on the general aims of the gild and the circumstances of its foundation, whilst others seem to have drawn up a statement especially for the return. The gild's choice of format thus governed the content of the return. Foundation dates often appear in the superscription of the manuscript. Information concerning the gild's finances and possessions is usually added at the end. Whilst the writ asked for such a financial statement, it was not a part of a gild's ordinances or charter and had to be added as a kind of appendix.

The returns from Yorkshire demonstrate these characteristics.[47] Three of the Beverley returns were based on ordinances. That of Corpus Christi claimed recent foundation following the precepts of Popes Urban IV and John XXII.[48] As the latter died in 1334, the return would appear to be a copy of ordinances from the first half of the fourteenth century. The document was described as a copy (*copia*). The St Helen and St Mary gild returns were both introduced as ordinances (*ordinacio*).[49] These three returns contain brief statements concerning possessions added in a separate hand. That from the Great Gild of St John of Beverley Hanshus is a special case.[50] It was evidently a response to the writ concerning occupational gilds.[51] It is a series of copies of charters, the oldest being

---

43 PRO C 47/46/454, 455.
44 PRO C 47/46/451.
45 PRO C 47/46/449, 450.
46 PRO C 47/46/444.
47 See Figure 1.3.

48 PRO C 47/46/445.
49 PRO C 47/46/446, 448.
50 PRO C 47/46/447.
51 Smith, *English Gilds*, p. 150, also suggests this.

from Archbishop Thurstan in the reign of Henry I and the latest being an inspeximus of Richard II. They all refer to the liberties granted to the town through its gild merchant. No ordinances were recorded. All three gilds in Hull supplied foundation deeds, rather than ordinances, including the names of founders and witnesses.[52] Whilst gild activities and objectives were included, these documents emphasized such factors as the responsibilities of membership, internal discipline and financial matters. The two York gilds made statements that seem to have been based on their ordinances.[53] At one point, the Paternoster Gild quotes a disciplinary clause from them. These statements were probably tailor-made for the occasion. Rotherham's return was also probably a statement based on ordinances but included an account of its extensive property-holdings.[54] Ripon provided two statements and Bedale one that was very brief.[55] In making any analysis of the content of the returns, it is vital to be aware of the sources used by their authors in compiling them.

That only thirteen returns are extant from Yorkshire is disappointing. It is, however, certain that this does not present a full picture of gilds in the county in 1389. Indeed, it is clear from Figure 1.2 that the whole corpus of documentation for all the returns is incomplete. The survival of the writs is random. They are extant for counties where no returns are present and are missing in the case of some counties where returns have survived. Returns exist in large numbers for Norfolk and Lincolnshire, and in moderate quantity for Cambridgeshire, London and Suffolk, to the virtual exclusion of most other areas of the country. They are absent in places such as Bristol, Southampton and Worcester, which all had merchant gilds that were, by this time, of considerable antiquity and which should have made returns under the terms of the writ.[56] There are examples of merchant gilds in Cornwall, too, that date back to the early thirteenth century in both Helston and Liskerret.[57] Even in counties where quite large quantities of returns survive, they may be far from complete. In Suffolk, apart from two from Beccles, most were made for Bury St Edmunds and the surrounding area. None has survived from the entire south-east of the county, although gilds are known to have existed in Ipswich, Framlingham, Kelsale and Woodbridge.[58]

---

[52] PRO C 47/46/449–51.

[53] PRO C 47/46/454–55.

[54] PRO C 47/46/453.

[55] PRO C 47/46/452–444.

[56] C. Gross, *The Gild Merchant* 2 vols. (Oxford, 1890), II, pp. 24–28, 213–214, 272–273.

[57] *Ibid.*, p. 108.

[58] P. Northeast, 'Parish Gilds', *An Historical Atlas of Suffolk*, ed. D. Dymond and E. Martin (Bury St Edmunds, 1988), pp. 58–9.

Figure 1.2: Distribution of Extant Writs and Returns

Sources: T. Smith, *English Gilds*, H. F. Westlake, *The Parish Gilds of Mediaeval England*.

County	Writ	Returns	Percentage
Norfolk	–	165	32.5
Lincolnshire	s	124	24.4
Cambridgeshire	c	60	11.8
London	cs	42	8.3
Suffolk	–	39	7.7
Yorkshire	cs*	13	2.6
Northamptonshire	cs	10	2.0
Derbyshire	s	8	1.6
Essex	–	8	1.6
Warwickshire	–	7	1.4
Oxfordshire	–	6	1.2
Gloucestershire	–	5	1.0
Hertfordshire	–	4	0.8
Leicestershire	–	3	0.6
Shropshire	–	2	0.4
Bedfordshire	–	1	0.2
Berkshire	–	1	0.2
Devonshire	–	?1	0.2
Dorset	–	1	0.2
Kent	–	1	0.2
Rutland	cs	?1	0.2
Lancashire	–	1	0.2
Somerset	–	1	0.2
Staffordshire	–	1	0.2
Sussex	cs†	1	0.2
Rutland	cs	?1	0.2
Somerset	–	1	0.2
Staffordshire	–	1	0.2
Sussex	–	1	0.2
Wiltshire	cs	1	0.2
Bristol	s	–	–
Cornwall	cs	–	–
Hampshire	cs	–	–
Surrey	cs†	–	–
Worcestershire	cs	–	–
Unknown	–	2	0.4

The evidence from Yorkshire also shows that more gilds were flourishing, in the late fourteenth century, than the returns indicate. Only one gild, figuring in the thirteen extant returns, also appears in the probate registers before 1389 but bequests were made to six other gilds in the county.[59] Furthermore, there generally seems to have been some interval between the foundation of a gild and the first bequest to it. Seven of the thirteen Yorkshire gilds mentioned in the returns first received bequests during the two decades 1389–1408.[60] It might, therefore, be fair to assume that at least some of the twenty-three other gilds appearing in the probate registers between 1389 and 1399 were founded before 1389 but did not make extant returns.[61]

Whilst it could be argued that, in the political atmosphere of the day, some gild officers were unwilling to make returns, and it seems certain that a number of fraternities in both London and Lynn avoided making them, it is hard to accept this as more than a minor cause of the preponderance of responses from the

---

[59] YML L2(4) 84v 1386 (St John the Baptist, York). BIHR Reg 10 346r–v 1349 (St George, Scarborough); YML L2(4) 45r–v 1365 (St Mary Fossgate, York); BIHR Reg 14 16r 1378 Corpus Christi, Weaverthorpe and Holy Trinity, Thwing; PR 1 8v 1387 Corpus Christi, Pontefract; PR 1 3v–4r 1389 Resurrection of Christ, Hull.

[60] BIHR PR 1 18v 1390 St Mary, Ripon; Corpus Christi, Hull, PR 1 62r–v 1393; PR 1 74v 1394 Paternoster, York; PR 3 4r 1398 Corpus Christi, Beverley; PR 3 252v–253r 1406 St John the Baptist, Hull; PR 2 575v 1408, St Mary in St Mary, Hull; Reg 18 344r–v St John of Beverley, Beverley.

[61] BIHR PR 1 6v, 1390 St John the Baptist in St Denys, York; PR 1 34r 1391 Holy Trinity in St Mary, Hull; PR 1 40v 1391 St Katherine, Rotherham; PR 1 66r 1394, 3 30v 1398 St Christopher, York; PR 1 74v 1394, PR 1 81v 1395, PR 2A 3v St George, York; PR 1 96r–v 1395 (St Mary of the) Weavers, York; PR 1 92r–v 1395 St Mary, Whitby; YML L2(4) 118r 1396, 117v 1397 St Mary, Pocklington; L2(4) 118r 1396, L2(4) 117v 1397 Holy Cross, Pocklington; BIHR PR 2 93v–94r Assumption of the Virgin, Tickhill; PR 2 2r 1396 Holy Cross, Whitby; PR 1 1396 St Mary in Holmkirk, Beverley; PR 2 9r 1397 Corpus Christi, Doncaster; PR 2 9r 1397 Paternoster, Doncaster; PR 2 9r 1397 St Katherine, Doncaster; PR 3 4r 1398 St Mary in St Mary, Beverley; PR 3 11r 1398 St Christopher, Hull; PR 3 11r 1398 St George in St Mary, Hull; YML L2(4) 121r 1399 St Thomas of Canterbury in St Michael le Belfrey, York; BIHR PR 3 26r–v 1399 SS Christopher and Andrew in St Helen Stonegate, York; PR 3 42v 1399 St Clement Pope, Scarborough; PR 3 42v 1399 St Katherine, Scarborough; PR 3 29r 1399 St Loy in Holy Trinity, Hull; PR 3 28v–29r 1399 St Mary, Malton.

Notes to Figure 1.2

*Smith (p. 132) says that Yorkshire had two writs, one 'social' the other 'craft', but both appear to be 'social', in Smith's terminology.

†Surrey and Sussex were treated as one county in the issuing of the writs.

Writs: 'c' and 's' indicate the survival of writs in respect of 'craft' and 'social' gilds respectively according to Smith.

Returns: the number of surviving returns in each county, calculated from Westlake.

Percentage: each county's percentage share of the total returns.

eastern central counties.[62] East Anglia was in a state of some social disarray during the years following the Peasants' Revolt, which might suggest a need for the sheriffs to carry out their duties vigorously, but local unrest would be likely to make the gathering of information from gilds in these areas more not less difficult.[63] The low numbers of returns from Essex and Kent, the epicentres of the revolt itself, also weakens such an argument.

Clearly the most likely explanation is that a major proportion of the documentation has been subsequently lost from the Chancery records.[64] This view is lent additional weight by the presence of four of the London returns in the Bodleian Library.[65] The central eastern counties might have made a particularly large number of replies, but this would be highly speculative. Clearly, the incomplete nature of the returns implies that generalizations based upon them, such as the distributional picture attempted by Scarisbrick, do not have a countrywide validity.[66] Furthermore, an overall view of those returns that have survived is further hampered by the lack of a satisfactory printed source.

In the absence of a comprehensive edition of the certificates, the only systematic view of them is Westlake's analysis.[67] He lists all the returns in the Public Record Office, but his summaries are not sufficiently detailed to show which format each gild used. Unfortunately this work, useful though it is, also introduces other variables into the information supplied by the returns. If the entries in Westlake's table are compared with more detailed accounts of specific groups of returns, such as Toulmin Smith's transcriptions of the English language ones, or those from the county of Yorkshire, it seems that they are generally reliable as regards such details as foundation dates, and in their accounts of the 'Origin, Purpose and Religious Provisions' and of 'Friendly Benefits to Members'. The column headed 'Remarks', however, should be approached with caution. Although the entries under this heading contain accurate information, it is not recorded with any consistency. For example, Westlake mentions the wearing of livery in seven of the forty-two returns from London gilds. Only two London gild certificates were transcribed by Smith. One of them, for St James, Garlickhythe, records the wearing of livery, but Westlake does not include this in his 'remarks'.[68] Clearly he did not intend to record every mention of livery in the returns. Twenty-five of Smith's transcriptions itemize gild goods, mainly sums of money, unmentioned by Westlake, in London, Lynn, Norwich, Oxborough and

---

62 Barron, 'The Parish Fraternities of Medieval London', p. 20. Owen, *The Making of King's Lynn*, p. 60.
63 Ed. R. B. Dobson, *The Peasants' Revolt of 1381*, 2nd edition (London, 1983), pp. xxvi, 233–64 *passim*.
64 On this point I disagree with Bainbridge, *Gilds in the Medieval Countryside*, p. 25.
65 Barron, 'The Parish Fraternities of Medieval London', p. 20.
66 Scarisbrick, *The Reformation and The English People*, pp. 28–9. See also Bainbridge, *Gilds in the Medieval Countryside*, p. 25.
67 Westlake, *Parish Gilds*, pp. 137–238.
68 *Ibid.*, p. 181, pp. 3–4.

Wiggenhall. Twenty reports of feasts, nineteen sets of disciplinary ordinances, and the presence of seven gild houses, all in Lynn, are also missing. Generally speaking, most of Westlake's more obvious omissions can be identified most readily in the returns from Lynn.[69] His purpose in compiling his list seems to have been to examine the religious and welfare aspects of gild membership. His additional comments are largely a selection of scraps of information that he felt were interesting, or curious, in the returns of particular gilds, or groups of gilds. Whilst much of this information is of anecdotal value, statistics based upon it are of limited use in providing an overall picture. Further examination of Smith's transcriptions also reveals that many of the documents he examined are damaged or incomplete. This is not always made clear in Westlake's list. As the conclusions of many of the individual returns in Smith's sample are missing or illegible, the gilds' lists of goods and possessions are often absent. Damage at the beginning of a manuscript sometimes explains the lack of a foundation date for a gild.[70]

Figure 1.3 compares the information contained in Westlake's summary with that yielded by Smith's sample of returns written in English. Although the latter provides complete transcriptions of a limited number of returns, they are, however, clearly atypical. Most replies were made in Latin. Gilds that chose to make their returns in English may well have been small, and possibly lacked clerical support. It is likely to be no coincidence that only one of them was wealthy enough to employ a chaplain. Thus Smith, too, presents an unbalanced picture.

In the case of the Yorkshire returns, the original manuscripts have been used and the information they offer is complete. Figure 1.4 is an attempt to collate this data. It is arranged under similar letter-headings to Figure 1.3 to aid comparison. Even this evidence, however, may not present a full picture. Whilst these gilds almost certainly carried out all the activities they described, they may well have pursued others that the officers did not think it worthwhile to mention. In Bedale, for example, the only gild function that the very brief return records is the maintenance of a chaplain to say mass at the Holy Cross altar in the church.[71] There is no mention of supplying a light, holding a feast or attending a gild mass or obit, which so many fraternities did. If these activities did not occur in Bedale, the Holy Trinity Gild there was unusual. It seems likely that the Nevilles were more concerned with reporting the pious expense of employing a priest than in commenting on social or ceremonial activities. Thus the content of each return must be viewed in the light of its format, even where the primary source has been used.

For all the imperfections of the source, it provides an essential snapshot of the

---

[69] *Ibid.*, pp.192–200, Smith, *English Gilds*, pp. 45–109.

[70] E.g. PRO C 47/46/455, St John the Baptist, York.

[71] PRO C 47/46/444.

Figure 1.3: Gild Activities from Smith's Sample and Westlake's Summary

	Smith		Westlake	
Activities	Returns	Percentage	Returns	Percentage
A Lights: altar lights and/or torches maintained	45	91.8%	409	80.5%
B Chaplains: clerics employed	1	2.0%	183	36.0%
C Funerals: provision of members' obsequies	44	89.8%	340	66.9%
D Feasts: celebratory meals or ales	18	36.7%	68	13.4%
E Processions: organized processions and/or plays	9	18.4%	62	12.2%
F Church: assistance with church maintenance	1	2.0%	69	13.6%
G Welfare: relief of sick or needy members	36	73.5%	185	36.4%
H Lands: recorded ownership of real estate	1	2.0%	30	5.9%
I Goods: cash in hand, valuables, church furnishings	25	51.0%	39	7.7%
J Discipline: regulation of members' behaviour	19	38.8%	47	9.3%
K Charity: relief of sick or needy non-members	2	4.1%	46	9.1%
L Premises: gild hall or chapel	7	14.3%	8	1.6%
M Livery: wearing of uniform dress or badges	4	8.2%	16	3.1%
O Pilgrimage: encouragement and/or financial support	1	2.0%	25	4.9%
N Subscription: annual levy and/or entrance fee	4	8.2%	10	2.0%
P Compulsory bequests	0	0%	12	2.4%
Total	49	100%	508	100%

Returns: The number of returns in which various activities are mentioned in each source.

Percentage: The above as a percentage of the total number of returns recorded in each source.

preoccupations and activities of English gilds in 1389. It enables us to build up a picture of what a gild was, and what it did, of the advantages its members enjoyed and the obligations they discharged. It provides us with a series of models against which other gilds, and similar organizations, can be measured and gives us a point from which later development can be discerned.

Figure 1.4: Yorkshire Returns

No.	Town	Parish	Founded	Gild	A	B	C	D	E	F	G	H	I	J	K	L	M	N	O	P
444	Bedale	–	–	Holy Trinity	–	B	–	–	–	–	–	–	–	–	–	–	–	–	–	1
445	Beverley	–	–	Corpus Christi	–	–	C	–	E	–	G	–	I	J	–	–	–	–	–	2
446	Beverley	Fr Friary	1378	St Helen	A	–	C	D	E	F	–	–	–	–	K	–	–	N	–	2
447	Beverley	–	1119–35	St John Han	–	–	–	–	–	–	–	–	–	–	–	–	–	–	–	4
448	Beverley	St Mary	1355	St Mary Purif.	A	B	C	D	E	–	G	–	–	–	–	–	–	N	–	2
449	Hull	–	1358	Corpus Christi	–	–	C	–	–	–	G	–	–	J	–	–	–	N	–	3
450	Hull	–	–	St John Baptist	–	–	C	D	–	–	G	–	I	J	–	–	–	N	–	3
451	Hull	St Mary	1357	St Mary	–	–	C	–	–	–	G	–	–	J	–	–	–	N	O	3
452	Ripon	St Wilfrid	–	Ss. Wilfrid Etc.	–	B	–	–	–	F	–	–	–	J	–	L	–	–	–	1
452	Ripon	St Wilfrid	–	unnamed	–	B	–	–	–	–	–	–	–	–	K	–	–	–	–	1
453	Rotherham	–	1356	Holy Cross	A	B	C	–	E	–	–	H	–	–	–	–	–	–	–	2
454	York	Minster	–	Paternoster	A	–	C	–	E	–	G	–	–	J	–	–	M	–	–	2
455	York	Minster	–	St John Baptist	A	–	–	–	E	–	–	–	–	J	–	–	–	N	–	2

No.: certificate number following C47/46/–. **Founded**: foundation date where known. Activities claimed by gild: **A**: lights maintained. **B**: chaplain employed. **C**: members' funerals held. **D**: feasts attended. **E**: ceremonial events conducted (including plays or processions). **F**: contributed to church upkeep. **G**: relieved members in need. **H**: owned lands. **I**: owned goods. **J**: disciplined members. **K**: did charitable works. **L**: owned chapel or hall. **M**: wore livery. **N**: paid subscription or entry fee. **O**: supported members on pilgrimage. **P**: indicates type of return: 1: Statements, 2: Ordinances, 3: Foundation Deeds, 4: Charters.

The basic purpose of all gilds was devotional. This is clear from Figure 1.3, although it is necessary to be aware of Westlake's interest in these matters, which he reported particularly fully. Presence at the gild's religious services was every member's duty and privilege. This was so universal a characteristic that it has not been listed in Figures 1.3 or 1.4. The eighty per cent of fraternities that reported maintaining lights and the sixty seven per cent stating that members attended the funerals and obits of their gild brothers and sisters, shows that corporate worship and care for the souls of members was clearly a central function of most gilds in 1389. Veneration of the gild's saint or cult through services and votive lights was a principal method of promoting this. The St John the Baptist Gild, York, for example, reported an annual service for all members, both living and dead, and the maintenance of a light on Sundays and feast days at the saint's altar in the Minster.[72]

Perhaps the ultimate, and the most expensive, method of expressing devotion to the gild's dedicated saint or cult, and of ministering to the pious aspirations of its members, was to employ a gild chaplain. In Westlake's account, thirty-six per cent of all gilds, including Holy Trinity, Bedale, and Holy Cross, Rotherham, did

[72] PRO C 47/46/455.

so.[73] Twenty-two gilds in his summary reported employing more than one, including the St John the Baptist Gild of Coventry which supported seven.[74] What is more, a further eight fraternities hoped to employ one when they could afford it. In some cases, such as that of the gild at Cirencester, the employment of chaplains seems to have been a gild's only declared function.[75] This was not necessarily based on a desire of the gild to compete with the parish. On the contrary, some gild chaplains were clearly intended to be assistants to the parish priest, as in the church of St Ebb, in Oxford, where the St Mary Gild provided one 'to assist the rector in choir at mattins, the hours etc. and especially at the Virgin's altar for the fraternity', or in the church of All Saints in Maldon, in Essex, where the Holy Trinity Gild's chaplain also assisted the incumbent at divine service.[76]

In some cases the duty of the gild chaplain, and, indeed, the function of the gild itself, was the maintenance of worship in a chapel in the parish church or churchyard, as in Waltham Cross where the Holy Sepulchre Gild provided services and lights for the dead in the charnel chapel, and in Ripon, where the gild members of St Mary, St Wilfrid and All Saints kept an ancient chapel in repair and provided a chaplain to say daily mass there.[77] Other gilds maintained chapels of ease at some distance from the parish church. In Thetford, the Fraternity of the Chapel of the Nativity provided three chaplains to say masses for the traders in their chapel in the marketplace, half a mile away from the other churches in the town.[78] In such cases it is hard to see whether the gild was supporting the parish, by providing an ancillary service, or competing with it by offering rival facilities. There may have been elements of both attitudes in the choices that such fraternities offered their members.[79] Overall, however, Eamon Duffy's impression that most fifteenth and sixteenth century gilds 'worked within and for the structure of the parish, not against it', could be extended to the late fourteenth century, on the evidence of the returns.[80]

General support of the parish is further indicated by the 13.6 per cent of gilds that reported making contributions to the upkeep of their parish church. This figure is drawn from the less reliable part of Westlake's table, and may not include all the data. Certain gilds, including, for example, the Assumption of St Mary at Pampesworth, Cambridgeshire, the Assumption of St Mary at Fincham, Norfolk, and the fraternity of Kettlebaston, Suffolk, stated this as their principal purpose.[81]

Most returns included statements to the effect that the fraternity encouraged peace and brotherly love. Beyond this, nine per cent of gilds in Westlake's list

---

[73] PRO C 47/46/444, 453.

[74] Westlake, *Parish Gilds*, p. 231.

[75] *Ibid.*, p. 152.

[76] *Ibid.*, pp. 223, 151.

[77] *Ibid.*, pp. 153, 234. PRO C 47/46/452.

[78] *Ibid.*, p. 211.

[79] Rosser, 'Parochial Conformity and Voluntary Religion', pp. 185–9.

[80] Duffy, *The Stripping of the Altars*, p. 145.

[81] Westlake, *Parish Gilds*, p. 145 (Pampesworth), p. 190 (Fincham), p. 229 (Kettlebaston).

mentioned the presence of regulations intended to control the behaviour of their own members. The three gilds in Outwell, Norfolk, for example, all condemned undue talking and the introduction of too many guests at gild meetings, and like many other gilds, discouraged disputes between members, whilst the Wisbech gild of St Peter recorded ordinances against brawling and gaming.[82] Disciplinary measures were included in seven of the thirteen Yorkshire returns, including that of St Mary in St Mary's, Hull, and St John the Baptist, York, which both prescribed fines, in quantities of wax, for misdemeanours within the gild, expulsion for those whose conduct might bring disgrace upon it, and a reconciliation process for quarrelling members.[83] This kind of regulation also appears in thirty per cent of Smith's transcriptions. A number of these are from returns that are clearly based on gild ordinances or foundation deeds and are therefore unlikely to have been influenced by recent local or national unrest.[84] Indeed, there is evidence for similar ordinances, and for their enforcement, throughout the late middle ages, especially in market towns and cities.[85]

Westlake devotes a whole column of his summary to the welfare, or 'friendly' benefits, that members derived from gild activities. The relief of distressed members and those who had fallen on hard times was undertaken by over a third of Westlake's list. The Paternoster Gild of York undertook to help members who had been impoverished as a result of robbery, fire or false imprisonment, and the St John the Baptist Gild of the city undertook to pay 7d. a week to members in need.[86] In Hull, the St Mary Gild in St Mary's distinguished between the poor and infirm, who received 7d. a week, and impoverished but able-bodied men and unmarried women who were to be granted 10s., which they must try to pay back over three years.[87] If they failed to do so the debt was then cancelled. In many returns the principal charitable provision offered to members was free, decent burial. The gild of St Mary in Beverley undertook to bury poor members of the gild honourably and solemnly, with five big candles, sung mass and burial, and members who failed to attend would be fined.[88] Eight of the Yorkshire returns made provision for funerals and obits and, in Westlake's list, over two thirds of the gilds reported on these activities.

Broadly speaking, at this time, gilds seem to have concentrated their charitable work on the needs of their own members. Calculations from Westlake's list show that only nine per cent of gilds extended such benefits to non-members and Smith's sample only yields four per cent. The gild of St Helen in Beverley, which

---

[82] *Ibid.*, p. 206 (Outwell), p. 148 (Wisbech).

[83] PRO C 47/46/451, p. 455.

[84] E.g. Smith, *English Gilds*, p. 20 (St Katherine, Norwich), p. 47 (St Thomas of Canterbury, Lynn).

[85] B. R. McRee, 'Religious Gilds and Regulation of Behaviour in Late Medieval Towns', in *People, Politics and Community in the Later Middle Ages*, ed. J. Rosenthal and C. Richmond (Gloucester, 1987), pp. 108–22.

[86] PRO C 47/46/454, 455.

[87] PRO C 47/46/451.

[88] PRO C 47/46/448.

maintained three or four poor, bed-ridden men and paid for their funerals, provides the only Yorkshire example.[89] Most accounts of gilds providing education or general poor relief are found in sixteenth rather than fourteenth century evidence.[90]

Records of fraternities, from the earliest times, place great emphasis on the holding of gild meals.[91] Westlake's list shows only thirteen per cent of gilds mentioning feasts in their returns, although over a third of Smith's sample does. However, even this latter figure seems remarkably low. Some of Westlake's notes mention them in a somewhat oblique way. The Trinity Gild in St Peter's in Ely, for instance, reported that thirty poor ate with the brothers and sisters at their Trinity feast.[92] The return of the gild of Our Lady, in Tideswell, Derbyshire, which was founded *circa* 1349, suggests a possible reason for the absence of feasting in some of the certificates.[93] It asserts that the members have not held a feast for seven years. They stopped, therefore, about the time of the Peasants' Revolt. This implies that the gild had, perhaps under pressure from local authority, modified its practices in the light of the political climate. Feasting offered an opportunity for riotous behaviour that could serve as a stimulus to even more serious social unrest.

Ordinances governing members' conduct at such gatherings suggest that rowdy behaviour was not uncommon, as exemplified by returns from Bishop's Lynn.[94] The gild of St John the Baptist, in Hull, also referred to feasting in the context of disciplinary regulations.[95] In Beverley, the feasts of the gilds of St Mary and St Helen were held in conjunction with the meetings that followed their annual processions, and which included the election of officers.[96] The return of the St Mary Gild states that the members ate their bread and cheese, and drank their beer, rejoicing in the praise of the Virgin. The gild feast was symbolic of fraternity and clearly had a eucharistic element.[97] Good behaviour was a matter of pious respect as well as civic order.

Another aspect of gild life that had implications for law and order lay in the holding of processions, plays and ceremonial events. Such activities lay at the heart of parish and civic life and the gilds were major contributors to them. Their incidence, as calculated from Westlake and Smith, was, however, surprisingly low. Only half of Lincoln's gilds reported carrying candles on their saints' days.[98] In Bury St Edmunds, out of seventeen gilds making returns, only that of St John

89 PRO C 47/46/446.
90 Scarisbrick, *The Reformation and the English People*, p. 30.
91 S. Reynolds, *Kingdoms and Communities in Western Europe 900–1300* (Oxford, 1984), pp. 67–8. Fryde, 'Gilds in England before the Black Death', pp. 217–18.
92 Westlake, *Parish Gilds*, p. 144.
93 *Ibid.*, p. 150.
94 PRO C 47/46/446, 448.
95 E.g. Smith, *English Gilds*, pp. 81, 84, 87, 89.
96 PRO C 47/46/450.
97 Rosser, 'Going to the Fraternity Feast', pp. 430–46.
98 Westlake, *Parish Gilds*, pp. 167–74.

the Baptist in the church of St James is mentioned as carrying a taper to the church on the Feast of the Decollation.[99] Bury might well have been a special case. The town was excepted from the general pardon of 1381.[100] It could be that the atmosphere there was still such that the gilds were encouraged to suspend this kind of activity, just as feasting had ceased at Tideswell since the revolt. If most gild processions were no longer held in Bury, it suggests that there may have been an awareness in some fraternities that this, too, was a politically dangerous activity. If this were the case, then some of those gilds which compiled replies for the return, rather than simply submitting their ordinances, might have failed to mention their processions.

In Beverley the three religious gilds laid considerable emphasis on their ceremonial activities. Their returns contained detailed descriptions of the processions of the gilds of St Helen, and the Purification of the Virgin, and directions for the costuming of the clerical members of the Corpus Christi Gild during its procession.[101] In York, ceremonial was also vital to the Paternoster Gild. Its principal stated purpose was to organize performances of the Paternoster Play, although it also sustained a light and a written explanation of the Lord's Prayer in the Minster, and held gild funerals and obits.[102] All these returns were based on gild ordinances which, by their nature, tended to include statements on the gilds' present purposes and current activities.

An adjunct to the question of ceremonial is that of livery. Westlake is not reliable here. Of those gilds that he notes as having liveries, a majority were in London. Clearly, public display was likely to be more common in urban areas, where there were many spectators to impress. It seems inconceivable that none of the great gilds of Coventry, Boston or Bury wore livery. Even in Smith's sample there were only two liveried fraternities reported in his group of Lynn gilds and only one in those of Norwich, although both towns had a large number of recorded gilds. In Yorkshire, only the York Paternoster Gild mentioned livery, which its members wore when riding through the city with their play.[103] Although the writs did not specify directly that gilds report on their liveries, the catch-all provision of 'all other things touching these gilds and brotherhoods', indicates that they were expected to do so.[104] It was specifically mentioned in the petition to the Cambridge Parliament.[105] Chaucer's *Prologue* indicates that livery was generally perceived as being stereotypical of gildsmen.[106] Any reluctance on the part of a gild to record the wearing of livery, unless it was referred to in its charter or ordinances, was probably a matter of political prudence.

---

[99] *Ibid.*, p. 227.
[100] Dobson, *The Peasants' Revolt*, pp. 233–64, *passim*.
[101] PRO C 47/46/454, 446. These activities are discussed in more detail in Chapter 3, pp. 105–6.
[102] PRO C 47/46/448
[103] *Ibid.*
[104] Smith, *English Gilds*, p. 128.
[105] See above, p. 14. Tuck, 'The Cambridge Parliament', pp. 234–5.
[106] Chaucer, *The Canterbury Tales: General Prologue*, ll. 363–4.

The instruction of the writs was very clear as regards recording the lands, buildings, rents and possessions of the gilds. As the ostensible reason for the proposed suppression was to raise revenue for the king's French war, this information was vital to the inquiry. Since the ordinances and charters of the gilds surveyed did not list these items, the financial state and material possessions of a gild generally took the form of an addition to its return. Such information, then, would have been based on the contemporary situation of the fraternity. It is also certain that, given the circumstances, gild officials would ensure that the financial statements would be pitched as low as possible. The writ shows that Chancery was aware of this as it required all persons who held any lands or possessions belonging to the gild to be named, thus attempting to block one method of concealment. This part of the writ was fulfilled by the Holy Cross Gild in Rotherham, which listed cottages, messuages and fields held by named members, including John Fledburgh, the vicar, Robert de Bollom, gentleman, Richard Ploghright, Richard FitzSimond and Robert Skynner.[107] Other gilds may have paid less attention to the detail of the writ. In Hull, for example, the Corpus Christi Gild made no reference to owning houses and lands but, only four years after the return was made, the will of Thomas de Styllyngflete used a messuage of the Corpus Christi Gild as a landmark to identify the position of one of his own properties.[108] It seems likely that the building was in gild ownership for some years prior to this for it to be used for such a purpose.

Concealment of chattels and cash-in-hand is more difficult to prove. Many gilds pleaded poverty, emphasizing the devotional or parochial uses to which they put all their funds. That of St John the Baptist of Whittlesford prayed that the gild's chattels be not touched because the church roof must soon be repaired.[109] Others, like the Lynn Young Scholars, said that they had already spent all their goods 'aboute honest werkys'.[110] The Lynn fraternities of St Anthony, St Thomas of Canterbury and St Leonard, affirmed that their 'katel' was 'redy to our lord þe kinges will', probably in the hope that such complaisance would buy off the threat of suppression.[111] The whole political background against which the returns were made encouraged the gild officials to minimize their assets.

There seems little doubt that the authorities believed gilds to be affluent and that their suppression would provide sufficient funds materially to assist the king to fight a war. The returns, however, gave little impression of a vast source of untapped wealth. The authorities may well have been disappointed, seeing the gilds either as being less affluent than they had believed, or more expert in concealment than they had thought. The confiscation of their assets could have

---

[107] PRO C 47/46/453.

[108] PRO C 47/46/449. '*messuagium Gilde corporis Christi*', BIHR PR 1 62r–v.

[109] Westlake, *Parish Gilds*, p. 147.

[110] *Ibid.*, p. 53.

[111] *Ibid.*, pp. 46, 48 50.

been so difficult as to prove unprofitable. This might provide a possible clue to the authorities' later inaction.

It seems probable that the gilds' sources of income were also under-reported. Only a few Yorkshire gilds admitted taking contributions from members. The forty-three men and women whose names appear as founders of the Corpus Christi Gild in Holy Trinity, Hull, each contributed ten silver shillings a year for five years for this purpose.[112] Thereafter they undertook to pay one penny and one farthing a week for life. The St John the Baptist Gild in Hull charged its members the much lower fee of two shillings each year.[113] The other Yorkshire returns did not report subscriptions or entrance fees, although some Beverley gilds mentioned an obligation to make small church offerings at their annual masses. Only the gild in Rotherham admitted an income from real estate. Again, it seems likely that some gilds were as reluctant to declare their sources of income as they were their assets.

Concealment, however, did not necessarily imply fabrication. There is every indication that gilds fulfilled all their devotional and charitable purposes to the best of their ability and that their financial obligations were considerable. The income from the property owned by the Holy Cross Gild of Rotherham was used for maintaining their chaplain, for torches and surges to be burned at the Holy Cross altar and at funerals and for alms.[114] It had no other goods or chattels. The gild of St Mary, St Wilfrid and All Saints in Ripon was founded for the restoration and maintenance of an old, ruined chapel of St Mary dating from the time of St Wilfrid.[115] All their money was spent on this and on the chaplain who sang mass there daily. The 'other fraternity', that is reported on in the same certificate, sustained a chaplain to sing mass at an altar in Ripon Minster (*le haut eglise*), this being its sole objective. Expenditure was implicit in all the charitable, funereal and devotional activities that the returns described, as well as in more public, social or administrative functions such as processions, feasts and the election of officers. Many gilds probably were poor, but it was clearly in their interests to emphasize, or even exaggerate, their poverty.

Some returns, perhaps from politically aware officials, called into question the status of their organizations. The gild of St Bridget in Fleet Street, in London, affirmed that its members had no obligations under oath, that, although they wore hoods on the saint's day, their gatherings were not malicious, and that they were not really a fraternity at all.[116] The officers of the St Mary Gild, in the same church, claimed that they were simply wardens of the light of St Mary and that this was not a gild either.[117] The societies of Corpus Christi and St Christopher in Great Yarmouth also denied that they were gilds and asserted that they had no

112 PRO C 47/46/449.
113 PRO C 47/46/450.
114 PRO C 47/46/453.
115 PRO C 47/46/452.
116 Westlake, *Parish Gilds*, p. 182.
117 *Ibid.*, p. 184.

goods or possessions.[118] That of Corpus Christi claimed simply to sustain a light. The St Christopher Society maintained an altar and a priest, but members subscribed on a yearly basis and could withdraw when they wished. However, even if they did not regard themselves as gilds, the sheriffs of London and Norfolk were clearly persuaded to the contrary view, as demonstrated by the very existence of the returns.

Such ambiguities beg the question as to what did, and what did not, constitute a gild in the Late Middle Ages. The official view, implicit in the writs, was that they were groups of lay men and women, bound by oaths and agreed rules, that met together, both regularly and on occasion. They feasted together and appointed their own officers.[119] They might also own lands, goods and money. However, the institution and wording of the inquiry itself shows that the authorities were aware that there were differences between individual gilds that required clarification. One such difference, that was officially recognized, was that between occupational organizations and the rest. The former were all expected to have royal charters or letters patent. It was evidently not compulsory for the latter, who were, nevertheless, to produce them if they had them (*si quas habent*). Occupational organizations were not called gilds in the writs; the instructions were to the masters, wardens and searchers of mysteries and crafts. The other writs were to the masters and wardens of gilds and fraternities.

In Yorkshire, the terms 'gild' and 'fraternity' seem to have been used interchangeably. The returns of Rotherham, Bedale and Ripon called such institutions fraternities. Those of Hull and Beverley, and the Paternoster Gild of York, defined them as gilds. The St John the Baptist Gild, in York, referred to its wardens as *custodes fraternitatis seu gilde*. This kind of double formula was also found widely in Yorkshire wills, including some that were contemporary with the returns.[120] The term 'service' which was applied, in the fifteenth and sixteenth centuries, to gild-like organizations, especially in the West Riding, did not appear in this documentation, nor did 'confraternity', which was rarely used in Yorkshire records.[121]

Although the writs asked for an account of the founding of each gild, they did not ask specifically for a statement of its purposes. These emerge from the returns in a variety of ways. All gilds were, to a greater or lesser degree, pious institutions, but their piety took different forms. As we have seen, a priority of some was the employment of chaplains, of others it was the maintenance of lights or buildings or in the holding of processions or plays. Yet others were especially concerned with deeds of charity, particularly towards their own members. Such preoccupations were generally related to the size, circumstances or geographical

---

[118] *Ibid.*, p. 219.

[119] See the translation of the writs in Smith, *English Gilds*, pp. 127–31.

[120] BIHR PR 1 3v 1389, Alice Sax of Hull, PR 1 6v 1390, Cecily Marshall of St Denys, York.

[121] Services are discussed in Chapter 2, pp. 72–77. 'Confraternity' appears in the ordinances of the Corpus Christi Gild of York interchangeably with 'fraternity', MS Lansdowne 304, fols. 5r–19v, *passim*, see Chapter 4, p. 128.

location of the gild in question. A city such as York could sustain the Paternoster Gild, despite its very specialized function. Beverley, with its ancient Minster and the shrine of St John of Beverley, supported gilds that added to the rich ceremonial already present in the town.[122] In Hull, a comparatively new town with little tradition of ceremony, the gild of St Mary in St Mary's chapel demonstrated its piety by waiving the annual subscriptions of members who were making pilgrimages to the Holy Land.[123] For a gild in a seaport, this was not surprising. In the rural setting of Bedale, however, the gild's only stated function was to finance a chaplain, as if it were simply a service.

Common to most gilds, as they appear in the 1389 returns, was a pious purpose and an administration capable of making a reply to the writ. Underpinning this, although they were not always made explicit, were a series of social and religious activities and a financial structure. The petitioners of 1388 believed that through these activities and structures the gilds constituted a threat to the established order and that they were increasing in number. How far they were correct in the latter assumption can be assessed by examining the foundation dates that appear on many of the returns.

The Proliferation of Gilds

The King's writ required the officers of each gild to state the date and circumstances of its foundation. Gild officers who were aware of the moves in the Cambridge Parliament to suppress gilds that were not ancient institutions must have realized that it was in their interests to emphasize the antiquity of their fraternities. 314, out of a total of 508, quoted actual dates of foundation in their returns.[124] Some of these referred to charters of incorporation, the rest were recorded or recalled in other ways, perhaps not always accurately. Sixteen gilds claimed to have been founded on dates prior to 1300. Others, while not citing actual dates, said they had been founded during the reigns of particular kings, including Henry I, John and Edward III. The borough gild in Malmesbury even claimed foundation in the reign of Athelstan. Thirty-five of them used formulae such as 'long ago', which might have indicated foundation beyond living memory in 1389. Three gilds were founded in the reign of Richard II, implying that they were twelve years old or less. A further thirteen gilds stated that they were of 'recent' foundation, or were 'newly founded'. Although such a statement is vague it does, nevertheless, suggest that some of these gilds were also founded within the current reign. A number of foundation dates are missing from damaged returns.

---

[122] See Chapter 3, below, pp. 105–6.
[123] PRO C 47/46/451.
[124] These figures are based on an analysis of the table in Westlake, *Parish Gilds*, pp. 138–238.

Figure 1.5: Fourteenth Century Gild Foundation Dates

Sources: H. F. Westlake, *Parish Gilds*, J. Hatcher, *Plague, Population and the English Economy 1348* (London, 1977), p. 25.

Events	Date	Foundations	Events	Date	Foundations
	1306	□1		1356	□□□□□□6
	1307	□□□3		1357	□1
	1309	□□□3		1358	□□□□□□□□8
	1310	□□2		1359	□□□□□□□□□9
	1313	□1		1360	□□□□□□6
	1315	□1	Plague	1361	□□□□4
	1316	□1	Plague	1362	□□□□4
	1317	□1		1363	□□□□4
	1320	□1		1364	□□□□□□□7
	1326	□1		1365	□□□□4
	1328	□□2		1366	□□□□□5
	1329	□□□□4		1367	□□□□4
	1331	□1	Plague	1368	□□□□□5
	1333	□1	Plague	1369	□□□□□□□□8
	1335	□□□3		1370	□□□□□5
	1336	□□□3		1371	□□2
	1337	□□2		1372	□□□3
	1338	□□2		1373	□□2
	1339	□□□3		1374	□□□□□□6
	1341	□□□□4	Plague	1375	□□□□□□□□8
	1342	□□2		1376	□□□□□□□□□□10
	1343	□□□3		1377	□□□□□□□□□□□11
	1344	□□□□4		1378	□□□□□□□□□□□11
	1345	□1	Plague	1379	□□□□□□□□□□□□12
	1346	□2	Plague	1380	□□□3
	1347	□□□□□□□7	Plague/Revolt	1381	□□2
Plague	1348	□1	Plague	1382	□□□□□□6
Plague	1349	□□□□□□□□□□□□□□14	Plague	1383	□□□□□□□□8
	1350	□□□□□□□□8		1384	□□□□□□□7
	1351	□1		1385	□□□□□□□□□□□□□13
	1352	□□2		1386	□□□□□□□□8
	1354	□□□□□5		1387	□□□□□□□□□□□11
	1355	□□2	Cambridge Parliament	1388	□1

Not included are 19 gilds founded before 1300, 35 founded 'long ago', 8 founded under 14th century kings and 13 founded 'recently'.

Figure 1.5 shows the chronological pattern of the foundations of the 298 four-teenth century gilds whose dates are given in the returns. Despite their short-comings, they give a clearer indication of the antiquity of individual gilds than that derived from testamentary sources, on which we are largely dependent for the following century and a half. These merely indicate a point in time in which a gild was known to be active. Even allowing for the disappearance of numbers of early fraternities, the table indicates a significant increase in gild foundations in the second half of the fourteenth century. Of the surviving returns that were pre-cisely dated, twenty per cent of gilds were founded before 1349 and eighty per cent from that date up to 1388. 1349 appears to represent a watershed, when four-teen gilds claimed to have been founded, representing the largest number recorded in any one year.

It seems certain that this increase was, at least in part, a response to the inter-national trauma of the Black Death. A proliferation of gilds and confraternities has been observed throughout Europe during the second half of the fourteenth century.[125] To some degree, perhaps, this could be put down to general panic and a flight to religion in the face of the pestilence. More particularly, however, it was a response of individuals to the need to confront sudden, unpredictable and widespread death with a dignity and ceremony that the parish alone could not always provide. This phenomenon has been analysed amongst the confraterni-ties of Florence by John Henderson and by Caroline Barron amongst the parish gilds of London.[126] Figure 1.5 indicates that peaks in gild foundation, in the areas covered by the returns, generally coincided with outbreaks of plague or other epidemics during the following forty years. An exception to this was the so-called 'children's plague' of 1361–62, where a peak in foundations preceded rather than followed the outbreak.[127] The victims here were mainly children, who had not been old enough to become immune in the 1348–49 outbreak or because the disease was not Bubonic Plague but some other sickness to which the young were particularly susceptible.[128] Child mortality was unlikely to have been a stimulus to gild foundation. Children's gilds, such as the Young Scholars' Gild of Lynn, founded in 1383, were rarities in the returns.[129]

The correlation between plague dates and increases in gild foundations cannot, however, simply be put down to a need for burial provision or to an increase in piety in the face of calamity. The Black Death was only one factor in

---

[125] J. Henderson, 'Religious Confraternities and Death in Early Renaissance Florence', in *Florence and Italy: Renaissance Studies in Honour of Nicholai Rubinstein*, eds. P. Denley and C. Elam (London, 1988), pp. 384–5.

[126] *Ibid.*, pp. 345–7. Barron, 'The Parish Fraternities of Medieval London', p. 25.

[127] J. Hatcher, *Plague, Population and the English Economy, 1348–1530* (London, 1977), pp. 58–61.

[128] P. J. P. Goldberg, 'Mortality and Economic Change in the Diocese of York, 1390–1514', *Northern History* 24 (1988), 39–55 (pp. 41–3).

[129] Smith, *English Gilds*, pp. 51–3. Seamer in the North Riding had a *gilde puerorum*. It is uncertain whether this was a gild of young boys, of children or of the Holy Innocents: BIHR PR 4 190r 1473 Alice Fewler of the parish of Seamer: 12d.

changes in population density and distribution that took place throughout the fourteenth century. There is evidence of the movement of individuals into towns and into the more fertile parts of the countryside, away from uplands and other areas of marginal farming.[130] In some agricultural areas there was a sharp decline in cultivated acreage and markets were disrupted, or disappeared, in a number of towns.[131] In these circumstances of social upheaval, when families were destroyed by sickness, or broken up by individuals emigrating from their familiar surroundings, a need for support of all kinds was paramount. There is some reason to suppose that parishes were unable to adjust to these social changes, their organization and boundaries having been fixed by the end of the thirteenth century.[132] An alternative form of association was readily to hand. Gilds offered their members spiritual comfort, social support and fraternal conviviality.

It is, however, easy to exaggerate the effects of the Black Death and its consequences, direct and indirect, on the formation of gilds. John Bossy argues persuasively that the plague merely stimulated the resurgence of a movement that was already well-established, almost universally throughout Europe, partly through the influence of the friars.[133] In an English context, it may be no coincidence that the petition to the Cambridge Parliament was contemporary with Lollard attacks on the mendicant orders.[134] One contentious aspect of the friars' role was their growing importance as confessors. During the fourteenth century, penance was increasingly being regarded as a private sacrament, its secrecy being more easily maintained by the employment of friars and, for the wealthy, private chaplains, than by the parish priest.[135] By contrast, the latter's most important activity was now the celebration of mass, which had become a more public ritual than it had been in previous centuries, providing powerful ceremonial demonstrations of unity, harmony and fraternity through the symbolism of Christ's body.[136] The establishment of gilds, especially in their role as employers of priests, enabled laymen to become involved in promoting, supporting and elaborating eucharistic ritual. A particular example of this trend grew out of the institution of the feast of Corpus Christi, which was established in England by 1318.[137] The response, in terms of gild foundations, was immediate. The 1389 gild returns recorded forty-four dedications to Corpus Christi.[138] This in itself was a major contribution to

---

130 See Chapter 2, p. 70.

131 R. H. Britnell, *The Commercialisation of English Society 1000–1500* (Cambridge, 1993), pp. 156–9.

132 Rosser, 'Communities of Parish and Guild', pp. 32–3.

133 Bossy, *Christianity in the West*, pp. 58–9. However, see also Bainbridge, *Gilds in the Medieval Countryside*, pp. 41–2.

134 Aston, ' "Caim's Castles" ', pp. 45–9.

135 J. Hughes, 'The Administration of Confession in the Diocese of York in the Fourteenth Century', in *Studies in Clergy and Ministry in Medieval England*, ed. D. M. Smith (York, 1991), pp. 87–163 (pp. 160–1).

136 James, 'Ritual, Drama and Social Body', pp. 8–9.

137 Rubin, *Corpus Christi*, p. 199.

138 *Ibid.*, p. 234.

gild proliferation in the fourteenth century, but it seems likely that the cult also helped to establish an ethos that encouraged the foundation of other gilds with allied dedications, such as Holy Cross, Holy Trinity, and St John the Baptist, whose head, presented on a platter, was symbolic of the host.[139]

Impelled by public manifestations of piety, and against a background of recurring epidemics and social disruption, gilds, at least in the areas covered by the returns, continued to proliferate up to and including the 1380s. If we take the foundations listed in Figure 1.5 and add to them both the number of those that were 'recently' founded and those that were established in Richard II's reign, some 34.7% of all gilds formed between 1300 and 1389 had been founded in the twelve years since the king's accession. This confirms the contention of the Cambridge Parliament that their number was increasing. In Yorkshire the fourteenth century evidence is sparse, and much of it belongs to the final two decades of the century. The evidence that there is, however, confirms that what appears to be a general trend occurred here too.

Conclusion

That gilds were proliferating throughout the country in the late fourteenth century seems certain. The Cambridge Parliament clearly viewed this as a threat, in its assumption that they provided opportunities for public unrest and sedition. Their growing affluence was also seen as an opportunity for central government to solve its economic difficulties. Contemporary criticisms of the wealth of the church as an institution may well have influenced the decision to petition that the gilds, whose orthodoxy was demonstrated through lavish public displays of their traditional beliefs, be suppressed. This initiative to persuade central government to take action against them was, however, ultimately unsuccessful and, at least by the early fifteenth century, there was a change in royal policy. The devotional ethos of the gilds now coincided with the Lancastrian crusade against heresy. In 1389, both the manner in which the writs were enforced and the various ways in which the fraternities responded show that gilds had established relationships with local authority in all its forms. The Yorkshire returns show us gilds that were closely associated with local lords, with ecclesiastical figures and with town governments. Their presence and distribution were known to central government through the agency of the county sheriff. It was perhaps inevitable that, as their activities became increasingly acceptable to the crown, their involvement with both national and local government should become ever closer. This was reinforced by two subsequent pieces of legislation.

We have already seen that gilds were made subject to mortmain legislation in 1391.[140] By subjecting real estate bequeathed to them to royal taxation, the crown

---

[139] *Ibid.*, p. 315.
[140] See page 14 above.

was not only benefiting economically from gilds, it was exercising a form of indirect control. Political control of a more overt kind grew from a further statute enacted by Henry VI in 1436.[141] At first sight this seems to be a measure attacking gilds. It complains that gilds and fraternities in various parts of the country have been enacting 'unlawful and unreasonable ordinances' to the detriment of the king's 'profits and franchises' and causing 'common damage to the people'. The 'Masters Wardens and People of every such Gild Fraternity or Company incorporate' are instructed to produce their 'Letters Patent and Charters' within a set time to be registered by the Justices of the Peace of the counties and the 'Chief Governors' of the cities, boroughs and towns. Any ordinances that are still not lawful and reasonable after they have been revised will render the articles of their charters void and attract a fine of £10 for each unsatisfactory ordinance. The force of the statute would remain at the king's pleasure.

Whilst this was clearly an attempt to exert national authority over gilds and their activities, it also had the effect of binding them ever closer to local government. The statute ensured this by employing justices of the peace and urban governors, rather than the king's sheriffs, to register gilds' ordinances. To function properly and legally a gild now required the approval of the local authority. Whilst it seems certain that this was, in many cases, a formalization of current practice, it offered justices and urban governors power over all local fraternities. Furthermore, it benefited the gilds by conferring upon them a formal legal status within the community. They became part of the local political and religious establishment. We shall see that the years immediately following this measure saw an increase in the recorded presence of gilds throughout Yorkshire and especially in York. It was inevitable that developments such as these would also stimulate changes within the gilds themselves and in their relationships with authority in all its forms. The various ways in which these processes took place will be investigated in subsequent chapters.

---

[141] *Statutes of the Realm*, II, pp. 298–9.

CHAPTER TWO

The Geographical Distribution and Chronological Development of Yorkshire Gilds

By the beginning of the fifteenth century, religious gilds were assuming an accepted role in the structure of society. This was apparent in that those of them that were large or wealthy enough to be identified were part of the orthodox, central strand of medieval public piety, that was generally supported by the king's government and by the local administrations of city, borough and manor that underpinned it. They were part of the establishment, embracing both church and state. This aspect of their role will be more fully investigated in later chapters, although it cannot be wholly ignored in this one. They were also probably almost universal. Westlake's assertion that any medieval church without a gild was unusual has received recent support through Rosser's estimate of the presence of 30,000 gilds in fifteenth century England.[1] An investigation of the distribution of the evidence for gilds in Yorkshire will be used to test these statements as they apply to the county. This will lead to a consideration of the economic and demographic characteristics of the places where gilds were found. How far identified gilds were associated with large, wealthy communities, and the power bases within them, and to what extent they also appeared in smaller, poorer places, will form a vital constituent in the discussion of their varying functions.

Medieval Yorkshire was a large administrative unit, embracing smaller areas with widely differing topographies. Although the gild, as an institution, was found throughout most of the county, there were local variations in the patterns of both their chronological development between 1389 and 1547 and their geographical distribution within the county. A complete list of all gilds identified in the county is supplied in Appendix 1. Following a general analysis, the gilds of two distinct geographical areas, the coastal East Riding and the textile areas of the West Riding, which present particular problems, relating to their economic circumstances and parish organization, will receive special attention. The development of fraternities in the county's five largest towns will also be given separate consideration, comparing common characteristics related to the urban environment with the differences between them. The gilds of the City of York will be used for comparative purposes only, as they will be discussed in detail in a later chapter. This chronological and geographical survey will provide essential background to arguments that will be developed in Chapter Three.

---

[1]   Westlake, *Parish Gilds*, p. 60. Rosser, 'Going to the Fraternity Feast', pp. 430–1.

The Nature of the Testamentary Evidence for Yorkshire Gilds

The principal body of documentation used in this chapter is testamentary. The disadvantages of using this kind of evidence have been widely discussed by historians.[2] Wills were made in significant quantity by a narrow band of the population that was wealthy enough to have sufficient possessions to bequeath. Furthermore, they are not always very informative in detail. Burgess, for example, makes the valid point that bequests to gilds fail to show what services they offered the testator.[3] They have been used here to identify the locations of gilds and the quality of individuals that made bequests to them. Generalizations based on this information can show only very broad trends. An additional problem, in the investigation, has been the sheer bulk of the material involved. The consequent use of the sampling system, described in the Introduction, and shown in Figure 2.1, naturally involves the omission of two-thirds of the potential information.[4] It should be noted that two of the sample periods shown in the table are inconsistent with the rest. Period one includes all the extant fourteenth century wills in the primary manuscript sources studied, spanning eighty years, rather than four. Period Fifteen covers one year only, that of the dissolution.

Another constraint lies in the way that the surviving probate records run. There are serious gaps in the probate registers of the Diocesan Exchequer Court, the principal source of this evidence, especially affecting sample period three, from 1416–1420. A further gap, in 1470, falls outside the sample. There are also significant geographical gaps in the records. The sequence of Richmondshire wills, for example, does not begin until the end of the fifteenth century, and Howdenshire was under the jurisdiction of the see of Durham. Whilst three local gilds were recorded in two Richmond wills, that have strayed into the probate registers, and a gild in Howden has been identified from other sources, fraternities in these two areas are less well documented than most others.[5] A smaller but

---

2 E.g. Goldberg, 'Mortality and Economic Change', pp. 38–40. Heath, 'Urban Piety', pp. 210–11, Burgess, 'Late Medieval Wills and Pious Convention', pp. 14–30, *passim*.

3 *Ibid.*, p. 18.

4 See above, pp. 9–10 and Figure 2.1.

5 Richmond: gilds of St Mary and St John Baptist: BIHR PR 5 248r–v 1484 William Walker of the parish of Richmond: 3s.4d., gilds of St Mary and St Thomas PR 5 248r–v 1484 Margaret Walker of the parish of Richmond: 3s.4d. Howden: Holy Trinity Gild: *Cal. Pat. 1549–1551*, p. 34: to Walter Wolflete of Howden and Robert Wright of Grimsby, yeomen, fields and a cottage in tenure of John Preston, belonging to the late gild of Holy Trinity within 'le Charnell' of the collegiate church of Howden. *Cal. Pat. 1549–1551*, pp. 21–23: to Sir John Wytheryngton and Cuthbert Musgrave (both of Northumberland) land in tenure of Thomas Webster in Barnby Yorkshire which belonged to the late gild of Holy Trinity in the collegiate church of Howden: yearly value 3s.4d. *Cal. Pat. 1549–1551*, p. 258: to Christopher Estoft of Ellerker and Thomas Dowman of Pocklington the messuage in Howden Yorkshire in tenure of Thomas Davye which belonged to the late gild of Holy Trinity in the collegiate church of Howden.

Figure 2.1: Testators Making Bequests to Gilds and Services in Yorkshire (excluding York) in Will Sample

No.	Sample Dates	Wills	Bequests		Testators	
1.	25 March 1320 – 24 March 1400	430	24	5.6%	23	5.3%
2.	25 March 1405 – 24 March 1409	131	19	14.5%	15	11.5%
3.	25 March 1416 – 24 March 1420	40	5	12.5%	2	5.0%
4.	25 March 1427 – 24 March 1431	250	21	8.4%	18	7.2%
5.	25 March 1438 – 24 March 1442	209	24	11.5%	15	7.2%
6.	25 March 1449 – 24 March 1453	118	19	16.1%	13	11.0%
7.	25 March 1460 – 24 March 1464	138	22	15.9%	18	13.0%
8.	25 March 1471 – 24 March 1475	274	51	18.6%	34	12.4%
9.	25 March 1482 – 24 March 1486	256	69	27.0%	46	18.0%
10.	25 March 1493 – 24 March 1497	110	16	14.5%	13	11.8%
11.	25 March 1504 – 24 March 1508	558	107	19.2%	77	13.8%
12.	25 March 1515 – 24 March 1519	355	52	14.6%	38	10.7%
13.	25 March 1526 – 24 March 1530	682	84	12.3%	66	9.7%
14.	25 March 1537 – 24 March 1541	1386	80	5.8%	63	4.5%
15.	25 March 1547 – 24 March 1548	324	3	0.9%	3	0.9%
Totals		5261	596	11.3%	444	8.4%

Wills: number of wills read in each sample period.

Bequests: number of bequests made to gilds in each sample period.

Testators: number of testators making bequests to gilds in each sample period.

Percentages relate to the total number of wills in each sample period.

important lacuna lies in the virtual absence of surviving medieval wills from the peculiar of Knaresborough, where the gild of St Robert was identified by bequests from Lincolnshire and Doncaster.[6]

With the exception of the probate registers of the Dean and Chapter of York and the few wills that appear in the Archbishops' registers, there are almost no extant Yorkshire wills before 1389. The raw figures in the table suggest an increasing interest in gilds, on the part of testators, that peaked in the early years of the sixteenth century. This impression, however, fails to take account of an increase in will-making over the same period, and the percentage figures indicate that the real peak in popularity was reached in the 1480s. Before attempting to analyse these patterns, however, it is important to establish the ways in which the data is affected by changes in the status, wealth and attitudes of the testators.

Many sixteenth century wills were made by the kind of individuals who had

6   P. J. P. Goldberg, 'From Conquest to Corporation', in *Doncaster: A Borough and its Charters*, ed. B. J. Barber (Doncaster, 1994), pp. 47–65 (p. 61), cites BIHR PR 5 183r 1480, the will of Katherine Travers. Foster, *Lincoln Wills*, III, p. 118: 1531 testament of Robert Brown of the parish of All Saints Welby, Lincolnshire: 'To the gylde of st Robert of Knavesborow iiijd'.

not made them at all in the previous century.[7] These were often husbandmen, with a few animals or small quantities of farm produce to leave to their children, who made brief wills and seldom made bequests to gilds. The large number of these wills made a high frequency of such bequests improbable. The low frequency of bequests to gilds in the fourteenth century, on the other hand, seems to have been due to entirely contrary factors. Here the testators were often gentry and high clergy who, in their long and elaborate wills, generally preferred to make pious bequests to religious houses or to found their own chantries. This group of testators made more bequests to gilds in the following century, when the latter became more politically acceptable.[8] Within the fifteenth century, however, urban merchants, craftsmen and their wives and wealthy husbandmen are found in increasing numbers in the probate registers. Such people were most likely to belong to gilds and to make bequests to them. If this analysis is correct, there was a greater likelihood of testators making bequests to gilds in the fifteenth century than in the fourteenth or sixteenth. Thus a higher proportion of bequests to gilds would be expected to appear in fifteenth century wills. Conclusions based on lower proportions during the fourteenth and sixteenth centuries should, therefore, be approached with some caution.

When a member of a gild made a will, his or her fraternity was not usually a principal concern. Bequests to gilds were made by a tiny minority of testators. Even the gild that received most legacies in the entire area, that of Corpus Christi in York, received only about 360 bequests from a total recorded membership of over 16,850.[9] Whilst a dozen gilds in other counties affirmed, in the 1389 gild returns, that they required their members to make bequests to them, this does not seem to have been the case with any Yorkshire fraternity.[10] However, there is some evidence to suggest that the York Corpus Christi Gild offered superior funerals in return for bequests, indicating that the two per cent of members that made bequests to it represents an atypically high figure.[11] Clearly, bequests to gilds were made only by the wealthiest and most highly motivated members.

One hundred and thirty-four gilds in the county received only a single bequest and, in most cases, this is the only proof of their existence. Of course, an isolated bequest to a gild does no more than show that it was operating in a specific location at a certain date. It cannot indicate recent foundation. There are frequent examples of gilds that were flourishing many years before they first received a bequest. Whilst the first testamentary evidence for the existence of the

---

[7] See Chapter 3, pp. 88–9 where evidence for these changing patterns of testators making bequests to gilds is presented and discussed.

[8] See Chapter 1, pp. 43–4.

[9] R. L. Skaife, *The Register of the Guild of Corpus Christi in the City of York*, Surtees Society 57 (1872), p. xii. For a complete list of bequests see gazetteer in Crouch, 'Piety Fraternity and Power'.

[10] E.g. St Christopher, St Edmund of Bury, St George, St John, all in Bury St Edmunds, Westlake, *Parish Gilds*, pp. 226–7.

[11] See Chapters 4, pp. 145–6, 5, pp. 170–1.

Corpus Christi Gild in Hull was in 1394, its gild return in 1389 claimed a foundation date of 1358.[12] The Holy Cross Gild of Hedon was first recorded in 1392, but did not receive its first bequest until 1472 and the St Mary Gild of Guisborough was operating by 1478 but was not mentioned in a will until 1547.[13] It is also obvious that where a gild was associated with more than one bequest, the interval between them is not an accurate guide to the fraternity's longevity. One can merely make the assumption that the gild was operating between the first and last record, although, even here, it is not beyond possibility that a gild might have lapsed and subsequently been re-founded during this period. Two bequests were received by forty-six gilds in the will sample. Those that attracted over ten, such as the gilds of Corpus Christi in Pontefract, St Mary in Swine, St George in Doncaster or the four gilds of Hornsea, were exceptional. The particular reasons for their popularity will be examined later.[14] As many as forty-one gilds, in the county, appeared in non-testamentary sources, but received no bequests in the sample. Twenty-four of these were manifestly wealthy fraternities, owning lands and houses, like that of St Mary in Ripley, where the disposal of its extensive former lands and properties is a matter of record, although there is no other extant evidence for its existence prior to the dissolution.[15] This being the case with a rich fraternity, it seems highly probable that a substantial number of smaller gilds either did not show up in the sample or disappeared without trace.

Another factor relating to the making of bequests may well have been fashion. In some cases all the bequests to a particular gild were concentrated within a short space of time. The four bequests to the St Botolph Gild in Bossall spanned the period from December 1527 to May 1539.[16] Similarly, the four to the St Mary Gild at Coxwold covered the period from September 1537 to October 1539.[17] It

---

[12] PRO C 47/46/449, BIHR PR 1 62r–v.

[13] Hedon: *Cal. Pat. 1391–1396*, p. 113, 1392: licence in mortmain for alienation of a toft by John de Burton and Hugh Maupas to the master and brethren of Holy Cross Gild in Hedon for finding a taper to burn before altar of St Augustine in Hedon. BIHR PR 4 84r–v 1472 Joan Elwyn widow of the parish of St Augustine: 3s.4d. Also 6s.8d. for painting the rood. Guisborough: St Mary Gild: ed. W. Brown, *Cartularium Prioratus de Gyseburne* 2, Surtees Society 89 (1894), pp. 409–10: 1498, indulgence of 40 days granted by Archbishop Lawrence Booth to all contributing to the gild of the BVM at Guisborough. BIHR PR 13A 313r 1547 Edmund Kendall goldsmith: 'Also I give unto the fynding of oure ladie preste and for the light a goode kendall Jackett'.

[14] See pp. 82 (Pontefract), 61–2 (Swine), 82–3 (Doncaster), 64 (Hornsea).

[15] *Certificates*, II, p. 226; *Cal. Pat. 1547–1548*, pp. 70–72.

[16] BIHR PR 9 378r 1527 Christopher Frere of Sand Hutton in the parish of Bossall: 12d. PR 9 397 1528 Brian Hodgeson of Herton in the parish of Bossall: 8d. and 4d. to Sir Robert White gild priest of Bossall. PR 9 459r 1529 Richard Wright of Herton in the parish of Bossall: 12d. PR 9 442v 1529 Edward Gradon of Claxton in the parish of Bossall: 12d.

[17] BIHR PR 11A 261r 1537 John Bell of the parish of St Michael: his best 'wedder' (sheep). PR 11A 348r–v 1538 George Davell gentleman of the parish of Coxwold: 20s. to Sir Thomas Swane the gild priest for prayers and 6s.8d. to the gild. PR 11A 322r 1538 Robert Orgraver of the parish of St Michael 12d. PR 11B 405r 1539 Thomas Webster of the parish of St Michael: 12d.

could be argued that both these gilds were briefly popular but ephemeral. However, the St Mary Gild of Patrington, whose two bequests were willed in October 1485 and March 1486, was still operating just prior to the dissolution sixty years later.[18] A more plausible solution may be that certain gilds were fashionable at a particular time, when testators either co-operated for a particular, unrecorded, gild project or wished to compete with one another in generosity to their fraternities.

Taking into consideration the imperfections of the records, the constraints of working with samples and the low probability of gild members making bequests to them, it seems likely that there were far more small gilds in late medieval Yorkshire than have emerged from records studied. It is also likely that they were more stable institutions than the tiny number of bequests that many of them attracted suggests.

Chronological Patterns of Gild Activity

Bearing in mind its shortcomings, and including bequests to services within the calculations, the testamentary evidence, nevertheless, offers some indication of the chronological ebb and flow of gild activity in late medieval Yorkshire.[19] The evidence of the county wills sampled, excluding York, indicates a steady increase in the number of previously unrecorded gilds that received bequests between 1349 and 1547. From the first recorded bequest, that to the St George Gild in Scarborough in 1349, to the end of the fourteenth century, twenty-four gilds were recorded.[20] In the first half of the fifteenth century there were bequests to thirty-two 'new' gilds. The second half of the century saw an additional seventy appearing in wills, whilst the half-century that culminated in the dissolution of the gilds in 1547 yielded a further eighty-two. This is, of course, a very rough indicator. More sophisticated information can be gleaned from the evidence laid out in Figure 2.1 and, especially, the graph at Figure 2.2, showing the peaks and troughs in the numbers of testators making bequests to gilds, and of the numbers of the bequests themselves, as a proportion of the total number of wills made in each sample period.

A general impression emerges that the popularity of gilds was at its highest between 1438 and 1530 when bequests to them maintained a level above the mean percentage of 11.3. It seems likely that both of these dates are, at least in part, related to national political events. The statute of Henry VI, of 1436, which required the registration of gild ordinances by local government agencies, whilst probably representing just one stage in the royal support of fraternities, appears

---

18 BIHR PR 5 282v 1485 William Barchard of the parish of Patrington: 6s.8d. PR 5 280r–v 1486 Thomas Raynes of the parish of Patrington: 40s., if he dies after his wife, Agnes. PRO E 301/119 m5 the priest was paid 75s. p.a. in 1548.

19 Services are discussed below, pp. 72–7.

20 BIHR Reg 10 346r–v 1349 Alan de Snayton cleric of the parish of St Mary Scarborough: 6s.8d.

**Figure 2.2: Graph: Percentage of Testators Making Bequests to Gilds
in Yorkshire (excluding York)**

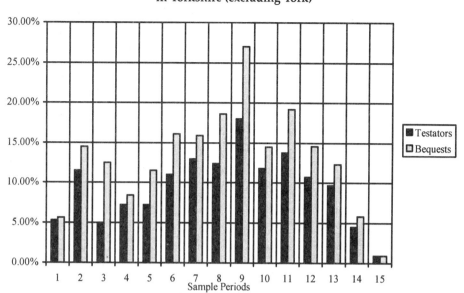

The columns show the number of testators making bequests to gilds expressed as a percentage of all testators in each sample period and the numbers of bequests they made similarly expressed.

Sample Periods: running from 25 March to 24 March as follows:

1. 1320 – 1400	6. 1449 – 1453	11. 1504 – 1508
2. 1405 – 1409	7. 1460 – 1464	12. 1515 – 1519
3. 1416 – 1420	8. 1471 – 1475	13. 1526 – 1530
4. 1427 – 1431	9. 1482 – 1486	14. 1537 – 1541
5. 1438 – 1442	10. 1493 – 1497	15. 1547 – 1548

to have acted as a stimulus to their growing popularity.[21] Although this measure seems to have had an immediate influence in York, it evidently took effect more gradually in the county at large.[22] At the other end of the sample sequence, the wills of 1537–41 immediately follow the Pilgrimage of Grace, coinciding with a period in which the gilds' devotional purposes were being attacked by central government. The bloody aftermath of the rebellion rendered a steep decline in bequests to gilds inevitable.[23]

A further indication of the popularity of gilds in the late fifteenth and early sixteenth centuries is in the multiple membership enjoyed by many testators. The

---

[21] *Statutes of the Realm*, II, pp. 298–9. See also Chapter 1, above, p. 44.

[22] See Chapter 4, below, p. 119.

[23] See Chapter 7, below, pp. 232–6.

divergence between the numbers of testators and bequests, found in the sample of 1416–20, may not be particularly significant, in view of its small size, but it is clear that during the peak periods of 1482–86 and 1504–08, this was a general trend. The fashion of supporting more than one gild at a time held sway from the 1440s until the first decade of the sixteenth century. This might point to a particularly high degree of gild activity during that time span, but there are other implications. Membership of one gild might have expressed an individual's loyalty to a particular saint or to a need for spiritual or material support from fellow members. Membership of several suggests involvement in a web of social contacts that often had commercial, or political, as well as devotional connotations. This could signal a shift in the nature and purposes of gilds, during this period, especially in urban areas, where such contacts were most readily made.

Within the broad pattern of proliferation and decline of bequests to gilds occur the two peaks shown in the samples of 1482–86 and 1504–08. It seems likely that these were the result of local variation. Before this can be established, however, it is essential to identify those areas where testamentary evidence is most likely to occur.

Gild Distribution

There is a high probability of gilds being found in large, prosperous locations. A township with a big population was more likely to provide a large number of wills, offering a greater likelihood that some of these might contain bequests to gilds. Furthermore, such a place would have a greater chance of supporting persons of sufficient wealth to enable them to make such bequests. The prosperity of a place, irrespective of its size, might also make the identification of gilds there more likely, especially if other factors were present to contribute to its importance, thereby attracting the presence or the attention of wealthy testators.

The size, wealth and importance of a medieval settlement can be measured in a variety of ways. Taxation returns can demonstrate the size or wealth of a community. The lay subsidy of 1334 is a useful indicator of the wealth of a community at that date. It was based on an assessment to the value of one fifteenth of the movable property in most locations. About two per cent of places were assessed at one tenth, but this is too small a proportion radically to affect totals. Because the way in which payments were made was determined locally, the lay subsidy is a guide to the wealth, not the population, of a community.[24] Clergy and their villeins were exempt from payment. This implies that townships, where there were concentrations of clergy and ancient, church-owned land, were wealthier than the figures suggest, although this factor is probably not very significant.

Some sixty per cent of all the locations in Yorkshire, that were assessed, paid

---

24 R. E. Glasscock, *The Lay Subsidy of 1334*, British Academy, Records of Social and Economic History NS 11 (Oxford, 1975), p. xxiv.

Figure 2.3: Distribution of Recorded Gilds within 1377 Poll Tax Populations

Population:	20–119	120–219	220–319	320–419	420–519	520–619	620+
All Locations:	898	157	24	27	4	3	8
Gild Locations:	62	33	13	10	3	3	8
Percentage:	6.9	21.0	54.2	37.0	75.0	100	100

Population:	Poll tax populations grouped according to size.
All Locations:	Total number of all locations appearing in each population group.
Gild Locations:	Number of locations where gilds and/or services were identified from all sources.
Percentage:	The number of gild locations expressed as a percentage of all locations within each population group.

Poll tax populations are taken from unpublished figures supplied by Richard Smith. 54 locations with 1377 poll tax populations of less than 20 had no recorded gilds. Gilds or services were found in 27 locations whose assessments were not recorded. The City of York is excluded from these calculations.

more than £1, and only nineteen, or 12.8%, of the 149 locations where gilds and services were later found, and whose assessments were recorded, paid less than that amount. The assessments for these nineteen places ranged from 9s. to 18s. The arithmetical mean valuation, for all locations where gilds were found excepting York, was £4.5s.8d. Clearly, the nineteen towns assessed at less than £1 had exceptionally low assessments for gild locations.[25] It must, however, be pointed out that some of these communities, such as Halifax, became considerably wealthier during the fifteenth century.[26] Evidence for services in Halifax first appeared, in the will sample, as late as 1526.[27] Equally exceptional were Market Weighton, Newbald and Yarm, the only three centres, out of a total of eighteen, with an assessment of £8 and over, where gilds were not identified from the will sample, or from other sources.[28]

However, it would be true to say that gilds developed, if they were not already present, in most communities that had been wealthy enough, in 1334, to be assessed at £1 or more. Unfortunately, for our purposes, this lay subsidy provides figures for a date that is earlier than any testamentary evidence for Yorkshire

---

[25] Elland (9s.), Kirkby Overblow (10s.), Spofforth (11s.), Halifax with Heptonstall (11s.), Foston (12s.), Stirton (12s.), Kirkburton (12s.), Huddersfield (13s. 4d.), Kirby Misperton (13s. 4d.), Penistone (14s.), Ripley (15s.), Keighley (15s.), Almondbury (16s.), Kirkheaton (16s.), Birstall (17s.), Alne (18s.), Bossall (18s.), Hawnby (18s.), Thorne (18s.).

[26] Goldberg, *Women, Work and Life Cycle*, p. 75.

[27] BIHR PR 9 349, Richard Ambler: St Mary, St George, Morrow Mass Services. For an explanation of the term 'service', see below, pp. 72–7.

[28] With the exception of Ravenser Odd (£15) which had disappeared under the sea by 1367, prior to most Yorkshire gild references. See J. A. Sheppard, *The Draining of the Marshlands of South Holderness and the Vale of York*, East Yorkshire Local History Series 20 (1966), p. 6.

gilds. All conclusions drawn from them are subject to later changes in the prosperity of an area.

Sixteenth century lay subsidy assessments do not provide a satisfactory
picture of all population centres in the county. Detailed information for parts of
the North and East Ridings may not have been returned by the government sur-
veyors, in the 1520s, and data for these areas is also missing from the returns of
the 1540s, although they do provide some indications of broad trends, especially
in York itself.[29]

Population can be measured by the poll tax of 1377.[30] It was paid by lay
persons over the age of fourteen, at a standard rate of 4d. per head. The question
of how far the figures provided by the returns have been distorted by evasion has
been widely discussed, but this is a more significant factor when applied to the
poll taxes of 1379 and 1380–1.[31] There are, however, several gaps in the Yorkshire
assessments and, whilst it is possible to fill some of these from later returns, they
have not been included in the following calculations.[32]

Whatever its shortcomings, the 1377 poll tax provides an essential rough
guide to the relative sizes of communities in the later fourteenth century. The
smallest community where gilds or services were found was Penistone with a
poll tax population of twenty. Fifty other places, with a poll tax population of less
than a hundred, also supported gilds. However, the arithmetical mean poll tax
population of the 132 locations, where gilds were found, was 236. If this figure is
compared with all the 1,027 Yorkshire locations taxed in 1377, with a population
of thirty taxpayers or more, excluding York, we can see a considerable disparity.
The arithmetical mean of this population is 103. This shows that gilds were found
preponderantly in communities with large populations. Certainly, most large
locations sustained gilds. Gilds or services were recorded in the will sample, or
from other sources, from fourteen out of a possible fifteen towns with poll tax
populations in excess of 400, Kirkbymoorside, with 511, being the only exception.

Figure 2.3 shows that gilds were present in most large population centres and,
that the larger the centre, the greater was the probability of gilds being found
there. However, it also indicates that gilds were discovered in ninety-five locations where poll tax populations were less than 220. This represents seventy-two

---

29 J. Sheail, 'Distribution of Taxable Population and Wealth in England during the Early Sixteenth Century', *Transactions of the Institute of British Geographers* 55 (1972), 111–26 (p. 116 and
   note, p. 118). A detailed return of 1524 from the City of York and the Ainsty is in E. Peacock,
   'Subsidy Roll for York and Ainsty', *YAJ* 4 (1877), 170–201.
30 I am grateful to Dr Richard Smith who has kindly allowed me to use his unpublished poll tax
   values of the surviving Yorkshire returns for 1377.
31 'Rolls of the Collectors in the West Riding of the Lay Subsidy (Poll Tax) 2Richard II', *Yorkshire
   Archaeological Journal*, 5, 6 and 7 (1879–1883), 5: 1–51, 241–66, 417–32, 6: 1–44, 129–71, 306–42,
   7: 1–31, 143–86. J. C. Cox, 'Poll Tax of the East Riding', *Transactions of the East Riding Antiquarian Society* 15 (1908), 1–70. B. J. D. Harrison, 'The 1377 Poll Tax Returns for the North Riding',
   Cleveland and Teeside Local History Society Bulletin 10 (1970), 1–8.
32 P. J. P. Goldberg, 'Urban Identity and the Poll Taxes of 1377, 1379 and 1381', *Economic History
   Review* 2nd series 43 (1990), 194–216 (pp. 194–5, 214).

per cent of all the places where gilds were identified. Such a high proportion might suggest that there were many more gilds in places with populations at all levels than have come to light. Indeed, bearing in mind the low probability of gild members making bequests to their fraternities, it tends to support the contention that gilds were an almost universal phenomenon. However, the question remains as to why testators made bequests to individual gilds in specific localities. Although the survival of evidence may be random to some degree, there seems little doubt that, in many cases, the gilds that can still be identified were of particular size or importance. The influences that made them so are best approached through an analysis of their geographical distribution.

Maps 2 and 3 show all the gilds and services that were found in the county, from all sources, before and after 1500.[33] The choice of the year 1500 as a watershed is not arbitrary. It falls after the peak in bequests to gilds that was identified in the sample period in the 1480s but before the later peak found in the very early sixteenth century.[34] Comparison of the maps shows that the changes in gild distribution taking place during this period are well illustrated by the selection of this date. The earlier map demonstrates a comparatively even distribution of locations where gilds were found throughout most of the rural areas of the county. They were, however, identified in greatest concentration in York, Hull, Scarborough, Doncaster and Beverley, all large urban centres. The later map shows a decline in the numbers of recorded gilds in all these places, although Doncaster almost maintained its earlier figure. Three other centres, Cottingham, Pontefract and Halifax, were found with more than four gilds after 1500. The most dramatic difference, however, is the discovery of 'new' gilds in quite small population centres. These were concentrated in two areas. The largest was found in the East Riding, in the wapentakes of Holderness and Dickering, between the Wolds and the sea. The other lay in the West Riding, largely between the River Aire and the southern county boundary. These two areas, and the five largest towns in the county, will be discussed in detail in later sections of this chapter, but the patterns displayed in the maps are also relevant to a general discussion of the characteristics of those locations where gilds were recorded. One characteristic might indicate a connection between gilds and economic activity. Many religious gilds were directly involved in the promotion of trade and commerce. The gild of St Mary in Holy Trinity, in Hull, was engaged in overseas trade on its own account and also lent money to its members for this purpose.[35] Gervase Rosser has shown that the Holy Cross Gild, in Stratford-upon-Avon, formed a focus for tradesmen both from the town itself and from a large number of villages in the surrounding countryside and he argues that this was a widespread practice.[36] It has also been suggested that the need of individuals to maintain social and

---

[33] For a discussion of the term 'services' see pp. 72–5 below.

[34] See Map 3.

[35] KHRO BRA/87, pp. 1–5.

[36] Rosser, 'Communities of Parish and Guild', pp. 33–4, Rosser, 'Going to the Fraternity Feast', p. 441.

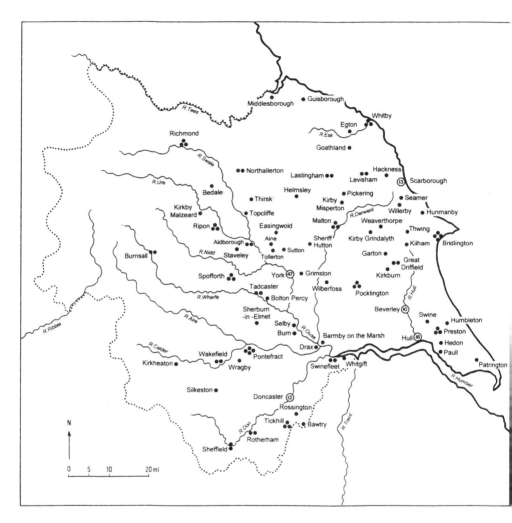

Map 2: Yorkshire Gilds and Services Recorded before 1500

The map shows gilds recorded before 1500. Sources include testamentary evidence and those gilds mentioned in the 1389 gild returns.

Each small black disk indicates the presence of a gild within the named location. Grouped disks indicate more than one gild in a location, up to a total of four.

Centres of population with more than four gilds are indicated by a larger disk with a number in it corresponding to the number of gilds recorded there.

56

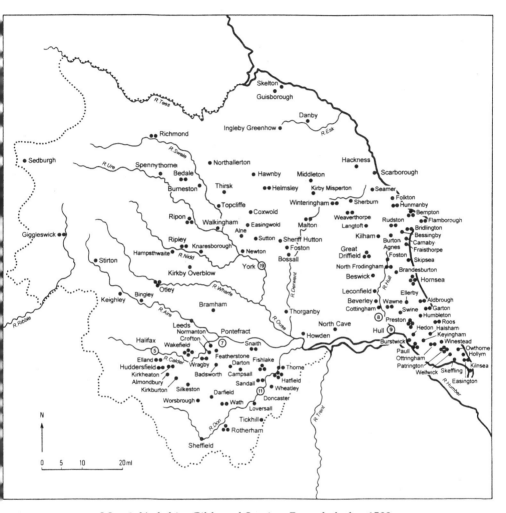

Map 3: Yorkshire Gilds and Services Recorded after 1500

The map shows gilds that are known to have existed between 1500 and 1550. It includes those that were first recorded between 1500 and their dissolution in 1547, and those that have been identified from evidence yielded by the process of dissolution. Sources include testamentary evidence, the commissioners' certificates of 1536 and 1538, the *Calendar of Patent Rolls*.

Each small black disk indicates the presence of a gild within the named location. Grouped disks indicate more than one gild in a location, up to a total of four.

Centres of population with more than four gilds are indicated by a larger disk with a number in it corresponding to the number of gilds recorded there.

business contacts, within a commercial centre, often led to their belonging to a range of gilds with different social profiles.[37]

Where Yorkshire gilds served as vehicles for such contacts, we would expect to find concentrations of them in places where there were opportunities for a high level of commercial activity. An essential prerequisite for this was a favourable position on the country's communications network. Places situated on established highways, and particularly where roads intersected, were likely sites for fairs and markets that would attract wealth into the community. If gild membership were linked with economic activity, gilds might be expected to be found there too. Despite our incomplete knowledge of the medieval road system, we know that Yorkshire was crossed by a number of well-known major thoroughfares.[38] For example, an important route passing through Doncaster, Pontefract, Boroughbridge and Northallerton is shown on the Matthew Paris maps. Although Boroughbridge wills fall largely outside the sample, the town being in the deanery of Richmondshire, the other three towns all sustained religious gilds, Doncaster supporting eighteen, Pontefract eight and Northallerton two.[39] Much smaller locations along this route also supported single gilds. Rossington had a poll tax population of only forty-five and Bramham, with 125, was also comparatively modest in size. An itinerary of King John mentioned a Yorkshire route that connected Tickhill, Doncaster, Pontefract, York and Northallerton. Tickhill sustained three gilds. This route also passed through, or least very close to, a number of gild centres of smaller population, including Sherburn-in-Elmet, with 133 poll tax payers, Bolton Percy, with ninety, and Sutton on the Forest, with 105, as well as Easingwold, that had the larger poll tax population of 206. There was also a route from York to Beverley, regularly used by Edward II, which would have passed through Wilberfoss, with 105 taxpayers, and Pocklington, with 341.

Of even greater importance to a local economy than roads was the availability of water transport, which was the best means of transporting goods in bulk. The county's two largest coastal or estuarial ports, Scarborough and Hull, supported thirteen and seventeen gilds respectively. Among the smaller coastal ports where fraternities were found, were Whitby with three gilds, Flamborough with two, Bridlington with three, Hornsea with four, and Paull with three. In the early sixteenth century, gilds were also recorded in a number of estuarine villages in South Holderness, including Easington and Kilnsea. Of more significance, perhaps, in terms of explaining the presence of fraternities in centres of low poll tax population, were ports with recorded gilds that were situated on navigable

---

[37] B. A. Hanawalt and B. R. McRee, 'The guilds of *homo prudens* in late medieval England', *Continuity and Change* 7 (1992), 163–79 (p. 167).

[38] B. P. Hindle, 'The road network of medieval England and Wales' *Journal of Historical Geography* 2 (1976) 207–21 (pp. 209, 215, 218 and Fig. 12, p. 220).

[39] For detailed referencing of gilds instanced in the following paragraphs see the gazetteer in Crouch , 'Piety, Fraternity and Power'.

rivers.[40] It has been shown that the only parts of the county that were more than fifteen miles from navigable water were the northern Pennines and the central portion of the North York Moors.[41] Gilds were not recorded in these areas. There was clear commercial advantage in being situated on a river bank, controlling shipping and tolls. Where navigable waterways were crossed by roads, or joined other rivers, this advantage was multiplied.

Research on the navigable rivers of the Humber estuary shows that many Yorkshire communities, of widely varying populations, known to be associated with gilds, were also favourably placed on the medieval waterways network.[42] York, of course, was the largest river port in the county, but taking the Ouse, and its tributaries to the north of the city, as an example of a navigable river system, the river flowed through several large communities, that had gilds recorded in the sample, and also through several smaller ones. Newton upon Ouse, for example, had a poll tax population of 107 and sustained a gild. Close to the confluence of the Ure and Swale, near Boroughbridge, Aldborough, with a population of seventy-eight, sustained two and was also on the main north-south road network. Further north, up the navigable Swale, Topcliffe, with a poll tax population of only fifty-six, maintained a gild that attracted eight bequests, that received mention in both of the commissioners' surveys and which ran a small choir school.[43] There may have been other reasons for the popularity of St Mary's Gild in Topcliffe, but its position on the river between Boroughbridge and Richmond, which was the highest possible navigational point, must have been a major factor. Similar examples could be found in other parts of the Humber river system.

As has been suggested, such favourably placed communities were usually the sites of markets and fairs. The presence of a weekly market, in particular, suggests that a place was able to attract commerce on a regular basis. The list of grants of fairs and markets, recorded in the charter rolls and calendared by

---

[40] J. F. Edwards and B. P. Hindle, 'The transportation system of medieval England and Wales', *Journal of Historical Geography* 17 (April 1991), 123–133 (pp. 127–9).

[41] *Ibid.*, Figure 2, p. 130.

[42] K. L. McCutcheon, *Yorkshire Fairs and Markets to the End of the Eighteenth Century*, Thoresby Society 39 (1940), p. 127.

[43] Topcliffe, St Mary Gild: YML L2(4) 364r 1483 Henry Wright chantry chaplain of the parish of St Columba: 3s.4d., BIHR PR 9 63v 1517 Richard Bell of the parish of St Columba: 40d., PR 9 427v 1528 John Dakitt of the parish of Topcliffe: 6d., PR 11A 337v 1538 Thomas Newsome husbandman of the parish of St Columba: a bushel of barley and 6 priests including lady priest and 6 lady children at his dirige. PR 11B 516r 1540 Thomas Dagget of the parish of St Columba: 4d., YML L2(5)a 186v 1540 William Carbot chaplain of the parish of Topcliffe: 8d., BIHR PR 11B 517v 1540 Thomas Newsome of Gricethwatte in the parish of St Columba: two bushels of barley. PR 12 6r 1540 Thomas Bell of the parish of St Columba: pardons a loan of 4s. that the masters owe him and 12d. of his own goods. He enfeoffs Richard Norton esquire of the gild lands in his possession. *Certificates*, I, 88–9 1546: Unfounded; in the parish church, maintaining a choir school for 6 singers and prayers for the dead and for parishioners. *Certificates*, II, 480 1548: 'The Service or Gilde of Our Lady in the said Parish of Topcliffe'. Yearly value £4 17s. No plate. Lands laid in mortgage to value of £12 p.a.

McCutcheon, does not provide a complete tally of all such institutions in medieval Yorkshire. However, thirty-three per cent of all those communities that were recorded, in the sample, as having gilds also appear in that list.[44] By contrast, only 9.5% of all the locations with a tax population of over thirty, that were assessed in 1377, were associated with such grants. Clearly gilds were generally much more likely to be found in centres with markets and fairs.

Five charters granting weekly markets were issued to centres whose poll tax assessments were not recorded in 1377. Of the rest, about half were to communities whose poll tax population was below the county's mean of 266 persons. Some of these places had particularly low populations. Whitgift, with a poll tax population of only fifty-three, had both a gild and market. Topcliffe and Newton upon Ouse have already been mentioned as small river ports. Skipsea, Ripley, Sheriff Hutton, Tollerton and Thwing all had poll tax populations of under 150 but had charters granting markets and fairs and sustained recorded gilds. Although most of these grants were made in the thirteenth and fourteenth centuries, pre-dating both gild evidence and the poll tax, some of the markets and fairs were still operating in the eighteenth century.[45] These included Whitgift, Topcliffe, and Tollerton.

Richard Britnell has argued that landlords' motives in obtaining grants for small markets such as these were mixed. There was a measure of self-interest, in that they would profit from tolls, but they would also be showing charity, in catering for the localized needs of their tenants: smallholders, tradesmen and craftsmen.[46] Such relationships between the lord and his tenants suggests that members of small communities might be employed by him in the routine of running local markets. It seems possible that, in at least some cases, fraternities of laymen with similar charitable motivations might have provided, under the supervision of lords or their agents, ideal administrative structures for this purpose. Some weight is added to this admittedly tenuous speculation by Skipsea's charter of 1338, which was granted jointly to Edmund, earl of Lancaster, his wife and the men of the town, although Skipsea's gild was not otherwise recorded until the sixteenth century.[47]

Commercial considerations were not, of course, the only reasons for the emergence of a gild in a particular location. Devotional or political factors could also play a part in determining the likelihood of a bequest being made to a fraternity in a particular place. The presence of friaries in urban centres has often been used

---

[44] McCutcheon, *Yorkshire Fairs and Markets*, pp. 161–71. R. H. Britnell, 'The Proliferation of Markets in England, 1200–1349', *Economic History Review* 2nd series 24 (1981), 209–21 (p. 210), draws attention to the incomplete nature of McCutcheon's information.

[45] 'Owen's Book of Fairs, 1770', calendared in McCutcheon, *Yorkshire Fairs and Markets*, pp. 172–7.

[46] Britnell, 'The Proliferation of Markets in England', pp. 220–1.

[47] McCutcheon, *Yorkshire Fairs and Markets*, p. 169.

as a broad indicator of the population and rank order of townships.[48] This is especially relevant to the thirteenth century when they were beginning to flourish in areas of high population. However, their presence in towns and cities can also be connected with a high degree of gild activity. The London friaries, for example, actively encouraged the development of gilds.[49] York's four houses between them supported no fewer than eleven gilds and there was at least one associated with a friary in Hull.[50] A relationship between friaries and gilds is hardly surprising, in view of the mendicant orders' desire to promote the concept of fraternity in general.[51]

Although this was not comparable to the situation in some continental cities, such as Florence, where forty-one per cent of gilds met in friary churches, the friars seem to have contributed significantly to the housing of fraternities in Yorkshire.[52] The only borough that contained one of the county's eighteen friaries, but had no recorded gild in the sample, was Yarm, which was, as we have seen, an unusually wealthy centre to have been without one. Although, by the Late Middle Ages, the number of friaries was no longer an indicator of the population size of a community, gilds were likely to flourish in communities where they were present, partly because such places were often large and prosperous, but also because of the friars' willingness to support them.

Some gilds maintained relationships with nearby ecclesiastical institutions of other kinds. In some cases this was because the institution was landlord and held the advowson of the parish. This was clearly the case in Middlesborough, that had a poll tax of only fifty-six. The St Thomas of Canterbury Gild there was connected with a nearby cell or priory (which it was is unclear) of Whitby Abbey. In the late fifteenth century, the 'prior' of the cell acted as parish priest in the impoverished church to which the gild was attached.[53] In other cases the relationship was much more direct. The presence, in the cartulary of Guisborough Priory, of an indulgence from Archbishop Booth offering a forty day indulgence to all who contributed to St Mary's Gild at Guisborough, which owned extensive property in the town and which is described as being 'of the priory', clearly indicates that the gild operated within the priory church.[54] It was undoubtedly subject to some control by the canons.

Not all gilds associated with religious houses were controlled by them, however. Swine in Holderness had a poll tax population of 240 and was remote

[48] E.g. R. B. Dobson, 'Yorkshire Towns in the Late Fourteenth Century', *Miscellany* 18, Thoresby Society 129 (1983), 1–21 (pp. 7–8).

[49] Barron, 'The Parish Fraternities of Medieval London', p. 23.

[50] St Ninian Gild in the Carmelite Friary: see Heath, 'Urban Piety', pp. 222–3.

[51] Bossy, *Christianity in the West*, p. 58.

[52] J. Henderson, 'Confraternities and the Church in Late Medieval Florence', in *Voluntary Religion*, Studies in Church History 23, ed. W. J. Shiels and D. Wood (Oxford, 1986), pp. 69–83 (pp. 70–5).

[53] *VCH*, III, pp. 105–6.

[54] Brown, *Cartularium Prioratus de Gyseburne*, II, pp. 409–10. *Cal. Pat. 1557–1558*, pp. 391–3.

from the principal routes of communication, with no market or fair, but it sustained a St Mary Gild, first recorded in the sample in 1484. It received seventeen bequests up to and including 1547.[55] This was a larger number of bequests from the sample than was made to any gild in either Hull or Beverley. Most of the testators were local husbandmen, but they included, unusually, a gentleman, William Hedon of Marton, and a widow, Isabella Salvayne, who was also of the gentry. There was also a bequest from the clearly wealthy John Gerves, from as far away as Hornsea, who coupled it with one to the famous *Scala Coeli* altar of St Mary's Gild in Boston.[56] These three bequests, together with the sheer number of the rest, suggest that the gild was larger and more highly regarded than the size or geographical position of the village might lead us to expect. Swine's parish church, however, was attached to a priory of Cistercian nuns that was the richest nunnery in the county in both 1291 and 1535.[57] The majority of the sisters were daughters of influential county families.[58] Although there were only nineteen nuns there at the dissolution, it survived until 1539, which suggests that the prioress, or the patron, wielded some influence.[59] The priory, however, did not control the gild directly. By 1480 it occupied premises either within or close to the priory precinct, but the territory was granted it by the lord of the manor, John Melton. In return, the gild was to pay him an annual rent of 6s. for life and a levy of 1d. on each of the five annual gild feasts. Melton was also given the right to veto the election of any gild priest who might celebrate in the priory church.[60]

In spite of the role of its lay patron, it seems likely that the presence of the nunnery was the reason for the gild's popularity. Whether this was because of the gentle status of the nuns, who might have attracted bequests from their relations and their affinities, or whether the nunnery's intrinsic sanctity was a factor, it is hard to say. It does seem, however, that there was some special reason for the popularity of this particular gild. The other Swine gild, that of St Peter, attracted only one bequest that falls outside the sample period.[61] Perhaps the presence of the St Mary Gild priest, who celebrated within the nunnery church, indicates a special relationship between the gild and the priory.

The role of John Melton in regulating the activities of the gild priest in Swine is of considerable interest. His relationship with the gild was one of patron and controller. There is no evidence to show whether he was a member. None of his family, nor that of its predecessors, the Hiltons, appeared among the recorded testators. His patronage of the St Mary Gild, however, illustrates a relationship

55 First bequest BIHR PR 5 212r, last bequest PR 13A 344r–v.

56 BIHR PR 11A 335v (Hedon), PR 2 564r (Salvayne), PR 9 389r (Gerves).

57 J. E. Burton, *The Yorkshire Nunneries in the Twelfth and Thirteenth Centuries*, Borthwick Paper 56 (York, 1979), p. 45.

58 N. Vickers, 'The Social Class of Yorkshire Medieval Nuns', *YAJ* 67 (1995), 127–32.

59 *VCH*, III, pp. 178–82.

60 G. Poulson, *The History and Antiquities of the Seigniory of Holderness* 2 vols. (Hull, 1841), II, pp. 209–10.

61 *Ibid.*

between gilds and secular power bases which seems to have led to the formation and development of fraternities in communities where the poll tax population was atypically small. The seats of lay magnates and their households sometimes constituted focuses of power that were not in proportion to their physical size. A gild might offer the local lord a structure through which he might control his most affluent tenants and followers, at the same time, perhaps, providing them with an organization through which they could approach him. It also allowed him control of the gild priest, strengthening his influence over the spiritual government of the parish. Of course, subsequent to the legislation of 1436 the agents of local government were obliged to record and approve gild ordinances but some evidence of a close relationship between local lords and gilds predates this statute.

The role of the Nevilles as founder members of the gild in Bedale has already been examined.[62] There are, however, other examples of gilds flourishing in the seats of Yorkshire nobility and gentry. Bossall, with thirty-three, had one of the smallest poll tax populations of any community with recorded gilds. Its St Botolph Gild, however, attracted four bequests in the sample. The village belonged to one of the branches of the Constable family. Spofforth's 1377 poll tax population was 111, less than half the mean for the county. The wills of Ralph Kylstern, a gild chaplain, and Richard Sudbery, rector of Crofton, in 1408 and 1428 respectively, both indicated the presence of three fraternities in the village, all active at the same time.[63] Spofforth was a major Percy seat. The parish containing the rival, Neville, castle of Sheriff Hutton had a poll tax population of 110, which was almost identical to that of Spofforth. It had no recorded market and was not adjacent either to a major road or to navigable water. Its Holy Cross Gild, however, attracted five bequests between 1472 and 1540.[64] In both Spofforth and Sheriff Hutton we see locations where gild activity was out of proportion to their comparatively modest populations. It is surely inconceivable that fraternities could have flourished in such places without the active encouragement of the families that ruled them. Although they did not usually figure in the wills of the aristocracy, some noble families, like the Nevilles of Bedale, might well have been both patrons and members.

Another important institution influencing the establishment and survival of gilds was the parish itself. Gervase Rosser's argument, that the foundation of many gilds was a response to the inability of the long-established parish struc-

---

[62] PRO C 47/46/444. See Chapter 1, p. 24.

[63] BIHR PR 2 576v 1408: Ralph Kylstern gild chaplain of the parish of Spofforth, PR 2 540v–541r 1428: Richard Sudbery rector of the parish of Crofton: 20d.

[64] BIHR PR 4 171v 1472 Robert Percy of the parish of Sheriff Hutton: £4 to the gild chaplain at 13s.4d. p.a. If there is no gild chaplain then the money is to be spent on daily masses for a year in the parish church. PR 9 35v 1516 Peter Letheley of the parish of Sheriff Hutton: 6s.8d. for his burial. Reg 27 143 1517 William Nelson vicar of the parish of Sheriff Hutton: 8d. PR 10 72r 1529 Dom. Henry Toplady chaplain of the parish of Sheriff Hutton: 3s.4d. PR 11A 377v 1540 Richard Bruke husbandman: 12d.

ture to cope with fourteenth century population movements, must be addressed at this point.[65] Using Stratford-upon-Avon as an example, he contends that, because the parish was insufficiently flexible to act as an agent for forming links between a trading centre and its hinterland, the Holy Cross Gild fulfilled this function. A similar situation has been seen in south-east Suffolk where surrounding parishes, without recorded gilds, supported fraternities in Framlingham and Kelsale, manors of the Duke of Norfolk, and in the market town of Woodbridge.[66]

Similar cases can be found in Yorkshire where, during the second half of the fourteenth century, there was a significant migration from the countryside into the larger population centres, supplying labour shortages created by the Black Death and subsequent epidemics.[67] In North Holderness, the four gilds of Hornsea formed a focus for local traders. Whilst most of those who made bequests to them were of the parish of St Nicholas, three belonged to other parishes. John Bowman of Skerne was one of ten testators who made money bequests to all four gilds, John Barker of Catwick was one of six who did so to the Corpus Christi Gild and John Dumbler, a yeoman of Sigglesthorne, left wheat and barley to the three other gilds of Holy Trinity, St Katherine and St Mary.[68] The attraction was probably the important fair granted to the Abbot of St Mary's of York, who had the lordship of the town.[69] Few other gilds were recorded within a ten mile radius. Elsewhere, whilst gilds were not recorded in close proximity to Rotherham, Sheffield or Malton, the small numbers of bequests to them were from testators within each location rather than from surrounding villages. Even the Corpus Christi Gild of Pontefract received only three of its fifty-one bequests from beyond the All Saints parish boundary.[70] It is, however, in York itself that Rosser's pattern can clearly be perceived.[71]

Whilst it is evident that commercially active gilds in some of Yorkshire's larger townships attracted members from outside them, it is difficult to support, in wider terms, Rosser's argument, that gilds presented their members with alternatives to inadequate parish organization. Yorkshire evidence shows that, in the vast majority of cases, parishioners made bequests to their own parish gilds and that they identified with both parish and fraternity. These gilds usually supported parish institutions. The relatively high proportion of bequests to parish gilds, by parish clergy, indicates a common interest between the two.[72] Indeed, there is evidence that in some parts of the county, especially in the West Riding,

---

[65] Rosser, 'Communities of parish and guild', p. 33.

[66] Northeast, 'Parish Gilds', *An Historical Atlas of Suffolk*, p. 58.

[67] P. J. P. Goldberg, 'Female Labour, Service and Marriage in the Late Medieval Urban North', *Northern History* 23 (1986), 18–38 (pp. 19–22).

[68] BIHR PR 9 422r 1528 (Bowman), PR 9 391v 1528 (Barker), PR 9 479v 1529 (Dumbler).

[69] McCutcheon, *Yorkshire Fairs and Markets*, p. 170.

[70] BIHR PR 5 261r 1485 William Fyxbe of Ruston, PR 6 102v 1504 John Bolton of Ledesham, PR 9 446v–447r 1529 James Illingworth of Friston Bywater.

[71] See Chapter 4, pp. 156–7.

[72] See Chapter 3, pp. 93–6.

gilds, or institutions very like them, were being used to reinforce the structure of the parish, rather than to work against it.[73] It is clear that the needs of particular parishes were, in some cases, a further factor in determining the distribution of recorded gilds.

To summarize, gilds were probably present in most late medieval communities. Those that were recorded were likely to include the largest and most important fraternities. These were usually identified from testamentary evidence in places that were populous and affluent. This is because such places produced wealthy testators in sufficient numbers for bequests to gilds to show up in the will sample. Gilds were also found in smaller locations which had chartered markets and fairs or where the local lord was powerful or influential. This suggests that they had a political or commercial function within their communities. In some cases they were in association with religious houses, either because the house in question was also their landlord or because they maintained some special relationship with it. Whilst devotional aspects of gilds will be examined in the next chapter, these distributional patterns will be investigated in chronological terms within particular geographical contexts in the following sections.

Gilds in the East Riding

The distributional patterns of recorded gilds can be illustrated by their presence in different topographical areas. They were, over the whole period of the sample, found most frequently in the Vales of York and Pickering, and in Holderness, where good agricultural soil supported high concentrations of affluent people. They occurred less commonly in uplands, such as the High Dales, the Wolds and the North York Moors, where the population was more widely scattered. In the North Riding generally, the sixteenth century lay subsidy returns, whatever their limitations as evidence, show particularly low populations of those wealthy enough to pay tax.[74] The extensive parishes of Bainbridge and Wensley, for example, were both situated in land that was largely composed of rough pasture. Bainbridge, with a 1377 poll tax population of 143, was as populous as forty per cent of all locations with recorded gilds. Even Wensley, with sixty-six, was as large as fifteen per cent of them. No gilds were recorded from the sample in either parish. By contrast, a particularly large number of references to gilds were found in the East Riding, with the exception of the Wolds. This is clear from Maps 2 and 3. Comparison between the two maps also shows a massive increase in the numbers of gilds after 1500. This increase was particularly evident in the eastern part of Dickering and, above all, in South Holderness, during the early sixteenth century. It is the purpose of this section to investigate why this was so.

In the area from Flamborough Head to Spurn Head, lying to the east of the Wolds and the River Hull, some nineteen gilds were identified before 1500. Most

---

73 See below, pp. 76–7.
74 Sheail, 'Distribution of Taxable Population', pp. 114–19, Figs. 1–3.

of these were recorded in communities of some size or wealth. These included Preston, Patrington, Bridlington and Hedon, all of which had 1377 poll tax populations of over 350. After 1500, some fifty-six gilds were found, many of which flourished in much smaller communities. Of these, seven are known only from non-testamentary sources dating from after the dissolution. Winestead, in Holderness, for example, with a 1377 poll tax population of ninety-five, had a cottage called a 'gilde house', which was granted to Sir Michael Stanhope and John Bellow in 1548, as part of a purchase of vast quantities of property related to former church lands.[75] From this it can been inferred that a gild was present in the village prior to the dissolution, and that it was large enough to own property. Figure 2.4 shows that other similar transactions in the East Riding reveal the presence of at least seven property-owning gilds in this area of south-east Yorkshire, in the mid-sixteenth century, that are known only through such records. A further nineteen figured in both post-dissolution land sales and testamentary evidence. In Carnaby, for instance, the St John the Baptist Gild received a bequest of barley in 1526, and was the owner of a gild house mentioned in an Elizabethan land deal.[76] Evidence of post-reformation land transactions is rare elsewhere in the county. A systematic study of the *Calendar of Patent Rolls* shows many dealings concerning former church real estate, but they rarely involved gild lands. This suggests either that North Riding gilds did not own property on the scale of the Holderness gilds, or else that they were more expert in concealing it from royal authority at the time of dissolution. The situation in the West Riding was rather different and will be discussed later.

The certificates of the commissioners' surveys carried out in 1546 and early in 1548 are missing for almost all of the East Riding. In July 1548, however, John Bellow undertook a further, less detailed, inspection to assess the pensions of the surviving chaplains, and much of this material for the East Riding is extant.[77] These certificates name gild priests in several of the larger locations, including Patrington and Ottringham.[78] They also show that the St Mary Gild in Swine survived the dissolution of the nearby nunnery and, presumably, continued as a parish gild.[79] Furthermore, some gilds seem to have survived as chantries. A number of chantry priests are reported on in places where a gild of the same dedication was previously known to exist. Whilst the majority of these were gilds and chantries celebrating the Virgin Mary and Holy Trinity, which were common dedications for both chantries and gilds, the survival of a chantry dedicated to the less popular St Laurence in Kilham, where a gild of that name had owned property, can surely have been no coincidence.[80]

---

[75] *Cal. Pat. 1548–1549*, p. 27.

[76] BIHR PR 9 348r, *Cal. Pat. 1569–1572*, p. 237.

[77] PRO E 301/19. See also Kitching, 'The Chantries of the East Riding', pp. 178–94.

[78] PRO E 301/19 m. 5.

[79] *Ibid.*

[80] *Ibid.*, m. 8. *Cal. Pat. 1548–1549*, pp. 27–9. For a discussion of terminology see pp. 72–7 below. The significance of the appearance of gilds as chantries in the commissioners' certificates is further explored in Chapter 7, pp. 240–1.

Figure 2.4: Gild Evidence in Holderness and East Dickering

The table is based on testamentary evidence, *The Calendar of Patent Rolls*, PRO E 301/119 and information from *VCH ER*.

Location	1377	Gilds	Beq.	–1500	1500+	Pens.	Land
Aldbrough	177	2	16	–	16	–	–
Bessingby	65	1	–	–	–	1	1
Beswick	76	1	1	–	1	–	–
Brandesburton	271	1	–	–	1	–	–
Bridlington	379	4	14	8	6	1	1
Burstwick	97	1	–	–	–	–	1
Burton Agnes	182	1	1	–	1	1	–
Carnaby	173	1	1	–	1	–	1
Cottingham*	767	8	30	–	30	2	1
Easington	262	2	3	–	3	–	1
Flamborough	278	2	1	–	1	–	1
Foston o t Wolds	118	1	1	–	1	1	1
Fraisthorpe	60	1	–	–	–	–	1
Garton o t Wolds	nr	1	1	–	1	–	–
Great Driffield	348	2	5	3	2	2	1
Halsham	164	1	–	–	–	–	1
Hedon	482	1	12	5	7	1	1
Hollym	116	1	2	–	2	–	1
Hornsea*	535	4	70	–	70	2	–
Humbleton	97	1	9	1	8	–	–
Keyningham	204	1	–	–	–	–	1
Kilham	363	1	1	1	–	1	2
Kilnsea	164	1	1	–	1	–	1
Langtoft	100	1	1	–	1	–	–
Leconfield	192	1	–	–	–	–	1
N. Frodingham	196	2	2	–	2	–	–
Ottringham	337	2	8	1	7	1	2
Owthorne	95	1	1	–	1	–	–
Patrington	372	4	5	2	3	2	2
Paull	229	2	3	1	2	–	–
Preston	371	4	19	5	14	2	–
Roos	149	–	–	–	–	–	–
Rudston	198	2	4	–	4	–	2
Skeffling	215	1	–	–	–	–	1
Skipsea	95	1	2	–	2	–	–
Swine	240	1	17	1	16	1	–
Wawne	nr	2	11	1	10	–	–

Location	1377	Gilds	Beq.	−1500	1500+	Pens.	Land
Welwick	185	1	1	–	–	1	1
Winestead	95	1	–	–	–	1	1
Totals	8302	63	244	29	215	19	26

1377:   poll tax population.
Gilds: number of different gilds identified in each location.
Bequests: total of all bequests to gilds within each location.
−1500:   total of all bequests to gilds within each location before 1500.
1500+:   total of all bequests to gilds within each location after 1500.
Pens: pensions survey by John Bellow for Court of Augmentations July 1548, PRO E 301/119: gilds and chantries with the same dedications as known gilds.
Land: references to gilds figuring in land transactions post-dissolution.

*The 11 bequests to all 4 gilds of Hornsea have been multiplied by 4 and the 3 bequests to all 8 gilds in Cottingham have been multiplied by 8.

Figure 2.4 shows that, in the area east of the Wolds, eighty-eight per cent of all bequests to gilds were made in the sixteenth century and, of the remaining twelve per cent, only one was made before 1450.[81] Beverley and Hull are not included in these figures. Nearby Cottingham, however, one half the size of Hull and a third that of Beverley in terms of the 1377 poll tax population, surpassed them both in numbers of sixteenth century bequests to gilds. Its flourishing local market was large enough to make it likely that gilds would be found there. The same could be said of the other established towns in the area that had supported gilds in the previous century. More unexpected is the number of villages with poll tax populations of less than 100 which recorded gilds within the sixteenth century sample or were identified from property transactions. Bessingby, Beswick, Owthorne, Skipsea, Winestead, Burstwick and Humbleton all fall into this category.[82] Although some of these places, such as Owthorne and Skipsea,

---

[81] BIHR PR 2 17r–v 1440, Alice Martyn to St Mary Gild of Wawne.

[82] Bessingby: poll tax population: 65. St Mary Magdalene Gild: *VCH ER* II, p. 20 quotes *Test. Ebor.*, V, 133–4. *Cal. Pat. 1549–51*, p. 148. 1549: gild house croft and land to Edward Pese and William Wynlove. *Cal. Pat. 1569–72*, p. 38. 1570: former gild lands granted to Hugh Counsell and Robert Pistor. Beswick, poll tax population: 76. Unnamed gild: BIHR PR 6 138r 1505 Robert Thomson of the parish of Lockington: a quarter of barley. Owthorne, poll tax population: 95. St Mary Gild: BIHR PR 9 457v 1529 William Fairbarne of the parish of St Peter: 4d. Skipsea: poll tax population: 95, Unnamed gild: BIHR PR 11A 371r 1537 John Mewdie husbandman of the parish of All Saints: a measure of barley. PR 11A 357v 1538 Peter Garton husbandman of the parish of Skipsea: two butts of wheat lying near Nowlawgait. Winestead, poll tax population: 95, unnamed gild: *Cal. Pat. 1548–1549*, pp. 27–9: Cottage called 'gilde house' granted to Sir Michael Stanhope and John Bellow. Burstwick, poll tax population: 97, St Mary Gild: *VCH ER* V, p. 19: former gild house and land, obit and light. Humbleton, poll tax population: 97, St Mary Gild: BIHR PR 5 272r 1486 Nicholas Grymston of the parish of St

received only one or two sixteenth century bequests to their gilds, Humbleton's St Mary Gild received nine. The St Mary and St Peter Gilds of Aldbrough, with a poll tax population of only 117, received sixteen between them.[83]

Clearly, both the evidence of land transactions and testamentary evidence from the sample point to a high degree of gild activity in the rural areas of south east Yorkshire in the early sixteenth century. Furthermore, the evidence of land transactions and of the July 1548 certificates also points to a high rate of survival of gilds right up to the dissolution. This is further supported by evidence from two testators in Hornsea in 1547, one of whom left 12d. each to all four gilds there 'over and beside there wagies', showing that the Hornsea gilds were still collecting subscriptions as late as April in the year of their suppression.[84] The St Mary Gild at Swine, too, received a bequest in 1547.[85]

Reasons for the late flowering and survival of gilds in Holderness are not immediately obvious. Apart from Hull itself, most of the area was not on the main inland communications system and, as we have seen, some of the communities had been small in 1377. However, there were estuarine havens at Hedon, Patrington, Paull, Winestead and Easington which supported a certain amount of coastal trade.[86] The area was generally fertile but in the thirteenth, fourteenth and fifteenth centuries had suffered badly from coastal erosion. By the early sixteenth

Peter formerly Rector of Gudmadame (?Goodmanham): 6s.8d. PR 6 109r 1504 William Drew of the parish of SS Peter and Paul: 3s.4d. PR 6 104v 1504 John Tod of Fytlyng in the parish of SS Peter and Paul: a bullock and two bushels of wheat for the light. Reg 25 162v 1505 Robert Benyngworth vicar of the parish of Humbleton: 20s.8d. PR 6 134v 1505 Agnes Drew of the parish of SS Peter and Paul: £4. PR 6 197v 1506 Richard Garthom of Fitling in the parish of SS Peter and Paul: 12d. PR 6 176r 1506 John Wheilpedall of the parish of Humbleton: a half quarter of wheat to gild and light. PR 9 58v 1517 John Garthom of the parish of SS Peter and Paul: 10d.

83 Aldbrough, St Mary Gild: BIHR PR 6 103v 1504 James Newton of the parish of Aldbrough in Holderness: 20d. for repairing the light. PR 6 157r 1506 Alexander Pudsey of the parish of Aldbrough 3s. 4d. PR 9 10r 1516 John Jenkenson husbandman of the parish of Aldbrough in Holderness: a measure of wheat. PR 9 42r 1517 Anthony Clerke of Great Coldome in the parish of St Bartholomew: a measure of wheat. PR 9 85r 1517 Margaret Garthom widow of the parish of Aldbrough Holderness: 3s.4d. PR 9 439r 1528 Robert Garthome husbandman of the parish of St Bartholomew: a measure of wheat. PR 9 428v 1528 William Dumler of the parish of St Bartholomew: a measure of wheat. PR 9 483r 1529 William Jenkynson of the parish of St Bartholomew: a bushel of barley. St Peter Gild: PR 6 103v 1504 James Newton of the parish of Aldbrough in Holderness: 2 measures of grain. PR 6 157 1506 Alexander Pudsey of Great Coldome in the parish of Aldbrough: 3s.4d. PR 9 42r 1517 Anthony Clerke husbandman of the parish of St Bartholomew: a quarter of wheat. PR 9 85r 1517 Margaret Garthom widow of the parish of Aldbrough in Holderness: 3s.4d. PR 9 432r 1528 Ralph Marshall carpenter of the parish of Aldbrough: a measure of wheat. PR 9 439r 1528 Robert Garthome husbandman of the parish of St Bartholomew: a quarter of malt. PR 9 428v 1428 William Dumler of the parish of St Bartholomew: a quarter of barley. PR 9 483r 1529 William Jenkynson of the parish of St Bartholomew: a bushel of barley.

84 BIHR PR 13A 352v 1547 Thomas Beverlay.

85 BIHR PR 13A 344r-v 1547 Hugh Andersone.

86 Sheppard, *The Draining of the Marshlands of South Holderness and the Vale of York*, p. 6.

century, however, this had largely ceased.[87] This clearly led to increased agricultural prosperity. By the late fifteenth century grain and legumes were being exported through Hull in years when the harvests were good.[88] By the 1530s, the trade, although still spasmodic, included exports of corn, to Calais and London, and of butter to Spain.[89]

A reversion of arable land into pasture, and consequent depopulation, has been noted generally in the East Riding in both the fourteenth and fifteenth centuries.[90] However, the epicentre of this movement seems to have been the more marginal arable land in the Yorkshire Wolds.[91] Where actual desertion of these areas did not take place, there was often a shift from arable to pastoral farming, which required a smaller workforce. Some seventy East Riding villages disappeared between 1334 and 1550.[92] Most of these were on the Wolds, although there were two villages in Holderness that were deserted due to encroachment of the sea.[93] Gilds that were recorded in Garton on the Wolds, Kirby Grindalyth and Kirkburn, before 1500, did not receive bequests in the sample during the sixteenth century when rural wills were more plentiful.[94] Even those of Pocklington, on the western edge of the Wolds, received their last bequest, in the sample, in 1494.[95] The evidence of bequests to gilds suggests that some emigrants from decaying communities in the Wolds found their way into South Holderness, as the threat from the sea diminished, and that this area enjoyed a prosperity that was lacking in some other areas of the East Riding.

This new affluence is reflected in the building and refurbishment of churches. Almost all the surviving medieval churches, in the area to the east of the Wolds, that had recorded gilds, also showed signs of rebuilding during the perpendicu-

---

87 *Ibid.*

88 W. Childs, *The Trade and Shipping of Hull 1300–1500*, East Yorkshire Local History Series 20 (1990), p. 13.

89 R. Davis, *The Trade and Shipping of Hull 1500–1700*, East Yorkshire Local History Series 8 (1964), p. 14.

90 A. R. H. Baker, 'Changes in the later Middle Ages', in *A New Historical Geography of England*, ed. H. C. Darby (Cambridge, 1973), pp. 186–247 (pp. 211–12).

91 *Ibid.*, p. 193.

92 M. Beresford, *The Lost Villages of England* (Lutterworth 1954), p. 170.

93 M. Beresford and J. G. Hurst, *Deserted Medieval Villages* (Guildford and London, 1971), Fig. 13, pp. 66, 21.

94 Garton on the Wolds, St Mary Gild: BIHR PR 2 652v 1430 Richard Collom of the parish of St Michael: a quarter of barley. Kirby Grindalyth, St Mary Gild: PR 5 226r–v 1484 Thomas Smyth of the parish of St Mary chapel Sledmere: a quarter of barley. Kirkburn, St Katherine Gild: PR 5 91r 1483 Robert Chow husbandman of Estburn in the parish of Kirkburn: 6s.8d.

95 Pocklington, Apostles Gild: YML L2(5)a 6r and 10r 1494 Robert Asshe of the parish of All Saints: a quarter of malt. Holy Cross Gild: L2(4) 118r 1396 John Skynner of the parish of Pocklington: 18d. L2(4) 117v 1397 Thomas Chaluner of the parish of Pocklington: 2s. St Mary Gild: L2(4) 118r 1396 John Skynner of the parish of Pocklington: 40d. L2(4) 117v 1397 Thomas Chaluner of the parish of Pocklington: 40d. L2(5) 6r and 10r 1494 Robert Asshe of the parish of All Saints: a quarter of malt.

lar period.[96] Skeffling church was completely rebuilt. Towers and steeples were constructed in many places, including Patrington, Hedon, Preston and Burton Agnes. Other churches, such as Ottringham and Hornsea, had large windows reconstructed at this period. Whilst there is little surviving evidence that gilds themselves either initiated or supported these activities, at least one Hull fraternity contributed to church furnishings.[97] It is surely no coincidence that communities which were able to expend large sums on their churches also included persons who wished to leave money and goods to their parish gilds, in this part of Yorkshire. Indeed, the evidence of the gild bequests themselves forms a compelling argument for the general prosperity of early sixteenth century Holderness.

This increasing affluence during the early sixteenth century clearly made it more likely that members, who had never done so previously, would make bequests to their gilds. As will be shown in Chapter Three, these persons were preponderantly wealthy husbandmen and their wives, many of whom continued to support their fraternities throughout the period leading up to their dissolution.

Gilds and Services in the West Riding

Compared with the East Riding, where a total of 126 gilds were identified from all sources, the West Riding, with only seventy-one, that were specifically described as gilds, showed an apparently low level of gild activity. This might have been partly due to the topography of the Upper Dales, where the economy was pastoral and the population sparse. Their absence elsewhere in the West Riding is, however, less easy to explain. The Humberhead Levels, with similar agricultural conditions to those obtaining in Holderness, and the prosperous Vale of York might have been expected to show a high level of gild activity. Furthermore, an increase in the rural manufacture of cloth was also stimulating the growth of both population and wealth in the Dales throughout the period, but especially by the late fifteenth century.[98] Gilds were, however, found in only a few of those West Riding towns that were involved in the textile trade. Leeds, for example, had a Jesus Gild which received six bequests between 1515 and 1537.[99]

---

[96] N. Pevsner, *The Buildings of England: Yorkshire: York and the East Riding* (Harmondsworth, 1972, repr. 1992), *passim*.

[97] KHRO BRA87 pp. 129, 130–2, 137. See Chapter 6 pp. 200–1.

[98] J. L. Bolton, *The Medieval English Economy 1150–1500* (London, 1980), p. 252. Goldberg, *Women, Work and Life Cycle*, p. 75.

[99] Although the Jesus Gild is not specifically named in the first three of the following bequests it seems likely that they relate to it: BIHR PR 9 24v 1515 William Musgrave of the parish of Leeds: 12d. PR 9 35v 1516 Nicholas Best of the parish of St Peter: 12d. PR 9 70v 1517 Brian Baynes ?merchant of the parish of Leeds: the proceeds of a bargain worth 46s.8d. or if it fails 13s.4d. PR 9 61r 1517 Robert Batty of the parish of St Peter: 12d. PR 9 366v 1527 William

Wakefield, too, supported four gilds known from sources relating to the 1520s but not associated with the will sample.[100]

The dearth of identifiable gilds in the West Riding seems to be at least partly due to a difference in local terminology. In the will sample, some thirty-six testators made forty-six references to thirty-one institutions that they called 'services' between 1427 and 1540.[101] These institutions were found in the West Riding but rarely occurred elsewhere in Yorkshire. Furthermore, many of them were flourishing in townships where gilds were not mentioned in the testamentary evidence but where the size and prosperity of the town might suggest that they were likely to have existed. In 1474, for example, William Hull made bequests to the services of St Mary and Holy Cross in Sheffield which, with a 1377 poll tax population of 585, was the largest town in the county where no bequests to gilds occurred in the sample.[102] Wills from three further towns, where the poll tax population had been in excess of a hundred, Hemsworth, with 182, Wath-upon-Dearne, with 103, and Kirkby Overblow with 102, also made reference to services or to service priests.[103] Other West Riding towns that had increased in prosperity during the expansion of the cloth trade in the fifteenth century, but where no bequests to gilds were found in the sample, also had testators who left money to services. In Wakefield, for example, John Leke, in 1452, made bequests to the services of St Mary and Holy Cross and both Richard Ambler, in 1526, and Robert Thomson, a clothier, in 1538, made similar bequests to services in Halifax, dedicated to St Mary, St George, the Morrow Mass and St John the Baptist.[104]

The principal and sometimes the only function of a service was to maintain a chaplain, whose duties generally included praying for the souls of parishioners, both living and dead, saying mass at the altar of the service and assisting the parson in parish duties. His stipend was usually paid by rents yielded by properties that had been donated or bequeathed by the founders of the service, who were normally unnamed parishioners. These impressions emerge not so much from the testamentary evidence as from the certificates of the king's commissioners, in 1546 and 1548, who recorded sixty 'services' in West Riding locations. It may also be significant that the four surviving gild returns from the West Riding, in 1389, all maintained that the employment of a chaplain was central to their

---

Atkynson butcher of the parish of St Peter: 3s.4d. PR 11A 264v 1537 Robert Mores of the parish of St Peter: 4d.

100   J. W. Walker, *Wakefield its History and People* (Wakefield, 1939), p. 149.

101   1427: BIHR PR 2 529v Richard del Turton of Holandswayne in Silkeston to the St Mary Service of Silkeston. 1540: PR 11 429v Thomas Dryvell of Pontefract to the St Mary Service in the Chapel of St Giles in Pontefract.

102   BIHR PR 4 124v 1474.

103   BIHR PR 11461 Sir Robert Buttle service priest 1540 (Hemsworth St Mary Service). PR 11 315r Richard Abson of Swinton 1538 (Wath St Mary and St Nicholas Services). PR 11 504 Robert Redman 1540 (Kirkby Overblow St Mary Service).

104   BIHR PR 2 261v 1452 John Leyke. PR 9 349 1526 Richard Ambler. PR 11 333v, 1538 Robert Thomson clothier.

intentions.[105] All these factors might lead us to leap to the conclusion that 'service' was an alternative term used in the fifteenth and sixteenth centuries by natives of the West Riding to describe their gilds. This is, however, to oversimplify the situation.

Eleven of the bequests made to services, recorded from the will sample, were to that of St Mary, in the parish church of Pontefract. Eight of the testators concerned also made bequests to gilds in the town or to their gild priests. Chief amongst these was the Corpus Christi Gild, but those of Jesus and St Thomas were also mentioned.[106] It is evident that, in the minds of Pontefract testators, there was a clear distinction between the St Mary Service and the Corpus Christi, Jesus and St Thomas Gilds. One of the testators, Robert Smalethorpe, asked for the two chaplains of the St Mary Service to attend his funeral as well as the two chaplains of the Corpus Christi Gild, amongst a list of clerics whose prayers he sought. However, distinctions are more blurred concerning an institution that sustained a priest in the Chapel of St Giles, also in Pontefract. Four testators referred to it as a service, but William Mures, in 1529, called it a gild.[107] Similar confusions occurred in Giggleswick. Hugh Lawkeland, in 1527, and James Car, in the following year, both left sums to the gild of St Mary 'if it procede and go forwarde'.[108] It may well be that the gild did not survive, despite their bequests of 10s. and 6s.8d. respectively. At all events, in 1538, John Malton, chantry priest in the town, left the large sum of £33.6s.8d. to found a St Mary Service.[109] If, however, the parish would not support the service, then the money was to go the 'chaplain'. No service was recorded by the commissioners in either 1546 or 1548, although they recorded three chantries, including one dedicated to St Mary.[110] There is nothing to link the St Mary chantry with any of the testators to the service or the gild. It is hard to say whether we are dealing here with three separate institutions or with a single one which was differently defined on separate occasions.

Inconsistencies in the testamentary evidence are, however, less confusing than those that occurred in the Yorkshire chantry certificates. The term 'service' did not appear in the instructions for the commissions of 1546 or of 1548.[111] It did, however, figure as a classification in seventy of the certificates, sixty of which referred to places in the West Riding. Whilst some of these were simply called

105 PRO C 47/444, 452, 453. See Chapter 1 above, pp. 31–2.
106 BIHR PR 3 518v–519r 1438 John Thornton vicar. PR 2 460v 1462 Robert Roper, PR 4 9r–v 1474 Robert Smalethorpe. PR 5 69v 1482 John Potter, 73r 1482 John York, 41r 1483 William Marton. PR 9 430r Roger Chapman alderman, 472r–v William Mures alderman.
107 BIHR PR 2 460v 1462 Robert Roper. PR 5 69v 1482 John Potter. PR 41r 1483 William Marton. PR 9 472r–v 1529 William Mures alderman. PR 11 429 1540 Thomas Dryvell.
108 BIHR PR 9 385r 1527 Hugh Lawkeland, PR 404r 1528 James Car.
109 BIHR PR 11 495r 1538 Sir John Malton chantry priest.
110 *Certificates*, II, pp. 253–5, 409–10. The undedicated Tempest chantry may have been that of St Sonday, which was to have been the recipient of Lawkeland's bequest if the gild did not 'go forwarde'.
111 *Certificates*, I, pp. 2–3. *Certificates*, I, pp. 371–2.

'services', 'service or gild', 'service or chantry', 'service or stipend' and 'service or salary' were all used quite frequently. Clearly, 'service or gild' indicated the presence of a gild. 'The Guylde or Service of the Rode wythyn the . . . Churche of Tykhyll', for example, had received three bequests as a gild in the previous century.[112] The incumbent was expected to say three masses during the week and 'do certen obites for the soules of theym which gave the lands' that financed his salary. However, these duties differed little in form from the two services, not alternatively described as gilds, in Rotherham.[113] The St Mary Service priest said mass every Saturday at eight o'clock, prayed for the souls of the benefactors and conducted divine service. The St Katherine priest's duties were similar except that he said mass at six in the morning, winter and summer. In 1391, John Norys left 13s.4d. to the fraternity of St Katherine.[114] The St Mary Service of Ripley, shown to have been a considerable landowner in the commissioners' certificate of 1546, was referred to as a gild or fraternity when the lands were sequestered in 1548.[115] Here the priest's duties included helping the curate to minister to over 700 'houslinge people' in a parish of 'grete circuyte', divided by the Nidd, which was subject to flooding. In this case there was no reference to his performing obits. Some of the revenues that supported his stipend were used by the churchwardens for maintaining the fabric of the church.

Although the majority of references to services appear in the West Riding certificates, a small number refer to institutions in other parts of Yorkshire. The case of the Corpus Christi 'service' of Holy Trinity in Hull is of particular interest. In 1546 two certificates were issued for the 'Stipend or Service of Corpus Christi'.[116] Thomas Atkynson received a salary, derived from rents, at the hands of the mayor and commons of the city. He was 'called the Corpus Christi preste' maintaining 'Goddes service' in the church. Robert Apulbie's stipend was founded by Adam Tutburie 'to singe at the saide alter and to pray for his sowle, his frendes sowle and all Christien sowles', the salary being paid by the mayor and commons of Hull. The Tuttebury chantry had been set up in 1384 to benefit the Corpus Christi Gild of Hull, one of the city's land-owning fraternities, and its endowment was further increased in Tuttebury's will in 1398.[117] The entry for the Tuttebury 'stipendary or service', in 1548, explained that the salary paid to 'Apilbie' was still maintained by the town despite the decay of the Tuttebury property, which had stood empty for twenty years. Here we have what are, undoubtedly, gild chaplains' posts being described as 'stipends or services'. These confusions, however, reflect a real ambiguity. The Corpus Christi Gild of Hull was not unique in running a chantry chapel and all gilds that employed

---

112 *Certificates*, I, p. 186. BIHR PR 3 241r Simon Auty 1405, PR 2 563v John Sandford 1429, PR 2 671r John Denby 1430.

113 *Certificates*, I, pp. 206–7.

114 BIHR PR 1 40 1391 John Norys.

115 *Certificates*, II, p. 226, *Cal. Pat. 1548–1549*, pp. 70–2.

116 *Certificates*, II, pp. 343–4.

117 *Certificates*, II, p. 344 note. BIHR PR 3 39v–40r 1398.

priests might also, with some accuracy, be described as corporate chantries. It was this aspect of them that the commissioners were investigating.

Some eighteen of the eighty-eight institutions, identified from all sources as services, were also described, either in the certificates or elsewhere, as gilds. This amounts to about twenty per cent of the total. Of the rest, some were certainly not. The *Valor Ecclesiasticus*, of 1535, in a very rare reference to services in York-shire, shows that Thomas Smyth, service priest of Rufforth, was simply a stipen-dary priest whose salary was directly paid by the Hospital of St Leonard in York.[118] In the commissioners' certificates, the 'Service or Perpetual Stipend' of the priest in the Chapel of Stainborne was a similar case, the salary being paid by the parson of Kirkby Overblow to maintain a chapel of ease three miles away from his church.[119] In Wath-in-Nidderdale, the stipendary or service for the chapel of Middleton Whernowe had previously been financed by Jervaulx Abbey and the unnamed service in Selby parish church had been recently founded by the king to 'serve the cure, by reason of the late dissolved monastery there'.[120] Services were also founded by magnates, often to sustain chapels of ease. This was the case in the Garsdale Chapel in Dent-in-Craven, where the stipend was paid by Lord Scrope, and in Bradfield where the Earl of Shrewsbury founded a chapel for his tenants of Bolsterstone Manor.[121] Eleven services, twelve and a half per cent of the whole, should probably be classified as stipends or chantries rather than gilds.

The remainder seem to have been gilds, in at least some respects. Each was usually financed by lands, money or goods donated or bequeathed by groups of founding parishioners, to employ a chaplain, who, as any gild priest, would pray for the souls of the founders, and of all parishioners, living and dead, say masses and assist the parson. A few services, in addition to lands, were shown by the commissioners to have possessed some wealth in terms of goods and plate.[122] Information on more fraternal activities was largely absent. There was no mention of the sustaining of lights or the holding of feasts and processions. However, the source of much of this information is the certificates of the commis-sioners, whose remit was to record assets, not activities. Furthermore, the burning of candles before images had been forbidden since 1538 and religious processions were also being discouraged by this date.[123] By the late 1540s the gilds' wealth and activities were largely concentrated on the one activity that could not be concealed from the crown, the employment of priests financed through income from real estate. Whilst 'service' was also employed by the com-

---

118 Ed. J. Caley, *Valor Ecclesiasticus Temp. Henry VIII Auctoritate Regia Institutus* (London, 1825),V, p. 38.

119 *Certificates*, II, p. 398.

120 *Ibid.*, pp. 505, 402.

121 *Ibid.*, pp. 413, 401.

122 E.g. St Mary Service Hatfield, *Certificates*, I, p. 149, Holy Trinity Service Badsworth, *Certifi-cates*, I, p. 168, Morrow Mass Service Wakefield, *Certificates*, I, p. 311.

123 Haigh, *English Reformations*, pp. 14, 156–8, 170.

missioners to identify an institution staffed by stipendary priests, who were not financed by parochial fraternities but by other agencies of church or state, they never used the term to denote gilds that did not intend to employ chaplains. In the few cases where a service no longer supported a priest, the reasons for this were explained.[124] In every case the service had done so once, even if the income was now used for other purposes.

Bequests of money and, less frequently, of lands and real estate, supplemented the income that services derived from their lands. Clearly some kind of organization was needed to administer this property; to collect rents and render accounts. Whilst this was undertaken by the town government in Hull, and in the case of the St John the Baptist Service in Ripley, by the churchwardens, the usual agency seems to have been the service itself.[125] Other bequests included several cows and a beehive.[126] These are reminiscent of bequests of livestock and produce to gilds in other rural areas.[127] It seems reasonable to assert that a service that was sufficiently organized to attract and administer bequests, in both money and kind, also had the character of a gild.

The question remains as to why this institution was particularly popular in the West Riding. This was probably directly related to the size and nature of parishes. Unusually large parishes made it difficult for incumbents to cope with parochial duties, especially in districts of rising prosperity and growth. This was a particular problem in Pennine valleys, where populations were scattered over wide areas and divided by rivers which were difficult to cross in times of bad weather, as we have seen was a problem in Ripley. The vast parish of Halifax is another case in point. The parish church attracted sixteenth century bequests to the services of St Mary, St George, the Morrow Mass and St John the Baptist.[128] Of these, only the Morrow Mass Service was reported on in 1546, but the 'Perpetuall Stipend or Service of the Rood Alter' also received a certificate.[129] Both of these services were supported by rents from lands given by parishioners and their priests carried out duties in the parish church. The certificate for the St Mary Service in the chapel at Heptonstall, six miles away, is more explicit.[130] The service priest was required 'to helpe the curate to mynystre all sacrementes and sacrementalles to the parocheners nigh adjoynynge to the said chapelle'. It claimed that the whole of Halifax parish numbered 2,000 people. There was clearly a need for a large staff of clergy to cope with them. Likewise, the service

---

124 E.g. *Certificates*, I, p. 168: the Holy Trinity Service of Badsworth, where there had been no chaplain for three years. The income was used for church maintenance.

125 *Certificates*, II, p. 268.

126 BIHR PR 5 464v–465r 1495 Thomas Beaumont of Whytlay to Kirkheaton St Mary Service. PR 4 25r 1471 Margaret Marshall of Ryhll to Wragby St Mary Service. PR 9 395v 1527 Robert Jub of West Hardwick to Wragby St Mary Service (cows). PR 1 541v 1539 William Shelito to Featherstone St Mary Service (hive).

127 See Chapter 3, pp. 113–15.

128 BIHR PR 9 349v 1526 Richard Ambler. PR 11 333v 1538 Robert Thomson clothier.

129 *Certificates*, II, pp. 299, 295.

130 *Ibid.*, p. 297.

priest of St Mary in Huddersfield was to assist the curate in similar duties, ministering to a population of 1,400 'or ther aboutes'.[131] In places such as these the provision of additional priests was a particularly valuable contribution that pious laymen could make to the well-being of their parish, for the health of their own souls. Such considerations would naturally take precedence over more social functions. Indeed, large populations spread over wide areas and difficult terrain must have made meetings for feasts and elaborate ceremonials difficult to organize, although we cannot be sure that they did not take place. The argument that many West Riding services were gild-like institutions whose main function was to provide a priest for remote communities in the Dales is given further force by the 1389 return from Bedale, where the sole stated function of the Holy Trinity Gild, founded by the Nevilles, was to fund a chaplain.[132]

The puzzle of the St Mary Service in Pontefract still remains. Perhaps it was a more loosely-organized fraternity than the Pontefract gilds, concentrating on the maintenance of the service priest and laying less emphasis on ceremonial and social activities. Maybe it owed its original foundation to immigrants from Pennine parishes who were used to calling this kind of gild a service. There is, unfortunately, insufficient evidence to pursue such speculation.

For the purposes of this book, all those services that received bequests and those which, from their certificates, seem to have been supported by groups of parishioners, are classified as gilds and are included as such in tables, maps and statistics. Those that appear to have been chantries or stipends, exclusively maintained by individuals or by other institutions, have been excluded.

When services are included in the calculations, the West Riding emerges as an area that contributed in a major way to the proliferation of recorded gilds, especially during the first half of the sixteenth century. Maps 2 and 3 show this trend. Services are also a factor contributing to the second peak in the percentage of bequests to fraternities that occurred in the first decade of the century which can be seen in Figures 2.1 and 2.2. However, the emergence of gilds in rural centres and the increase in bequests to them is counterbalanced by a different pattern that can be discerned in the development of the county's urban gilds.

Gilds in Urban Centres

Apart from York, which was by far the largest of Yorkshire's urban centres, five large towns formed the principal concentrations of population in the late medieval county. They fall into two natural groups. The three established boroughs of Beverley, with a 1377 poll tax population of 2,663, Hull, with 1,557, and Scarborough, with 1,480, shared a somewhat similar pattern of gild bequests. The testators of Pontefract, with a poll tax population of 1,085, and Doncaster, with 800,

---

131 *Ibid.*, p. 282.
132 PRO C 47/46/444. See Chapter 1, p. 29.

Figure 2.5: Bequests to Gilds in Larger Urban Centres

	Sample Dates	Wills	Hull	Beverely	Scarborough	Pontefract	Doncaster
1.	Aug 1320 – Mar 1400	430	9	3	4	2	3
2.	Mar 1405 – Mar 1409	131	5	3	2	–	–
3.	Mar 1416 – Mar 1420	40	3	–	–	–	–
4.	Mar 1427 – Mar 1431	250	1	2	–	5	–
5.	Mar 1438 – Mar 1442	209	11	–	–	4	–
6.	Mar 1449 – Mar 1453	118	6	1	1	1	–
7.	Mar 1460 – Mar 1464	138	3	2	2	6	–
8.	Mar 1471 – Mar 1475	274	1	–	–	6	6
9.	Mar 1482 – Mar 1486	256	3	1	–	14	12
10.	Mar 1493 – Mar 1497	110	2	–	–	1	1
11.	Mar 1504 – Mar 1508	558	–	–	–	8	26
12.	Mar 1515 – Mar 1519	355	4	–	1	2	1
13.	Mar 1526 – Mar 1530	682	–	–	–	12	1
14.	Mar 1537 – Mar 1541	138	2	1	–	1	–
15.	Mar 1547 – Mar 1548	324	–	–	–	–	–
Total			50	13	10	62	50

behaved rather differently. The distribution of bequests to gilds in these five urban centres, throughout the sample periods, is shown in Figure 2.5. The figures indicate that, in Hull, the largest number of bequests was recorded over the sample periods up to 1453. In Beverley and Scarborough, there were very few bequests to gilds at all and the majority of these were also made in the fourteenth and early fifteenth centuries. By contrast, bequests to Pontefract gilds occurred most frequently in the late fifteenth and early sixteenth centuries and those in Doncaster were mainly concentrated between 1471 and 1508. Whilst the general trend that we have seen in the county at large is, to some extent, reflected in bequests to Pontefract and Doncaster gilds, it in no way represents the situation in Beverley, Hull or Scarborough.

When bequests to gilds in these five towns are examined as a proportion of all such bequests, their share of the total decreased rather than increased over the sampling period. Between them they received 87.5% of all fourteenth century bequests. By the first decade of the sixteenth century, their share of the sample had declined to 32.4%. As a group, these five large towns received, progressively, a lower proportion of bequests from the sample. Individually, however, each town had its own particular pattern within this general trend, although, admittedly, we are dealing with very small numbers of testators.

Hull's bequests, within the sample, were spread amongst eighteen recorded gilds, twelve of which belonged to Holy Trinity parish and five to the smaller, but still wealthy, St Mary's.[133] Most of the known gilds were operating up to the

---

[133] They were, technically, chapels of ease rather than parish churches. The gild of St Ninian in

middle of the fifteenth century. Joan Gregg, in 1438, made bequests to ten named gilds and, in 1451, John Harpham left a total of 40s. to sustain every gild light in Hull, at a rate of 3s.4d. each, indicating a total of twelve.[134] Of the fifty bequests to Hull gilds, seventy per cent were made before 1454. By contrast, only two were recorded between 1485 and 1517, but a further six appeared in the sample between 1517 and 1540. This pattern points to some correspondence between the town's prosperity and the incidence of such bequests. Hull suffered a general economic decline in the second half of the fifteenth century, but began to recover in the early sixteenth.[135] Certainly, the number of bequests to gilds fell dramatically during the nadir of Hull's fortunes, but the total of six, recorded in sixteenth century samples, hardly suggests a large-scale revival of interest at this later period. This does not necessarily indicate, however, that gilds were not active at this time. Rather than make bequests directly to gilds, some Hull testators preferred to make them to the fraternities' maisonsdieu and to the poor persons that inhabited them.[136]

Other evidence confirms that several Hull gilds were active at periods when bequests to them were rare. The Corpus Christi Gild of Holy Trinity parish, whose rent book of 1522 indicates that it was a considerable property owner in the town, was reported on by the commissioners in 1548.[137] The account book of the St Mary Gild in Holy Trinity continued to be kept up to 1536, although the quality of the accounts shows a marked deterioration after 1512.[138] The Holy Trinity Gild, founded in the mid-fourteenth century, constructed its hall between 1465 and 1476, at a time when bequests to Hull gilds were at a low point.[139] It also continued to perform its Noah Play annually on Plough Day after the dissolution, although detailed accounts ended in 1531.[140] This gild, however, had, in 1456, become a shipmen's gild, exclusive to mariners skilled in navigation.[141] A similar take-over of an existing gild by a commercial group took place in 1499, when the gild of St George was incorporated by the town as a merchants' gild, discharging both devotional and mercantile functions.[142] The ordinances of other occupations, published in the same decade, show that craft associations in Hull now fulfilled some of the functions of religious gilds. Whilst the weavers simply maintained a votive light, the glovers also bore lights at members' funerals, and

---

the Carmelite Friary appears in the probate registers outside the sampling period. See Heath, 'Urban Piety', pp. 222–3 and note.

[134] BIHR PR 3 555v–556v 1438 Joan Gregg widow. PR 2 231r–v 1451 John Harpham.

[135] J. I. Kermode, 'Merchants, Overseas Trade, and Urban Decline: York, Beverley, and Hull c. 1380–1500', *Northern History* 13 (1987), 52–73 (pp. 55–6).

[136] E.g. BIHR PR 11 470 1540 James Clerke. PR 11 480r 1504 Sir Thomas Henrison priest.

[137] *Certificates*, II, p. 571, KHRO BRA 88 10.

[138] KHRO BRA 87/8, p. 142. See Chapter 6.

[139] Woodward, 'The Accounts of the Building of Trinity House, Hull', pp. 153–170.

[140] A. J. Mill, 'The Hull Noah Play', pp. 504–8 and note.

[141] Woodward, 'The Accounts of the Building of Trinity House, Hull', p. 153.

[142] KHRO BRE 5/4.

the walkers and shearmen additionally attended members' burials and weddings en masse.[143]

Beverley was a town that was rich in gilds. Its thirteen fraternities were very active in the early fifteenth century.[144] The low number of bequests to them, however, makes it difficult to draw meaningful conclusions from testamentary evidence alone. What there is shows that, while the thirteen recorded bequests to gilds, in the sample, ranged in date between 1396 and 1538, almost half of them were made before 1408. This period is, of course, very close to the beginning of the main probate registers. It suggests a high degree of gild activity around 1390 when the regulations for the Corpus Christi procession were written, naming six gilds that did not appear in the will sample.[145] Only two bequests to Beverley gilds were identified after 1500. That recorded in 1538 was, however, unusual, in that it was a musicians' gild whose membership may have been countywide.[146] The only gild in the town to receive more than three bequests from the sample was the Great Gild of St John of Beverley, four of whose five legators came from outside the borough.[147]

By the second quarter of the fifteenth century, Beverley's mercantile economy had declined to that of a local market town, showing further deterioration, with falling rents and a declining population, towards the century's end.[148] The admittedly thin testamentary evidence suggests that religious gilds were active before most wills were systematically recorded and that, while gilds survived, they did so in an atmosphere of economic decline in which few bequests were made to them. It has also been argued that their devotional functions were partly replaced by craft associations.[149] This mirrors the situation that we have seen in Hull, although the timing of these trends in Beverley was rather earlier. The foundation, or re-foundation, of young men's gilds in both St John's and St Mary's churches, during the first decade of the sixteenth century, shows, however, that gilds unconnected with crafts were still active, although the level of bequests to them was low.[150]

Despite its high poll tax population in 1377, there were only ten bequests in the sample to the thirteen recorded gilds of Scarborough. Five gilds are known

---

[143] KHRO BRE 5/1 (weavers), 2 (walkers and shearmen), 3 (glovers).

[144] They are listed in Appendix 1.

[145] Leach, *Beverley Town Documents*, pp. 35–6.

[146] BIHR PR 11A 365r–v 1538 George Wilson luter, living in York, to the officers of the brotherhood of Our Lady called the Red Ark.

[147] BIHR PR 3 270r 1407 Reginald Gerrard of Scarborough. Reg 18 344r–v 1408 John Mayer mercer of Beverley. PR 2 539v–540r 1428 Thomas Beauchamp chaplain of Hull. YML L2(4) 301r–v 1462 John Haliday gentleman of Heslington. BIHR Reg 168r–v 1506 Robert Dunler vicar of Garton.

[148] *VCH ER* VI, pp. 55–6, Kermode 'Merchants, Overseas Trade and Urban Decline', p. 55.

[149] D. A. Lamburn, 'Politics and Religion in Sixteenth Century Beverley' (unpublished D.Phil. thesis, York, 1991) pp. 293, 296, 305. See Chapter 3, pp. 106–7, for further discussion of this point.

[150] HCRO BC/II/3 fol.47.

only from evidence from outside the sample.[151] The chronological spread of the three bequests to the St Clement Gild, the only fraternity to receive more than one, indicates that it was active for a span of at least 108 years, between 1400 and 1518.[152] No other bequest to a gild was found in the sample after 1462. However, economic decay and a decline in population has been detected in Scarborough from the early years of the fifteenth century.[153] It seems likely that many of the thirteen gilds of Scarborough were founded in the years of its affluence, before the beginning of the main probate registers, and that there had been a decline in gild activity before testamentary evidence was widely recorded. A single bequest to the St George Gild, in 1349, the earliest recorded in the county, gives some support to this view.[154] There is insufficient evidence from the town to indicate whether there was a commercialization of gilds, of the kind detected in Hull and Beverley.

Figure 2.5 shows that in both Pontefract and Doncaster the majority of bequests to gilds were made much later than in the three larger towns. It appears that, as in Beverley, Hull and Scarborough, bequests to gilds tend to have been made in periods of economic prosperity but that this prosperity occurred later here. Both were important, long-established market towns that were flourishing particularly in the second half of the fifteenth century. A symptom of this is the promulgation of royal charters, incorporating Doncaster, in 1467, and Pontefract, in 1484, as boroughs.[155] The reasons for their prosperity were, however, somewhat different. Pontefract, dominated by its Duchy of Lancaster castle, was a town of well-established strategic importance. Doncaster, although smaller than Pontefract in 1377, was to become the premier wool market in the north by the

---

151 *VCH NR* II, p. 558. Ed. A. Rowntree, *The History of Scarborough* (London, 1931) p. 378, lists the following gilds in the town in 1426 without giving detailed references: All Saints, Corpus Christi, Holy Trinity, St Clement, St George, St James, St John Baptist, St Mary Assumption, St Nicholas, St Sitha. The following bequests were found in the will sample: St Clement Gild: BIHR PR 3 42v 1400 William Carter of the parish of St Mary formerly of Flamborough: 6s.8d. and a chest. PR 3 276r–v 1407 Simon Qwaynte of the parish of St Mary: 6s.8d. PR 9 80v 1518 Richard Smyth burgess merchant of the parish of St Mary: 3s.4d. St George Gild: Reg 10 346r–v 1349 Alan de Snayton cleric of the parish of St Mary Scarborough: 6s.8d. St John Baptist Gild: PR 2 229r–v 1451 Alice Burton widow of Robert burgess of the parish of St Mary: 3s.4d. St John Baptist Gild in St Sepulchre Chapel (may be the same gild as St John Baptist): PR 2 470r 1462 Peter Provest burgess of the parish of St Mary: 3s.4d. St Katherine Gild: PR 3 42v 1400 William Carter of the parish of St Mary: 6s.4d. and a chest. St Mary in Jerusalem Gild: PR 1 13r 1390 John Rottese of the parish of St Mary: 3s.4d. to the light (this may be a bequest to a gild in the Holy Land). St Nicholas Gild: Reg 18 12v–13r 1408 John Norman of the parish of St Mary 6s.8d. St Sitha Gild: PR 2 470r 1462 Peter Provest burgess of the parish of St Mary 20d.
152 BIHR PR 3 42v 1400 William Carter. PR 3 276r 1407 Simon Qwaynte. PR 9 80v 1518 Richard Smyth burgess and merchant.
153 P. Heath, 'North Sea Fishing in the Fifteenth Century: the Scarborough Fleet', *Northern History* 3 (1968), 53–69 (p. 65).
154 BIHR Reg 10 346r–v 1349 Alan de Snayton cleric of Scarborough.
155 Dobson, 'Yorkshire Towns in the Late Fourteenth Century', pp. 4–8.

early seventeenth century and was already expanding.[156] The pattern of bequests to gilds in each town seems to reflect this contrast.

Although it had a lower poll tax population than Beverley, Hull or Scarborough, the gilds of Pontefract attracted more bequests than any other centre, apart from York. This high figure was largely due to the popularity of its Corpus Christi Gild, which received fifty-two bequests from the sample between 1387 and 1529. Only seven of these were made prior to 1460, whilst fourteen belonged to the sample period 1482–86. The coincidence between this period and the promulgation of the town charter, in 1484, may be significant. Unfortunately, this extremely popular fraternity is known only from testamentary evidence. It is tempting to speculate that a gild of this importance, in a town controlled, throughout most of fifteenth and sixteenth centuries, by the crown, had royal support and membership. The other gilds of the town included the Jesus Gild, which was operating between 1507 and 1529, and which seems to have absorbed the St Roch Gild at some point between 1507 and 1515.[157] This amalgamation might suggest some particular difficulties in the town, at this time, as it also coincided with a fall in bequests to the Corpus Christi Gild.

Doncaster, with only just over half Hull's poll tax population, made the same number of bequests to its twenty-four gilds.[158] The largest number of these bequests, fourteen, were to the gild of St George and covered the period from 1471 to 1529. The testamentary evidence for gilds in Doncaster prior to 1471 rests entirely on the contents of one will made in 1398 by William Millot, who left quite substantial sums of money to the gilds of Corpus Christi, Paternoster and St Katherine.[159] Otherwise, seventy-eight per cent of all bequests to Doncaster gilds were made in the last two decades of the fifteenth century and the first of the sixteenth. Bequests by individuals to more than one gild were particularly common in Doncaster at this time. In 1492, William Bakehouse made bequests to as many as nine.[160] This trend is further exemplified by a series of six blanket bequests to all the gilds of Doncaster, of which each testator was a member, during the thirteen months between June 1505 and July 1506.[161] As in Pontefract, however, this

---

156 A. Everitt, 'The Marketing of Agricultural Produce, 1500–1640', in *Chapters from The Agrarian History of England and Wales*, gen. ed. J. Thirsk, 5 vols. (Cambridge, 1990), IV, pp. 15–156 (p. 43).

157 Jesus Gild: BIHR PR 6 122r–v 1507 John Bule. PR 9 40r–v 1515 Hugh Austwyk mercer. PR 9 430r 1529 Peter Chapman alderman. PR 9 472r–v 1529 William Mures alias Purser alderman. St Roch Gild: PR 6 226v–227r 1507 Thomas Waldyng. Jesus and St Roch Gild: PR 9 22r 1515 Thomas Cooke burgess.

158 Goldberg, 'From Conquest to Corporation', supplies a large number of references to gilds that fall outside the sample.

159 BIHR PR 2 9r.

160 BIHR PR 5 31r 1482 William Bakehouse to the gilds of Corpus Christi, Holy Cross, Holy Trinity, St Christopher, St George, St James and St Sitha, St Mary, St Mary Magdalene, St Thomas of Canterbury.

161 BIHR PR 6 194v, 1505 Joan Pereson widow. PR 6 203r 1505 William Multiclyffe. PR 6 209r–v 1505 Thomas Dey. PR 6 195v 1505 William Wod. PR 6 212r 1505 Thomas Vance ?merchant. PR 6 221r 1506 Thomas Cook cordwainer.

high point in bequests to gilds coincides with the granting of a charter, further extending the power of its burgesses. In 1505, the lordship of the borough was granted by Henry VII to its mayor and commonalty.[162] This suggests a strong connection between civic sentiment and gild membership. It has already been argued that multiple gild membership might indicate a place where gilds displayed a strong political and commercial dimension.[163] Although direct evidence of a commercialization of Doncaster gilds is lacking, a bequest to a cordwainers' gild in 1505, might hint that its fraternities were, at this time, developing along the lines of those in Beverley and Hull.[164]

Two forces seem to have been at work in urban centres during periods of decline in bequests to gilds. One was the disincentive of economic difficulties. This varied according to the fluctuating prosperity of each town. Although non-testamentary evidence suggests that gilds were active in some towns even during periods when there were no bequests to them, it might be fair to assume that such bequests were a barometer, if a somewhat unreliable one, of the economic health of both town and gild. The other force may have been a perceptible secularization in the nature of the gilds themselves. The commercialization of some gilds that occurred in Hull, Beverley and, probably, Doncaster during the second half of the fifteenth and the early sixteenth century was, perhaps, a symptom of this. Their role as property owners and landlords was also increasing as bequests and donations accumulated. Furthermore, we shall see that their involvement with local government was enhancing their political influence. Such changes in the nature of some urban gilds probably affected the attitude of potential testators. A bequest to a fraternity was basically a pious act offering spiritual rewards to the dying. If, however, the gild was perceived as offering worldly advantage as a priority, its spiritual efficacy might be called in question. Increasing secularization may account for the decline in bequests to urban gilds in the sixteenth century, even though they continued to be active.

Conclusion

The indications are that gilds were as common an institution in Yorkshire as they were elsewhere in the country. The testamentary evidence on which this research is heavily dependent, however, generally reveals only the large and important fraternities. Nevertheless, the frequency with which such gilds appear can be used as a measure of their popularity over a period of time. The chronological pattern that has emerged is an increase in the popularity of gilds in the county, from 1389, which reached its zenith in the late fifteenth and early sixteenth centuries, followed by a decline prior to their dissolution in 1547. Fluctuations within

---

[162] Goldberg, 'From Conquest to Corporation', pp. 51–2.

[163] See pp. 51–2 above.

[164] BIHR PR 6 149r–v 1505 Thomas Cook cordwainer: 'Item gilde Allutarii xxiiij lb. rosyn', also bequests to the gilds of St George, St Sebastian, St Barbara.

this pattern were caused by local variations. The larger urban centres, for example, attracted progressively fewer bequests to gilds throughout the period, whilst they increased in rural areas and in the smaller boroughs of Pontefract and Doncaster. One effect of these contrary trends was a peak in bequests in 1482–46 and again in 1504–08.

Most gilds were identified in centres of high population, economic affluence, political power or religious significance. The variable importance of these factors in different areas, however, was further modified by local conditions. The proliferation of gilds in Holderness in the early sixteenth century was a response to a new-found prosperity based on its agriculture. West Riding services supplied a need for additional parish clergy in large parishes, with difficult terrain. Each town was subject to different commercial and political pressures. These variables result in a diversity that renders classification and generalization, except in the widest terms, almost impossible. Variation was not only seen between gilds but was also found within the changing functions and memberships of those few individual fraternities where documentary evidence survives. Aspects of this diversity can only be investigated further by examining what we can discover of the people who belonged to them.

CHAPTER THREE

The Membership and Activities of Yorkshire Gilds

From the evidence of the gild returns of 1389 and from some of the other surviving literature, it is possible to discover the aspirations of gilds as corporate bodies. It has been shown that these were basically devotional and fraternal.[1] They were expressed in a wide variety of ways. In order to fulfil these aspirations, however, gilds needed to raise finance and to gain and sustain the approval of the individuals and groups who governed the communities where they operated. In many cases they became commercial entities in their own right, owning real estate or engaging in trade. Many also became increasingly identified with local ruling groups. This was probably part of a two-way process, whereby gilds sought influential members, who would give them access to local government, and members joined successful gilds as a step to political power within the wider community, through fraternal links. The key to the gilds' successful relationship with local authorities was their conservative piety which was acceptable, not only to local magnates and corporations, but to the crown as the ultimate source of power.

This chapter will test these propositions by investigating the kind of person who, as a member of a Yorkshire gild, was able and willing to make a bequest to it. It will examine the occupations of such members, as far as they can be determined, and their status within their communities, in an attempt to illustrate general themes within the wide variations that the special characteristics of individual gilds displayed in particular places and at particular times. The bequests made to fraternities by these testators, supplemented by other evidence, will throw further light on their social and economic activities, as well as leading to a discussion of their devotional preoccupations and the ways in which these were expressed. Material from the City of York will only be used for comparative purposes in pursuit of these arguments. Detailed discussion of York gilds is undertaken in the next chapter.

The Occupations and Status of Testators

In the absence of membership registers for fraternities outside York itself, any investigation of the kinds of people who belonged to gilds in the county rests largely on an analysis of the testamentary evidence. This is not a wholly satis-

[1]   See Chapter, 1 pp. 31–5.

factory process. The disadvantages of using a sample of data from a group that was restricted to the wealthier members of society, and the problems related to incomplete probate registers, have already been discussed.[2] A further difficulty is that many testators, especially in small towns and rural areas, did not specify their occupations or social status. In the larger towns, and especially in York, the existence of a franchise system, and of elaborate structures of local government, led to this kind of information being frequently included in the preambles to wills or in the marginal notes of the registers. In the county will sample, by contrast, the vast majority, especially of rural testators, were known simply by their names. Their status and occupations can only be deduced, where possible, from the content of their wills. Figure 3.1 makes it clear that only a minority of the occupations of testators can be identified up to the 1520s. Thereafter, the proportion of testators of unknown occupation never fell below forty per cent.

Despite these constraints, we would expect to find that a high proportion of urban testators making bequests to gilds came from the mercantile classes. This group dominated civic government throughout the Late Middle Ages, although high office was sometimes achieved by a few wealthy artisans.[3] If a significant proportion of the civic elite were gild members, then we can assume, with some confidence, that there was a relationship between the government of a town and its gilds.

Figure 3.1 shows that the nineteen merchants and wholesalers who made bequests to gilds were scattered thinly throughout the sample, making it difficult to discern any overall chronological trend spanning the whole period from 1398 to 1538. Six of them were from Hull.[4] Pontefract yielded eight and Beverley just two merchants.[5] Doncaster and Scarborough were each represented by one.[6] These figures seem very low for mercantile centres, where high numbers of gilds were identified. However, fifteen urban testators identified themselves by status, claiming the rank of burgess or alderman.[7] The majority of such testators were of Hull and Beverley but, by the early sixteenth century, bequests to gilds were more commonly made by aldermen and burgesses of Pontefract and Doncaster.

2 See Introduction, pp. 9–10, Chapter 2, pp. 46–7.
3 J. I. Kermode, 'Obvious Observations on the Formation of Oligarchies in Late Medieval English Towns', in *Towns and People in the Fifteenth Century*, ed. J. A. F. Thomson (Gloucester, 1988), 87–106 (p. 97).
4 BIHR PR 3 11r 1398 John Hornsee, merchant. PR 2 575v 1408 Alan Wilcok, merchant. PR 2 233r–v Richard Bille 1451, merchant. PR 5 87v 1483 George Busshell (Bussell), merchant. PR 5 250v 1484 William Barron, draper. PR 11A 324r–v 1438 Henry Lamley draper.
5 Pontefract: BIHR PR 3 549r 1438 Thomas Wrote, clothier. PR 5 250v 1484 John Illyngworth, draper. PR 9 40r–v Hugh Awstyk, mercer. PR 9 442v Thomas Hodgeson, merchant. Beverley: Reg 18 344r–v 1408 John Mayer, mercer. PR 2 243v–244r 1452 Richard Patryngton, merchant.
6 BIHR PR 6 212r 1505 Thomas Vance merchant of Doncaster. PR 9 80v 1518 Thomas Hodgeson, merchant of Scarborough.
7 Civic officeholders making bequests to gilds called themselves burgesses in Hull, Beverley and Scarborough. In Doncaster they were aldermen and in Pontefract both terms were used, although both towns had achieved borough status prior to the dates of all the sampled wills. Two of the testators were the widows of burgesses.

**Figure 3.1: Occupation and Status of Lay Testators Making
Bequests to Gilds and Services (excluding York)**

Date	Merchants	Craftsmen	Husbandmen	Civic	Gentry	All Women	Unknown	All
1320–1400	1	2	–	3	–	2	20	23
1405–1409	2	–	–	2	1	1	14	16
1416–1420	–	–	–	–	–	–	2	2
1427–1431	–	2	1	–	1	2	17	19
1438–1442	2	1	1	–	–	2	12	16
1449–1453	2	1	–	1	–	1	10	13
1460–1464	–	2	1	1	1	3	19	22
1471–1475	–	2	–	–	2	4	32	34
1482–1486	4	6	8	–	1	4	34	51
1493–1497	–	1	3	–	–	–	10	13
1504–1508	2	1	19	2	1	10	58	80
1515–1519	3	–	13	4	–	5	22	38
1526–1530	1	3	25	4	2	4	29	68
1537–1541	2	2	23	–	2	4	27	62
1547–1548	–	1	2	–	1	–	2	5
Totals	19	24	96	17	12	42	308	462

Date: period of will sample.
Merchants: including mercers, drapers, clothiers and their wives and widows.
Craftsmen: persons of urban occupation and their wives and widows.
Husbandmen: including yeomen and those with wills indicating agricultural livelihood and their wives and widows.
Civic: burgesses, aldermen, civic officeholders and their wives and widows.
Gentry: lords, knights, esquires, gentlemen and their wives and widows.
Unknown: all testators of unknown occupation.
All: all testators making bequests to gilds and services.

N.B. Some testators appear under several headings.

It is reasonable to assume that most of this civic group and the partially overlapping mercantile group together comprised the wealthiest and most influential individuals in their communities. They seem, indeed, to have supported gilds as a relatively high proportion of the will-making population at large, accounting for some 54.3% of all testators making bequests to gilds, in the county's five largest towns, whose occupations are known. The political significance of the size of this grouping will be pursued in the next chapter, in the context of the relationship between gilds and the civic government of York, where the evidence is more plentiful. In social and commercial terms, it is clear, however, that gilds attracted bequests from leading figures in the county's urban centres.

Sixteen of the twenty-four testators who came from what might be seen as the social stratum below that of merchant and wholesaler were also from the five large towns. This whole group, identified in Figure 3.1 as craftsmen, comprised five from textile manufacture, six from victualling, three leatherworkers, two metalworkers, two mariners, a carpenter, a potter, a musician and a lawyer. Several of these testators, however, either by their occupations or from the nature of their bequests, were evidently men of considerable wealth. One of the Hull mariners was part-owner of his ship.[8] William Scoforth, walker of Beverley, left 5s. and a pound of wax to the St Mary Gild, and 6s.8d to Corpus Christi, and John Cryche, baker of Doncaster, left 20d. and a helmet, for ceremonial use, to the St George Gild of Doncaster.[9] It seems likely that such men were sufficiently prosperous members of their communities to be included within the ruling group.

This was also the case with the handful of testators of known occupation from smaller towns. Individual merchants made bequests to gilds in Bridlington and Leeds.[10] In Middlesborough, a clothier made a bequest to a gild there and another, in Halifax, left money to a local service.[11] William Marshall, a lawyer from Middleton by Pickering, who left the receipts from a croft and toft to the masters of the local gild of St Mary for a ninety-nine year period, was clearly a man of local importance and an owner of agricultural land.[12] William Barker, a barker from Whitby, left the large sum of 13s.4d. to his Holy Trinity Gild, butchers from Leeds and Ripon both left 3s.4d. to local gilds and a carpenter from Aldborough in Holderness bequeathed a measure of wheat to the St Peter Gild there.[13] This latter bequest, however, suggests that the carpenter combined his craft with agriculture. Typically of craftsmen in small rural communities, he was evidently also a husbandman.

Husbandmen might, in some respects, be regarded as the rural equivalent of wealthy urban artisans, and the marketing activities of the two groups overlapped.[14] Figure 3.1 shows that husbandmen accounted for sixty-nine per cent of all known occupations. Furthermore, they were found in sufficient quantity for a real trend to be perceived. Although not all of these individuals actually stated that they were husbandmen, it is reasonable to assume, from the contents of their wills, that they all gained their living from the land, leaving quantities of produce and animals to their legatees, as well as farmland and meadows. These characteristics appeared in the wills of the twenty testators who called themselves husbandmen and the five who styled themselves yeomen. It seems logical to group with them those who did not do so but whose wills showed similar features.

8   KHRO BRA 87/1522 1523 John Armstrong mariner of Hull, BIHR PR 3 4r 1398.
9   BIHR PR 3 4r William Scoforth walker of Beverley. PR 5 256r 1484 John Cryche baker of Doncaster.
10 BIHR PR 5 40v 1507 John Smyth of Bridlington. PR 9 70v 1517 Brian Baynes of Leeds.
11 BIHR PR 3 987v–988r 1439 Robert Thomson of Middlesborough. PR 11 333 1538 Robert Thomson of Halifax.
12 BIHR PR 9 436r 1528 William Marshall.
13 BIHR PR 1 92r–v 1396 William Barker. PR 9 366v 1527 William Atkinson butcher of Leeds. PR 5 275r 1485 Richard Ellington butcher of Ripon. PR 9 432r 1538 Ralph Marshall carpenter of Aldbrough.
14 Rubin, 'Religious Culture', pp. 16–17.

There were no testators who appeared to be husbandmen making bequests to gilds in the sample prior to 1428. The first to describe himself thus was John Faceby, of Sutton-on-the-Forest, in 1463.[15] From the 1480s, however, the proportion of husbandmen rose steadily from fifteen per cent of all those making bequests to gilds to forty per cent by 1547. Although a small sample makes this final percentage of questionable significance, the two preceding periods yielded values of around thirty-seven per cent from groups of over sixty testators. The reason for this steep rise is related both to an overall increase in the proportion of rural testators and to a growing interest in gild membership.[16] Whilst a number of these wills are so brief that it is difficult to judge how wealthy a testator might have been, some of the husbandmen who made bequests to gilds were clearly substantial farmers and landowners. Richard Hull and John Pryston, both of Coniston in the parish of Swine, each left a bushel of barley to the St Mary Gild and made other bequests of livestock and produce.[17] Peter Asy, who bequeathed barley to the gilds of St Mary and St Katherine in Preston, was wealthy enough to commission a trental of masses.[18] John Bell of Coxwold parish, who owned property for rent and an array of farm implements, gave a sheep to the St Mary Gild.[19] These men were wealthy enough to wield considerable influence, as landowners and employers, within their communities and to be important members of the affinities of the local lords, at least some of whom controlled gilds within the areas they governed.

Bequests to gilds from lords themselves, however, were rare. Those noblemen and gentry whose wills were locally proved comprised only three per cent of testators to gilds in the county. No more than two appeared in any one sample period. They included no titled aristocracy, although some were men of local importance, such as Sir Thomas Reedness, lord of Whitgift, who left 6s.8d. to its Holy Trinity Gild, and Robert Roos esquire of Ingmanthorpe, who bequeathed 3s.4d. to the Holy Cross Gild of Ripon.[20] Others called themselves gentlemen, like George Davell who left 6s.8d. to the St Mary Gild of Coxwold and a further 20s. to Sir Thomas Swanne, the gild priest, to pray for him.[21] How far the Nevilles in Bedale, the Reednesses in Whitgift and the Meltons in Swine personally participated in the activities of their parish gilds is a moot point. Their political and economic control of local fraternities was probably exerted, at least partly, through their agents.

This does not necessarily indicate that noble and gentle laymen and women were not members of gilds. Their names often appear in the membership lists of large or exclusive urban fraternities. Membership of such gilds offered public

---

15 BIHR PR 3 295v.

16 See Chapter 2 above, pp. 50–1.

17 BIHR PR 9 443v 1529 Richard Hull husbandman. PR 9 483 1529 John Pryston.

18 BIHR PR 11A 275v 1537 Peter Asy husbandman.

19 BIHR PR 11A 261r 1537 John Bell.

20 BIHR PR 3 276v 1407 Sir Thomas Re[e]dness. PR 11 12r–v 1529 Robert Roos esquire.

21 BIHR PR 11A 348r–v 1538 George Davell.

figures a wider or more influential network of political and economic contacts than more local gilds could possess. The register of the Corpus Christi Gild of Boston, Lincolnshire, for example, shows that it attracted many aristocratic members.[22] The three extant bequests to it in the Lincoln will registers, however, were all made by members of the urban elite.[23] The membership register of the Corpus Christi Gild of York is also rich in the names of county families, and whilst some of this group were prepared to pay higher membership fees than most other entrants, few of them made bequests to it.[24]

That the nobility and gentry were members of influential gilds, yet were not in the habit of making bequests to them, suggests that their interest in them was, unlike that of some other testators, not centred on their funerary practices or intercessory role. In his analysis of aristocratic wills, J. T. Rosenthal found that, amidst a plethora of pious legacies, the nobility of the fourteenth and fifteenth centuries founded chantries and commissioned obits from religious houses and, especially, from the mendicant orders.[25] He records only one bequest by an aristocrat to a gild and implies that this was prompted by charity towards the fraternity rather than a request for its prayers.[26] Since persons of noble status preferred to cater for their daily devotional needs by maintaining family chapels in their houses and to provide for the care of their souls after death by founding chantries, the motives for their membership of gilds were as likely to be social and political as pious.[27] However, the large and exclusive gilds, where membership attracted the benefits of indulgences or other tokens of especial sanctity, which were as relevant to the piety of the living as to the testaments of the dead, offered them devotional benefits as well as socio-political influence.[28] The Corpus Christi Gild of York, for example, possessed several indulgences and a large collection of relics, besides being governed by churchmen.[29]

Mixed motives for joining gilds are discernible in all lay groups and this is equally true of one that cuts across them all, but demands separate consideration. Women accounted for just over nine per cent of all testators to gilds. Here there is no doubt of the size of the group as, unlike artisans or mercers, individuals are almost always easily identified. The incidence of their bequests, fluctuating between six and fourteen per cent of the total of the various sample periods,

22 BL MS Harley 4795. See also H. Fenning, 'The Guild of Corpus Christi', *The Guilds in Boston*, ed. W. M. Ormrod (Boston, 1993), pp. 35–9.

23 Foster, *Lincoln Wills*, I, pp. 175–8 1526 Joseph Benson, Merchant of the Staple, II, pp. 40–3 1527 John Leek mercer, III, pp. 42–3 Thomas Murre roper.

24 See Chapter 5, below pp. 173, 184.

25 J. T. Rosenthal, *The Purchase of Paradise – Gift Giving and the Aristocracy 1307–1495* (London, 1972), pp. 81–122, *passim*, pp. 121–2, p. 128.

26 *Ibid.*, p. 109. Isabella Morley made a bequest to the gild of St Andrew, Buxton.

27 J. Hughes, *Pastors and Visionaries, Religion and Secular Life in Late Medieval Yorkshire* (Woodbridge, 1988), pp. 10–11.

28 Bainbridge, *Gilds in the Medieval Countryside*, pp. 135–7, adduces both pious and political motives for gild membership on the part of both aristocracy and gentry in Cambridgeshire.

29 See Chapter 5, pp. 189–91.

roughly follows the general pattern of all bequests. The 1389 gild returns and surviving gild registers clearly show that almost all gilds had sisters, as well as brothers, amongst their members, and that men and their wives usually joined gilds as couples, often at a reduced entrance fee.[30]

This latter point provides one clue as to why many women became gild members, and why more of them did not make bequests to them. Eighty-six per cent of female testators to gilds were certainly widows, and some of the rest may have been, their wills containing insufficient evidence to confirm their status. Wives that pre-deceased their husbands seldom made wills.[31] Furthermore, it is clear that, in a number of cases, the husband's bequest to a gild included that of the widow. Instructions by husbands concerning their obits generally included provision for their wives. The elaborate orders for gild obits that are bound with the register of Corpus Christi Gild in Boston, Lincolnshire, are a case in point.[32] That of Henry and Katherine Basse was a joint affair, and the gild bellman was enjoined to urge the citizens, at each station where he announced the service every year, that they should 'pray for the sawles of Herry Basse of Boston mercer and Kateryn hys wyfe brother and sister in Corpus Christi gilde'.[33] Several male testators left real estate that would revert to a gild on the death of their widows. In 1472, John Sturmy of Hedon left a house to the officials of the gild of Holy Cross on the death of his wife and son and, in 1474, Robert Smalethorpe left a tenement in Bondgate to the Corpus Christi Gild of Pontefract under similar conditions.[34] In these cases the widow might have considered that any obligation to the gild had already been discharged. Widows also made arrangements with gilds for their dead husbands. The assignment of John Haynson's property to the St Mary Gild of Holy Trinity in Hull, in 1476, seems to have been the decision of Margaret, his widow, whose name was subsequently added to the obit.[35] Since female gild members were less likely to make bequests to their fraternities than males, the testamentary evidence produces an underestimate of their numbers.

Joint membership by married couples suggests that wives shared their husbands' motives, whether devotional, social or political. The wives of Chaucer's craftsmen saw their gild as a route to social aggrandizement, through their husbands' political manipulation of the gild.[36] This is not, however, the whole story. There is some indication of both independence and an enthusiasm for gilds on the part of individual women. For example, they did not always belong exclu-

---

[30] E.g. MS Lansdowne 304; ed. M. D. Harris, *The Register of the Guild of the Holy Trinity, St Mary, St John the Baptist and St Katherine of Coventry*, Dugdale Society 13 (London, 1935); ed. P. Basing, *The Gild of Trinity and SS Fabian and Sebastian in St Botolph without Aldersgate in London*, London Record Society (1982).

[31] C. Burgess, 'Late Medieval Wills', p. 19.

[32] MS Harley 4795 fols. 78r–89.

[33] *Ibid.*, fol. 83.

[34] BIHR PR 4 179, 49r–v.

[35] For a full discussion of this episode see Chapter 6 below, pp. 207–11.

[36] See Introduction, p. 1.

sively to the same gilds as their husbands. William Walker of Richmond left 3s.4d. each to the gilds of St Mary and St John in his will of 8 September 1484. Ten days later Margaret Walker, his wife, left 3s.4d. to the gild of St Mary too, but she also bequeathed 20d. to St Thomas' Gild.[37] She left nothing to St John's Gild. An even greater degree of independence was shown by Agnes Maners, widow, who founded a obit within the gild of Corpus Christi in York, that was to be celebrated in St Margaret's Walmgate, for her soul, those of her parents, her friends and all the faithful dead.[38] She made no mention of her husband, Thomas, with whom she had joined the gild in 1441–42, and whose will, if he made one, has not survived.[39] Particular enthusiasm for gilds appears in the will of Joan Gregg of Hull who left 20s. each to ten gilds in the town and to one in London.[40] Such examples suggest that gild membership offered particular benefits to women.

Whilst there is no evidence that women were eligible for office in any Yorkshire fraternity, there is an indication that, in at least two Beverley gilds, they were regarded as a special group which, in a ceremonial context, commanded its own particular place.[41] In the gild processions of both St Helen and the Purification of the Virgin, all the gild sisters followed immediately after the tableaux of the saints, carrying lights, ahead of the other members.[42] In view of the popularity of female saints, especially St Mary, as gild patrons, it seems likely that women were regarded as a distinct group in other gilds.[43] There is evidence, albeit inconclusive, of a wives' gild in Roos, Holderness, that endowed a window in the church there.[44] Religious gilds may well have been particularly important to pious laywomen. Opportunities for a communal lay religious life, which the beguinages and tertiary orders provided for continental women, were lacking in England.[45] To those who did not wish to live the solitary life of an anchoress and preferred to remain within the world, gilds were the only available means of pursuing piety in the company of other women. It was, after all, the solution adopted by Margery Kempe, who, after her many pilgrimages, joined the Holy Trinity Gild of Lynn in 1438.[46]

Such considerations are a reminder of the basically devotional purposes of

---

37 BIHR PR 5 235r–v. Both wills appear on the same folio and received probate on the same date (11 February 1485); it is not known which partner died first.

38 MS Lansdowne 304, fol. 12r.

39 *Ibid.*, fol. 38v

40 BIHR PR 3 555v–556v 1438.

41 Scarisbrick, *The Reformation and the English People*, p. 25, points out that women could, in theory, become officers of gilds, although they rarely did so. There is evidence from Cambridgeshire of females participating in gild organization, see Bainbridge, *Gilds in the Medieval Countryside*, pp. 47–50.

42 PRO C 47/46/446, 448.

43 See below, pp. 100–1 and Figure 3.4.

44 Poulson, *History of Holderness*, p. 97, refers to a fragment of inscribed glass in the church clerestory. I am indebted to Richard Marks for this reference.

45 R. N. Swanson, *Church and Society in Late Medieval England* (Oxford, 1989), p. 274.

46 *The Book of Margery Kempe*, ed. and transl. B. A. Windeatt (London, 1985), pp. 30, 328.

gilds. We have seen that lay testators came principally from groups that might be supposed to be politically and economically active, both in town and country. By and large, these are the gild members that we know about, but they may not have been typical. Many of the comparatively wealthy men and women who cared enough about their fraternities to make bequests to them were probably leading members of gilds, insiders who were fully conversant with the micro-politics of their organization and its control. It is possible that the rank and file were more concerned with the devotional and fraternal aspects of membership than with political and economic undercurrents. On a macro-political scale, however, it is difficult to separate politics from piety. The Lancastrian suppression of heresy had the active support of the church hierarchy.[47] If gilds were manifestations of orthodox lay piety, we would expect them to be seen as allies of the church, as well as the state, in this process.

The attitudes of the higher clergy towards gilds do not emerge through testamentary evidence. Like the aristocracy, they did not support gilds in this way. The only cleric in the sample, above the rank of rector, who made a bequest to a gild, was James Clapeham, Master of the College of Holy Trinity in Pontefract, who left 20s. to the Corpus Christi Gild in the town.[48] Membership registers show, however, that large numbers of higher clergy were members of influential urban gilds, including those of Corpus Christi, in both York and Boston, Lincolnshire, but they do not seem to have recorded many bequests even to them.[49] The inventory of the Corpus Christi Gild in York shows, however, that high clerics were generous to such gilds in their lifetimes, rather than at their deaths.[50] This suggests that gifts to fraternities were seen, by such dignitaries as the bishops of Carlisle and Hereford, as enhancing their political or social influence rather than inducing the intercessionary prayers of gildsmen and women. Most gilds, outside York, that emerged through the will sample, were too small to wield this kind of influence, although the Corpus Christi Gild in Pontefract was probably an exception.

There is little doubt, however, of a general support for gilds, on the part of testators from lower secular clergy, especially within the context of the parish. That an average of twelve and a half per cent of all testators making bequests to gilds in Yorkshire were clerics should be seen in the context of a country where secular clergy accounted for four per cent of all males.[51]

It has been argued that the institutions of gild and parish represented opposing influences.[52] Certainly, on the face of it, the position of a gild priest, appointed by a body of laymen to work within the parish, but not entirely under

---

[47] R. N. Swanson, *Church and Society*, p. 340.

[48] BIHR PR 5 446r–v 1494.

[49] For Corpus Christi York see below p. 176. For Corpus Christi Boston see Fenning, 'The Guild of Corpus Christi', p. 36.

[50] MS Lansdowne 304, fols. 2r–5v.

[51] C. Haigh, *English Reformations*, pp. 4–5.

[52] G. Rosser, 'Communities of Parish and Guild', pp. 39–44.

Figure 3.2: Status of Clerical Testators Making Bequests to Gilds (excluding York)

Date	All Clerics	High Clerics	Rectors	Vicars	Chaplains	All Testators
1320–1400	2	–	–	1	1	23
1405–1409	2	–	–	–	2	16
1416–1420	1	–	–	–	1	2
1427–1431	3	–	1	–	2	19
1438–1442	2	–	–	2	–	16
1449–1453	2	–	–	1	1	13
1460–1464	3	–	–	1	2	22
1471–1475	7	–	2	–	5	34
1482–1486	9	–	1	2	6	51
1493–1497	3	1	1	1	–	13
1504–1508	8	–	–	6	2	80
1515–1519	4	–	–	3	1	38
1526–1530	2	–	–	1	1	68
1537–1541	3	–	–	–	3	62
1547–1548	1	–	–	–	1	5
Totals	52	1	5	18	28	425

Date: period of will sample.
All Clerics: all clerical testators who made bequests to gilds or services.
High Clerics: all clerics above the rank of rector.
Rectors: all rectors.
Vicars: all vicars.
Chaplains: all unbeneficed clergy including gild and service priests.
All: all testators making bequests to gilds and services.

the direct control of the incumbent, seems anomalous. The parish itself, however, has been described as a kind of fraternity in its own right.[53] Viewed in this way, a parish gild can be seen as an association of leading lay parishioners, who were responsible to the churchwardens.[54] In parishes where there were several gilds, the presence of numbers of bequests to, for example, the four gilds of Hornsea or the eight gilds of Cottingham, shows that their memberships overlapped to a considerable degree, and suggests that gilds were complementary, not antagonistic to one another in their support of the parish.[55] It is likely that, in these cases,

---

[53] Swanson, *Church and Society*, p. 280.

[54] *Ibid.*, p. 281.

[55] General bequests to the four gilds of Hornsea: BIHR PR 6 193r–v 1505 Joan Jakson of the parish of St Nicholas: 2s.8d. to the four gilds, PR 6 241r 1506 Richard Parkour of the parish of St Nicholas: 4s. to be divided into equal portions, PR 9 388r 1428 Robert Meteham gentleman of the parish of St Nicholas: half a quarter of barley to each gild, PR 9 412v 1528 Thomas Smyth of the parish of St Nicholas: 10s. to the four gilds, PR 9 422r 1528 John Bowman of the parish of Skerne St Leonard: 6s.8d., PR 9 454v 1529 Agnes Don of the parish of St Nicholas:

individual gilds had their own responsibilities in terms of ritual and of the maintenance of their chapels.

If, on the other hand, conflict between parish and gild were the norm, we would not expect beneficed clergy to make bequests to them. However, rectors and vicars together accounted for 43.4% of all the clerics who made bequests to gilds, in the sample, suggesting that they regarded them as allies, not opponents, in the context of the parish. Of the five rectors who made bequests, one did so only to gilds outside his parish and four of the eighteen vicars did the same.[56] These exceptions might have been expressing loyalty to fraternities in places where they had family connections or that had played a part in earlier phases of their careers, although it is tempting to speculate that Richard Sudbury's bequest to gilds in Spofforth showed a Percy connection. The majority, however, supported local fraternities.

As chaplains formed the majority of all clerics, especially in northern counties, during the late fifteenth century, it is only to be expected that, as Figure 3.2 shows, they comprised the largest single group, in the sample, of clerical testators making bequests to Yorkshire gilds.[57] Of the twenty-nine chaplains recorded, five were employed by gilds, four were chantry chaplains, one was a service priest and the remaining nineteen were unspecified. Apart from their duties to gild, service or chantry, chaplains also had a parochial role. Most of them assisted the incumbent in a variety of duties, either in the parish church or in chapels of ease. This was particularly evident in the large rural parishes of the West Riding, where chapels of ease made a major contribution to parochial care.[58]

It is, of course, hardly surprising that a gild or service chaplain should support, in his will, an institution that had employed him and to which he had devoted at least some of his life's work. His bequests would also secure the

---

12d. to each gild, PR 11A 309v 1538 Jennet Smarte of the parish of St Nicholas 12d: to each gild and a towel to each altar, PR 11A 356v–357r 1539 William Tyndale of the parish of St Nicholas: a bushel of barley to each gild, PR 11B 426–2r–v 1539 John Beverlay of the parish of Hornsea: 12d. to each gild, PR 11B 484–1v 1540 Richard Birde of the parish of St Nicholas: a bushel of wheat to each gild 'and I wit to my wif a cowe and my take in the gilde lande', PR 13A 352v 1547 Thomas Beverlay of the parish of St Nicholas: 12d. to each gild 'over and beside there wagies'. General gild bequests to the eight gilds of Cottingham: PR 6 169v 1506 Thomas Seman of the parish of St Mary: 2 sheep to the eight gilds of Cottingham, PR 9 41v 1517 William Sheffelde of the parish of St Mary: 12d. to each gild, PR 9 379 1538 William Jenkynson of the parish of St Mary: 8d. to every gild.

56 BIHR PR 2 540v–541r 1428 Richard Sudbury rector of Crofton made bequests to three gilds in Spofforth. PR 2 483r–v 1464 Thomas Covell vicar of Topcliffe made bequests to gilds in Bridlington. Reg 25 161v–162r 1505 John Holme vicar of Garton made a bequest to Holy Trinity Gild Sherburn in Hartford Lythe. Reg 25 168–v 1506 Robert Dunler of Garton made a bequest to the gild of St John of Beverley.

57 A. K. McHardy, 'Careers and Disappointments in the Late-Medieval Church', in *The Ministry: Clerical and Lay, Studies in Church History* 26, eds. D. Wood, W. J. Sheils and D. B. Foss (Oxford, 1989), pp. 111–30 (p. 114–15).

58 See Chapter 2, pp. 76–7.

prayers of his gild brothers and sisters and of the gild priest, his successor, whose post his bequest might help to maintain. Such bequests were sometimes generous. Thomas Rawson, chaplain of the fraternity of St Mary in Easingwold, left 6s.8d. to the gild in 1541 and, in 1506, the same gild received 10s. to repair its chalice, 13s.2d. for its 'works' and cooking utensils, already in the keeping of its wardens, from William Robynson, chaplain of the parish.[59] Most chaplains made bequests to gilds in their own parishes, implying that they were local members. Some also made bequests to gilds in other places, or to several gilds in the same parish.[60] Only one chaplain made a bequest to a gild elsewhere and not to one of those in his own parish.[61]

As many as eighty-three per cent of clerical testators to gilds, in the county sample, were working in rural parishes. In the five largest towns, there were no clerical bequests in the sample from Scarborough or Hull and both Beverley and Doncaster provided just one testator each.[62] The remaining seven were all from Pontefract, all made bequests to the Corpus Christi Gild and none was later than 1494. Thus, thirteen per cent of all clerics made bequests to a single urban gild which attracted an unusually large number of bequests from all groups of testators. These bequests were made at the period when the gild was at its most popular and, of course, contributed to a high number of bequests at this time. The popularity of this Pontefract gild with local clergy might also indicate that, like the Corpus Christi Gilds of Beverley and York, it was run by the chaplains of the town.[63] If this fraternity is seen as a special case, support for gilds and services by the clergy could be viewed as a largely rural, rather than an urban, phenomenon. This reflects their role in providing chaplains for large rural parishes.

Clerical support for gilds was not evenly distributed over time. If we discount the numbers of clerical testators, making bequests to them in the atypically small samples for 1416–20, where the main probate register is defective, and for 1547–48, when dissolution was actually taking place, we can see that they were found with the greatest frequency between 1470 and 1500. A decline in the early years of the sixteenth century accelerated in the 1520s and 1530s. No rectors made bequests to a gild, in the sample, during the sixteenth century, and the last vicar did so in 1528.[64] This suggests that clerical bequests to gilds followed the

---

[59] BIHR PR 2 247r 1451.

[60] E.g. BIHR PR 2 1408 Ralph Kylstern gild chaplain of Spofforth made bequests to three gilds in Spofforth and also to St Mary Gild Staveley. PR 10 72r 1529 Sir Henry Toplady chaplain of the chapel of Farlington in the parish of Sheriff Hutton left 3s.4d. each to gilds in Sutton-on-the-Forest and Sheriff Hutton.

[61] YML L2(4) 330v 1475 William Paynter chantry priest of Preston, Holderness, left 3s.4d. to the Holy Cross Gild of Hedon.

[62] BIHR PR 2 539v–540r 1428 Thomas Beauchamp chaplain of Beverley. PR 1 5 25r 1471 Thomas Tynlay gild chaplain of Doncaster.

[63] BIHR PR 3 668v 1430, PR 3 518v–519r 1438, PR 1 5 33r 1471, PR 5 83v 1482, PR 5 31v 1482, PR 5 211v 1484, PR 5 446r–v 1494.

[64] BIHR Reg 27 164r Henry Smythson vicar of Hunmanby bequeathed a quarter of barley to the St Mary Gild there.

general pattern of bequests that was seen in Figures 2.1 and 2.2. However, it might also imply changes in clerical attitudes towards gilds, throughout the whole period, although the numbers involved are very small and the totals derived from them could be misleading.

Reasons for some of these changes in attitude can be sought in government religio-political policy. The impetus towards orthodox spirituality, that had been set in motion by official opposition to Lollardy, led the governments of Henry V and Henry VI to promote the use of confession as a means of preventing the spread of heresy. The resulting measures were codified and eventually accepted by the convocations of Canterbury and York in 1462.[65] The pastoral demands that they laid upon priests might explain the need for parishes to employ more chaplains. This need would be fulfilled, in part, by gild and service priests, especially in rural areas far from urban friaries. Their appointment being the indirect result of official promptings, it is not surprising that most chaplains were orthodox in their beliefs and practices, following the regimes laid down in the recommended priestly manuals, that were in general use at this time.[66] As both employees and confessors of gild members, their involvement with them would have become increasingly close. They probably developed loyalties to what were basically religiously conservative institutions, to their lay members and to their saintly cults. Furthermore, the content of the teachings derived from the books that they used served to reinforce the doctrine of purgatory, which was central to so many of the funerary and intercessionary activities of gilds.[67]

It is tempting to ascribe the decline in clerical bequests to gilds, in the early sixteenth century, to changing attitudes towards spiritual orthodoxy. There is, however, little evidence to support this. A more mundane, but perhaps more probable, explanation is the poverty of parochial clergy, both beneficed and unbeneficed, that has been widely observed at this period.[68] From the 1530s, however, the reasons for the cessation of bequests to gilds by beneficed clergy probably lie in the process of reformation that was driven by government actions. They were charged, in 1536, through Cromwell's injunctions, with enforcing the Act of Ten Articles that contained provisions attacking beliefs and practices central to the whole ethos of religious gilds.[69] In particular, the official line included an attack on saints' cults and images. The Vicar General's officers were already destroying nationally venerated shrines.[70] Whatever the attitude of individual clerics to these changes, support for local gilds had already become politically and doctrinally questionable. Nevertheless, three bequests to gilds,

---

[65] J. Hughes, *Pastors and Visionaries*, pp. 262–3.

[66] P. Mackie, 'Chaplains in the Diocese of York, 1480–1530: The Testamentary Evidence', *YAJ* 58 (1986), 123–33 (pp. 132, 127). Hughes, 'The Administration of Confession in the Diocese of York', p. 107.

[67] *Ibid.*, pp. 114–15.

[68] Mackie, 'Chaplains in the Diocese of York', p. 124.

[69] See Chapter 7, pp. 228–9.

[70] M. Aston, *English Iconoclasts* (Oxford, 1988), p. 224. Duffy, *The Stripping of the Altars*, pp. 402–3.

appearing in the sample after 1536, made by chaplains, demonstrate a persistent religious conservatism amongst the lower ranks of the clergy, in rural parts of the county, despite the actions of government.[71]

Lay Piety and the Dedications of Gilds

The doctrinal orthodoxy that rendered gilds acceptable to the establishment of both church and state can clearly be seen in their choices of dedication. A gild's piety was focused upon the veneration of its own particular saint or cult. The nature of its rituals and their place within the calendar were dependent on its choice of devotional patron. The physical manifestation of the dedication, the cult image, was usually a central feature of the members' worship through votive lights, decoration and ceremonial use. A gild's character and sometimes the parameters of its membership were dictated by the dedication. The vast majority of choices reflected the mainstream preoccupation with the humanity of Christ and his sacrifice.

The most popular cult, in terms of gild dedications, that was directly connected to the godhead was that of Holy Trinity. By the late Middle Ages, this concept, a symbol of Christian orthodoxy and unity, was often related iconographically to that of Corpus Christi.[72] God the Father was depicted supporting the crucified Christ. In some versions, known as the Throne of Grace (*Gnadenstuhl*), the seated Father was portrayed supporting the crucifix with the Holy Ghost in the form of a dove hovering above it.[73] Later examples show the Father standing, supporting the bleeding body of Christ in its manifestation as the Man of Sorrows. Both symbolize God offering the broken body of his Son in remission for sins of the world, an act that was replicated in every celebration of the Eucharist. These images, in both versions, appear frequently in the glass of York parish churches.[74] It was the subject of a full-page miniature in the York-produced Bolton Hours of *circa* 1420 and appears on the obverse of the fifteenth century Middleham Jewel.[75] The comparatively recently instituted feast of Corpus Christi was also linked to Trinity Sunday in the church calendar, falling

---

71 BIHR PR 11A 243r 1537 Sir Thomas Ladestoke chaplain of Foston. YML L2(5)a 186v 1540 William Carbot chaplain of Topcliffe. BIHR Reg 29 73r 1540 Robert Ketland priest of St Mary, Alne. PR 13A 401v–402r 1547 Thomas Hodgeson former gild priest of Corpus Christi in St Nicholas Hornsea did not make a bequest.

72 Duffy, *The Stripping of the Altars*, pp. 35–40.

73 G. Schiller, *Iconography of Christian Art*, II , transl. J. Seligman (London, 1972), pp. 122–3.

74 J. A. Knowles, *Essays in the History of the York School of Glass-Painting* (London, 1936), pp. 169–73. Windows displaying a Man of Sorrows Trinity are in Holy Trinity Goodramgate (I 2c), St Martin Coneystreet (sIV 1–2c), and the Minster (nXX 4–5). The Minster window originated in St John Ousebridge. Also in the Minster (sXXVII 2a) is a *gnadenstuhl* Trinity originally from St Martin Coneystreet.

75 York, Minster Library MS Add. 2 fol. 33r (*gnadenstuhl*). The Middleham Jewel (*gnadenstuhl*) is in the Yorkshire Museum.

Figure 3.3: Frequency of Yorkshire Gild and Service Dedications (excluding York)

No.	%	Dedication	No.	%	Dedication	No.	%	Dedication
105	37.1	St Mary Virgin*	2	0.7	All Saints	1	0.4	St Hilda
32	11.3	Holy Trinity	2		Apostles	1		St John Apostle
14	4.9	Holy Cross†	2		Morrow Mass	1		St Leonard
13	4.6	St Katherine	2		Paternoster	1		St Loy
12	4.2	Corpus Christi	2		St Erasmus	1		St Margaret
10	3.5	St John Baptist	2		St John Beverley	1		St Peter Milan
7	2.5	St Christopher	2		St Lazarus	1		St Roch
6	2.1	Jesus	2		St Michael	1		St Saviour
6		St George	2		Young men	1		St Sebastian
6		St Nicholas	1	0.4	Puerorum	1		St Sitha
5	1.8	St Helen	1		Resurrection	1		St Sonday
4	1.4	Plough	1		St Andrew	1		St Thomas Apostle
3	1.1	St Anne	1		St Anthony	1		St Thomas Lancs.
3		St James	1		St Barbara	1		Sepulchre
3		St Laurence	1		St Bega			
3		St Mary Magdalene	1		St Botolph			
3		St Peter	1		St Clement			
3		St Robert	1		St Gregory			
3		St Thomas Cant.	1		St Giles			

*Also to Our Lady etc. including Assumption (2), Purification (1), Coronation (1), The Mother (of Pity) (1)
†Also to The Rood, St Crux etc.

Number: number of known gilds bearing each dedication.
%: percentage of known gilds bearing each dedication.

There were nineteen gilds of unknown dedication. Not included are the following composite dedications: Holy Trinity and St Mary; St Mary and St Helen; Jesus and St Mary; St George, Corpus Christi and Saviour; St Anthony and St Sitha; St James and St Sitha; St Christopher and St George; Jesus and St Roch; St Mary, St Wilfrid and All Saints; Holy Cross and St Mary.

on the following Thursday. Figure 3.3 shows that Corpus Christi, itself, had a dozen gilds dedicated to it in the county. This cult was, in many ways, the apex of the worship of Christ as God in man, and of the late medieval obsession with the physical nature of Christ's redemptive sacrifice. The host, that was seen literally as his body, was revered through its new liturgy, through processions and, in some places, through plays.[76] It is not surprising that Corpus Christi gilds were

[76] M. Rubin, *Corpus Christi*, pp. 243–87 *passim.*

found in many of the larger population centres in Yorkshire.[77] A large town was a suitable setting for mounting a worthy procession, or for providing a fitting audience for a play cycle, such as those of York, Wakefield and Beverley. It has been argued that, symbolically, the body of Christ could also stand for the body politic of a town or city, and the processions and ceremonies of the cult can be seen as means of ritually binding together its inhabitants, with their conflicting interests in an act of social harmony.[78]

Other gilds were concerned with various aspects of the life and passion of Christ. The fourteen dedications to Holy Cross, the Rood or St Crux might indicate that some of the gilds in question, apart from maintaining the parish rood, supported the elaborate rituals of Holy Week, in particular, on Good Friday, which was also known as the *Adoratio Crucis*.[79] Others, however, might have been connected, rather, with the feasts of the Invention or the Exaltation of the Cross. Testators tended not to be specific as to which aspect of the Rood was venerated. According to its 1389 gild return, the Holy Cross Gild of Rotherham seems to have held its annual procession on the feast of the Exaltation.[80] The five gilds dedicated to St Helen, the finder of the True Cross, were also connected with the cross as an object of veneration in itself. Gilds of the Resurrection and the Sepulchre were more clearly connected with the celebration of Holy Week.[81]

The late medieval cult of The Holy Name of Jesus was represented in Yorkshire by six single and two composite gild dedications, as a token of its wide popularity elsewhere.[82] The principal function of the Paternoster Gild in York was to promote the Paternoster Play in celebration of the words of Christ. The gild in Beverley may also have been connected with the town's Paternoster Play, although recent research throws some doubt upon this.[83] The existence of Doncaster's Paternoster Gild is proved from a single testamentary source and whether there was a play there is unknown.[84] Gild dedications in general, however, emphasize the humanity of Christ and the sacrifice of his passion rather than his ministry or his resurrection, which attracted only one gild dedication in the county.

The most popular cult of all was that of the Virgin Mary, through whom Christ received his human form through his incarnation.[85] Figure 3.3 shows that over a third of all the gilds identified in the county were dedicated to her. In most cases,

---

[77] Corpus Christi gilds were found in Bempton, Beverley, Cottingham, Doncaster, Hornsea, Hull, Ottringham, Patrington, Pontefract, Scarborough, Wakefield and Weaverthorpe.

[78] James, 'Ritual, Drama and the Social Body', pp. 6–9.

[79] Duffy, *The Stripping of the Altars*, pp. 22–3.

[80] PRO C 47/46/453.

[81] Duffy, *The Stripping of the Altars*, p. 34.

[82] *Ibid.*, pp. 113–16.

[83] D. J. K. Wyatt, 'Performance and Ceremonial in Beverley before 1642 – an annotated edition of local archive materials' (unpublished D.Phil. Thesis, York, 1983), p. xxxiv.

[84] BIHR PR 2 9r 1398 William Millot.

[85] Bossy, *Christianity in the West*, pp. 8–11. E. Cameron, *The European Reformation* (Oxford, 1991), pp. 16–17.

bequests to St Mary gilds were made to 'Our Lady', in English language wills, and *beate Marie* (*virginis*), in those in Latin. Gilds dedicated to specific aspects of the Virgin and her life were much rarer, although, as with Holy Cross gilds, testators did not always refer to the dedication in full. The gild of St Mary in the church of St Mary in Beverley was dedicated to the Purification, and held its procession on that date according to the 1389 gild return, but none of the bequests made to it referred to this.[86] Similarly, the gilds of her Assumption in Tickhill, and her Coronation in Doncaster are referred to as St Mary gilds in the testamentary evidence, perhaps due to a desire for brevity on the part of testators or their scribes.[87]

In some cases, however, the lack of a dedication to a specific aspect of the cult might indicate a merger of gilds, especially in the larger population centres. In Preston, Holderness, there were two complementary St Mary gilds. That of St Mary the Virgin attracted ten bequests between 1472 and 1537. Five of the same testators also made bequests to the gild of the Mother (*matris*) or, in one case, to St Mary of Pity (*beate Marie pietatis*).[88] No testator who made a bequest to the gild of the Mother failed also to leave something to that of the Virgin. It seems likely that the two gilds celebrated different parts of the Marian calendar in their ceremonial, the former commemorating Christ's incarnation, on such feasts as the Annunciation, Nativity and Purification, and the latter his passion, enhancing the parish rituals of Holy Week. They evidently worked closely together and shared a gild hall.[89] Perhaps they merged at some time after 1507, as testators in Preston, after this date, made bequests to St Mary the Virgin only.[90]

Christ's humanity was further emphasized at this period by placing him in the wider context of the rest of his immediate family, his friends and his disciples, as shown, not only in the Bible, but also in the *Golden Legend* of Jacobus de Voragine.[91] A number of county gild dedications demonstrate this trend. The most popular male saint was St John the Baptist, the forerunner and cousin of Christ. St Anne, St Mary Magdalene and St Lazarus and the apostles James, Andrew, John, Peter and Thomas, were all represented with varying degrees of popularity, and there were two gilds dedicated to the Apostles as a group.

Gild dedications to other saints were generally conservative, being made to legendary and semi-legendary martyrs and miracle workers whose popularity had been long established. St Katherine of Alexandria was especially favoured, with thirteen dedications. As the 'bride of Christ', the intercessory saint for the dying and the patroness of young girls, students, nurses, spinners, wheelwrights

---

[86] PRO C 47/46/448. BIHR PR 2 639r–v, 3 4r, 5 212v.

[87] BIHR PR 3 241r 1405 (Tickhill), PR 6 191v 1505, PR 5 31r 1482 (Doncaster).

[88] BIHR PR 6 77r 1472, PR 6 221r 1474, PR 6 114v 1504, PR 6 152r 1505, PR 6 233v 1507.

[89] *VCH ER* V, p. 199.

[90] BIHR PR 9 33v–34r 1516, PR 11A 275v 1537.

[91] Bossy, *Christianity in the West*, pp. 9–10. *The Golden Legend of Jacobus de Voragine*, trans. W. G. Ryan, 2 vols. (Princeton, 1993).

and millers, her appeal was wide.[92] *The Golden Legend* claimed that she possessed a particular dignity, having been granted, at her death, five 'privileges' that God bestowed only singly upon other saints.[93] St Christopher's popularity was related to his role as the bearer of Christ's body and that of St Nicholas by his ability, like Jesus, to resurrect the dead and by his patronage of children. The popularity of the national patron, St George, had been boosted by Henry V's invocation of the saint at Agincourt.[94]

A few gilds were dedicated to local saints. St Hilda of Whitby was commemorated in a gild in nearby Hackness.[95] St Robert of Knaresborough had gilds dedicated to him in Knaresborough itself and in Aldborough and Burnsall.[96] St John of Beverley was the dedicatee of two gilds in Beverley itself: the Great Gild of St John and the gild of St John in May.[97] There was a gild of the uncanonized St Thomas of Lancaster in Pontefract, where he had been executed and where he was buried in the Cluniac Priory.[98] St Wilfrid shared a gild dedication in Ripon with St Mary and All Saints.[99] No gild of St John of Bridlington or St William of York was identified within the will sample. Other northern saints, such as St Oswald, St Cuthbert, St Edwin and St Paulinus, were also absent. Southern English saints attracting gild dedications were St Thomas of Canterbury, whose cult was nationwide, and the East Anglian St Botolph, whose gild in Bossall was probably related to the place-name.[100] The dedication of the Beverley Gild of St Peter of Milan probably indicates that it was a Dominican confraternity.[101]

The presence of a Gild of St Sonday, in Doncaster, is less easy to explain.[102] Although there was only one gild identified, parish lights of St Sonday were found in Stirton and in Sherburn where there was also a bequest to the St Sonday banner.[103] It is unclear whether he was a personification of the Lord's Day or an actual saint, probably St Dominic. If it was the former, then, like the Morrow Mass Services of Halifax and Wakefield, the dedication was a practical descrip-

---

92 Duffy, *The Stripping of the Altars*, p. 164. D. H. Farmer, *The Oxford Dictionary of Saints* (Oxford, 2nd edition, 1987).

93 *The Golden Legend*, II, p. 341. I am indebted to Katherine Lewis for this reference.

94 D. H. Farmer, *Oxford Dictionary of Saints*.

95 Ed. J. C. Atkinson, *The Whitby Cartulary*, 2 vols, Surtees Society 69 and 72 (1878–79), II p. 746. BIHR PR 3 601v–602r 1440, PR 5 73v 1472, PR 9 77v 1518, PR 11B 415r 1539.

96 Foster, *Lincoln Wills* III, p. 118 (Knaresborough 1531). YML L2(4) 336v 1474 (Aldborough). BIHR PR 1 5 174r (Burnsall).

97 PRO C 47/46/447. Leach, *Beverley Town Documents*, p. 36.

98 BIHR PR 2 537v–538r 1428.

99 PRO C 47/46/452.

100 St Thomas of Canterbury Gilds included Doncaster: BIHR PR 6 191v and Middlesborough: PR 3 987v–988r. St Botolph Gild in Bossall: PR 9 378r 1527, PR 9 397r 1528, PR 9 459r, PR 9 442v 1529.

101 Leach, *Beverley Town Documents*, p. 36.

102 BIHR PR 7 10v–11r 1507.

103 BIHR PR 9 372 1527 Roland Dumwith (light in Stirton), PR 9 370 1527 John Atkynson (light in Sherburn), PR 9 394 1527 Janet Atkynson (banner in Sherburn).

tion of the function of the fraternity.[104] Both services provided a chaplain, one of whose duties was to say early morning mass. Also descriptive were the titles of the two Youngmen's Gilds, also known as gilds of the Four Yeomen, that were founded, or re-founded, in Beverley, in 1503, in St Mary's parish and, in 1508, in the Minster parish.[105] The young men of each parish were to elect four officials, called Yeomen, to rule the gild, to ensure the maintenance of seven serges of wax, that were to burn before the altar of St Mary and to bear torches in the Corpus Christi procession. The *Gilde Puerorum* of Seamer might have been a similar organization, although it could, alternatively, have been a gild of The Holy Innocents.[106] Indeed, it might even have been a children's fraternity in both senses, as boys' gilds sometimes participated in the celebration of a variety of feast days, including those of St Nicholas, St Clement and St Katherine, as well as Holy Innocents.[107]

The Plough Gilds found in the four East Riding towns of Brandesburton, Cottingham, Preston and Wawne represented a different and older tradition than the cults of saints.[108] The ceremonies of Plough Monday were, in origin, pre-Christian fertility rites that had been absorbed into the calendar of the church.[109] The money raised by young men, harnessed to a plough and demanding payment from householders, on pain of ploughing up their doorways, would, probably, have been put into a stock to be managed by the gild for pious purposes. In Preston the gild seems to have sustained a Plough Light, which received bequests in 1506 and 1507.[110] Plough lights were also found in the Holderness villages of Burton-Pidsea and Sproatley.[111] Here, in this remote corner of the county, were gilds which did not belong to medieval Christian orthodoxy so much as to popular superstition, to beliefs and rituals that predated the church and were to survive the Reformation.[112] In intention and function they represent the antithesis of the Corpus Christi gilds of the towns and cities.

The general impression left by the dedications that Yorkshire people chose for their gilds is one of religious conservatism. The rare occurrence of occasional local saints and non-devotional dedications was far outweighed by the veneration paid to the Virgin, the Holy Trinity, to Christ in his various aspects and to saints whose appeal was common to late medieval Christendom. The details of how the cults were publicly celebrated by rural gilds is sparse, however, and can

---

[104] Halifax: *Certificates*, II, p. 299, BIHR PR 9 349 1526, Wakefield: *Certificates*, II, pp. 311, 416.
[105] HCRO B C/II/3 fol. 47.
[106] BIHR PR 4 190r 1473. Duffy, *The Stripping of the Altars*, p. 13.
[107] Duffy, *The Stripping of the Altars*, p. 13.
[108] BIHR PR 9 1517 (Brandesburton), PR 9 41v 1517 (Cottingham), PR 5 282v 1485, PR 6 233v 1507 (Preston), PR 6 102r–v 1504, YML L2(5)a 42r–v (Wawne).
[109] Duffy, *The Stripping of the Altars*, p. 13.
[110] BIHR PR 6 184 1506, PR 6 231 1507.
[111] BIHR PR 11 252 1537 (Burton Pidsea), PR 9 413 1528 (Sproatley).
[112] Cameron, *The European Reformation*, pp. 9–12.

only be deduced from testamentary evidence. Outside York, other documentation is extant only in Hull and Beverley.

Religious Ceremonial in Yorkshire Towns

A gild's procession and feast, which usually took place on the same day, formed the highlight of its year. The procession was a public expression of its identity and its devotion to its cult. In an urban context, gilds were often also major participants in civic ceremonial, which gave each fraternity the opportunity to make a public statement of its role within the structure of the community of which it was a part. The manner and scale of this participation varied widely, not only in relation to the size and purposes of each gild, but also to the nature of the community and its structures. In a city such as York, ceremonial relationships between the city and its gilds were complex, and there are extant records through which they can be examined.[113] Elsewhere in the county, there are few accounts of gild ceremonial. Despite the large numbers of fraternities identified in Scarborough and Doncaster and the many bequests made to the Corpus Christi gild of Pontefract, no such records survive, and even in Hull and Beverley the evidence is patchy.

Hull, in the late Middle Ages, was, in ecclesiastical terms, poorly provided for.[114] As a result of its late foundation, its two churches lacked full parochial status. There were only two friaries and one monastery in the city. A relative lack of parish clergy had led to the establishment of chantries and of the organization of chaplains in Holy Trinity church, known as the Priests of the Table, to compensate for this, but, even so, Hull had an estimated total of less than fifty priests, in the early sixteenth century, compared with 600 in York. Peter Heath, from a study of testamentary evidence, detects a general lack of enthusiasm both for religious change and for the status quo as the forces of the Reformation gathered strength elsewhere.[115] This view is, to some extent, reflected in its gild records. Although some eighteen fraternities were found in Hull, none attracted more than eight bequests from the sample, most of which dated from before the sixteenth century.[116]

Three of Yorkshire's surviving 1389 gild returns relate to Hull. They all seem to have been based on documents concerning the foundation of the gilds in the late 1350s.[117] They contain information concerning membership conditions, dis-

---

[113] See Chapter 4, pp. 142–5, where the relationships between city and gild is examined in some detail.

[114] Cross, 'Parochial Structure and the Dissemination of Protestantism', pp. 270–1.

[115] Heath, 'Urban Piety', pp. 228–9.

[116] See Table 3.5 above.

[117] PRO C 47/46/449–451. St Mary was founded in 1357, Corpus Christi in 1358. St John the Baptist's foundation date is missing from the damaged return but its provisions are similar to the other two, although it is rather briefer.

cipline and payments, and make provision for the relief of poor members. There are references to feasts and meetings, but not to public ceremonial or the maintenance of lights. These omissions, however, are probably related to the Hull returns being based on foundation deeds rather than ordinances.[118] Hull seems to have differed from Beverley in its attitude to plays and processions. There is no record of a Corpus Christi cycle here or accounts of large-scale religious events. The Plough Day 'Noah' play, of the Holy Trinity Gild, which is known to have been performed annually between 1461 and 1536, involved just one elaborate pageant.[119] No script has survived, if indeed the event was not a moving tableau or dumb-show, and whether it was part of a larger civic ceremonial is not known. The account book of the gild of St Mary in Holy Trinity church, however, shows that the Rood was borne through the streets, annually, on Holy Cross or Rogation Day, by the fraternity, and that lights and torches were carried in the Corpus Christi Day procession and on its gild day.[120] This fraternity, then, took part in two processions apart from its own. The Rogation Day procession might have been parochial, that of Corpus Christi was possibly civic. This evidence hints that Hull was richer in civic and gild ceremonial than its otherwise sparse gild documentation implies.

Beverley, by contrast, was a borough with a strong ecclesiastical ethos. Although it had only three parish churches, one was the Collegiate Minster of St John, one of the four 'Mother' churches of the diocese. It was immensely wealthy and the destination of pilgrims visiting the shrine of St John. St Mary's, too, was a large and affluent church. St Nicholas Holmkirk served a rather poorer district and only one gild is known to have been connected with it.[121] Although, like Hull, Beverley had two friaries, theirs were the more powerful and influential Dominicans and Franciscans, whilst Hull housed Augustinians and Carmelites. There was also a Preceptory of the Knights of St John. Unlike Hull, Beverley was an old-established borough and religious centre with a tradition of drama and pageantry. This is made clear by the 1389 gild returns from three religious gilds which laid considerable emphasis on their ceremonial activities.

The gild of St Helen, based on the church of the Friars Minor, described its St Helen's Day procession in some detail.[122] It was led by a fair young man, dressed as the saint, accompanied by two old men, one with a spade and one with a cross. This symbolized St Helen's discovery of the True Cross. The sisters of the gild came next, two by two, then the brothers and, finally, the gild aldermen. The procession, to the sound of music (*cum maxima melodia*), passed to the conventual church where mass was held at the saint's altar. This was followed by a feast of bread, cheese and beer. The gild of the Purification of St Mary, of the parish

---

118 See Chapter 1, p. 25.
119 A. J. Mill, 'The Hull Noah Play', pp. 489–505.
120 KHRO BRA 87, pp. 2, 107, 118. See Chapter 6, pp. 198–9, for a more detailed account.
121 BIHR PR 1 98r 1396 John Jakeson to the gild of St Mary in Holmkirk: 5s.
122 PRO C 47/46/446.

church of St Mary, had a similar procession on the Feast of the Purification.[123] A young man, dressed as a virgin queen, seeming to have a baby in his arms (*quasi filium in ulnis suis*), with two men as Joseph and Simeon, attended by two angels carrying twenty-four candles on a framework, and other lights, headed the procession. Then the sisters of the gild, followed by the brothers, two by two, carrying lights, to the accompaniment of music, processed to St Mary's Church. There the 'virgin' offered the 'child' to Simeon at the high altar, and the members offered their candles and a penny. There was a feast in the evening, and, on the following Friday, a solemn mass for the souls of departed brothers and sisters. The clerically-run Corpus Christi gild spent less space describing its ceremonial but laid down that every member who was a chaplain must attend the Corpus Christi Day procession in alb, stole and maniple.[124]

The twin climaxes of Beverley's ceremonial year were the spectacular Rogation Day procession, in which all the city's major gilds participated, and the Corpus Christi plays. These events were recorded in The Great Gild Book of Beverley but references to them also appear in other parts of the town records.[125] The Rogation Day procession, in which the shrine of St John of Beverley was carried through the town, was probably organized by the gild of St John in May.[126] On Rogation Monday the craft gilds of Beverley built, covered and decorated wooden castles before which the masters of each craft sat, in rich clothing, to wait for the procession to pass.[127] In the afternoon there was a riding of the masters. Music was played in some of the castles according to the 1555 ordinances of the minstrels' gild.[128] The Corpus Christi procession, in 1431, included the gild lights of Corpus Christi, St Mary, St Helen, Paternoster, St John the Baptist, St John in May and St Peter of Milan, as well as the merchants' gild of St John of Beverley and nineteen craft organizations.[129] The plays, however, seem to have been entirely the responsibility of the craft associations.[130] This was certainly so in York, and there are indications that it might also have been the case in Wakefield.[131]

In his examination of sixteenth century Beverley, David Lamburn suggests that the religious activities of the crafts and trades of the borough might have led

---

[123] PRO C 47/46/448.

[124] PRO C 47/46/445.

[125] 'The Great Gild Book': HRO BC/II/3, printed transcriptions in Leach, *Beverley Town Documents*. A recent edition of the records pertaining to ceremonial and drama is Wyatt, 'Performance and Ceremonial in Beverley before 1642'.

[126] Wyatt, 'Performance and Ceremonial in Beverley', p. xxxiv.

[127] Leach, *Beverley Town Documents*, pp. 34–5, 77, 99.

[128] KHRO BC/II/3 fols. 41v–42r.

[129] Leach, *Beverley Town Documents*, pp. 35–6.

[130] *Ibid.*, pp. 33, 34.

[131] For York see Chapter 4, p. 142. Ed. A. C. Cawley, *The Wakefield Pageants in the Towneley Cycle* (Manchester, 1958), p. xv.

to a decline, that he perceives, in the influence and activities of religious gilds.[132] From an assessment of their ordinances he points out that, in addition to their participation in civic drama and ceremonial, the craft associations were carrying out the funereal, memorial, charitable and devotional activities that authorities such as Scarisbrick and White regard as being the province of religious gilds. He goes on to cite the decline in bequests to religious fraternities, the need to re-found the Youngmen's Gilds and the lack of a political focus for religious gilds as evidence of their dwindling importance in the town.[133] No religious gild was recorded as participating in the processions of Rogation Day or Corpus Christi after the 1520s.[134] He asserts that the craft and merchant organizations of Beverley were exceptional in 'having a more notably religious aspect' than other towns, 'especially Hull'.[135]

There is, however, evidence from Hull that, by the 1490s, gilds exclusive to particular occupations were being incorporated, either as new foundations, or by taking over existing fraternities, and that these new gilds made wide provision for religious observances, including the keeping of obits.[136] They all kept lights before images in Holy Trinity Church, the weavers before St Peter, the walkers and shearmen before St Christopher, the glovers before Our Lady of Pylo and the merchants before St George. In Beverley, several occupations behaved in the same way, maintaining lights in St Mary's Church, the mercers in honour of the Holy Trinity, the drapers before the image of St Michael Archangel and the barbers before the image of St John the Baptist.[137] In both Hull and Beverley a blurring of the distinction between gilds and occupations seems to have been taking place towards the close of the fifteenth century. Whilst there is insufficient evidence to tell how far this process was taking place in other towns and in smaller places in the county, the changing relationship between gilds and crafts will be further pursued in the next chapter in the context of the City of York.[138]

In more general terms, it is clear that, in both Hull and Beverley, gilds had an important ceremonial role in the community, not only through the public expression of their devotion to their own cults and images, but also by participating in civic and parish processions, where their individual identities formed part of a larger whole. Whilst the different characteristics of Hull and Beverley might have been reflected in a larger scale of religious ceremony in Beverley, the contrast could have been more apparent than real. It is likely that at least some of the differences are a product of the survival of a smaller quantity of relevant material in Hull. Clearly, the testamentary evidence for Pontefract and Doncaster, as well as

---

132 D. A. Lamburn, 'Politics and Religion in Sixteenth Century Beverley' (unpublished D.Phil. thesis, York, 1991), pp. 293, 296, 305.
133 *Ibid.*, pp. 305–6.
134 *Ibid.*, p. 311.
135 *Ibid.*, p. 295.
136 KHRO BRE 5/1–4. See Chapter 6, p. 214.
137 Leach, *Beverley Town Documents*, pp. 76, 99, 109.
138 See also Chapter 2, pp. 79–80.

for smaller places, such as Hornsea, shows the presence of gilds that were, in many cases, more popular than those of Hull and Beverley. It seems certain that their ceremonial practices, although sadly unrecorded, must have been equally important to their smaller communities.

Some indication of the scale of the ceremonial, liturgical and social practices of gilds can be gleaned from the articles of intrinsic worth or practical value that members bequeathed their fraternities in smaller towns and villages.[139] The quality both of the gild's worship and its feasting was enhanced by the will of William Robinson, chaplain of Easingwold, who, in 1506, besides forgiving a debt of 13s.2d. to the Master of the St Mary Gild, left 10s. for the repair of the gild chalice and also bequeathed it the cooking utensils that were already in the hands of the Wardens.[140] Spectacular gifts of jewellery included a silver horn left by Henry Lokwod, in 1489, to the Gild of St Mary in the Porch at Thirsk.[141] John Sandford of Tickhill, in 1429, instructed his executors 'forto gyfe to þe rude gylde of Tykill his best girdell harnest wit apare of lambre bedes and a nothir girdell harnest wit S and a ryng of golde wit a diamant to Sancte Christopher Gilde'.[142] More directly devotional were the mass book and vestments that Robert Ketland left to the St Mary Gild of Alne in 1540.[143] Of both devotional and practical use were bequests of wax, such as the pound of it given by Thomas Ledys of Ripon to the fraternity of the Holy Cross, in 1474.[144] Useful bequests included the chests that William Carter left to the gilds of St Clement and St Katherine in Scarborough in 1400.[145]

This range of gifts, whilst giving us a tantalizing glimpse of the wealth of gilds, demonstrates that much of it was related to religious display and ceremonial. The burning of Robert Ketland's wax, in the form of votive or funeral lights, lit the various ceremonies but also symbolized prayer. The feasting, too, that William Robinson's cooking pots would have been used to supply, had its devotional aspects. The fraternal and sororal meal was a symbol of the Last Supper, and the feeding of the five thousand, besides being a social event to cement the gild's unity in brother and sisterhood. If processions, masses and obits were the focus of the religious life of a gild, its social focus was the feast, and the two were closely bound together as Rosser has demonstrated in a recent article.[146] Information relating to feasting in the county's rural fraternities is sparse, although occasional bequests of malt and cooking utensils indicate that it was probably as common here as elsewhere.[147]

---

[139] See Figure 3.4.
[140] BIHR PR 6 244r.
[141] BIHR PR 5 250v.
[142] BIHR PR 2 563v.
[143] BIHR Reg 29 73r.
[144] BIHR PR 4 10v.
[145] BIHR PR 3 42v.
[146] G. Rosser, 'Going to the Fraternity Feast'.
[147] See also Chapter 6, pp. 201–2, where evidence relating to the feast of the St Mary Gild in Holy Trinity, Hull, is discussed.

The general indications are that the activities that were recorded in Beverley and Hull also occurred in gilds throughout the county. If they took place, perhaps, on a smaller scale in Hull than in Beverley we might deduce that they did so on an even smaller scale elsewhere. There is no reason to suppose, however, that the gilds of Alne, Thirsk or Tickhill performed rituals and held processions that were any less important to their members or to the communities in which they operated than those of Beverley or even York. The evidence of testators suggests the contrary. By establishing the identity of its membership group within a community a gild might also provide that community with a ritual and devotional service and a focus for political and economic power.[148]

Gild Administration

The capacity of a gild to play its part in the life of a community was obviously related to its ability to administer its affairs. At the heart of this lay its economic strength. Many of those gilds that were sufficiently successful to have been recorded, in one way or another, were not only dependent on the continuing membership of wealthy members, although their presence was one indicator of success. They also became wealthy institutions in their own right, owning lands and buildings and engaging corporately in business or agriculture. We have seen that identified gilds were found most frequently in prosperous locations.[149] In some cases at least one factor in a community's prosperity might have been the presence of a successful fraternity.

In the absence of gild accounts outside the larger urban areas, clues to the ways in which gilds administered themselves can be sought only through testamentary evidence, and, in particular, by an analysis of bequests. Figure 3.4 shows the kinds of bequest that were made to gilds during each of the sample periods. Clearly, by far the most usual kind of bequest to a gild was a sum of money. The actual amounts varied widely. In the early part of the period covered, when the wills were, as we have seen, predominantly those of wealthy individuals, bequests of 13s.4d. and more were not uncommon. In the sixteenth century sums were generally lower, and 12d. was more usual. This reflects the higher proportion of people of more modest means making wills by this period.

Most money bequests were simply that. The testators gave no indication of what the sum was to be used for. They trusted the gild to use the bequest wisely. Other testators attached specific conditions. In such cases it is possible to draw inferences from them. In 1394, Thomas de Styllyngflete, burgess of Hull, paid 13s.4d. each to the gilds of Corpus Christi and the Resurrection, on condition that they burn candles at his obsequies.[150] This suggests that both gilds provided a

---

148 M. Rubin, 'Small Groups', pp. 132–48.
149 See Chapter 2, pp. 52–5.
150 BIHR PR 1 62r–v.

Figure 3.4: Analysis of Types of Bequests to Gilds and Services in Yorkshire (excluding York)

Date	Money	Land	Livestock	Produce	Jewels	Other	All
1320–1400	28 (90.3%)	1 (3.2%)	–	–	–	3 (9.9%)	31
1405–1409	20 (100%)	–	–	–	1 (5.0)	2 (10.0%)	20
1416–1420	4 (100%)	–	–	–	–	–	4
1427–1431	16 (76.2%)	–	1 (4.8%)	1 (4.8%)	1 (4.8%)	3 (14.3%)	21
1438–1442	24 (92.3%)	–	1 (3.8%)	–	–	–	26
1449–1453	17 (100%)	–	1 (5.9%)	–	–	–	17
1460–1464	18 (72.0%)	3 (12.0%)	1 (4.0%)	–	–	1 (4.0%)	25
1471–1475	40 (83.3%)	4 (8.3%)	3 (6.3%)	1 (2.1%)	1 (2.1%)	1 (2.1%)	48
1482–1486	61 (84.7%)	1 (1.4 %)	–	8 (11.1%)	3 (4.2%)	2 (2.8%)	72
1493–1497	6 (42.9%)	1 (7.1%)	1 (7.1%)	2 (14.3%)	1 (7.1%)	–	14
1504–1508	84 (77.8%)	6 (5.6%)	4 (3.7%)	12 (11.1%)	–	4 (3.7%)	108
1515–1519	37 (71.2%)	1 (1.9%)	3 (5.8%)	9 (17.3%)	–	1 (1.9%)	52
1526–1530	64 (77.1%)	1 (1.2%)	1 (1.2%)	29 (34.9%)	–	–	83
1537–1541	46 (52.9%)	–	6 (6.9%)	25 (28.7%)	1 (1.1%)	3 (3.4%)	87
1547–1548	2 (40.0%)	–	–	–	–	1 (20.0%)	5
Totals	464 (60.4%)	18 (2,3%)	24 (3.1%)	87 (11.3%)	8 (1.0%)	21 (2.7%)	773

Date: date of will sample.

Money: number of money bequests.

Land: real estate including farmland, houses. tenements and messuages both as outright bequests and reversions.

Livestock: including cattle, sheep, beehives.

Produce: including wheat, barley, malt, peas.

Jewels: valuables including silverware, rings, girdles, beads, embroidery.

Other: other goods including wax, chests, furniture, armour, plain utensils, plain fabric.

All: total number of bequests to individual gilds (not the number of testators). This includes wills containing references to gilds or bequests where the amount is not specific. The sums of categorized bequests may not, therefore, tally with the totals.

Percentages are related to the total number of bequests in each period.

basic funeral for their members but required extra payment for lights. Bequests to gilds outside the testator's parish were sometimes conditional on a particular service. Ralph Kylstern, gild chaplain of Spofforth, left money to three local gilds in 1408, but also bequeathed 20s. to the gild of St Mary in Staveley, for prayers for the souls of his parents.[151] They had, presumably, lived there and he might still have been a member of the gild. In 1504, James Newton of Aldburgh in Holder-

---

[151] BIHR PR 2 576v.

ness left 20d. towards the repair of the St Mary Gild light.[152] Here Newton was making a practical contribution to necessary maintenance, as well as sharing in the prayers associated with the light. In 1516, Peter Letheley of Sheriff Hutton left 6s.8d. to the Rood Gild of the town for his burial. He left a further 6s.8d. to St Mary's Gild in Sutton-on-the-Forest. He also bequeathed a house in Huby to Thomas Sted on condition that he and his heirs 'gyff yerley to our ladys gilde in Sutton xxd'.[153] Whilst Letheley was paying for his local gild to conduct his funeral, he was also providing an income to another gild through the agency of his legatee.

Where the bequest was not specific, the uses to which a gild would have put the money bequeathed to it can be adduced from extant gild accounts, such as those of St Mary in Holy Trinity, Hull, and Corpus Christi, York, which showed expenditure on feasts and ceremonials, on the salaries of officials, on the maintenance of lights, on the provision of masses and obits and on contributions to civic or parish causes.[154] For example, some gilds took a lead in the discharge of the laity's parochial obligations towards the upkeep of parts of the church and its furnishings. In Hull, the gild of St Mary in Holy Trinity bought and repaired church organs.[155] There is little surviving evidence for such activities in the more rural areas of Yorkshire, but it seems likely that gilds behaved similarly to that of St Peter in Boxford, Suffolk, which contributed 43s.4d. to the repair of the pinnacle of the church steeple in 1537, or the gild of St John the Baptist in Dunstable, which repaired the church roof, installing wooden sculptures, probably of fraternity members.[156] An unnamed gild in Roos, in Holderness, endowed a window in the parish church. This was clearly a modest donation compared with the sumptuous glass provided by the great Palmers' Gild of Ludlow, Shropshire, but was probably a significant gesture in a small rural parish.[157] Other gilds in the county took responsibility for the repair of their own chapels, or for parts of the church appropriate to their dedications and some testators reflected this in their bequests. Joan Elwyn of Hedon, for example, left 6s.8d. in 1472 to the Holy Cross Gild in St Augustine's parish church for painting the rood there.[158]

These outlays financed the outward and visible, social and devotional manifestations of gild life. More mundane were payments in respect of repairs to gild property, the laundering and cleaning of vestments and the payment of taxes.

---

152 BIHR PR 6 103v.

153 BIHR PR 9 35v.

154 See Chapters 6 and 7 below for a full discussion of these accounts.

155 KHRO BRA 87/8, pp. 130–2, 137.

156 Ed. P. Northeast, *Boxford Churchwarden's Accounts 1530–1531*, Suffolk Records Society 23 (1982), p. 26. J. Lunn, 'Medieval Figures in Dunstable Priory Church', *Bedfordshire Magazine*, vol. 24 number 186 (Luton, 1993) reprinted as a pamphlet available in the church.

157 G. Poulson, *History of Holderness*, p. 97. E. W. Ganderton and J. Lafond, *Ludlow Stained and Painted Glass* (Ludlow, 1961), pp. 46–52, east window (No. 16) of Chapel of St John, in St Laurence parish church, 'appropriated to the Palmers [gild]' (p. 47) and embellished in fourteenth century.

158 BIHR PR 4 84r–v.

The St Mary Gild in Holy Trinity, Hull, also laid out money in trade.[159] It used some of its own funds in international commerce through the agency of its merchant members and also made loans to some of them, on which they were able to make a personal profit. The benefits of membership were not only social and devotional, they were, in this case, also commercial. Other Yorkshire fraternities in the county laid out funds on building works. Accounts relating to the building of halls are extant for Holy Trinity Gild in Hull and for two gilds in York.[160]

Expenditure on a large scale, however, could not be covered by bequests and entrance fees only. A more regular and reliable income was provided by the acquisition and exploitation of lands and buildings. Bequests of real estate were, naturally, much rarer than those of money. Almost all of them were made in the sample periods between 1460 and 1530. Their purpose was, almost always, to provide an income in rents to the gild. Hugh Awstwyk's direction, in 1515, that a room 'be devised to the use of Jesus gilde in pontefract', in return for annual prayers, was unusual.[161] A more typical example was Edmund Portyngton of Beverley who, in 1463, left two houses in Keldgate to revert to the Corpus Christi Gild after the deaths of his legatees.[162] Other testators, such as John Bule of Pontefract, left land. He bequeathed half an acre to the Jesus Gild in 1507.[163] Like the 'sellio', or field strip, called Scaylyland, that William Dowse left to the fraternity of St Mary in Easingwold, in 1430, it was almost certainly agricultural land intended to provide an income in rent.[164] There is also much non-testamentary evidence for gilds owning large tracts of agricultural lands. In 1546, for example, the Tickhill gild or service of the Rood was reported as owning cottages, crofts, barns, meadows, tofts and other 'parcells' of land to an annual rental value of £7.8s.7d.[165]

Gild real estate seems to have been administered by two principal methods. The rental book of the Hull Corpus Christi Gild, which covers 1522–25, relates to the tenements of the gild.[166] They comprised eleven houses, five little houses, a hall and five gardens. Rents were collected at Pentecost and Martinmas and account was kept of expenses, such as labour and materials for repairs. The nature of the account suggests that it was kept directly by gild officers. The way in which they administered their property was probably similar to that shown in

---

[159] E.g. KHRO BRA 87/8, p. 5. See Chapter 6, pp. 203–6 below.

[160] Woodward, 'Hull Trinity House Accounts', pp. 153–70. York, Merchant Adventurers' Hall, Archives of The Company of Merchant Adventurers, Guild of St Mary, Account Rolls c.1357–1367, 1–5, Account Book 1358–1369. YCA G4, fol. 16. White, *The St Christopher and St George Gild of York*, pp. 3–4.

[161] BIHR PR 9 40r–v.

[162] BIHR PR 2 595r–v.

[163] BIHR PR 6 122r.

[164] BIHR PR 2 666r.

[165] PRO E 301/67 item 47.

[166] KHRO BRA 88.

extant correspondence between Holy Trinity Gild of Coventry and its tenants, showing that the fraternity was a careful and caring landlord.[167]

The St Mary Gild in Holy Trinity in Hull also derived some income from rents, according to its accounts, although no rental book has survived.[168] Its most profitable tenement, however, which it obtained from the estate of John Haynson, in return for celebrating an annual obit, was farmed out to a succession of influential gild members. They provided the gild with an annual income and, presumably, made a personal profit in return for the responsibility and risk of maintaining the property. This was not always a profitable arrangement, as the terms sometimes had to be re-negotiated when the farm changed hands, as the general level of rents declined. In 1504, for example, the current mayor of Hull, Richard Garner, agreed to take over the Haynson property and repair it paying a much reduced farm.[169] By 1507 it was held by John Meteson at the same lower farm.[170] It also seems likely that, even when not formally farmed out, rents were not always collected directly from the householders. It is explicit in some of the rentals of the Holy Trinity Gild in Coventry that the gild was receiving rents from individuals in respect of several tenements or cottages, which were certainly sub-let.[171] The 1546 chantry certificate of the York Corpus Christi Gild indicates that this was also happening in York.[172]

By 1540 there are indications that individuals were regarding their tenure of gild land as heritable property. Richard Birde of Hornsea left his wife his 'take in the gilde land' and Thomas Bell of Topcliffe made 'Master Richard Norton Esquire . . . feoffe in same possession of the landes of oure ladie gilde of Topclif that I was in my lif tyme'.[173] Both these bequests were, however, made under the shadow of the Reformation, and might represent attempts to claim land that could already be seen as vulnerable to royal sequestration.

From the late fifteenth century, an increasingly important type of bequest was that of livestock. This reflects the growing proportion of testators who were husbandmen. It seems likely that the cow, worth 8s., that Thomas Beaumont left to the St Mary Service in Heaton, in 1495, the two calves that Thomas Crispyn, rector of Lastingham, bequeathed to the gilds of Holy Trinity and St Mary respectively, in 1475, and the beehive that Robert Newell, chaplain of Pontefract, left to the Corpus Christi Gild, in 1471, were intended, by the testators, to provide an income for the gild, rather than directly to provide food for gild feasts.[174] The

---

[167] L. Fox, 'The Administration of Gild Property in Coventry in the Fifteenth Century', *English Historical Review* 55 (1940), 634–47.

[168] For a fuller description of the gild's financial dealings see Chapter 7 below.

[169] KHRO BRA 87/8, p. 116.

[170] *Ibid.*, p. 120.

[171] Ed. G. Templeman, *The Records of the Guild of Holy Trinity, St Mary, St John the Baptist and St Katherine of Coventry*, 2 vols. (Dugdale Society, Oxford, 1944), II, pp. 81–92, *passim.*

[172] *Certificates*, I, p. 55.

[173] BIHR PR 11B 484–1v 1540 Richard Birde, PR 12 6r 1540 Thomas Bell.

[174] BIHR PR 5 464v–465r Thomas Beaumont of Heaton, PR 4 118v 1475 Thomas Crispyn rector of Lastingham, PR 4 33r Robert Newall chaplain of Pontefract.

practical details of the way in which such property was administered are provided by a reference relating to sheep.

These were by far the most usual animals for fraternities to receive from testators in the sample, and, of these, breeding ewes were the most common. In 1538, John Roger of Danby left *unam ovem matricem* to the St Mary Gild and, in 1506, John Symondson of Helmsley bequeathed as many as four mother sheep to the Holy Trinity Gild in the town.[175] In the commissioners' certificates of 1548, a note relating to the assessment for Ryedale, referring to the parish of Helmsley, explains how a group, not described as a gild, but behaving very like one, kept sheep for a pious purpose.[176] The entry is worth quoting in full.

> Memorandum That there was in tyme paste gathered amongest the tenandes belonging to the chapell of Pokley a stok of shepe to the nomber of foure score yewes and was put in diverse of the tenandes handes paing therefore yerely for the occupieing of the same iijd apece and for every yewe decaed xijd to thintent to have a preste to do dyvine service in the said chapell at such tymes as the tennandes there could not come to the paryshe churche for water the whiche iiijxx yewes[[177]] are now decaed and iiij li remaining in the tennandes handes for the same Towardes the finding of the said incumbent iiij li.

The average value of a sheep in the period 1450–99 was approximately 22d.[178] In 1530 it had risen to about 26d. The tenants who were keeping the stock were paying about an eighth of each sheep's value as a kind of rent. In the case of a loss in numbers, the tenant was charged about half the value of each missing sheep.

Whilst it would be dangerous to assert that all gilds receiving bequests of sheep operated stock systems like that of Pockley Chapel, it seems reasonable to suggest that many did so. In rural areas this kind of arrangement probably suited all three parties. The testator could leave livestock directly to the gild rather than give his executor the trouble of selling it. The gild received a steady income, in cash, from the tenants, with the minimum of administrative trouble. The tenants of the stock were able to make a small profit as well as performing a useful, and possibly prestigious, service to the gild. The arrangement was similar to the way in which gilds farmed out lands and tenements that had been left them, although the agreements might have been less formal in the case of livestock and therefore less likely to be recorded.

Second in frequency to money bequests were those of produce. Figure 3.4

---

[175] BIHR PR 11A 364r 1438 John Roger of Danby, PR 6 162r 1506 Robert Symondson of Helmsley.

[176] PRO E 301/63 item 124. Bainbridge, *Gilds in the Medieval Countryside*, pp. 132–3, describes the activities of gild stockholders in Cambridgeshire.

[177] Page in *Certificates*, II, p. 509 reads this word mistakenly as 'years'.

[178] P. J. Bowden, 'Economic change: wages, profits and rents 1500–1750', in *Chapters from The Agrarian History of England and Wales*, gen. ed. J. Thirsk, 5 vols. (Cambridge, 1990) I, pp. 13–187 (p. 171). The price actually cited is 1.84s. Prices of sheep are calculated from tables on p. 136.

shows a marked increase in bequests of this kind in the sixteenth century, especially in the sample periods between 1526 and 1541. This, of course, also coincides with the increase of bequests from husbandmen. Apart from one bequest of peas, these were of three commodities, wheat, barley and malt.[179] They were most commonly bequeathed by the half quarter, a weight of approximately 14lbs., or by the mette or *medius* which was a capacity measure of approximately two gallons.[180] The average price of a half quarter of wheat, between 1450 and 1499, was 3s.2d. and barley was cheaper at 1s.5d. per half quarter.[181] However, this type of bequest was becoming more frequent at a time when the sums of money left to gilds were becoming smaller. Bequests in kind did not, therefore, imply that the testator was necessarily employing a cheap option.

Testators did not indicate how the gilds were to use these gifts. Grain by the half quarter might have been sown in the agricultural lands owned by the gilds or be sold for profit. However, it seems likely, in at least some cases, especially where grain was donated in smaller measures, that the wheat was used to make bread and the barley to make beer, the staple diet for annual gild feasts.[182] In the case of bequests of malt, it is inescapable that brewing was intended. Although there is no record of gilds in Yorkshire storing ale for their own use, the 1389 returns for several gilds in Lynn, in Norfolk, reported fraternities with a supply of ale, a place to keep it and regulations concerning its use.[183] It seems likely that bread-making and brewing offered trade and, possibly, profit to members who were bakers, brewers, millers and maltsters, although Bainbridge believes that brewing and baking might have been communal.[184] In the absence of membership registers, there is no direct evidence from Yorkshire sources, but a parallel case can be found in York, where the butchers who supplied meat for the feasts for the Corpus Christi Gild, in 1415, were all members.[185] The presence amongst the county testators of a cook, a baker, an innkeeper and two butchers suggests an interest in gilds by members of the victualling trades.[186]

Clearly, gild membership presented economic opportunity at many different levels. These groups of bequests reinforce the evidence of registers, account records, rentals and surveys, not only that gilds flourished in prosperous places,

[179] BIHR PR 11A 261r 1537 John Moryson of Wawne left St Mary Gild 2 bushels of peas.

[180] G. V. Harrison, 'Agricultural Weights and Measures', in *Chapters from The Agrarian History of England and Wales*, gen. ed. J. Thirsk, 5 vols. (Cambridge, 1990) I, pp. 307–413 (pp. 307–18). J. L. Fisher, *A Medieval Farming Glossary* (London, 1968).

[181] Calculated from Bowden 'Economic change', p. 171. This price for wheat is probably too high for Yorkshire, as the average is distorted by high prices in the home counties, *ibid.*, p. 210.

[182] See Chapter 4, p. 145, and Chapter 7, p. 201, below.

[183] Smith, *English Gilds*, pp. 90, 95, 98, 101, 104, 107, 109. The fullest and best preserved example is the gild of St Nicholas, West Lynn, p. 98.

[184] Bainbridge, *Gilds in the Medieval Countryside*, p. 20.

[185] See Chapter 6, pp. 178–9, below.

[186] BIHR PR 2 203v–204r 1449 Bernard Gerardson cook of St Katherine's Gild Hull. PR 5 266r 1485 Robert Hill baker of St George Gild Doncaster. See also pp. 87–8 and Figure 4.1 above.

but that they themselves were contributors to the prosperity of the places where they flourished. The evidence from rural testators suggests that the parish gilds in small towns and villages were as involved with the agrarian economy, and with extracting profit from it, as the urban gilds were within the trading and craft context of the larger towns and cities.[187] Here, the distinction between the craft and the gild is somewhat blurred, the craft in question being husbandry. This blurring is underlined, perhaps, by the identification of four gilds in the county dedicated to The Plough, rather than to any recognized saint or religious cult.[188]

Conclusion

As basically pious institutions, fraternities needed wealth and influence in order to pursue their devotional, ceremonial, charitable and fraternal functions effectively within their communities. An indicator of their success, in the absence of local records, is the status and occupations of the testators who made bequests to them. A number of these were prosperous and powerful people. Whilst this was most obviously the case in an urban context, the yeomen and rich husbandmen of the countryside were probably as influential as the aldermen, burgesses and merchants of the towns. Clerical support for gilds was also important. Bequests from the lower clergy underlined the contributions made by gilds to parish life. Individuals who wielded power on a larger scale, higher clergy and nobility, did not, however, generally make bequests to gilds, although they were often members of large urban fraternities. Whilst they might have joined for political and social reasons, the devotional aspects of the gilds could well have been equally important to them, especially as they reflected the attitude of the government in their religious orthodoxy. Piety might also have been a principal motive of many female members, whose numbers were probably greater than testamentary evidence might suggest. Gilds offered them an identity within a devotional association that was denied them elsewhere.

The conservative nature of the piety of fraternities is demonstrated by the objects they chose as their dedications, which were often Christo-centric, emphasizing the Marian and eucharistic cults that were typical of late medieval orthodoxy.[189] The other saints they adopted were usually the traditional figures of medieval hagiography.[190] Their allegiance to their chosen dedication was demonstrated through public ceremonial. This was shown not only through the processions that celebrated fraternities' own cults. In urban areas they also participated in pious events related both to the parish and to the town as a whole, where they celebrated their identity as a group within a structure of relationships

---

[187] Involvement of urban gilds with crafts and commerce is investigated in Chapter 4, in the context of York, and illustrated in Chapter 6 by material from Hull.

[188] See p. 103, above.

[189] See pp. 98–101, above.

[190] See pp. 101–2, above.

with other institutions.[191] These included occupational groups, with whom they became increasingly identified, and the town government. Such groups became anxious to control gilds, especially those that were acquiring wealth and political influence.[192]

As expenditure by gilds on pious objectives led to the development of administrative machineries and, as they became property owners, traders and corporate farmers, they began to display what we might perceive as secular characteristics. Whether this is to view the situation with post-reformation hindsight, and how far members were able to reconcile the contrary roles played by their gilds, are matters for further discussion.[193] So, too, are the complex relationships between gilds and other institutions in the course of their development. Further investigation of these questions is best pursued through an examination of the more plentiful records of York itself.

[191] See Chapter 4, pp. 144–5.
[192] See Chapter 4, pp. 137–8.
[193] Rubin, 'Small Groups and Identity', pp. 147–8.

CHAPTER FOUR

The Religious Gilds of Medieval York

From about the third decade of the fifteenth century, the larger urban religious gilds, now encouraged by royal approval, can increasingly be seen as agents of religious orthodoxy. This stance led them to be favoured by individuals with commercial and political ambitions, whose conventional piety chimed with official policies. In York, many gild members were of the mercantile classes, who were striving to maintain power. Others, from the artisan groupings, were trying to gain it. We can see an increasing symbiosis between the largest gilds and the city government, resulting in an enhancement of their more secular aspects. Membership of the Corpus Christi, St Christopher and St Anthony Gilds may not have actually been a qualification for city office, but many officeholders were members. Conversely, the activities of these great gilds were also closely monitored and controlled by the city government, which encouraged the amalgamations that made the largest gilds even larger. Their ceremonial activities became progressively more concerned with display, as their wealth in treasure and real estate burgeoned. At the same time, the relationship between religious gilds and occupations underwent a change, during the fifteenth century, that seems to have led to an increasing commercialization of the former.

This chapter will examine these changes and attempt to interpret their significance. A central question is how far the gradual subjection of devotional objectives to secular pressures affected a relative decline in urban fraternities, as the recipients of pious bequests, when compared with the continued increase in such bequests to rural gilds, prior to 1536. If this decline signalled a growing disenchantment with the great urban gilds as devotional institutions, it does not, however, follow that they ceased to be seen as pathways to political power, for as long as they continued to receive the support of central government and the church hierarchy. It seems likely, however, that patterns of gild membership were more complex than this, and that national political factors and shifting economic circumstances also played a part.

The Chronological Distribution of Testamentary Evidence

The testamentary evidence relating to York fraternities, used in this chapter, is based on a substantially complete list of gild bequests rather than a series of samples.[1] It is possible, therefore, to look at trends in more detail here than in the

---

1   Based on Eileen White's list in the BIHR, see Introduction, p. 9, above.

Figure 4.1: Numbers of York Testators Making Bequests to Gilds and of the
Bequests they Made to them

Period	Date Range	Testators to Gilds		Bequests to Gilds	
		Number	*Mean Variation*	*Number*	*Mean Variation*
1	1365–1400	17	–20.4	18	–44.6
2	1401–1410	22	–15.4	30	–32.4
3	1411–1420	15	–23.4	24	–38.6
4	1421–1430	37	–0.7	57	–5.6
5	1431–1440	84	+43.6	135	+72.4
6	1441–1450	73	+32.6	134	+71.4
7	1451–1460	54	+15.6	114	+51.4
8	1461–1470	37	+0.4	70	+7.4
9	1471–1480	66	+28.6	117	+54.4
10	1481–1490	59	+21.6	105	+43.8
11	1491–1500	24	–14.4	45	–17.6
12	1501–1510	56	+18.6	80	+17.4
13	1511–1520	13	–24.4	18	–44.6
14	1521–1530	20	–17.4	24	–38.6
15	1531–1540	15	–22.4	23	–39.6
16	1541–1550	7	–30.4	7	–55.6
Totals		599	Mean: 37.4	1001	Mean: 62.6

rest of the county. In York, this evidence can be supplemented by city, ecclesiastical and even gild records in a profusion not found elsewhere in the county. Many of these have proved to be accurately calendared and there is a wealth of secondary sources supplied by three centuries of scholarship. Some of the most important evidence relates to the Corpus Christi Gild, which receives detailed consideration in the next chapter, although its place in the general picture of the city's gilds cannot be wholly ignored here. Figures 4.1 and 4.2 show that both the numbers of York testators who made bequests to gilds and the numbers of bequests that they made to them increased dramatically from the beginning of the fifteenth century to a maximum between 1430 and 1450. The rise is distorted only by the absence of records for 1409–25 in the York Exchequer Court registers which creates an artificial dip in bequests at that period. The peak in the 1450s does not coincide with the point when most bequests were recorded from the sample taken from the rest of the county, in 1504–08.[2] This latter period was the last decade in which bequests to York gilds were recorded in significant numbers. Thereafter the steady decline in bequests to gilds in the city, that had been taking place since the 1440s, accelerated sharply. Within the general decline, however, are a series of peaks and troughs which can be related to a variety of factors.

2 See Figures 2.1 and 2.2.

One factor was undoubtedly economic. The comparatively slow decline in bequests to gilds, from the middle of the fifteenth century, accelerating sharply after the first decade of the sixteenth, roughly follows the pattern of the city's economic difficulties. York's mercantile decline from a high level of prosperity in the early fifteenth century to a state of some urban decay in the mid-sixteenth has been long established.[3] Whilst the causes of the decline have been hotly debated and its universality, beyond the textile industry, convincingly questioned, there is no doubt that the process, at least to some extent, took place.[4] It is also clear that the city's economic fortunes fell during a period when those of some other areas in the county, notably the West Riding, were rising.[5] This is reflected in the later peak in bequests to gilds elsewhere in the county. The largest occupational group in York that made bequests to gilds was mercantile.[6] This was the group that was most affected by economic decline, and, whilst it continued to represent about a quarter of all testators to gilds, their number declined from the peak of 1431–40, suggesting a link between the prosperity of this particular group and the number of bequests it made to gilds. Furthermore, a general shrinkage of the city's population, associated with its economic decline, also led to decreasing numbers of testators, and bequests to gilds.[7]

Wealth, however, is not the only measure of prosperity. Social harmony and a sense of security are also important factors in generating a sentiment of corporate well-being. In late medieval society such feelings were often expressed through pious ceremonial. In urban areas, these activities were generally focused on the concept of the 'honour' of the city.[8] Mervyn James discusses this in terms of the Corpus Christi cult, and, indeed, the York Corpus Christi Gild, in its *Primo Constitutio*, proclaimed that its annual procession was 'to the honour of god and the city of York'.[9] From the decade 1411–20 up to its dissolution, the bequests made to it averaged 61.3 per cent of all those made to gilds in the city.[10] This proportion indicates that it was a trend-setter amongst the city fraternities. Its contribution to the harmony of the city, through its rituals and ceremonials, and to York's place within the structures of the diocese, the county and beyond, through its wide membership, was a major factor in maintaining the city's public image and a symbol of its wealth, piety and security.[11]

If gilds played a part in maintaining civic stability, then we would expect them to be affected by instability, whether its causes were local or national. The trough

---

3   E.g. J. N. Bartlett, 'The Expansion and Decline of York in the Later Middle Ages', *Economic History Review*, 2nd series, 12 (1959) 17–22. Palliser, *Tudor York*, pp. 111–45. Kermode, 'Merchants, Overseas Trade, and Urban Decline', pp. 51–73.

4   Goldberg, *Women, Work and Life Cycle*, pp. 76–7.

5   *Ibid.*

6   See Figure 4.9 below.

7   Palliser, *Tudor York*, pp. 204–6.

8   James, 'Ritual, Drama and Social Body', pp. 12–13.

9   '. . . ad honorem Dei et civitatis Ebor', MS Lansdowne 304, fol. 17v.

10   See Figure 5.3.

11   See below, pp. 143–5.

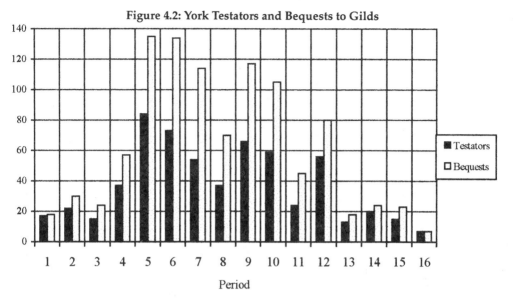

Figure 4.2: York Testators and Bequests to Gilds

The columns show the numbers of testators making bequests to gilds in the City of York and the number of bequests they made. The first point on the graph shows all such bequests made in the fourteenth century. Thereafter each point refers to totals per decade from 1400–1550.

Period refers to the date ranges displayed in Figure 4.1.

in gild popularity, that took place in the 1460s, as reflected in the testamentary evidence, occurred at a time of insecurity and chaos, when the city was exposed to the hazards and divisions of civil war. In particular, the events surrounding the battle of Towton, and its aftermath, were viewed by the city as a time of great disruption and a root cause of subsequent economic decay.[12] Only three testators made bequests to gilds in 1461 and only one did so in 1462.[13] Thereafter some recovery took place, although the figures for the end of the decade are artificially depressed by a gap in the probate register in 1470.

The trough in bequests to gilds in the 1490s is less easy to explain in national terms. It was, however, a particularly violent decade during a longer period of unrest within the city itself.[14] Annual enclosure riots over grazing rights claimed by the vicars choral, lasting from 1485 to 1495, eventually led to royal interven-

12 *VCH York*, pp. 59–60. A. Goodman, *The Wars of the Roses: Military Activity and English Society, 1452–97* (London, 1981), p. 52. Palliser, *Tudor York*, p. 203.

13 BIHR PR 2 451v–452v 1461 Alderman Thomas Barton, spicer, to St Christopher Gild, PR 2 446r–v 1461 Roger Lasselles esquire, to St Christopher Gild. YML L2(4) 298v–299r Agnes Marsshall wife of Alderman John Marsshall, Merchant of the Staple, to Corpus Christi Gild shrine. BIHR PR 2 465v–466r 1462 Agnes Staneburn, widow of John Staneburn, to Corpus Christi and St Christopher Gilds.

14 Palliser, *Tudor York*, p. 45.

tion.[15] The violent and protracted dispute between the crafts of the cordwainers and the weavers over their precedence in the Corpus Christi procession disrupted the city's ceremonials between 1490 and 1493.[16] Internal political dissensions in the city's government, unsolved by royal revisions of the electoral regulations in 1464 and 1473, underlay these symptoms of malaise and continued until Henry VIII's intervention in 1517.[17] Fiscal problems ran counterpoint to these difficulties which caused the city authorities to increase the number of city chamberlains appointed to oversee and underwrite the city's finances between 1487 and 1499.[18] Similar expedients were again adopted in the 1530s and 1540s, accompanied by a further decline in bequests to gilds, but by this time, the gilds themselves were under the reforming pressures that were to lead to their dissolution.[19]

A further explanation of the early sixteenth century decline in bequests might lie in general attitudes to piety. Heath has found general lack of religious enthusiasm in pre-reformation Hull, and Tanner sees a similar trend in Norwich.[20] This does not, however, seem to have been a universal phenomenon. Burgess's account of contemporary Bristol churchwardens gives an entirely contrary impression.[21] Although there was a decline in bequests to gilds in York, the content of the wills, especially with regard to their funereal provisions, suggests that pious concerns rooted in an acceptance of the doctrine of purgatory survived the trauma of the Pilgrimage of Grace.[22]

So far we have been examining only the troughs in the general pattern of testators and bequests. Its peaks were probably enhanced by other factors, including demography. In years of pestilence, more wills were made and there was a higher probability of gild bequests being recorded. Jeremy Goldberg notes that there was particularly high mortality in the whole county, including York, in 1391, 1429, 1436, 1438, 1459, 1467, 1471–72, 1474, 1483, 1505–06 and 1508–9.[23] The high number of bequests to gilds, especially in the 1430s, the 1470s and in the first decade of the sixteenth century, may be viewed in the light of this. If the number of bequests to gilds in these decades increased for this reason, then the figures for the 1440s, most of the 1450s and the 1490s must have been correspondingly depressed during periods of apparently lower mortality. High mortality is,

---

15 *YCR*, II, p. 123.

16 *Ibid.*, pp. 56–8, 70, 73–4, 90–1, 93–4, 96–100.

17 *VCH York*, pp. 82–4. Palliser, Tudor York, pp. 68–9.

18 J. I. Kermode, 'Urban Decline? The Flight from Office in Late Medieval York', *Economic History Review* 2nd series 35 (1982), 179–94 (p. 187). R. B. Dobson, *York City Chamberlains' Account Rolls 1396–1500*, Surtees Society 192 (1980), pp. 212–13.

19 *FR*, I, pp. 250–69. See Chapter 7, below.

20 Heath, 'Urban Piety', pp. 228–9. N. P. Tanner, 'The Reformation and Regionalism', p. 140.

21 C. Burgess, ' "A fond thing vainly invented": an essay on Purgatory and pious motive in later medieval England', in *Parish, Church and People: Local Studies in Lay Religion 1350–1750*, ed. S. J. Wright (London, 1988), 56–84 (pp. 77–8).

22 See pp. 145–6 below.

23 Goldberg, 'Mortality and Economic Change', pp. 41–2.

however, an insufficient explanation for the major peak in bequests between 1431 and 1450.

It seems certain that the promulgation, in 1436, of the statute of Henry VI, requiring local governments to approve all new gild ordinances, was an important stage in the development of gilds.[24] It offered official recognition to fraternities that were not incorporated by royal charter. It also gave the city authorities direct control of all gilds and their ordinances. The measure was, in many cases, a recognition of current practice. The Corpus Christi Gild, for example, was founded in 1408, and included, in its early membership, numbers of the city elite.[25] Although there is no record of its formal recognition by the city authorities at that time, the agreement of 1431 makes it clear that there was a close relationship between the two, prior to the statute of 1436.[26] Unlike the St Christopher Gild, incorporated in 1396, it was dependent on local recognition until the royal charter of 1458.[27] Royal approval of all fraternities, through the agency of the city, conferred a new status upon unchartered gilds. That this initiative took place in a decade that saw an explosion in bequests to York gilds is unlikely to be coincidental, although there was a general increase in will-making in the 1430s.[28] The members, and would-be members of the urban elite were presented with fraternities that, in addition to offering established spiritual benefits, now had an official connection with the city's government. That the measure had an immediate effect in the principal centre of both lay and ecclesiastical administration in the North, is hardly surprising. It has already been shown that the response was less immediate further afield, in the remoter parts of the county, although, even there, the secular benefits of gild membership were eventually perceived.[29]

The statute of 1436, however, was a manifestation of wider governmental concerns. It can be seen as part of a royal policy of support for traditional doctrine and practices. This had been set in train by the Leicester parliament of 1414 which introduced legal sanctions against Lollard opinions and practices.[30] Now, by controlling the ordinances of all gilds through the agents of local government, the Lancastrian monarchs were ensuring their co-operation as potential allies in their crusade against heresy and encouraging their maintenance of conservative religious beliefs and ceremonials. Clearly, the larger gilds, such as Corpus Christi in York, were already unequivocally orthodox in their stance.[31] The process of licensing ensured the compliance of lesser gilds containing less traditionally minded members. From this point, religious orthodoxy is a common thread

---

[24] *Statutes of the Realm*, II, pp. 298–9.

[25] See Chapter 5, pp. 168–9.

[26] YCA BY fols. 116Av–117v.

[27] *Cal. Pat. 1391–1396*, pp. 711, 716. YCA G 11.

[28] Goldberg, 'Mortality and Economic Change', p. 42, Fig. 1.

[29] See Chapter 2, pp. 50–1.

[30] J. Catto, 'Religious Change under Henry V', in *Henry V: The Practice of Kingship*, ed. G. L. Harriss (Oxford, 1985), pp. 97–115 (p. 97).

[31] See Chapter 5, p. 60.

running through the complex web of those gild institutions that we can identify, uniting them in their diversity. The weaker that thread was to become, the greater was the vulnerability of all gilds to the initiatives that eventually destroyed them. These processes, however, varied greatly from gild to gild and it is appropriate, at this point, to investigate the range of fraternities found in York, and to examine their different purposes and evolution.

Parish Gilds

Like Norwich and Bristol, but unlike the urban centres in the rest of Yorkshire, York had a multiplicity of parishes. During most of this period there seem to have been about forty.[32] Whilst Doncaster's single parish church of St George sustained some eighteen identified gilds, no York parish can be shown to have supported more than two.[33] Thus, whilst gilds were concentrated in one large parish church in Doncaster, Pontefract and Scarborough, in two in Hull and in three in Beverley, in York some fifty-four fraternities were distributed more thinly over a much larger number of churches and other institutions. This gives the impression that the specifically parish gild was less highly regarded in the city than elsewhere. Only thirteen of the parish churches of York and its immediate suburbs possessed, between them, some nineteen identified gilds that attracted bequests, or which were otherwise recorded. These are listed in Figure 4.3. Gilds were generally found in the wealthier parishes, but their numbers were not great and they did not generally receive many bequests.[34]

With such a small number of bequests and in the virtual absence of other information, the activities and functions of York parish gilds can only be deduced on the basis of evidence from elsewhere. Twenty-two gilds associated with parish churches, excluding those with occupational connections, made returns in 1389, from Lynn in Norfolk.[35] They give a picture of some of the functions which were fulfilled by parish gilds in an urban area divided into a large number of parishes. Ordinances governing the maintenance of lights, the conduct of gild masses and funerals and the holding of feasts and processions indicate that they were organized along much the same lines as parish gilds elsewhere. It is clear, however, that the Great Gild of Holy Trinity dominated gild life in Lynn in much the same way as those of St Christopher, Corpus Christi and St Anthony did

---

[32] The precise number is unclear. Some parishes, especially in the suburbs, were at various times assessed for taxation purposes jointly with others, suggesting that their churches may have become derelict. See Peacock, 'York Subsidy Roll', pp. 172–91 and *YMB III B/Y*, pp. 184–5. Furthermore, some testators referred to non-parochial chapels, such as Holy Trinity Fossgate, as if they were parishes: e.g. BIHR PR 2 501v–502r 1426 John Clerk, fishmonger.

[33] See Figures 4.3 and 4.4.

[34] Tax assessments of York parishes are shown in Figure 4.8.

[35] Westlake, *Parish Gilds*, pp. 192–200. Smith, *English Gilds*, pp. 45–109.

Figure 4.3: York Bequests to Parish Gilds

Parish	Gild	BeqF	BeqL	Total	Life	Notes
All Saints Pavement	St Mary	1485	1512	2	27	–
Chapel of St Thomas	St Nicholas	1430	1430	1	–	Hospital?
St Andrew Fishergate	St Mary	1428	1428	1	–	–
St Crux	St Crux	1440	1458	2	18	–
St Crux	Jesus and St Mary	1365	1365	1	–	Hospital
St Denys Walmgate	St John Baptist	1390	1390	1	–	–
St Denys Walmgate	St Katherine	1503	1506	2	3	–
St John Hungate	St John Baptist	1449	1449	1	–	–
St Laurence Walmgate	St Anne (or Agnes)	1404	1508	104	–	1548 CC
St Laurence Walmgate	St Mary	1404	1404	1	–	–
St Michael le Belfrey	St Thomas Martyr	1398	1399	2	2	16th C glass
St Michael le Belfrey	St Mary	1486	1509	4	23	–
St Helen Stonegate	SS. Chris & Andrew	1399	1399	1	–	–
St Helen Stonegate	St Mary	1478	1478	1	–	–
St Margaret Walmgate	St Anne	–	–	–	–	BIHR Y/Marg 36
St Mary Bishophill Sr	St Mary	1453	1453	1	–	–
St Nicholas Micklegate	St Mary	1486	1486	1	–	–
St Olave	St Mary	1434	1434	1	–	St Mary Abbey?
St Saviour	Corpus Christi	1416	1416	1	–	Light
St Saviour	St Anne	1527	1527	1	–	–

BeqF: date of first bequest.
BeqL: date of last bequest.
Total: total number of bequests.
Life: interval in years between first and last bequest.
CC: *Certificates.*

York.[36] The Trinity Gild in Lynn owned extensive properties, was involved in trade and lent money to the corporation. It employed thirteen chaplains in three different churches and, as the York Corpus Christi Gild, conducted especially elaborate funerals. Whilst the smaller, parish gilds may have aspired to follow similar practices and to fulfil a variety of charitable functions, in imitation of the Trinity Gild, they operated on a much smaller scale and confined their activities to a single parish or cause, such as the maintenance of a hospital or almshouse.[37] It is likely that most York parish gilds also operated on this scale and, although the number of bequests to each was modest, this was also the case in the rest of the county.

Associated with parish gilds were a number of fraternities devoted to specific

[36] Owen, *The Making of King's Lynn*, pp. 60–3.
[37] *Ibid.*, p. 61.

causes. There was, for example, considerable gild activity surrounding two York hospitals. The gild of Jesus and St Mary, that seems to have been connected with St Crux parish, was founded in 1357 with the stated object of creating a hospital in Fossgate.[38] When this function had been fulfilled, the gild was probably dissolved in 1391.[39] Subsequently, altars were sustained by several gilds in the hospital chapel, one of which was the gild of Holy Trinity that was later associated with the Mercers' mistery and which eventually administered the hospital.[40] The gild of St Nicholas in the Chapel of St Thomas, which received a bequest in 1430, could have been a gild of the parish of St Nicholas Micklegate.[41] However, an alternative, and perhaps more likely, explanation is that it sustained an altar in the chapel of the Hospital of St Thomas which, at the time of the bequest, was run by Holy Trinity Priory, with which St Nicholas parish church was associated. The hospital was sold to the Corpus Christi Gild by the Priory in 1478.[42] The three bequests to an unspecified St Nicholas Gild between 1491 and 1509 may also refer to this fraternity.[43] That all three testators also made bequests to the Corpus Christi Gild supports this theory. If this is correct we have the interesting situation of a gild flourishing for over thirty years within an institution owned by another much larger fraternity, underlining the general proposition that individuals were often members of several fraternities and that gilds were not necessarily competitive with one another.

Most of the other gilds shown in Figure 4.3 seem to have been parish fraternities that were not associated with any particular cause. The majority of them were situated in the wealthier parishes, whose inhabitants were, presumably, more able to make bequests to them. It is, however, clear, from a comparison of Figures 4.3 and 4.8, that even wealthy people who lived in less affluent parishes were more likely to make legacies to the larger gilds in the city. None of the five testators of the relatively poor parish of St Margaret Walmgate made a bequest to the local parish gild of St Anne.[44] Its existence is attested by a brief account for the year 1397, on a scrap of parchment preserved in the parish records.[45] Even in the richest city parishes, bequests to local parish gilds were rare. Of the fifty-five

---

38 L. R. Wheatley, 'The York Mercers' Guild, 1420–1502 – Origins, Organisation and Ordinances' (unpublished MA dissertation, York, 1993), pp. 22–30.

39 *Ibid.*, p. 75.

40 *Ibid.*, pp.78–83. Also see below, pp. 139–40.

41 BIHR PR 2 666v 1430 John Wilson of the parish of St Nicholas Micklegate.

42 YCA G 13, 14.

43 BIHR PR 5 391r–392r, 1491, Richard Wakefeilde, chaplain of All Saints Northstreet, 12d. PR 5 510r–v, 1497, John Robynson, butcher of Holy Trinity King's Court, 12d. YML L2(5)a 82r–83v 1509, Alison Clark widow of St Michael le Belfrey, 6s.8d.

44 BIHR PR 2 523r, 1427, John de Man, merchant, bequest to St George. PR 3 408r–409r, 1435, William Barton, skinner, bequests to Corpus Christi, St Christopher, Paternoster, St Mary of the Skinners, St John the Baptist. PR 3 156v, 1478, Richard More, yeoman, bequest to Corpus Christi. PR 5 65r, 1482, Thomas Rede, bequest to Corpus Christi. PR 7 62r–v, 1508, Ranald Home bequest to Corpus Christi.

45 BIHR Y/Marg 36.

testators of St Crux parish, who made bequests to gilds, only two did so to the gild of St Crux in the parish church.[46] In All Saints Pavement, just two out of thirty-two testators to gilds made bequests to the parochial gild of St Mary.[47] Of the forty-seven testators of St Michael le Belfrey, who made bequests to gilds, only three did so to the parish gild of St Mary and one to that of St Thomas of Canterbury, which probably installed windows in the rebuilt church in the early sixteenth century, about 120 years later.[48]

Other parish gilds also seem to have operated for long periods without receiving bequests. That of St Anne, in the suburban church of St Laurence, received bequests in 1404 and 1427 but was not mentioned again until 1493, when, in a sudden burst of popularity, it received six bequests between 1503 and 1508, and was finally recorded, as the gild of St Agnes, at its dissolution, in 1546.[49] It seems likely that the gild enjoyed an unbroken existence of at least 142 years, but the various intervals, such as the sixty-six years between 1427 and 1493, which included the period when bequests to all York gilds were at their zenith, shows how infrequent and random surviving legacies to parish gilds are. All the evidence suggests that there were numbers of unrecorded parish gilds in the city. Whilst it cannot be inferred that parochial fraternities must have existed in such wealthy parishes as St John Micklegate, Holy Trinity King's Court or St Martin Coney Street, where none have been recorded, it would be equally dangerous to assert that they did not.

They were, however, much less popular with testators than the larger gilds. 82.2 per cent of all bequests to York gilds were made to those of Corpus Christi, St Christopher, St Anthony and the smaller gilds that they absorbed, during the course of the fifteenth century. There are a number of possible reasons for this. A parish gild, in the context of York's plethora of small parishes, would have little political influence beyond its limited boundaries. Membership offered fraternity between close neighbours, who might already be friends, rather than powerful contacts city-wide or beyond. Low memberships, even in wealthy parishes, would often mean that parish gilds were modest economic units with corre-

---

[46] BIHR PR 3 600r–v, 1440, Thomas Carlile tailor. PR 2 375r–376r 1458 Katherine Radclyff widow of John mercer.

[47] BIHR PR 5 260v–261r, 1485, Thomas Kendale dyer. PR 8 117r 1512, Ralph Close.

[48] St Mary Gild: YML L2(4) 367v 1486 Thomas Rowson baker: 12d. L2(5)a 43r–v 1505 John Elward alderman: 13s.8d. L2(5)a 82r–83v 1509 Alison Clark widow: 6s.8d. St Thomas of Canterbury Gild: L2(4) 121 1399 Simon de Lastyngham: a missal and 26s.8d. for his brothers' prayers. One series of panels is still in situ, others are now in the York Minster Chapterhouse.

[49] BIHR PR 3 111r 1404 Thomas Telar of the parish of St Laurence: 18d. PR 2 527 1427 John Dunkan chaplain of the parish of St John Ousebridge: 3s.4d. PR 5 445v 1493 William Arthure of the parish of Heslington: 6d. PR 6 34v 1503 Thomas Hemyngburgh clerk of the parish of St Laurence: 12d. PR 6 201v–202r 1505 Thomas Freman tanner of the parish of St Laurence: 3s.4d. for torches. PR 6 202v–203r 1505 Margaret North widow of William of the parish of St Laurence ex Walmgate: 20d. PR 6 174r 1506 John Gudryk of the parish of St Laurence extra Walmgate: 12d. PR 7 51v–52r 1508 Margaret Campynott of the parish of St Laurence: 6s.8d. PR 7 62r–v 1508 Agnes Leys widow of the parish of St Laurence extra Walmgate: 12d.

spondingly limited opportunities for charitable activities. It seems likely that they catered primarily for those who were not wealthy enough to make wills. The vestigial account of the St Anne Gild in St Margaret's parish indicates this.[50] Above all, however, their popularity was probably most affected by the circumstances of will-making. A large gild, employing chaplains, or, like the Corpus Christi Gild, run by them, offered much more powerful prayers, to help the soul through purgatory, than a small fraternity of parishioners. The larger gilds also provided lavish funerals which offered both spiritual advantages and a statement of the status, piety and wealth of the deceased.[51] Such inducements were offered, not only by the largest gilds, with their civic connections, but also by medium-sized gilds, or confraternities, based in the religious houses of the city.

Monastic Gilds and Confraternities

The term 'confraternity' does not seem to have been much used in late medieval York, except in the case of the Corpus Christi Gild.[52] It is employed here to describe a gild of laymen that was based in a religious institution, monastic, mendicant or episcopal, and that enjoyed an arrangement of mutual support with its inmates and governors. The religious house benefited economically from the confraternity, that gave it gifts and offerings for conducting religious services. The confraternity, in return, enjoyed the special religious and funerary advantages that association with a religious house might imply. In addition, the house could also attempt to prevent interference in the confraternity's affairs from secular authorities or from local parishes. This might be of particular significance in the complex political context of a city. Such confraternities were common throughout Europe and, it has been argued, weakened the authority of the parish.[53] Although the citizens of York did not usually call them confraternities, gilds based in religious houses were more popular with testators than were their parish fraternities. However, the relationships that monastically-based gilds enjoyed with their parent houses did not invariably imply conflict with parishes. It is the purpose of this section to investigate the range of relationships that existed between gilds and religious institutions.

Figure 4.4 shows bequests made to those recorded York gilds which had a direct link with monastic houses within the city, including a number where the

---

50 BIHR Y/Marg 36. Ed. P. Hoskin, 'Some late fourteenth-century Gild Accounts and Fabric Wardens' Accounts from the Church of St Margaret's, Walmgate, York', in *The Church in Medieval York, records edited in honour of Professor Barrie Dobson*, gen. ed. D. M. Smith (York, 1999), pp. 75–86.

51 See below, pp. 145–6.

52 It is used in the preamble and ordinances of the Register of the Corpus Christi Gild interchangeably with 'fraternity', MS Lansdowne 304 fols. 15r–19v. Here it seems to describe the relationship between the clerical and lay members of the gild.

53 J. Henderson, 'Confraternities and the Church in Late Medieval Florence', in *Voluntary Religion*, Studies in Church History No. 23, ed. W. J. Shiels and D. Wood (Oxford, 1986), pp. 69–83 (p. 69).

Figure 4.4: York Bequests to Confraternities

Institution	Gild	BeqF	BeqL	Total	Life	Notes
Minster	St Christopher	1394	1543	241	149	Incorporated 1396, *CC*20
	SS. Christopher & George	1466	1535	36	80	*CC*20
Abbey of St Mary	St Mary at the Abbey	1420	1487	45	67	–
St Giles Chapel	St Mary (Skinners)	1435	1445	5	10	Occupational
?Holy Trinity Priory	Corpus Christi	1413	1550	379	137	Founded 1408 Incorporated 1458 CC546
	St Nicholas	1491	1509	3	18	?In St Thomas' Hospital
St Andrew (Gilbertines)	St Mary	1428	1428	1	1	–
Austin Friars	St Katherine	1414	1537	10	123	–
	Holy Trinity	1438	1471	2	33	?Occupational
	St Mary & St Austin	1506	1509	2	14	–
	St Augustine (Cordwainers)	1520	1520	1	1	Occupational
	Resurrection (Carpenters)	–	–	nil	1	Occupational
Dominican Friars	Holy Trinity	–	–	nil	1	–
Carmelite Friars	St Mary (Cordwainers)	1402	1527	30	125	Occupational
Franciscan Friars	St Francis	1428	1453	6	25	–
	St Mary	1420	1420	1	1	–
	St Mary & St Francis	1429	1429	1	1	–

BeqF: date of first bequest.
BeqL: date of last bequest.
Total: total number of bequests.
Life: interval in years between first and last bequest.
CC: *Certificates.*

connection is open to some doubt or where individual gilds are discussed in other contexts elsewhere in this book. These include the two largest fraternities in the city. The arguments for an association between Holy Trinity Priory and the Corpus Christi Gild will be pursued in the next chapter.[54] The second most popular gild with testators, that of St Christopher, later St Christopher and St George, had a relationship with the Minster. Subsequent to its first bequest, in 1394, it was incorporated by letters patent from Richard II, during his visit to York, in 1396.[55] These provided that the gild was to be based in the Minster. This connection was confirmed in 1426 by the foundation of a chantry at the altar of St Christopher that, in 1546, still employed two chaplains.[56] These were selected by the gild, but approved by the Dean and Chapter, underlining the former's status

---

[54] See Chapter 5, pp. 164–5.

[55] *Cal. Pat. 1391–96*, p. 711.

[56] BIHR PR 1 66r Richard Byrd tanner of All Saints North Street. White, *St Christopher and St George*, p. 2.

within the ambit of the latter.[57] Whether it ever had the full standing of a confraternity within the Minster is unclear. Although it continued to pay oblations, given at the St Christopher chantry, to the Minster, from about 1448 it worshipped in its own chapel in Coney Street, and feasted in the new Guildhall.[58] The chantry, however, was maintained and was later used as a kind of civic enclave.[59] The city was evidently able to use the gild to gain official entry to the Minster and to make its presence felt within its Liberty.

The only other fraternity that had a demonstrable connection with the Minster was that of Paternoster, whose 1389 return recorded that it maintained a candelabrum and a board, hanging against a pillar there, to explain the content and meaning of the Lord's Prayer.[60] It does not seem to have met in the Minster and the performances of the play, which was its principal function, took place in the city streets not in the cathedral precinct.[61] Whilst the Dean and Chapter were prepared to accept the presence of gild chantries and shrines within the Minster, however, they did not promote confraternities as did the city's religious houses.

The gild of St Mary at the Abbey, which received forty-five bequests between 1420 and 1487, making it the fourth most popular in the city, had its chapel in the gatehouse of the Benedictine Abbey of St Mary's, outside the city walls.[62] It was certainly sited there between 1438 and 1485, during which period seven testators described the gild as being next to the abbey gates.[63] Whilst sixteen testators were of the parish of St Olave, by the abbey walls, and two were from nearby Clifton, twenty-three were members of other parishes in York and its suburbs. It may be significant, however, that all but two of these bequests were made in the period up to 1444, when an acrimonious and expensive lawsuit over fishgarths between the abbot and the city began.[64] This strife might have affected the city-wide nature of the gild, which seems to have taken on a more parochial character thereafter. The gild appears to have been both a confraternity and a parish fraternity acting principally, at least after 1444, as a focus for the interests of a suburban neighbourhood. Its role here may have been similar to that of the gild of St Anne in St Laurence, whose popularity may have reflected a similar feeling of community amongst the inhabitants of areas outside the walls of the city to the south.[65] The paucity of gild bequests from other suburban York churches, unconnected with monastic houses, and the presence of a probable confraternity of the Gilber-

---

57 YCA G70 33. PRO E 301/66 20, 21.

58 Dobson, 'Citizens and Chantries in Late Medieval York', pp. 318–20.

59 White, *St Christopher and St George Gild*, pp. 8, 3–4.

60 BIHR PR 3 520r, PR 3 560v–561r, PR 3 597v, PR 5 27r–v, PR 5 35r, PR 5 211r, 286r–v.

61 PRO C 47/46/454.

62 A. Raine, *Medieval York* (London, 1955), pp. 92–1. L. T. Smith, *York Plays: The Plays Performed by the Crafts or Mysteries of York on the day of Corpus Christi in the 14th, 15th and 16th Centuries* (Oxford, 1885), p. xxix.

63 See gazetteer in Crouch, 'Piety Fraternity and Power' under St Mary Gild at the Abbey and also St Mary in St Olave.

64 Dobson, *York City Chamberlains' Account Rolls*, pp. 37–58.

65 See p. 127 above.

tines in St Andrew Fishergate, however, supports the contention that the piety connected with a religious institution was a major factor in the promotion of many gilds.[66] Unfortunately, there is little evidence of suburban gilds near the other major urban centres in the county with which to make comparison.

Although they did not support gilds on the scale of the mendicant orders in Florence, it was clearly the policy of York's four friaries to support lay fraternities, and they did so to varying extents and with differing degrees of success.[67] Unlike Florentine confraternities, none of them seems to have been regarded as Tertiary Orders of their friary. It may be that the agreement drawn up between the gild of the Resurrection, the carpenters' mistery, and the prior and convent of the Austin Friars, in which the friary undertook to provide religious services for the gild in return for payment, indicates a typical arrangement.[68] A majority of friary confraternities were gilds sustained by specific crafts within the city, and this aspect of their functions will be discussed in the next section.

The Augustinians maintained three recorded gilds in addition to two that were definitely craft related. Their popularity with gilds might have been connected with the friary's central location in the city. The gild of St Katherine seems to have been its major confraternity. It attracted ten bequests, between 1414 and 1537, four testators describing it as being based in the friary, and two others referring to it as the gild of St Katherine and St Mary Magdalene, inferring that it absorbed another gild before 1480.[69] The friary also supported a Holy Trinity Gild which received three bequests, between 1438 and 1471.[70] However, it may be no coincidence that all three testators were tailors. It seems likely that, although none of the wills confirms this, the gild was associated with this craft. The dedication of a possible St Mary and St Austin Gild, or of two separate gilds of St Mary and St Austin, recorded in 1509, might refer to a cordwainers' gild dedicated to St Augustine in the friary or possibly to a separate amalgamated fraternity.[71]

Although the Dominicans do not seem to have been deeply involved with lay confraternities, the fate of their Holy Trinity Gild, wound up by the city authori-

[66] BIHR PR 2 529r 1428 William Gaynesby of the parish of St Andrew outside the walls: 6s.8d.

[67] J. Henderson, 'Confraternities and the Church in Late Medieval Florence', pp. 70–2.

[68] YCA E 20A B/Y fol. 207v. See below p. 137.

[69] Testators mentioning the Augustinian friary: BIHR PR 2 128v–129r, 1446, William Gyslay. PR 2 417r, 1459, Richard Wighton dyer of St John Ousebridge. PR 2 485r–v, 463, William Touthorp butcher of Holy Trinity Kings Court. PR 4 43r–44r, 1467, Alice Langwath widow of St Andrew. Testators to St Katherine and St Mary Magdalene: BIHR PR 5 177r, 1480, William Broune cooper. PR 11 249r, 1537, John of Burton gentleman and city macebearer, of St Martin. Other testators to St Katherine: YML L2(4) 172r, 1414, Robert Wakefeld glazier of St Helen Stonegate. L2(4) 323v–324, 1470, Isabella Saxton widow of St Michael le Belfrey. BIHR PR 8 62r–v, 1508, Ranald Home of St Margaret. YML L2(5)a 82r–83v, 1509, Alison Clark widow of St Michael le Belfrey.

[70] BIHR PR 3 511r, 1438, Robert Dote, tailor of Coneystreet. PR 2 405r, 1459, John Carter tailor of All Saints Pavement. PR 4 162v 1471, Ralph Moyses tailor of St Crux.

[71] BIHR PR 8 26v–27r 1509 Richard Rawlyn of St John del Pike.

ties in the early fifteenth century, throws light on the relationships between the city, the gilds and the friaries.[72] All but a minority of about thirty-seven of its members wanted to amalgamate the gild with that of St Anthony. Those who wished to secede had removed the long box, in which the gild kept its torches and other goods, from the friary. The prior and convent were threatening to excommunicate them if they did not return it. John de Moreton, and other trustworthy men, had inquired into the case and found that the gild was unlicensed by the crown and should be suppressed. They ruled that the prior and convent should retain the image of Holy Trinity, which the gild had been founded to venerate, and its candelabrum. The long box that figured so prominently in the dispute was to be kept in the Chapel of St William on Ouse Bridge and the torches that were stored in it should be burned at divine service there. The gild's funds were to be used by the Lord Mayor towards building the new Chapel of St Anne, on Foss Bridge.

This dispute and its resolution raises a number of interesting points. Beyond the provision of religious services, the convent also provided space for the gild's principal image and for its material possessions. Although the confraternity afforded some protection for gild assets from the secular power of the city and the parent house could use excommunication as a weapon, it was possible for the lay power to override friary opposition in special circumstances. In this case the desire of a majority of the gildspeople to leave the protection of the priory was an important factor. The authorities also made great play with the unlicensed nature of the gild. Although this seems to have been a convenient excuse, it underlines the precarious status of unchartered gilds prior to the Statute of 1436. It is likely that only a small minority of York gilds had royal licences or charters; certainly, very few are extant or are known to have existed. The St Anthony Gild itself did not receive its royal licence of incorporation until 1446, considerably later than this dispute.[73] The Holy Trinity Gild's assets were confiscated into the city coffers, but the friary's ability to complain about this was diminished by their being put to pious uses, albeit to pious uses that were directly sponsored by the city. The convent would find it difficult, physically, to recover the long box, as the gild had been abolished and the box was no longer in the convent church, but in a different consecrated place. The brothers and sisters of Holy Trinity who wished to join the St Anthony Gild were obviously now free to do so, but their gild assets did not follow them. Basically, the city authorities could control gild affairs, and profit from them, even where the fraternity was based in a conventual church.

Only two confraternal gilds were recorded in the Franciscan Friary. In 1420, Thomas Rygton left 18d to the fraternity of St Mary in the conventual church of the Friars Minor in York.[74] Six bequests to a gild of St Francis between 1428 and 1453 suggest an important, if short-lived, confraternity but, although one testa-

---

72 YCA E 20 YMB AY II, fols. 194v–195r, undated. A. Raine, *Medieval York*, p. 92 note, suggests 1418.

73 *Cal. Pat. 1441–1446*, p. 442.

74 YML L2(4) 194r–v, 1420, Thomas Rygton of St Andrew parish.

tor, Alice Poumfreyt, was buried in the friary, none actually identified the gild with the Franciscans, and the connection is largely based on its dedication.[75] A bequest in 1429 to a gild of the Blessed Mary and St Francis in York probably indicates a merger of the two gilds, although no connection with the friary is established by the will.[76]

Although the Carmelite friary housed only one fraternity, it was, with thirty testators, the most popular in testamentary terms connected with any mendicant convent in the city. The St Mary Gild of the Carmelites was, however, sustained by the craft of the cordwainers, and it will be discussed in the following section.[77]

The popularity of friaries as locations for gilds was probably related to their popularity with testators generally. Bequests to friaries, often in return for intercessionary prayers, were common in late medieval wills generally and were certainly so in both York and Yorkshire.[78] The prayers of professional mendicants, who were also religious, were evidently seen as being particularly efficacious in ensuring the swift passage of souls through purgatory. Such power was clearly advantageous to the devotional and funerary aspects of gilds. There were also physical advantages in making use of large friary churches. When the Corpus Christi Gild outgrew its accommodation in Holy Trinity Priory, its master and stewards celebrated a general obit in the four friary churches every four years.[79] It is easy to overstate the importance of the siting of non-parochial gilds within institutions that can be seen as neutral, in terms of local politics, and comparatively free from civic influence. The fate of the Holy Trinity Gild of the Dominicans shows that the corporation could interfere in confraternities of mendicant houses, even before the Statute of 1436 increased its powers. Such considerations might, nevertheless, have encouraged the establishment of craft-related gilds within the city's friaries.

Gilds and Occupations

There is a widely-held misconception that York, in the early fifteenth century, supported a large number of 'craft guilds'. The problem is one of definition. The majority of the crafts and occupations of the city did not refer to themselves as gilds and were not described as such by their contemporaries. Membership of a craft, mistery, or art consisted of the masters who were franchised to it within the city. It was compulsory, when working or trading within the city's jurisdiction, to belong to it and, under penalty, to obey its ordinances. These were enforced by the craft's searchers, who have often been seen as the agents of the city authori-

[75] BIHR PR 2 660r–v, 1429, Alice widow of Roger Poumfreyt skinner.
[76] BIHR PR 2 660r–v, 1429, Richard Vender spicer of St Martin Coney Street.
[77] See pp. 136–7 below.
[78] R. Southern, *Western Society and the Church in The Middle Ages* (London, 1970), p. 290. *VCH York*, p. 110. Heath, 'Urban Piety', pp. 220–1.
[79] YCA G 11A, Skaife, *Corpus Christi Gild*, p. 267.

Figure 4.5: City of York Bequests to Occupational gilds

Craft	Gild	Location	BeqF	BeqL	Total	Life
Carpenters	Resurrection	Austin Friars	–	–	–	–
Chantry Chaplains	Chantry Chaplains	–	1399	1407	2	8
Cordwainers	St Mary	Carmelite Friars	1402	1527	30	125
Cordwainers	St Augustine	Austin Friars	1506	1520	2	16
Mercers/merchants	Holy Trinity Fossgate	Hall and Hospital	1410	1525	20	115
Skinners	St Mary	St Giles	1435	1445	5	10
Tailors	St John Baptist	Hall	1386	1546	44	161
Tailors?	Holy Trinity	Austin Friars	1438	1471	3	33
Weavers	St Mary	–	1406	1528	12	122
Weavers	Holy Ghost	–	1528	1528	1	1

BeqF: date of first bequest.
BeqL: date of last bequest.
Total: total number of bequests.
Life: interval in years between first and last bequest.

ties.[80] Most recorded regulations concerned the conduct of business. The principal socio-religious activity that they governed was their participation in the city's annual Corpus Christi play cycle. This activity was closely regulated by the city.[81] Individual crafts could only vary their contributions to the event by formal consent of the mayor and council.[82] It is difficult to reconcile such tightly circumscribed associations with the voluntary and devotional characteristics of late medieval religious gilds.

There were, however, exceptions. The Weavers' Gild of York was incorporated by royal charter, granted by Henry II, with the right of making coloured cloth for most of the county, in return for an annual tax of ten pounds.[83] Clearly, this was the kind of craft gild that was instructed to produce copies of its charters and letters patent in the writs for the 1389 gild returns.[84] The weavers' ordinances, of 1400, referred to the craft as a gild, insisting that membership be exclusive to weavers and that all female members be properly trained.[85] The question arises as to whether this was the same gild as that of St Mary of the Weavers, which, as shown in Figure 4.5, received twelve bequests between 1406 and 1528.[86] A major-

---

80 H. Swanson, *Medieval Artisans* (Oxford, 1989), pp. 107–26.
81 H. Swanson, 'The Illusion of Economic Structure', pp. 29–48.
82 E.g. Permission was granted to the painters and stainers to combine their pageant with that of the pinners and latteners: 31 January 1422, YCA A/Y Memorandum Book, E 20, fol. 247r–v.
83 *YMB A/Y*, I, pp. xxvii–xxx.
84 See Chapter 1, pp. 16–17.
85 *YMB A/Y*, I, pp. 242–3.
86 BIHR PR 3 228v–30r 1406 Agnes Hulott widow of Thomas litster of the parish of St John

ity of these were, indeed, from weavers. In each case the connection between the craft and the gild is made clear. However, the list of testators contains individuals who were not weavers, although they all probably had a close connection with the craft. They were a dyer, a mercer, a merchant and Margaret Plumpton, of unknown occupation. Their presence seems irreconcilable with the exclusive nature of the weavers' ordinances. The last recorded bequest, that of William Robynson, in 1528, also made the only recorded bequest to a second weavers' gild, that of the Holy Ghost.[87]

> Item I yeve to the maister of the wevars to the stoke of our ladies Gilde iijs ivd
> Item I yeve to the holie gost gilde of the wevars ijs

The example of the weavers gives rise to several questions. These principally concern the relationship between gild and craft. Were the memberships of the two identical? Did they fulfil the same function? Was the relationship between them static? If the answer to such questions is in the affirmative, what was the function of a possibly new weavers' gild in the sixteenth century? If it were a rival organization, it is strange that Robynson made a bequest to both gilds. These problems arise from a craft that could legitimately claim to be a gild. Similar questions are posed by some of those which could not.

The gild of St Mary of the Skinners in St Giles received only five bequests but, as one of these was made by a tailor, it was obviously not exclusively a skinners' gild.[88] The bequests to this fraternity were all made over a period of ten years, between 1435 and 1445. If this indicates that the gild was comparatively short-lived, then it also implies that it was, in some sense, separate from the craft, which continued to exist, and to collect pageant money, up to at least 1582.[89] In the case of the cordwainers, there is a further series of difficulties. In 1391, William de Kirkby, *allutarius*, left 12d. for the Corpus Christi light of his art.[90]

Ousebridge: 10s. PR 3 244v–245r 1406 Alan de Hamerton mercer of the parish of St Peter the Little: 20s. YML L2(4) 165v 1412 William Hull weaver: 20s. L2(4) 164v 1413 Thomas Catton weaver of the parish of St Michael le Belfrey: 6s.8d. BIHR PR 2 586v 1429 William Percy weaver of the parish of St Saviour: 3s.4d. for a trental as use and custom provides. PR 3 487v–490r 1436 Thomas Bracebrigg merchant of the parish of St Saviour: 20s. PR 3 483r–v 1437 William Beverley weaver of the parish of St Crux: 3s.4d. PR 2 312r–v 1455 John Watton weaver of the parish of All Saints Pavement: 3s.4d. PR 4 256r 1475 William Holme weaver of the parish of St Michael Ousebridge: 13s.4d. PR 5 151r–v 1479 Margaret Plumpton of the parish of St Olave: 3s. PR 5 424r 1492 John Kendale weaver of the parish of St Sampson: 12d. PR 9 394r 1528 William Robynson weaver of the parish of All Saints Pavement: 3s.4d. to the master of the weavers and the gild stock.

[87] BIHR PR 9 394r.
[88] BIHR PR 3 408r–409r 1435 William Barton skinner of the parish of St Margaret: 3s.4d. to the gild light. PR 2 81v–82r 1436 Helen Dorham widow: 20d. PR 3 511r 1438 Robert Dote tailor of the parish of St Martin Coneystreet: 2s. PR 2 45r 1442 John Northfolk skinner of the parish of St Martin Coneystreet: the remainder of the torches that the gild should carry at his funeral. PR 2 121v 1445 William Leeston skinner of the parish of St Crux: 20d.
[89] *REED York*, pp. 400–1.
[90] BIHR PR 1 35r–v.

Whether or not this light continued to be maintained by the cordwainers is not known, but, in 1408, William Byrgrefe, a cordwainer, made the first of thirty bequests to the gild of St Mary of the Carmelites.[91] This gild seems to have been the friary's principal confraternity. William Byrgrefe did not make any connection between the St Mary Gild and his craft. Others, however, did. In 1444, John Marton, also a cordwainer, asked to be buried in the friary and left 3s.4d. to the St Mary Gild sustained by the cordwainers there. Richard Paynot, who described himself as a shoemaker, also identified the gild as being of the cordwainers (*allutari*), in 1478. Two widows of uncertain occupation, Helen Hekke, in 1487, and Alice Clerk, in 1506, also mentioned the gild as being sustained by the cordwainers. Alice Clerk, however, simply referred to it as being St Mary of the Cordwainers and did not connect it with the friary. She also made a bequest to the gild of St Augustine of the Cordwainers, which was still in operation in 1520, when Edward Wayde, shoemaker, asked for its torches to attend his funeral. The wills of Marton, Paynot and Hekke clearly identify the gild with both the friary and the craft, and those of Byrgrefe and Clerk support this. However, none of the other testators mentioned the cordwainers' role in sustaining the gild and, although most of their occupations are known, none were cordwainers. Furthermore, a significant number of them belonged to occupations totally unrelated to shoemaking. Ten of them belonged to the victualling trades, and whilst it might be argued that the four butchers had a connection with leather production, bequests to the gild from three bakers, a cook and a fishmonger are less easy to explain. It would be also difficult to ascribe the presence of a plumber, a plasterer, a spicer and an apothecary to medieval fluidity of labour.

It is hard to see why, if it were a cordwainers' gild, so few of the craft made bequests to it. Three possible explanations present themselves. The gild was active for at least 125 years. It is possible that it was sustained by the craft for only part of its life. However, even if Byrgrefe's bequest is not included, the interval between the wills of Marton and Clerk is over sixty years and the bulk of the other wills falls within this period. An alternative explanation is that we are dealing with two separate gilds of St Mary in the Carmelite convent, one sustained by the cordwainers, the other a confraternity open to all. However, it has already been shown that gilds sustained by crafts received bequests from members whose occupations were unconnected with that craft. It also seems unlikely that two gilds with identical dedications would be competing for space in the same location on the same feast days. The most probable explanation is that the gild, sustained by the cordwainers, but open to all, including the families of cordwainers, attracted members from other occupations as a commercial or political forum where they could maintain contact with cordwainers. This might have eventually been seen as dilution by the cordwainers. It is possible that an increasing preponderance of members of other crafts, amongst the membership

---

[91] BIHR PR 3 88r–v 1402 William Byrgrefe cordwainer of the parish of St Nicholas Micklegate: 3s.4d.

of the St Mary Gild, led them to found a new, more exclusive, gild, probably, in view of its dedication, in the Augustinian Friary, which served cordwainers only. It could be that the appearance of the Holy Ghost Gild of the Weavers, recorded in 1528, was in response to similar pressures in their St Mary Gild.[92] Parallel circumstances seem to have led to the foundation (or re-foundation) of the merchants' gild of St George in Holy Trinity in Hull, to the eventual detriment of that of St Mary in Holy Trinity.[93]

What we may be seeing is a general movement towards occupationally based gilds during the latter part of the fifteenth and early sixteenth centuries. This can be further illustrated by documentation relating to the carpenters of the city, whose ordinances were renewed by the mayor and council, in 1482, at the prayer of twenty-four masters of the craft.[94] The new ordinances formalized 'a broderhode had and usyd emong the occupacion and craft', providing for an annual subscription of 6d., two meetings each year and the appointment of four keepers to manage the accounts. The new fraternity would offer help to members fallen into poverty and provide elaborate funerals and prayers for the dead, including two trentals of masses, to be sung twice every year for the souls of former brothers and sisters, by the Augustinian friars. This latter intention was pursued in an indenture, drawn up in 1487, between the prior and convent of the Augustinian Friary, the two searchers 'of the occupacion of the carpenters', and the four 'Keepers of the holy fraternite of the Resurreccion of our Lord mayntened by the carpenters of the said citie'.[95] One searcher, Richard Bysshop (Bischope), and one keeper, James Whynsell (Wynfell), had been amongst the petitioners to the council in 1482. The indenture agreed an annual payment of 10s. to the friars in respect of the trentals that had figured in the 1482 ordinances, and additional payments of 5s. each for a further five trentals to be sung following the death of 'every brother that truly doeth his dutye'. The annual payments were partly to be discharged by granting the friars the farm of two properties beside St Leonard's landing. Throughout the document, the keepers and searchers were mentioned together and seem to have had joint responsibility for the arrangements. By this date, the fraternity had adopted the dedication of The Resurrection of Our Lord, although this did not appear in the ordinances. The Resurrection was the theme of the craft's Corpus Christi pageant, and was therefore a natural dedication for the gild to adopt. The craft and the new gild were working very closely together, although they were still distinct entities, each being represented by its own officials. Here we see a gild being formed from an existing nucleus within a craft.

Other craft-related gilds showed different patterns of development. That of St John the Baptist made no mention of the tailors' craft, with which it was later

---

92 See p. 135 above.
93 See Chapter 7, pp. 215–16.
94 *YMB A/Y*, II, 277–83.
95 YCA E 20A B/Y fol. 207v, *YMB A/Y*, II, pp. xxxviii–xl and *YMB B/Y*, pp. 254–5. See p. 131 above.

associated, in its 1389 gild return.[96] The earliest recorded ordinances of the tailors, in 1387, concerned the regulation of the craft and its pageant through the agency of its searchers.[97] In 1415, the gild of St John the Baptist leased land from the mayor and commonalty, in order to build a gild hall.[98] That four of the five gild masters representing the fraternity were tailors suggests that the craft had already secured some control over the affairs of the gild. This was not put on an official footing, however, until 1453, when it was incorporated by royal licence, sanctioning the tailors of York to found a gild of St John the Baptist.[99] In this case, then, an existing gild was adopted by a craft which eventually took it over and ran it. However, the testamentary evidence shows that the St John the Baptist Gild was, at no time, exclusive to the tailors. Only eleven testators, a quarter of the total, can be identified as such, and these are by no means concentrated after the date of incorporation. Three of the eleven bequests occurring before that date were made by tailors, as were six of the thirty-three recorded subsequently.[100] The testators included six drapers, but this allied occupation did not formally combine with the tailors' gild until 1552.[101] By that time the religious function of the former St John the Baptist Gild had disappeared prior to the formation of the Merchant Taylors' Company.

The gradual drawing together of craft and gild was by no means exclusive to York. Similar take-overs of existing religious gilds by groups of craftsmen have been noted in fourteenth century London.[102] It has been shown that religious

[96]   PRO C 47/46/455. The development of this gild is traced in the opening chapters and appendices of B. Johnson, *The Acts and Ordinances of the Company of Merchant Taylors in the City of York* (York, 1949), on which this paragraph is partly based.

[97]   *YMB A/Y*, I, pp. 94–100.

[98]   YCA E 20 A B/Y, fol. 39r–v.

[99]   PRO C 66/477, transcribed by Johnson, *Acts and Ordinances of the Company of Merchant Taylors*, pp. 121–2.

[100] Pre 1453: YML L2(4) 84v 1386 John de Seuenhaus tailor of the parish of St Michael le Belfry: 10s. BIHR PR 2 116r–v 1445 John Hull tailor of the parish of St Crux: 3s.4d. PR 2 140r–v 1446 John Loncaster tailor of the parish of St John Ousebridge: 6s.8d. Post 1453: PR 4 241r–v 1467 Robert Duffeld tailor of the parish of St Denys: 20d. PR 5 71v 1482 Thomas Thirske tailor of the parish of St Martin Coneystreet: 6s.8d. PR 5 46r–v 1483 William Letwyn tailor of the parish of St Denys Walmgate: 3s.4d. PR 5 463v–464r 1494 James Lonnesdale tailor: a tenement with a croft outside Micklegate in the suburbs on condition that the gild presbyter says masses etc. for his soul. YML L2(5)a 45v 1505 William Beene tailor of the parish of St Michael le Belfrey: 2s. BIHR PR 11 185r 1536 Thomas Lame tailor: a brass pot.

[101] BIHR PR 2 525r–v 1425 William Newland draper of the parish of St Martin Coneystreet: 6s.8d. PR 2 79v–80v 1444 Thomas Carr draper of the parish of St Sampson: 10s. PR 4 86r 1472 John Croft pewterer of the parish of St Sampson: 12d. PR 6 15v 1501 Edward Foster draper of the parish of All Saints Pavement: 3s.4d. PR 8 3r–v 1508 William Chymney alderman draper of the parish of St Sampson: 6s.8d. YML L2(5)a 199r–200r 1541 John Litster draper of the parish of St Michael le Belfrey: reversion of 3 tenements in All Saints Pavement parish to the master and 4 wardens of the gild worth 20s. per annum to pay for an annual obit. Any surplus to go to the gild. B. Johnson, *The Acts and Ordinances of the Company of Merchant Taylors in the City of York* (York, 1949), p. 42.

[102] Barron, 'The Parish Fraternities of Medieval London', pp. 14–16. E. M. Veale, 'Craftsmen

gilds and occupations combined earlier in the capital than the evidence suggests was the case in York. In London, as in York, there seems to have been an initial separation of the organizational elements of craft and gild but their gradual rapprochement culminated in the establishment of livery companies in the early sixteenth century.[103] The Society of Merchant Adventurers of York, by contrast, was not formed until 1581.[104]

The gild of Holy Trinity in Fossgate of the Mercers was probably the wealthiest of all the city's gilds that were sustained by occupations and it is the best documented. The complex question of its foundation and early development has been the subject of a recent study by Louise Wheatley, which discusses its relationship with the mercers' mistery and the Hospital of St Mary and Jesus in Fossgate.[105] The fraternity's genesis lay in the establishment, in 1357, of a gild of Jesus Christ and the Blessed Virgin Mary, connected with the parish church of St Crux.[106] A principal object of the gild was the foundation of a hospital, which was completed in about 1371 and licensed by Edward III, who provided for the employment of a chaplain and for the formal changing of the gild into a hospital.[107] The hospital chapel contained five altars.[108] The gild of St John the Baptist ran a chantry of the same dedication at one of them; according to an agreement made in 1396, although what seems to have been an attempt by the gild to take over the running of the hospital must have been unsuccessful.[109] By 1397, a Holy Trinity Gild, probably based on the Holy Trinity altar in the hospital chapel, was the major fraternity supporting the hospital.[110] The gild was associated with the mercers' craft and, in 1420, more than two thirds of the brethren supervising the hospital were mercers.[111] However, they do not, at this stage, seem to have had any formal connection with the mercers' mistery. The only attempt to establish a mercantile gild in the city had ended with the suppression of an unlicensed Holy Trinity Gild by the crown in 1306.[112] The mercers seem to have had no organization, beyond the supervision of their searchers, until they were incorporated by

and the Economy of London in the Fourteenth Century', in *The Medieval Town: a Reader in English Urban History 1200–1540*, ed. R. A. Holt and G. Rosser (London, 1990), pp. 120–40 (pp. 125–9).

[103] Veale, 'Craftsmen and the Economy of London', p. 126.

[104] Palliser, *Tudor York*, p. 273.

[105] Wheatley, 'The York Mercers' Guild'. This work and subsequent discussion with Louise Wheatley form the basis of much of this paragraph.

[106] Sellars, *YMA*, pp. 1–3. YML L2(4) 45v–46 1365 Emma widow of William de Huntington apothecary of St Wilfrid is the only testator.

[107] *YMB B/Y*, p. 143.

[108] Wheatley, 'The York Mercers' Guild', p. 56. Sellars, *YMA*, pp. 96–7, in an undated sixteenth century inventory, lists three surviving altars: Holy Trinity, St Thomas the Martyr and St John the Baptist.

[109] YMA, Trinity Hospital Administration, 3.

[110] Wheatley, 'The York Mercers' Guild', pp. 92–3.

[111] *Ibid.*, pp. 94–7.

[112] G. O. Sayles, 'The Dissolution of a Gild at York in 1306', *English Historical Review* 55 (1940), pp. 83–97.

charter as a mistery in 1430.[113] The charter made no mention of the Holy Trinity Gild, however, which probably remained a separate institution. At all events, the twenty recorded testators who made bequests to the Holy Trinity Gild in Fossgate were not exclusively mercantile. Although the majority consisted of mercers or merchants, they included a mason, a draper, a clerk and two bakers amongst their number.[114] Once again, a highly prestigious occupational gild counted amongst its membership a number of individuals who did not belong to its mistery and whilst one of these, the mason, Hugh Grantham, made his bequest prior to the incorporation of the mercers, all the rest did so afterwards.

Occupational gilds and craft organizations, however closely they were associated, remained technically separate, allowing those who were not mercers, tailors, weavers or cordwainers, to join an occupational gild, for reasons of business, friendship or piety, and to contribute to it socially and financially. This arrangement seems to have generated popular fraternities, that, as Figure 4.5 shows, lasted well into the sixteenth century. However, the original gild sometimes proved too popular, especially with members of other crafts, and new, additional, exclusive gilds were formed which allowed craft members to associate in their devotional practices without outside interference.

The Civic Gilds of York

Important as the craft-related gilds probably were to the groups that controlled them, the vast majority of all bequests to York gilds were made to the three largest, Corpus Christi, St Christopher and St Anthony, and to the gilds which they absorbed. Each had its own devotional character, fulfilled different functions and made its own distinctive contribution to the public life of the city, maintaining its relationship with civic government. Large numbers of testators saw fit to make bequests to all three.[115]

Although the Corpus Christi Gild is the subject of the next chapter, the way in which its public activities impinged on the city at large is relevant to this one, in respect of its annual procession, its role as a provider of funerals and its position as link between the city government and the secular clergy. The St Christopher Gild, and its close relationship to the city government, has been thoroughly examined by Eileen White in a relatively recent Borthwick Paper, which includes accounts of its amalgamation with the St George Gild, of its role in the building of the city's gildhall and of the scandals which tarnished its image in the 1530s.[116] The character of the smallest of the three, the St Anthony Gild, is less easy to

---

113 YMA, Royal Charters and Grants 1/1A–B.
114 White's list in the BIHR is incomplete as regards this gild.
115 E.g. BIHR PR 3 539r–v 1438 John Shirwodd. PR 3 515v 1438 Margaret Horneby, PR 2 79v–80v 1444 Thomas Carr draper. PR 2 138v–139v Thomas Lyverton. PR 2 137v–138v William Revetour chaplain.
116 White, *The St Christopher and St George Gild*, pp. 6, 14.

Figure 4.6: Bequests to Paternoster, St Anthony and Allied Gilds

Gild	BeqF	BeqL	Total	Life	Notes
Paternoster	1395	1439	21	50	gild return 1389
Paternoster & St Anthony	1444	1487	4	43	St Anthony absorbs Paternoster
St Anthony	1428	1540	75	112	first recorded 1418
St Martin & St Anthony	1449	1475	2	26	–
St Mary & St Martin	1450	1494	21	48	–
St Martin	1451	1451	1	1	founded 1446
St Mary St Martin & St Anthony	1460	1467	2	7	–
St Mary & St Anthony	1473	1473	1	1	–

BeqF: date of first bequest.
BeqL: date of last bequest.
Total: total number of bequests.
Life: interval in years between first and last bequest.

define, especially since it absorbed, or merged with, a variety of other fraternities whose functions it then assumed. The process illustrates the way in which such amalgamations took place, showing how some gilds were dynamic, and even predatory, in their development over the period of the Late Middle Ages.

We have seen that the St Anthony Gild was already so popular in 1418 that a majority of the members of the gild of Holy Trinity in the Dominican friary demanded an amalgamation with it.[117] At some point before 1444 it absorbed the Paternoster Gild, whose play, in which sins were reproved and virtues commended, had been described in its return in 1389.[118] Members in livery were to ride with the players through the streets and manage the procession. The properties used in the play were kept safe in a wooden chest. The text has been lost but its content and manner of presentation may have been related to episodes from the Corpus Christi cycle.[119] According to Angelo Raine, an account roll of the gild for 1399, since lost, showed that the Paternoster Gild was based in a room in a hospice in Aldwark, belonging to the Priory of Bridlington, had a membership of ninety-six brothers and fifty-seven sisters and contained details of expenditure on feasting and funerals.[120] A bequest to the Paternoster and St Anthony Gild in 1444 shows that the merger with the St Anthony Gild was completed by then.[121] It was not, however, formalized until 1446, when the gild was incorporated by charter.[122]

---

[117] See above p. 132.
[118] PRO C 47/46/454.
[119] A. F. Johnston, 'The Plays of the Religious Guilds of York: The Creed Play and the Pater Noster Play', *Speculum* 50 (1975), 55–90.
[120] Raine, *Medieval York*, pp. 91–2. See also Smith, *York Mystery Plays*, p. xxix.
[121] BIHR PR 2 79v–80v 1444 Thomas Carr draper of St Sampson.
[122] *Cal. Pat. 1441–6*, p. 442.

At this point it was also officially merged with the gild of St Mary and St Martin, whose dedication suggests that it was itself the result of a previous amalgamation. The charter of incorporation stated that the new united fraternity would be known as the St Martin Gild and gave permission for a hall and hospital to be constructed on the site of St Martin's Chapel in Peaseholme. The new name evidently caused some confusion amongst testators, as shown in Figure 4.6, although the dedication to St Anthony eventually persisted, suggesting that it was the senior partner. Bequests to gilds dedicated to various combinations of St Anthony, Paternoster, St Martin and St Mary were probably all manifestations of the St Anthony Gild in various stages of metamorphosis.

The Paternoster play continued to be performed under the management of the St Anthony Gild. In 1495, it was minuted in the city's House Book that the gild could not 'conuenyently bryng furth þe play Called þe pater noster play'.[123] It was subjected to an unrecorded fine and instructed to prepare it for the following year. The gild was still associated with the play in 1558, despite the Council's protestations, in 1548, that the fraternity no longer existed.[124] In this year the Paternoster Play was performed instead of the Corpus Christi cycle.

None of the city's religious gilds participated directly in the Corpus Christi plays. Its pageants were put forth by the misteries or crafts. All of the three large gilds, however, were responsible for dramatic events in the city. The gild of St George organized an annual 'riding', which was maintained after its merger with the St Christopher Gild and revived during the Marian period.[125] The City Chamberlains' Account Books for 1554 show that the event included a play upon a pageant with a cast that included a dragon, a king and queen and St George himself, with his followers.[126] The procession and play were accompanied musically by the city waits. Perhaps the actor portraying the saint was wearing the fine sallet that Sir William Tode bequeathed in 1503 for use in the 'riding'.[127] The cast of characters and the use of a pageant suggests a higher level of dramatic content than the riding and joust performed by the St George Gild in Norwich.[128] In 1446, the St Christopher Gild itself was bequeathed a six-page play of St James the Apostle, although there are no records of its performance.[129]

The Corpus Christi Gild's Creed Play was another major contribution to the city's dramatic life. Although, once again, the script is lost, it seems to have been played on pageants and to have consisted of biblical episodes related to the text of the creed.[130] The play was bequeathed to the gild in 1446 and was first

123 YCA B7, fol. 135r.
124 YCA B22, fol. 125v. See Chapter 7, p. 238.
125 *REED York*, pp. 289, 326–7.
126 YCA CC4(2) p. 162.
127 BIHR PR 6 59r–v, 1503, Sir William Tode.
128 McRee, 'Unity or Division?', pp. 195–7.
129 BIHR PR 2 137v–138v 1446 William Revetour, chaplain of St John Micklegate.
130 Johnston, 'The Plays of the Religious Guilds of York', pp. 61–2.

recorded as being performed in 1449.[131] Its success led the corporation to commission a performance to be played before Richard III, in 1483, and to direct, in 1495, that it should replace the Corpus Christi cycle once every ten years.[132]

The dramatic activities of the gilds provide a further example of their orthodoxy and of their opposition to the attitudes of the Lollards, who condemned such plays as frivolous and idolatrous.[133] Apologists for the plays saw them as living books and pictures which, to the honour of God, informed and entertained the people, providing examples of piety and offering them the opportunity of empathising with the sufferings of Christ and his saints. It is also clear, from the way in which such public performances were ordered, controlled and policed by the city authorities, that the latter regarded them as civic as well as gild events.

The principal ceremonial function of the Corpus Christi Gild, however, was not the Creed Play. It was to form the focus of the Corpus Christi procession, which, at the suggestion of Friar William Melton in 1426, was held on a different day from the performance of the Corpus Christi cycle.[134] By the period 1465 to 1476, it was taking place on the day following the feast.[135] Whilst the evolution of the procession is a matter for the next chapter, its significance in terms of the relationship between the gilds and the city must be addressed here. It reflected a complex web of overlapping interests and power bases. It was, in essence, a civic occasion. In 1492, for example, the Lord Mayor, sheriffs, aldermen, members of the ruling council of The Twenty-four, and the representatives of every 'Gild, frat[er]nite art & occupac[i]on' took part, accompanied by their appropriate banners and torches, under pain of forfeit, as they had always done, by ancient custom, since the mayoralty of Thomas Wrangwish, in 1476.[136] It seems likely that the householders along the route of the procession hung their best beds and coverlets outside their doorways, as the council directed in 1544.[137] In this way they identified with and adorned the occasion.

The climax of the procession was provided by the Corpus Christi Gild.[138] Following its cross, and led by its ten torchbearers, who were supervised by the gild beadle, with his silver-gilt badge of office, its clerical members, clad in surplices, with the best singers in the middle, directed by two suitable chaplains in silk copes, marched together, singing litanies and appropriate songs.[139] Four of the year's six elected wardens, wearing silk stoles and bearing white rods, marshalled the whole procession. The two most senior wardens, similarly equipped,

131 BIHR PR 2 137v–138v 1446 William Revetour chaplain of St John Micklegate.

132 Johnston, 'The Plays of the Religious Guilds of York', pp. 61–2.

133 R. Woolf, *The English Mystery Plays* (Berkeley and Los Angeles, 1972), pp. 84–6.

134 D. J. F. Crouch, 'Paying to see the Play', *Medieval English Theatre* 13 (1991), 64–111 (pp. 97–8).

135 R. Beadle, 'The York Cycle', *The Cambridge Companion to Medieval English Theatre*, ed. R. Beadle (Cambridge, 1994), pp. 85–108 (p. 90).

136 *REED York*, p. 164.

137 *Ibid.*, p. 283.

138 YCA G 11A *Approbatio Statutorum* 1477. For the route see Crouch, 'Paying to see the Play', pp. 65–6.

139 YCA C99:3 m. 2. The beadle's badge was valued at 41s.4d., MS Lansdowne 304, fol. 3v.

guarded the shrine. The master for that year, in a silk cope, was flanked by two former masters of his choice. The shrine itself, housing the host, was an object of dazzling magnificence. Given to the gild, in 1449, by Thomas Spofford, then Bishop of Hereford, it was of silver-gilt, covered with images of saints and angels, in precious metal, and embellished with jewels, and other valuables, bequeathed by generations of members.[140] Although a large proportion of such bequests had been made in the middle part of the fifteenth century, when the new shrine was being furbished, its power as an emblem of sanctity was still being demonstrated by testamentary evidence from as late as 1534.[141] Under its canopy, carried by four deacons, and borne on its bier, it proclaimed the special status of the gild, binding together all its members, clerical and lay, from York and from the country at large, in the common pious objective of venerating the eucharist, and, at the same time, defining the relationship of the gild and its governing clerics to the city and its government.[142]

Indeed, every group in the procession, whilst confirming its devotion to the eucharist, was also re-establishing, on an annual basis, its place in the hierarchy of the city by honouring its representatives chosen for the year. It is hardly surprising that, within such a spectacle of urban solidarity, frictions arose between sectional interests, exemplified by the conflict between the weavers' and cordwainers' crafts, in the 1490s, over their precedence in the procession.[143] There was, however, a powerful factor at work that limited opportunities for sectional strife. Each participating individual combined a variety of interests by belonging, typically, to several interlocking groups: a mistery, a craft-related gild, a parish fraternity and a place in the governmental hierarchy, for example. It was also common for a person to be a member of several gilds at the same time, the honour of each of which he, or she, would be obliged to uphold. A range of loyalties and personal perceptions of their priorities on the part of such individuals, led to occasional confusions. In 1533, for example, the city council tried to solve one problem of priority by prohibiting the wearing of the 'ray gowns', which were the livery of the St Christopher and St George Gild, by members of the city council in processions.[144] However, the overlapping partisanships, of what was probably the bulk of the more influential, franchised citizens, ensured a web of unity that militated against factional violence. Those with political ambition, who were most likely to plot for their own advancement, would find it difficult to manipulate an event that displayed such a complex system of loyalties. It is, surely, significant that the only major, recorded, public order problems were presented by craftsmen who might have had gild affiliations and who were unlikely

---

[140] MS Lansdowne 304, fols. 2r–3v.

[141] BIHR PR 11 85r 1534 Janet Sparke bequeathed her coral beads to the Corpus Christi shrine.

[142] YCA C 99:3 m. 2.

[143] See p. 122.

[144] White, *The St Christopher and St George Gild*, p. 17. In Marian times (1553) aldermen were directed to wear scarlet cloaks in processions. This might have been a revival of earlier civic livery (*YCR*, V, p. 98).

to achieve high civic office.[145] The procession represented a coming together of a variety of interests in which all the city shared, to a greater or lesser degree. Politically it made statements about the relationship between the city and its lesser clergy, about the civic dignity symbolized by the role of the Lord Mayor, and about its place in the world at large. Within this picture, the Corpus Christi Gild itself demonstrated a union between clerics and laity, focused on the shrine that housed the eucharist and which was venerated by the city and by the world beyond its walls, in a rich display of public piety.

After walking through the more affluent streets of the city, the procession demonstrated the city's relationship with the Archbishop and the Dean and Chapter, by hearing a sermon, preached in the chapterhouse of the Minster, and finally deposited the host in the Hospital of St Leonard in a public act of charity.[146] The progress was concluded by a feast, provided in the sixteenth century, by the city. In 1520 it was of lavish proportions.[147] In the mid-fifteenth century, however, the arrangements had been different. In 1449 the mayoral party spent 49s.9½d. on bread, wine and fruit, but was also invited to the Corpus Christi Gild's own feast, which cost £4.18s.½d., including bread, meat, poultry, spices and beer.[148] The later practices suggest that identification between the gild and the city had become closer.

Corpus Christi was clearly a very special occasion. However, lesser processions by smaller gilds must have been commonplace throughout the year. Although we lack detailed descriptions of the ceremonial of parish fraternities or friary gilds in York, the accounts of the gilds of St Helen in the Franciscan friary and of the Purification of the Virgin in St Mary's parish church, both in Beverley, that appear in their returns of 1389, probably provide a good impression of similar events in York.[149]

Another important function of the city's gilds that contained elements of public ceremonial was the funeral. This aspect of the gilds' services was one that grew in popularity, especially during the sixteenth century. Figure 4.7 shows that funerary bequests accounted for 33.8% of legacies to gilds, in 1501–1510, and rose steadily to 57.1% in 1541–1550, demonstrating an increasing demand on gilds as funeral providers. The most popular fraternities in this respect were those boasting large memberships: those of St John the Baptist, St Anthony, St Christopher and St George, and, above all, Corpus Christi. A typical series of bequests was made by John Bollyng, priest of the parish of St Saviour.

Also I will that the maister and the kepers of Corpus Ch[rist]i gilde be at my saide dyrige and beriall messe the Maister have viijd & ev[e]ry keper vjd And

---

[145] See p. 122.

[146] YCA A/Y Memorandum Book E 20 fols. 278r–v.

[147] *REED York*, p. 221.

[148] YCA F C 2:5 m. 2v, C99:3 m. 2.

[149] PRO C 47/46/446, 448. See Chapter 3 above pp. 105–6.

the bedell to haue for his torches as the custome is and the beadell of Saynte
Ch[ris]tofors gild for his torches as the custom is.[150]

In addition he left a shilling to every priest of Corpus Christi who attended his
funeral. In later wills, testators increasingly asked for the masters and keepers of
Corpus Christi to be paid 'as costume is', or 'accordynge to the custome of the
Citie', stressing the normality of the gild's role in this respect.[151]

The growing demand for elaborate funerals affirmed the presence of the righteous dead as a continuing part of the community, whose duty it was to ease their
passage through purgatory to heavenly bliss, whilst commemorating their
earthly achievements.[152] The funeral was a public celebration, marking the
passage of a soul from one stage of its journey to another and assisting through
intercessory prayer. It also set in motion charitable provisions of the deceased's
will, fulfilling, for the last time, the testator's obligations towards the Acts of Corporal Mercy, so prompting the valuable prayers of the poor and needy in a
process that was often repeated at set intervals, through obits, anniversaries and
chantries.[153] Clive Burgess's account of a typical urban parish funeral, based on
documentation from Bristol, is equally typical of York.[154] The obsequies of the
urban elite, such as Richard Wartre, twice Lord Mayor and witness of the incorporation of the Corpus Christi Gild, were undoubtedly impressive occasions, as
the detailed instructions for torchbearers, weepers and charitable largess demonstrate.[155]

For the wealthier members of fraternities, especially of the Corpus Christi
Gild, however, parish funerals were not impressive enough. There were probably
two reasons for testators asking for the added pomp of a Corpus Christi funeral.
One lay in the nature of the gild. The prayers of its officers, being clerics, were
probably regarded as being especially effective and the sheer size of the membership guaranteed a large quantity of fraternal intercessors. The other reason was
probably related to the pretensions of the deceased. This large fraternity conducted particularly spectacular funerals in response to specific bequests. Such a
funeral made a powerful statement about the mortal prestige, wealth and influence of the deceased and his or her family.

---

150 BIHR PR 9 33v 1516.
151 BIHR PR 9 313v 1525 John Sympson cardmaker of St Denys. PR 11, 1534, Jane widow of
    William Nelson merchant of Holy Trinity Micklegate.
152 Duffy, *The Stripping of the Altars*, p. 303.
153 C. Burgess, 'The Benefactions of Mortality: The Lay Response in the Late Medieval Urban
    Parish', in *Studies in Clergy and Ministry in Medieval England*, Borthwick Studies in History 1
    (York, 1991), 65–86 (pp. 70–2).
154 *Ibid.*
155 BIHR PR 4 1458 (probate 1465).

Figure 4.7: Analysis of Bequests Made to York Gilds

Date	Money	Funerary	Land	Jewels	Household	Other	All
1365–1400	16 (88.90%)	2 (11.10%)	1 (0.60%)	–	–	1 (0.60%)	18
1401–1410	24 (80.00%)	3 (10.00%)	1 (3.30%)	2 (6.70%)	2 (3.30%)	1 (3.30%)	30
1411–1420	16 (69.60%)	4 (17.40%)	–	1 (4.30%)	4 (17.40%)	2 (8.70%)	23
1421–1430	54 (100.00%)	5 (9.30%)	–	–	–	–	54
1431–1440	122 (92.40%)	8 (6.10%)	–	5 (3.80%)	2 (1.50%)	3 (2.40%)	132
1441–1450	116 (88.50%)	3 (2.30%)	–	8 (6.10%)	4 (3.10%)	3 (2.30%)	131
1451–1460	103 (91.20%)	5 (4.40%)	1 (0.90%)	6 (5.30%)	–	3 (2.70%)	113
1461–1470	62 (88.60%)	–	–	4 (5.70%)	4 (0.70%)	–	70
1471–1480	103 (88.00%)	12 (10.30%)	–	12 (10.30%)	1 (0.90%)	–	117
1481–1490	100 (95.20%)	15 (14.30%)	–	4 (3.80%)	1 (1.00%)	–	105
1491–1500	37 (84.10%)	10 (22.70%)	1 (2.30%)	4 (9.10%)	1 (2.30%)	1 (2.30%)	44
1501–1510	70 (87.50%)	27 (33.80%)	–	8 (10.00%)	–	2 (2.60%)	80
1511–1520	15 (83.30%)	8 (44.40%)	1 (5.60%)	1 (5.60%)	1 (5.60%)	–	18
1521–1530	19 (79.20%)	6 (25.00%)	3 (12.50%)	2 (8.30%)	–	–	24
1531–1540	20 (87.00%)	11 (47.80%)	1 (4.30%)	1 (4.30%)	1 (4.30%)	–	23
1541–1550	6 (85.70%)	4 (57.10%)	1 (14.30%)	–	–	–	7
Totals	883 (89.30%)	123 (12.40%)	10 (1.00%)	58 (5.90%)	21 (2.10%)	6 (0.60%)	989

Date:	decade.
Money:	total number of money bequests.
Funerary:	money bequests conditional on funerary services.
Land:	all real estate.
Jewels:	valuables including silverware, rings, girdles, beads, vestments, embroidery, armour.
Household:	chests, furniture, clothes, plain utensils and plain fabric.
Other:	other goods including foodstuffs, livestock, wax and non-funerary candles and torches.
All:	total number of bequests to individual gilds (not the number of testators). This includes references to gilds and bequests where the amount is not specific. It does not take into consideration more than one item given to the same gild by a testator. Thus the sums of categorized bequests will not necessarily tally with the totals.

All percentages are related to the total number of bequests to gilds and are placed in brackets.

The Membership of York Gilds

The quality of those testators who made bequests to York gilds is central to assertions that the fraternities of the city increasingly represented the interests of various sections of its elite classes. A brief analysis of what can be discovered of their wealth, status and occupations is essential to support or refute such arguments. One method of measuring an individual's wealth might be the parish in which he or she lived. Parishes formed units of taxation and assessments, such as that carried out by the city in 1420 and the Lay Subsidy of 1524, are useful indicators of relative prosperity.[156] It is possible to identify, with some certainty, the parishes of almost ninety per cent of testators, living in York, who made bequests to gilds. Many wills describe the testator as being of a particular parish. Others, by directing that they be buried in a particular church, probably implied that they were parochial members of it. Testators' parishes can also be identified where they specified the destination of their compulsory mortuary bequest, even when they preferred to be interred in one of York's friaries, or simply asked to be buried where God willed it. Table 4.8 shows the number of bequests to gilds made by parishioners of York parishes and the tax rating of each parish in 1420 and 1525.

The correlation between high numbers of parishioners making bequests to gilds and parishes with high assessments is very clear. Only the suburban parishes of All Saints Fishergate, St Helen Fishergate and St Mary Layerthorpe and, within the city walls, that of St Cuthbert Peaseholme did not yield a testator. The vast majority dwelt in wealthy parishes within the city walls. There were two exceptions. The parish of St Olave, although suburban, was associated with the Abbey of St Mary, as well as containing the important market in Bootham. All but six of its twenty-two testators made a bequest to the local gild of St Mary at the Abbey. The only other suburban parish to yield a significant number of testators was St Laurence Walmgate, more than half of whom made bequests to its parochial gild of St Anne.[157] More personal details of testators, making bequests to gilds, can be sought in a variety of sources. York wills often give the franchised occupations of testators, or those of their husbands, and frequently mention the status of former mayors and aldermen. Their names can also be checked against the Freemen's Register, to establish their occupations, and against its lists of city officials, as well as in a number of other printed and manuscript sources.[158] These

---

[156] *YMB B/Y*, pp. 184–5, Peacock, 'York Subsidy Roll', pp. 172–91.

[157] See p. 127.

[158] *FR*, I. Dobson, *York City Chamberlains' Account Rolls*. F. Drake, *Eboracum* (London, 1736), Smith, *Archives of the Merchant Adventurers*, Sellers, *YMA*, W. R. Childs, *The Customs Accounts of Hull 1453–1490*, YAS 144 (1986), MS Lansdowne 304, Skaife, *Corpus Christi*, YCA G C100: 1–6, C101: 1–4, C102: 1–3, C103: 1–2, YCR, YMB A/Y, YMB B/Y, Goldberg, *Women, Work, and Life Cycle*, pp. 40–71, *passim*. See Appendix 3 for a list of York civic officials, their occupations, where known, and their membership of the Corpus Christi Gild.

have been used, in addition to testamentary material, in the compilation of the tables in this section. In Figure 4.9, analysing the occupations of gild testators, the categories used are those employed by Jeremy Goldberg in his analysis of the occupational structure of the city.[159] This permits comparison to be made between movements in the total population of various crafts in the city, as shown by Goldberg, and variations in the total members of particular occupational groups making bequests to gilds. In particular, the portion of his Table 2.6, which applies to York, is especially apposite, as it is largely based on the franchise material that is also used here.

The most striking feature of Figure 4.9 is the large number of testators from the mercantile group that made bequests to gilds. Admittedly, the figures are too small to bear close statistical analysis, but they seem to show that members of this occupation were particularly likely to make such bequests. They comprise over twenty per cent of all testators making bequests to gilds, a proportion that remained substantially steady throughout the period. This is in contrast to the trend found by Jeremy Goldberg, who shows that the overall mercantile population of York decreased, as a proportion of all occupational populations, between 1350 and 1509.[160] Over this period, the mercantile group was, therefore, increasingly more likely to make bequests to gilds than its share of the overall population suggests. This phenomenon is directly related to mercantile involvement in the large gilds of Corpus Christi, St Christopher and St Anthony, all of which had a relationship with the city government, and with the Mercers' Gild of Holy Trinity in Fossgate, many of whose members were prominent in its ruling clique.

None of the other occupational groups made a proportion of bequests to gilds in excess of their share of the franchised population. Significant numbers of such bequests were made by members of the victualling trades, perhaps because they gained some advantage as suppliers of gild feasts.[161] Members of some other crafts made comparatively large numbers of bequests to the gilds they sustained. Textile workers, for instance, made bequests to St Mary of the Weavers, leather workers to St Mary of the Carmelites, and tailors to St John the Baptist, although, as we have seen, these gilds were not exclusive to those crafts.[162] Membership of such gilds may have had a commercial motive, or even have been a pathway to political advantage for those ambitious craftsmen who were competing for public office.[163]

---

[159] Goldberg, *Women, Work and Life-cycle*, p. 61. The categories are tabulated on p. 45, and are based on those used by C. Phythian-Adams, *Desolation of a City*, pp. 311–15.

[160] Goldberg, *Women, Work and Life Cycle*, p. 61.

[161] See Chapter 5, pp. 178–9.

[162] See pp. 134–8 above.

[163] H. Swanson, Medieval Artisans, pp. 23–5.

Figure 4.8: Parishes of Testators Making Bequests to York Gilds

	Parish	Testators	%	Date Range	Tax 1420	Tax 1524
1	St Crux	55	9.4	1390–1540	280	277
2	St Michael le Belfrey	47	8.0	1386–1546	236	736
3	St John Micklegate	37	6.3	1398–1528	200	202
4	All Saints Pavement	32	5.5	1395–1528	160	260
5	St Michael Spurriergate	31	5.3	1391–1535	260	446
6	Holy Trinity King's Court	26	4.3	1399–1535	280	301
7	St Denys	22	3.7	1390–1527	100	133
	St Martin Coney Street	22	3.7	1425–1537	160	180
	St Olave	22	2.7	1404–1490	–	76
10	St Helen Stonegate	19	3.2	1399–1546	120	81
11	Minster	15	2.5	1422–1542	–	–
	St Sampson	15	2.5	1405–1527	160	151
	St Saviour	15	2.5	1416–1527	100	67
14	All Saints North Street	14	2.4	1394–1543	170	78
	St Martin Micklegate	14	2.4	1427–1534	160	35
	St Mary Bishophill Senior	14	2.4	1431–1550	150	23
	St Mary Castlegate	14	2.4	1397–1492	130	110
18	St Laurence Suburbs	12	2.0	1404–1509	60	24
19	St Peter the Little	11	1.9	1402–1535	90	56
20	Holy Trinity Goodramgate	9	1.5	1436–1482	160	46
	St Nicholas Micklegate	9	1.5	1402–1529	80	129
22	St Andrew	8	1.4	1420–1474	60	12
23	St Wilfrid	7	1.2	1365–1489	70	209
24	Holy Trinity Micklegate	6	1.0	1503–1537	–	–
	St John del Pyke	6	1.0	1429–1509	–	45
26	All Saints Peaseholme	5	0.9	1442–1507	60	–
	St Margaret	5	0,9	1435–1437	60	51
28	St Edward Suburbs	4	0.7	1398–1464	60	–
29	St Gregory	3	0.5	1448–1506	–	10
	St John Baptist Hungate	3	0.5	1439–1449	60	–
	St Maurice Monkgate	3	0.5	1440–1523	60	62
32	Holy Trinity Fossgate	2	0.4	1426–1434	–	–
	St Clement	2	0.4	1475–1479	–	–
	St George Fishergate	2	0.4	1435–1503	60	–
	St Helen (unspecified)	2	0.4	1438–1482	–	–
	St Mary (unspecified)	2	0.4	1434–1439	–	–
	St Mary Bishophill Junior	2	0.4	1453–1501	25	39
	St Peter le Willows	2	0.4	1479–1535	60	18
39	Holy Trinity (unspecified)	1	0.2	1433	–	–
	St Andrew Suburbs	1	0.2	1428	–	–
	St Helen on the Walls	1	0.2	1460	60	12

Figure 4.9: Occupations of Lay Testators Making Bequests to York Gilds

	01	02	03	04	05	06	07	08	09	10	11	12	All
1365–1400	1	2	1	3	1	–	1	–	–	1	–	1	17
1401–1410	–	2	2	1	6	4	1	1	–	1	–	–	22
1411–1420	2	1	2	–	4	1	1	–	–	1	–	1	14
1421–1430	5	4	4	1	4	2	1	–	–	–	1	2	34
1431–1440	11	3	5	5	23	2	2	3	1	2	1	2	81
1441–1450	6	7	2	5	15	2	2	2	1	–	1	4	70
1451–1460	3	2	2	2	13	4	–	–	–	–	–	6	53
1461–1470	4	2	2	1	5	2	1	–	–	–	–	1	37
1471–1480	6	2	4	1	2	6	1	2	–	2	–	7	66
1481–1490	6	2	5	4	15	1	–	–	–	1	–	5	59
1491–1500	2	–	1	2	6	1	1	–	1	–	–	1	23
1501–1510	9	3	1	2	12	2	2	–	–	–	1	3	56
1511–1520	3	1	1	1	3	–	–	–	–	–	–	–	13
1521–1530	3	1	4	1	4	2	1	–	–	–	1	3	20
1531–1540	3	–	–	1	4	1	1	–	–	–	–	–	15
1541–1550	–	1	1	–	1	1	–	–	–	–	–	–	7
Totals	64	33	37	30	118	23	15	8	3	8	5	36	587

	Category	*Occupations Included*	*Occupations Excluded*
01.	Victuals	hucksters, millers, grocers	chapmen
02.	Leather	cordwainers, sutors, etc.	cappers, glovers
03.	Textiles	spinsters	
04.	Clothing	shepsters, cappers, glovers, pointers	mercers, drapers
05.	Mercantile	mercers, drapers, chapmen	grocers
06.	Metal	grinders, armourers, potters	
07.	Building	glaziers, painters, stainers	
08.	Wood	wrights, sawyers	wrights, sawyers
09.	Transport	mariners, carters, porters, boatmen	
10.	Armaments	bowyers, stringers, fletchers	armourers
11.	Chandlers	soap-makers	
12.	Others	barbers, clerks, doctors, gardeners	yeomen, gentlemen

The classifications are those used by P. J. P. Goldberg in *Women, Work, and Life Cycle in a Medieval Economy* (Oxford, 1992), pp. 45, 46, 48, 60–1 in his analysis of poll tax returns and franchise admissions.

Notes to Figure 4.8

%:	percentage of members in each parish of all York testators making bequests to gilds.
Date Range:	of first and last bequest to any York gild from a testator of that parish.
Tax 1420:	from *YMB III B/Y*, pp. 184–5, city tax assessment *circa* 1420, values to nearest shilling. Holy Trinity Goodramgate includes St John del Pyke, St Martin Micklegate includes St Gregory, St Nicholas Micklegate includes Holy Trinity Priory, St Mary Bishophill Senior includes Clementhorpe.
Tax 1524:	from Peacock, 'York Subsidy Roll', *YAJ* 4 (1877), pp. 172–91, values to the nearest shilling. St Laurence in the Suburbs includes St Edward.

Figure 4.10: Status of Lay Testators Making Bequests to York Gilds

Date	Civic	Gentry	All Women	All
1365–1400	1	1	4	17
1401–1410	2	–	4	22
1411–1420	2	–	5	14
1421–1430	1	–	8	34
1431–1440	15	3	18	81
1441–1450	12	3	10	70
1451–1460	10	3	11	53
1461–1470	7	2	8	37
1471–1480	7	4	10	66
1481–1490	16	1	7	59
1491–1500	4	–	1	23
1501–1510	17	4	14	56
1511–1520	3	--	1	13
1521–1530	10	1	–	21
1531–1540	3	1	4	15
1541–1550	4	–	2	7
Total	114	22	107	587

Civic: former mayors, sheriffs, chamberlains, common clerks and their wives and widows. Names of testators checked against York Freemen's Register, Merchant Adventurers' Records, City Chamberlains' Account Rolls, etc.

Gentry: lords, knights, ladies, esquires, gentlemen and their wives and widows, including those with recognized gentle names and whose wills indicate gentle status.

All Women: all female testators. Some may be also listed as civic or gentry.

All: all testators making bequests to gilds.

There was a predictable correspondence between the numbers of mercantile testators who made bequests to gilds and those who had held civic office. It is not entirely coincidental that 116 merchants or mercers made such bequests and that, as Figure 4.10 shows, 114 of such testators had held the civic offices of chamberlain, sheriff or mayor. Whilst the two lists are not identical, in many cases the same individuals have been counted in both. Thus the mercantile elite, which dominated the government of the city throughout its economic and political vicissitudes, by maintaining its grip on the principal civic offices, also made bequests to the gilds of the city in more than average numbers.[164] As we have seen, their bequests especially favoured the large civic gilds that were becoming increasingly enmeshed with the city government. Membership, especially of the

---

[164] J. I. Kermode, 'Urban decline?', pp. 193–4.

Corpus Christi and St Christopher Gilds, was very common amongst Lord Mayors and the most powerful merchants of York.[165]

The number of gentle and titled laypersons making bequests to York gilds was low. This follows the pattern that we have seen in the county at large. Some of those that did so owned houses in the city. Lord John Scrope, for example, in his will of 1441, left 3s.4d. to the gilds of Corpus Christi and St Christopher, asking for their lights to attend his lavish funeral in the Scrope Chapel of the Minster. He described himself as being of the parish of St Martin, Micklegate.[166] Other gentry made bequests to gilds in several places. Robert Roos esquire, of Ingmanthorpe, in his will, dated 1529 at York, asked to be buried in South Deighton, but made bequests to the Corpus Christi and St Christopher Gilds of York, as well as to the Rood Gild of Ripon and the St Mary Gild of Boston, Lincolnshire.[167] The numbers of the gentry who made bequests to gilds were swelled by the presence of knighted civic dignitaries such as Sir William Tode, who, as we have seen, left a helmet to the St George Gild in 1503, and Sir John Gilliot, who made bequests to the gilds of Corpus Christi, St Christopher, St Anthony, St John the Baptist and Holy Trinity Fossgate.[168]

Comparison between Figures 4.10 and 3.1 suggests that women were twice as likely to make gild bequests in York than in the rest of the county. This seems to be partly related to the high proportion of testators of mercantile occupation and civic rank that has been previously discussed. Many of the female testators were widows of aldermen or merchants. As such, they would be likely to have suffi-cient wealth to make wills and might wish to leave something to the gilds that they typically joined with their husbands. A case in point was Marion Kent, widow of John, merchant and former Lord Mayor, who, in 1488, left two shillings to the Corpus Christi Gild, which they had both entered in 1549.[169] She also made bequests to the gilds of St Christopher and St George, St Anthony, St John the Baptist and Holy Trinity Fossgate. After her husband's death in 1468 she became a merchant in her own right and, in 1475, was listed as one of the councillors of the mistery.[170] Other wealthy mercantile widows of city officials included Margaret Kirkham and Joan Ince, who both made bequests to the Corpus Christi Gild, as had their spouses.[171] Occasionally, wives who pre-deceased their hus-

165 Bequests to both gilds were made, amongst many others, by William Ormeshead BIHR PR 3 503r–504v 1435, John Giliot PR 5 237r–238r 1484, John Marshall PR 5 311r–v 1487, John Tong PR 5 398r–399r 1488, William Nelson PR 9 305r–v 1525, all former Lord Mayors and members of the mercantile group of occupations.

166 BIHR PR 2 321v–234r.

167 BIHR PR 11 12r–v.

168 BIHR PR 6 59r–v (Sir William Tode), PR 8 32v–34r 1509 (Sir John Gilliot).

169 BIHR PR 3 320r–321r, MS Lansdowne 304, fol. 45v, Skaife, *Corpus Christi*, p. 49.

170 Sellers, *YMA*, p. 64.

171 BIHR PR 2 61r–v 1443, Margaret Kirkham widow of Thomas merchant, Lord Mayor 1435, who died in 1435 (PR 3 486v–487v) making a bequest to Corpus Christi Gild. PR 5 362v–363r 1489, Joan Ince widow of John, chamberlain 1448, sheriff 1456, who died in 1483 (PR 5 308r–v), making bequests to Corpus Christi, St Christopher and St Anthony Gilds.

bands made bequests to gilds. Agnes Marsshall, in 1461, left her coral beads, with gaudes and a crucifix in silver-gilt, to be hung on the Corpus Christi Gild shrine.[172] Her husband, John, a Merchant of the Staple, subsequently became Lord Mayor twice and left 20s. each to Corpus Christi, St Christopher and St George, and St Anthony Gilds.[173] Although the widows and wives of affluent artisans and victuallers also made bequests to gilds, their wills generally suggest that they were also women of wealth and status.[174] Most female testators followed the general trend, of all persons of mercantile occupation or civic status, by belonging to the larger gilds. There is, however, a hint that some women's gild membership was of a different kind.

Although the numbers of bequests involved are very low, there is an indication that female testators supported parish gilds in proportionally greater numbers than their overall total might suggest. Of the twenty-two bequests made to parish gilds by all testators, ten were made by women. These included four of the ten bequests to the St Anne Gild in St Laurence in the Suburbs, and two of the four bequests to the St Mary Gild in St Michael le Belfrey. This points towards the proposition that the women might have enjoyed a special status in some parish gilds, especially those with female patrons.[175] By contrast, there is no indication of such a status being conferred on women in the large civic gilds, none of which had female dedicatees.

In an ecclesiastical centre such as York it was only to be expected that there would be a large number of clerical testators.[176] Figure 4.12 shows that, with 106 bequests to gilds, they almost rivalled the mercantile group. This was a higher proportion of the whole than the 12.5% of clerical testators derived from the county will sample.[177] The small number of higher clergy in the city who made bequests to York gilds had connections either with the Minster or with St Mary's Abbey and all made bequests to the clerically run Corpus Christi Gild and to no other city fraternity.[178] They reflected the trend, already seen in the county, of

172 YML L2(4) 298v–299r.

173 BIHR PR 5 311r–v 1487. Lord Mayor 1467 and 1480, Dobson, *Chamberlains' Accounts*, pp. 211–12.

174 E.g. Margaret North, widow of William tiler, chamberlain in 1497, BIHR PR 6 202v–203r 1505, and Maud Hancoke widow of alderman Robert grocer, PR 7 52r–53v 1508.

175 See Chapter 3, pp. 90–2.

176 R. B. Dobson, 'The Foundation of Perpetual Chantries by the Citizens of Medieval York', *The Province of York: Studies in Church History* 4 (Leiden, 1967), pp. 22–38 (pp. 37–8), has calculated that there were approximately 260 parish chaplains, excluding personal chaplains, in York in 1436.

177 See Figure 3.2.

178 YML L2(4) 238–239, 1434, Canon William Pelleson. BIHR PR 3 473v–474v, 1434, Canon John Carleton prebend of Riccall. PR 2 249r–v, 1452, John Affordeby master of the hospital of Stillingfleet, former master of St Mary's Hospital in Bootham. PR 2 305r, 1454 John Huet Procurator General. PR 5 252v–253v, 1480, William Lambert master of Staindrop College, who also left 13s. 4d. to Holy Trinity Gild, Staindrop and was buried at St Mary's Abbey,

Figure 4.11: Clerical Testators to York Gilds

Date	All Clerics	Higher	Rectors	Vicars	Chaplains	All
1365–1400	1	–	–	–	1	17
1401–1410	1	–	–	–	1	22
1411–1420	–	–	–	–	–	14
1421–1430	4	–	–	1	3	34
1431–1440	9	2	–	–	7	81
1441–1450	12	–	2	1	9	70
1451–1460	11	2	–	1	8	53
1461–1470	11	–	2	2	7	37
1471–1480	17	1	1	2	13	66
1481–1490	14	1	2	2	9	59
1491–1500	8	–	1	1	6	23
1501–1510	11	1	–	2	8	56
1511–1520	3	–	–	–	3	13
1521–1530	–	–	–	–	–	21
1531–1540	1	–	–	–	1	15
1541–1550	3	–	–	1	2	7
Totals	106	7	8	13	78	587

Date: date of will sample.
Clerics: all clerical testators making bequests to York gilds.
Higher: all clerical testators above the rank of rector and holders of offices within the Minster.
Rectors: all rectors who made bequests.
Vicars: all vicars who made bequests.
Chaplains: unbeneficed clergy including gild priests.
All: all testators making bequests to gilds.

members of this group making donations to gilds in their lifetimes rather than bequests.[179]

Beneficed clergy formed a smaller proportion of the total in York than elsewhere. Indeed, it was even smaller than Figure 4.11 implies, as six vicars choral are listed with the parochial vicars.[180] Discounting these, as it is not clear whether they also acted as parish clergy, bequests from beneficed parochial clergy appeared only between 1441 and 1510. The first date coincided with a surge in

York. YML L2(4) 363v, 1485, William Lasyngby vestry clerk of the Minster. L2(5)a I 73r, 1508, John Rumpton sacristan of the Minster.

[179] See Chapter 3, p. 93.

[180] YML L2(4) 263v–264r 1449, Thomas Northus, L2(4) 120v, 1469, William Esyngwold, L2(4) 325r–v 1471 Robert Gillesland, L2(4) 350v, 1481, John Anstan, L2(4) 377v–378r 1492, John Tanfield, L2(5)B 206r–207r 1542, Thomas Robynson.

the membership of the Corpus Christi Gild.[181] All the York vicars and rectors, making bequests to gilds, included one to Corpus Christi, emphasising its unique position in the city, as a fraternity run by clerics.[182] The lack of bequests from this group after 1510 may be related to economic factors. The value of benefices did not increase in a time of inflation and tithes in urban centres were difficult to collect.[183] Furthermore, by the 1530s, it was becoming increasingly obvious that the position of the gilds was becoming insecure.[184] The clerics of York, bearing in mind its political and ecclesiastical importance, might be expected to be particularly aware of the implications of changes in doctrine and practice following Henry VIII's break with Rome. Even if they could have afforded to make bequests to gilds, to do so might not have been politically wise. The bequests made to gilds by chaplains, who formed the vast majority of the clerical group, followed similar patterns, and probably for similar reasons. The stipends of chantry priests also remained static in a time of inflation, and there is no reason to believe that chaplains were less politically aware than rectors or vicars.

Membership of York gilds was not confined to its inhabitants. Forty-six testators who made bequests to them came from outside the city and its suburbs. Their distribution, and that of their bequests to gilds in York, is shown in Figure 4.12. As they were largely identified from the one-third sample of county wills, they represent a minority of the probable total. Those who lived nearest to the city supported local gilds, testators from Clifton and Heslington making bequests to the gilds of St Mary at the Abbey and St Anne in St Laurence.[185] The two testators from outside the county were special cases. William Lambert was buried in York and Robert Ormyshede came from a well-known family of city merchants.[186] A slightly larger group dwelt within ten miles of York.[187] Their

181 See Figure 5.1.
182 See Chapter 5, pp. 162–3.
183 Palliser, *Tudor York*, p. 229.
184 See Chapter 7, pp. 227–31.
185 BIHR PR 2 197v 1449 Richard Thurkilby mason of Clifton, to St Mary Abbey. YML L2(4) 353v–354r 1482 Thomas Kirkby of Clifton, to St Mary Abbey. BIHR PR 4 175r 1471 Thomas Dalton of Fulford, to Corpus Christi. YML L2(4) 301r–v 1462 John Haliday of Heslington, to Corpus Christi, St Christopher. BIHR PR 5 445v 1493 William Arthure of Heslington bequest to Corpus Christi, St Anne in St Laurence.
186 BIHR PR 5 415v–417v 1490 William Lambert Master of Staindrop College in County Durham and vicar of Gayneford, to Corpus Christi, St Christopher. YML L2(4) 61r–v, 1443 Robert Ormyshede advocate of Carlisle, to St Christopher.
187 BIHR PR 2 469v 1462 William Lassels chaplain of Bolton Percy, to Corpus Christi. PR 5 415v–417v 1490 Mgr. Thomas Pereson subdeacon of Minster and rector of Bolton Percy to Corpus Christi, St Christopher. PR 4 211r–v 1474 Hugh Goodrich parson of Escrick, to Corpus Christi, St Christopher, St Mary Abbey. PR 4 128r, 1474, William Wanton of Fangfoss, to St Christopher. YML L2(5)A 198v–199r 1541 Brian Godson chantry priest of Newton upon Ouse, to Corpus Christi. BIHR PR 3 1438 Thomas Harrald vicar of Overton, to St Mary Abbey. PR 9 359r 1526 John Smyth of Overton, to Corpus Christi. PR 6 162v 1506 John Richardson of Sheriff Hutton, to St Anthony. PR 2 249r–v 1452 John Affordeby of Stillingfleet former master of St Mary's Hospital York, to Corpus Christi. PR 6 113v–114r 1504 William Cliveland vicar of Tadcaster, to Corpus Christi, SS Christopher and George.

Figure 4.12: Testators and Bequests to York Gilds from outside the City

	Total	Zone 1	Zone 2	Zone 3	Zone 4
Numbers of testators:	46	5	11	28	2
Numbers of bequests to gilds:					
St Christopher	27	1	4	21	2
Corpus Christi	25	3	8	13	1
St Mary Abbey	5	2	2	1	
St Anthony	4	–	1	3	–
SS Christopher and George	3	–	1	2	–
Paternoster	1	–	1	–	–
St Anne in St Laurence	1	1	–	–	
SS Mary and Martin	1	–	–	1	–
St John the Baptist	1	–	–	1	–
Total bequests to gilds:	68	6	17	42	3

Zone 1: within approximately three miles of the city centre.
Zone 2: beyond three miles but within approximately ten miles of the city centre.
Zone 3: beyond ten miles from York but within the ancient county boundary.
Zone 4: outside the county.

bequests, like those of the much larger group who lived more than a day's return journey from York, were generally made to the three largest gilds of the city and to those gilds that became associated with them.[188]

---

[188] YML L2(4) 330v 1473 John Marston chantry chaplain of Aldborough WR, bequest to Corpus Christi. BIHR PR 4 171 1471 William Hawk rector of Barwick in Elmet, to Corpus Christi. PR 2 252r–v 1452 John Lokwood of Broughton Parva NR, to St Christopher. PR 2 336v 1456 Thomas Aleby of Broughton WR, to St Christopher; PR 2 298v–299r 1494 Thomas Kirkeham rector of Burnsall in Craven, to St Christopher, St Mary and St Martin. PR 3 292v 1463 Thomas Sprott rector of Denton, to Corpus Christi. PR 2 195r 1449 Joan Schipwyth of Fryston, to St Christopher. PR 2 465v 1462 Helen Aleby of Guisborough, to St Christopher; PR 9 65r 1517 Sir Robert Brown priest of Heptonstall, to SS Christopher and George. PR 11 12r–v 1529 Robert Roos of Kirk Deighton, to Corpus Christi, SS Christopher and George. PR 2 18v–19r 1441 Robert Stanlay vicar of Kirkby Overblow, to Corpus Christi. PR 5 372r–v 1490 John Smerte senior rector of Leconfield, to Corpus Christi, St Christopher, St John Baptist. PR 2 466v 1462 Marion Stokeslay of New Malton, to St Christopher. PR 5 456r 1494 John Pape of New Malton, to St Christopher. PR 5 446r–v 1494 James Clapeham master of Holy Trinity College Pontefract, to St Christopher. PR 4 10v 1474 Thomas Ledys of Ripon, to Corpus Christi, St Christopher. PR 3 548r 1438 Adam Middleton tailor of Ripon, to St Christopher. YML L2(4) 362r–363r 1485 Robert Fairbarne husbandman of Rockcliffe, to Corpus Christi, St Christopher, St Anthony, St Mary Abbey. BIHR PR 5 30r 1482 John Preston vicar of Rothwell, to St Christopher. PR 5 495r–v 1496 Thomas Sage, of Scawton to St Christopher, Corpus Christi. PR 2 24v–25r, 1441, Dom. Thomas Garton rector of Scarborough, to Corpus Christi. PR 4, 1472, Richard Lassells of Sowerby, to St Christopher. PR 2 484r 1461 Richard Wetwang rector of Stokesley, to Corpus Christi, St Christopher, St Anthony. PR 2 483r–v 1463 Thomas Covell vicar of Topcliffe, to Corpus Christi, St Christopher, St Anthony. PR 9 38r–39r 1516 Richard Peke of Wakefield, to St Christopher. PR

Between them, the three large civic gilds, and the fraternities that they absorbed, attracted about ninety per cent of all bequests made to York gilds, from this sample of testators living outside the city. That the gild of St Christopher, with its connections with the city government, received slightly more bequests from county testators than the Corpus Christi Gild, which received a larger proportion of city bequests, might reflect an interest in political or commercial contacts in the city on the part of some of these individuals. It also further emphasizes the funerary role of the Corpus Christi Gild, which could not be discharged in the remoter parts of the county, for obvious practical reasons.

Conclusion

During the fifteenth century generally, the gilds of York were agents of public and official piety. The larger gilds, especially, were supported by the corporation, licensed by the king and promoted by the church hierarchy through indulgences.[189] However, they became, to some extent, victims of their own success. The initiatives of the crown towards the promotion of orthodox piety led the city to make use of basically pious institutions for political ends. The expansion of the St Christopher and St Anthony Gilds, by their absorption of smaller fraternities, had the effect of reducing the number of gilds in the city, concentrating their influence in fewer hands. Whilst the outward display of these great gilds grew ever more magnificent, there is an impression that their ethos was becoming gradually more secular. Other important gilds increasingly came under the control of occupations within the city. It seems certain that the foundation of a craft-related gild, or the take-over of an existing gild by a craft, represented a successful bid for power and influence within the city by the craftsmen concerned. In the cases where existing gilds were taken over, it seems probable that there would be a change in its ethos, perhaps at the expense of its devotional functions. Promotion of the craft might be afforded a higher priority than veneration of the dedication.

Testamentary evidence suggests that the popularity of gilds in York was in sharp decline after the end of the first decade of the sixteenth century. The circumstances of will-making, when the testator's mind was concentrated on the hereafter, could, however, indicate that a decline in bequests was not necessarily related to a decline either in membership of gilds, or in the general level of orthodox lay piety. It lay perhaps, rather, in a general perception of decline in the quality of gilds as devotional organizations. Parish gilds, with their limited objectives, had never attracted many bequests in York and only two were made to them after 1510.[190] Gilds related to occupations continued to be supported, but

---

3 553r–v William Pillyng of Yarm, to St Christopher; PR 2 65v, 1440, Thomas Blawfrontt of Yarm, to St Christopher.

[189] Skaife, *Corpus Christi*, pp. 253–5, J. A. Twemlow, *Papal Letters, 1404–15*, p. 458.

[190] St Mary Gild in All Saints Pavement: BIHR PR 8 117r 1512 Ralph Close merchant of the parish of All Saints Pavement: 12d. to the master and prefect of the gild. St Anne Gild in St

at a lower level than before. The increasingly close identification of the St Christopher Gild with the city authorities emphasized its political nature, and its reputation was tarnished by financial scandal and riot in 1533.[191] It is impossible to judge how far a noticeable diminution in bequests to it, after that date, was due to the scandal, and how much to the influence of national political events.

There is no doubt, however, that the St Christopher and St Anthony Gilds, whilst not maintaining the number of bequests they had been receiving in the late fifteenth century, continued to flourish as political, charitable and ceremonial institutions right up to their dissolution. For many of York's inhabitants they still represented traditional piety, as shown by their continued support for ceremonial, elaborate gild funerals and obits. For others they had, perhaps, become too worldly, too big and the creatures of the richest and most ambitious elements in the city government. The continued popularity of the Corpus Christi Gild, however, especially as a provider of funerals, was a significant exception to the general decline. Its success proclaimed the importance that York testators placed upon the veneration of the eucharist, the doctrine of purgatory and the efficacy of the prayers of the priesthood.

Saviour: PR 11 28v–29r 1527 Thomas Addyson husbandman of Heworth in the parish of St Saviour (detached) 4d.

[191] White, *St Christopher and St George Guild*, p. 14.

CHAPTER FIVE

Case Study One:
The Corpus Christi Gild of York

The membership book of the York Confraternity of Corpus Christi is prefaced by a homily on the theme, 'This is my body'.[1] Quoting extensively from scripture, it emphasizes the need for universal harmony, under the rule of God, denounces the evils of rebellion, symbolized by the fall of man, and discusses the importance of Christ's sacrifice in redeeming the sins of the world that ensued from that act of disobedience. It explains the power of the eucharist, not merely as a commemoration of his sacrifice but through its mystic transformation into the actual body of Christ. A concluding passage on the importance of fraternity proposes that the members be guided by the seven rules of charity, before the seven constitutions of the gild are laid down.[2] The fifth of these regulations prohibits lay members from participating in the council or government of the gild.[3] Both the theological principles of the confraternity and its practical rules indicate that in its ceremonial purpose, that of bearing the host in solemn procession on Corpus Christi Day, and in its fraternal functions, the clerical membership was intended to form the senior and ruling partner. Although not unique, this structure was unusual. Only two other clerically governed Corpus Christi fraternities have been identified in England: in Beverley and in the collegiate church of St Mary-in-the-Fields, Norwich.[4] How far the clerics of York actually controlled the gild, or wielded real power through it, and to what extent they became agents of the city government, and of other political groupings, will be one of the themes of this chapter.

This question is closely linked to the gild's membership. It is possible to investigate this in more detail here than in any other fraternity in the county, because the entire membership list is extant.[5] Shifts in the patterns of membership can be shown to be part of the evolving relationship between York's gilds and government, that was discussed in the previous chapter. The gild's prosperity, its responsibilities and the way in which it governed itself all changed during the course of its history, from its genesis, in 1408, to its dissolution at the hands of the

---

[1] 'Hoc est corpus meum', MS Lansdowne 304, fols. 15r–17v, St Matthew 26, 26.
[2] MS Lansdowne 304, fols. 17r–v. I Corinthians 13, 4–6.
[3] MS Lansdowne 304, fol. 18v: 'Qui tamen seculares quamvis ad preces et ad fraternitatem recipientur ad nostra consilia nec ad gubernationem fraternitatis non admittantur'.
[4] M. Rubin, *Corpus Christi*, p. 242.
[5] MS Lansdowne 304, fols. 19v–27v, 32r–154v.

royal commissioners in 1547. This chapter will discuss the gild's development thematically, omitting detailed consideration of those aspects of its ceremonial and funerary functions, which were dealt with in the previous chapter. Prior to this, however, there will be a brief account of the gild's evolution, and a discussion of its ordinances, to provide a context for later discussion, followed by an attempt to reconstruct the background to its foundation, which will form a logical starting point for argument.

The gild's history can be traced through its Register, supplemented by the papers bound with it in MS Lansdowne 304. These are all available in an elderly, but substantially accurate, printed edition, compiled by R. L. Skaife, who also included further documents, relevant to the gild's history, from local archive sources.[6] He did not, however, consider the gild's extant account rolls in his edition, which add considerably to our understanding of the gild's affairs.[7] Although the sequence of accounts is far from complete, it provides snapshots of the fraternity, its members and its concerns, at various points in its development.

The Evolution of the Gild

The gild was founded in 1408, as a confraternity of chaplains and lay persons, with the encouragement of the city government, probably to form the focus of the civic Corpus Christi Day procession. It was ruled by six chaplains, who were elected annually as masters.[8] The new gild seems to have owned no land and to have had few possessions of intrinsic value at this stage. In 1431, the year following the construction of a wooden shrine for carrying the host, the gild made a formal agreement with the city concerning the ordering of the procession and the storage of the shrine in the civic chapel of St William.[9] In 1449, the wooden shrine was replaced by one in silver-gilt.[10] In 1458, the gild was incorporated by royal charter.[11] This reorganized its governing body, which was henceforth ruled by a single master, who might be a chaplain, or a vicar or rector, to whom six chaplains were to be responsible as keepers (*custodes*). In 1477, a new set of ordinances

---

6   Skaife, *Corpus Christi*.

7   YCA G C99:1–8, C100:1–6, C101:1–4, C:102:1–3, C:103:1–2. These account rolls have been accidentally omitted from the index of the Archive's *Catalogue* (York, 1908). Some extracts from them, relating to drama and ceremonial, have been edited and translated in *REED York*.

8   MS Lansdowne 304, fol. 17. Skaife, *Corpus Christi*, p. 10. The gild year as regards the entry of members seems to be the same as its financial year, as shown in its accounts. They were originally intended to be presented on the feast of St Clement (23 November) but appeared variably on dates ranging between late November and early December. I follow the register in referring to the year in which each annual list was begun: thus 1408 ran from November 1408 to November 1409.

9   YCA E 20A fols. 116Av–117v, A15. MS Lansdowne 304, fol. 42v.

10 The gift of Thomas Spofford, then Bishop of Hereford, MS Lansdowne 304, fol. 2r.

11 YCA G11.

were drawn up and approved by Laurence Booth, the archbishop of York.[12] In the following year the gild acquired, from Holy Trinity Priory, the Hospital of St Thomas, outside Micklegate Bar, which it continued to administer until the dissolution.[13] In 1483, it played its Creed Play before Richard III, who was already a member of the confraternity. In 1495, the city decreed that the play should replace the Corpus Christi cycle once in every ten years.[14] By this time the gild was an important landowner in the city and beyond, was the possessor of much treasure and had a wide and prestigious membership which included noble and gentle families from throughout the whole of the North.[15] In many ways it had become a national institution.[16] In its later history, it survived the problems of The Pilgrimage of Grace, which caused a sharp decline in its membership, and was showing signs of a revival in its popularity on the eve of its dissolution in 1547.[17]

The Ordinances of 1408 and 1477

The gild's purposes and organization were laid out in its ordinances.[18] It is difficult, however, to be precise about their dating. Clearly they were first composed and written down at the same time as the homily and the early membership lists, probably soon after 1408. However, large sections of them have been erased and overwritten.[19] These passages represent various updatings of both doctrine and practice, but it is not possible to know when these occurred or what they replaced. It seems likely that they pre-date the gild's incorporation, as an alteration to the sixth ordinance refers to masters in the plural. However, in the seventh ordinance, *sex magistri* has been struck out and *magistri et sex custodibus* interlined, showing that the ordinances were still being amended after 1458, but without erasing the original.[20]

The first two ordinances lay down the regulations for the ordering of the gild's contribution to the Corpus Christi procession and the election of officers. The third provides for the admission of members through the gild officers, without oath, on payment of a fee that was left to the individual's discretion. The fourth and fifth deal with the duties of the chaplains in conducting masses and funerals and with those of lay members in attending them, although it is stressed that the laity should have no voice in the gild's councils and must all be of good charac-

---

[12] *Approbatio Statutorum*, YCA G11A.

[13] YCA G13,14.

[14] See Chapter 4 above, p. 143.

[15] Pollard, *North Eastern England During the Wars of the Roses*, p. 189.

[16] Swanson, *Church and Society*, p. 281.

[17] See Figure 5.8.

[18] MS Lansdowne 304, fols. 17v–19v.

[19] Most, but not all, of the erased and overwritten passages are indicated in Skaife, *Corpus Christi*, pp. 6–8. There is a section that he missed at the top of MS Lansdowne 304, fol. 19r, which is the conclusion of the sixth ordinance.

[20] MS Lansdowne 304, fol. 19r. This is not shown in Skaife, *Corpus Christi*.

ter. The sixth ordinance makes provision for the annual obit and the seventh includes a variety of rules for the carrying of lights, the reception of legacies and gifts and the collection of subscriptions by the masters.

The *Approbatio* of 1477 deals with a similar range of topics in rather more detail, taking in various changes in practice and structure laid down in the charter.[21] Although the new master is to be elected, from a short list of three, by all members who are parochial clergy of the city, each of the six keepers is to nominate his own successor. There are elaborate regulations for safeguarding the gild's shrine and treasure chest. The arrangements for the procession, the anniversary for the souls of deceased members on the Saturday after Corpus Christi, the mass to be held on the next day and the *missa mortuorum* to be sung on the Monday of the Octave are all described. In addition it is laid down that there were to be four general obits held within the four friary churches once every four years. Provision is also made for the funerals of all priests who are members.

Both sets of ordinances are concerned with the duties, responsibilities and privileges of the gild's clerical members. The role of lay members is almost wholly ignored. If only these two documents had survived, we might easily assume that the York Corpus Christi Gild was entirely dominated by the city's parochial clergy and that its functions were exclusively pious. Lay interest in its business is, however, demonstrable even from its foundation.

The Origins and Foundation of the Gild

The gild's membership register states, both in the preamble to the ordinances and in that to the list of its members, that it was founded in 1408 by chaplains and other honest persons.[22] How this came about, however, is less obvious, and a number of theories have been advanced. Westlake suggests that the gild was formed to regulate the annual Corpus Christi procession, implying that the foundation was a result of a civic initiative.[23] The Corpus Christi procession and play cycle had been celebrated annually in York since the previous century. In 1366 Thomas de Bukton, the rector of Rudby, had bequeathed five pounds to sustain the solemnities of Corpus Christi celebrated every year in the City of York.[24] By 1387 three crafts are known to have owned pageant waggons, for use in the Corpus Christi plays, and, in 1394, the City Memorandum Book was already referring to them as being performed in *locis antiquitatus assignatis*.[25] There is, however, no evidence to suggest that the Corpus Christi Gild ever controlled the plays in any way. From 1426, when it was proposed that the procession and plays

---

[21] YCA G 11A. Transcribed in Skaife, *Corpus Christi*, pp. 259–70.

[22] MS Lansdowne 304, fols. 15r, 20r.

[23] Westlake, *Parish Gilds*, p. 55.

[24] '. . . ad sustencionem solempnitatis corporis Christi in Civitate Ebor singulis Annis celebrate centum solidos', YML L2(4) 43r.

[25] *REED York*, pp. 4–5, YMB A/Y E 20 fol. 17v.

should take place on separate days, the gild clearly had no involvement in the cycle, which the authorities governed through the agency of the searchers of the city's crafts.[26] By the mid-fifteenth century, the gild's keepers had the duty of marshalling the procession, but this may not have been the case in 1408, prior to the construction of the first shrine.[27]

It could be argued that the gild might have had a parochial origin. At the time of its dissolution it was referred to by the King's Commissioners as, 'The gulde of the fraternyte of Corpus Christi in the Trynte parisshe in Mikelgate in the Cyte of Yorke'.[28] Following the suppression of the Benedictine Priory of Holy Trinity, in 1538, the nave of its church was used as a parish church. Before this the parish was also known as that of St Nicholas Micklegate. The relationship between the priory and St Nicholas's church is unclear.[29] The church seems to have adjoined the conventual church and the priory appointed vicars, at various times, both to St Nicholas and Holy Trinity.[30] That the new gild, in 1408, had a connection with Holy Trinity as a parish seems unlikely, however, although John Wyot, vicar of St Nicholas, was one of the clerical members listed in the founding year of 1408 and in 1414 Prior John Castell of Holy Trinity was admitted.[31]

There is, however, information from another source that links the early years of the gild's activities with the priory. The earliest of the surviving gild account rolls, of 1415, shows evidence of a special relationship between the two institutions and may suggest that the annual feast (*cena*) was held within the priory precincts or, at least, nearby.[32] The account includes 5d. for a pottle of wine bought for the clerics of Holy Trinity Priory and an item of 5d. for beef for a breakfast (*iantaculum*) for them. These gifts imply that the gild was under an obligation to the priory, although a separate meal for the monks might suggest that they were not members. Earlier in the account, the men, who were paid 3s.4d. to carry the gild's ten torches in the Corpus Christi procession, were given a further 4d. to bring them from the Holy Trinity Hospital to the monastery of Holy Trinity, implying that they were stored there. The comparatively small sum suggests that the torches were not being carried ceremonially on their return journey. The 4d. paid out for carrying water from the Ouse for the feast might also suggest that the site of the feast was, at least, some distance from the river.

At a later point in the history of the gild it may well have outgrown any accommodation that the priory could offer. Certainly by the *Approbatio* of 1477,

[26] For a recent interpretation of how this control might have been exercised see H. Swanson, 'The Illusion of Economic Structure'. For the separation of procession and plays see Chapter 4 above, p. 143.

[27] In MS Lansdowne 304, fol. 17v the portion of the *Prima Constitutio* relating to the marshalling of the procession is written in over an erasure. See p. 162 above.

[28] *Certificates*, I, p. 54.

[29] *VCH York*, pp. 374–5. *RCHM York*, III, p. 12.

[30] L. Solloway, *The Alien Benedictines of York* (Leeds, 1910), p. 254.

[31] *Ibid.*, p. 249. MS Lansdowne 304, fols. 20r, 22r. BIHR PR 3 541r–v 1438 John Wyot vicar of St Nicholas Micklegate.

[32] YCA C99:1. m. 2.

the gild was making use of Holy Trinity Fossgate, the headquarters of the mercers' gild of Holy Trinity, for its general meetings, and it is recorded as paying a hire charge of 3s.4d. to the mercers for this privilege as early as 1459.[33] However, a relationship with Holy Trinity Priory was sustained. The gild's take-over, in 1478, of the priory's hospital of St Thomas seems to have been amicable, to the extent that the priory granted the gild the alms and oblations associated with the hospital eight years later.[34] The gild's new base may have strengthened the link between priory and gild, which were now close neighbours, explaining the commissioners' perceptions of a parochial connection between the two. It seems likely that, when the gild was founded, it was based in Holy Trinity Priory. This was the point from which the Corpus Christi civic procession set out, and where, later, the script of the Corpus Christi pageants was housed. The standards and banners for the procession, listed in the 1415–16 account, might also have been kept in the priory.[35] There is, however, no evidence to imply that the gild's foundation was the result of any initiative by either the parishioners of St Nicholas, or of Holy Trinity or by the priory itself.

Jonathan Hughes has suggested two further influences that might have been brought to bear on the formation of the gild.[36] He speculates that Archbishop Arundel, formerly of York but, by 1408, of Canterbury, 'may have encouraged the foundation' and cites a number of his circle who figured in the gild register. In particular he believes that the residentiary canons of the Minster were influential in the composition of the gild ordinances. Furthermore he notes that Nicholas Love's 'Mirrour of the Blessed Lyfe of Jesu' was begun in 1408 and he argues that the work might have been composed for the gild. However, this textually based argument does not necessarily imply more than encouragement and consultation. There is no evidence to suggest an active involvement by the Minster clergy, as a group, in the foundation or the later affairs of the gild. Minster clergy were never more than a tiny minority in the clerical membership, although their presence is recorded in most years' admissions. More persuasively, Hughes also links the gild to the developing cult of 'Saint' Richard Scrope, who was executed in York just three years prior to the gild's foundation. He notes that many of the early members were figures connected with the archbishop's family and cause.[37] He shows that the cult was attractive both to the city and to a web of supporters amongst some of the major county families. It was not rendered politically respectable until the executed archbishop's memory had been rehabilitated by

---

[33] YCA G11A. Skaife, *Corpus Christi*, p. 260 n.r.

[34] YCA G13 and G14 are the two matching copies of the agreement. The text is identical. G13 is sealed with the seals of the Lord Mayor and the Corpus Christi gild. G14 has the seal of St Thomas' Hospital affixed. The agreement over alms and oblations is inscribed into MS Lansdowne 304, fol. 11.

[35] YCA C100:1.

[36] Hughes, *Pastors and Visionaries*, p. 234.

[37] *Ibid.*, pp. 213–14.

Henry V and the cult legalized.[38] A link between the gild and the Scrope cult can be found in the 'The Bolton Book of Hours', which contains two miniatures of St Richard and a prayer to him.[39] It also contains, amongst other Corpus Christi related iconography, a Trinity miniature that is similar in style to Corpus Christi Trinities found in contemporary York glass.[40] The names of John and Alice Bolton, who became members of the gild in 1430, and of Thomas Scauceby, who joined in 1439, are written into its calendar.[41] A more detailed consideration of this tempting theory is beyond the scope of this present account, but it certainly cannot be ruled out. At all events the gild quickly attracted numbers of wealthy and powerful people, both clerical and lay, from the city and beyond.

It seems likely that, whatever the various influences that combined to sponsor the foundation of the gild were, there was already a structure in place to build upon. Two bequests that pre-date the foundation suggest the existence in York of another gild that may well have formed the nucleus of this movement. In 1399, Edmund de Balderstone, chaplain of the St Michael chantry in St Helen's Stonegate, left 6s.8d. to the Fraternity of the Chantries in York and, in 1407, Bernard de Everton, chantry chaplain in St Mary Castlegate, probably of the chantry of St Thomas of Canterbury, bequeathed a similar sum to the Fraternity Gild of Chantry Chaplains, York.[42] The presence of a Chantry Chaplains' Gild in the city at the turn of the fifteenth century points to a focal point for the formation of a new gild, controlled by chaplains. This theory is given added weight by a will of 1416, in which William Welton, former chantry chaplain of the altar of St Michael, in St Helen's, Stonegate, left 13s.4d. to the gild of the Chaplains of Corpus Christi, suggesting that the chaplains' gild had been superseded by the new confraternity.[43]

Further evidence that York's chantry and stipendary priests formed an organized body prior to the foundation of the Corpus Christi Gild is provided by a case heard before the mayor in 1388.[44] The dispute concerned the right of rectors and vicars to exact mortuary bequests from chantry and stipendary priests in the city. Both groups, referred to as communities, were represented by delegates at the meeting. Although neither was actually described as a gild, both were able to behave in a corporate way. The mayor and a committee of twelve citizens found in favour of the chantry priests, arguing that chantries and stipends were funded by the citizens and nobility of York and their heirs. The priests that were so employed were therefore entitled to their special protection. This demonstration of a relationship between the chantry chaplains, as a body, and the city authori-

---

38 J. W. McKenna, 'Popular Canonisation as Political Propaganda: the Cult of Archbishop Scrope', *Speculum* 45 (1970), 608–23 (p. 618).

39 YML, MS Add. 2, fols. 100r, 202v (Richard Scrope), fol. 33r (Trinity).

40 This iconography is discussed in Chapter 3 above, p. 98.

41 MS Lansdowne 304, fols. 42v (Bolton), 34v (Scauceby). YML MS Add. 2, fols. 27r–32v.

42 Balderstone: BIHR PR 3 16r–v, Everton: PR 3 262v–263r.

43 YML L2(4) 175v–176r 1416 William Welton chaplain of St John del Pyke. The bequest is in the codicil.

44 *YMB AY*, II, pp. 17–24, lxiii–lxvi.

ties is a further indication that the Chantry Chaplain's Gild might have formed the nucleus of the new Corpus Christi Gild, at the instigation of the city authorities.

A model for a chaplains' gild involved in a civic procession of Corpus Christi was not far to seek. The ordinances of the Corpus Christi Gild of Beverley make it clear that it too was a clerical gild that was formed for this purpose. They are to be found in its return of 1389, nineteen years before the York gild was formed.[45] These ordinances are less detailed and complex than those of York. Whilst no date of foundation was given, its claim to reverence the feast that had been newly established by Popes Urban IV and John XXII, might suggest that it originated in the early fourteenth century. It is unlikely to be coincidental that two of three known clerically-run Corpus Christi gilds were to be found in the same county, although other gilds of this dedication were governed by laymen.[46] It is clear, for example, that the Corpus Christi gild of Holy Trinity in Hull was not run by clerics.[47] Unfortunately, it is not possible to discover how the Corpus Christi Gild of Pontefract was organized. Whilst there is much testamentary evidence suggesting wide popularity and a substantial clerical involvement, no other documentation relating to it has survived.[48] It is likely that the founding members of the York gild were aware of the one in Beverley and based their new fraternity upon it.

Who the founding members were, however, is far from certain. In two of his footnotes, Skaife points out what he regards as several inconsistencies in the early part of the membership register.[49] He notes that there is no list of 'founders' and that the obituary, bound with it, contains over a hundred names that are not recorded in the list.[50] He implies, perhaps, that many of the distinguished names in the early part of the obituary might have helped to promote the gild's foundation. Certainly a number of very influential York names appear there. The families of Aldestanemor, Blakburn, Bolton, Gare, Morton, Ormeshede and Wyman, leading merchants of the city, all provided individuals who rose to the rank of Lord Mayor of York during the early fifteenth century.[51] It is also clear that the obituary, containing 457 names, does not include more than a fraction of the members listed in the register over the same period.

Skaife's assertion that a list of founding members is missing is not unreasonable. The register of the Holy Trinity and Saints Fabian and Sebastian Gild of St

---

45 PRO C 47/46/455.

46 See p. 160 above.

47 PRO C 47/56/449.

48 E.g. BIHR PR 3 518v–519r 1438 John Thorneton vicar of the parish of All Saints: 6s.8d. PR 4 33r 1471 Robert Newall chaplain of the parish of All Saints: a beehive. PR 5 83v 1482 Thomas Chaloner chaplain of the parish of All Saints Pontefract: 3s.4d.

49 Skaife, *Corpus Christi*, p. v, note, p. 10, notes.

50 The gild obit is bound into MS Lansdowne 304 interrupting the sequence of the register at fols. 28–31. The following folio has been misplaced to fol. 42 before the register continues in its proper sequence at fol. 32. The obit is printed in Skaife, *Corpus Christi*, pp. 238–49.

51 R. B. Dobson, *York City Chamberlains' Account Rolls*, pp. 208–9.

Botolph without Aldersgate, in London, is prefaced with three names of whom it is said that 'þes weren þe bygynneres þer of'.[52] Several of the Yorkshire gilds which made returns in 1389 listed their founding members in their certificates, including Holy Cross Gild, Rotherham, the gild in Bedale, St John the Baptist Gild, St Mary Gild, and Corpus Christi Gild in Hull, St Helen Gild and St Mary Gild in Beverley besides the Holy Trinity Gild in Grimsby in neighbouring Lincolnshire.[53] Although all of these lists are much briefer than the obituary of Corpus Christi in York, Skaife's suspicion that the latter may contain the names of 'missing' founder members, as well as some of those who entered at a later date, is probably correct.

The obituary seems to have been a bede book, perhaps largely for the remembrance of Skaife's 'founders', who were missing from the membership book, and for particularly generous or distinguished members. It was probably intended for use at the annual solemn obit on the Saturday evening after Corpus Christi and the mass that followed it on Sunday morning.[54] Such lists were common in late medieval gilds as well as in the parishes of the period.[55] The book was discontinued in 1437, perhaps because it was, by then, duplicating the information recorded in the register and the account rolls, but it was preserved with the register, and bound with it, probably in order that the 'founder members' would continue to be remembered in the prayers of the gild.

If the obituary included the names of the founder members as well as those of subsequent members who had died before the list closed in 1437, then it is possible to compile a putative founders' list by selecting all the names in the obit that do not appear in the membership register. Such a list does not, of course, include founder members who died after 1437. This must have been the case with four of the six chaplains who were elected as keepers of the gild for 1408, and were therefore already members. Roger Bubwith, William Wyntryngham, William Swerde and John Cayle do not appear in the obituary, although William Eston and Adam Wyntryngham do.[56] Even so, Skaife's estimate of 'upwards of one hundred' proves to be conservative: there are just over two hundred names of possible founder members that can be discerned in the obituary.[57] Taking into consideration the numbers of individuals who might have survived beyond 1437, the actual number of founders was probably considerably larger than this. The results of the exercise, imperfect though it is, are interesting. The 'founders' list shows sixty-one clerics, about a third of the total, of whom the vast majority seem

---

52 Ed. P. Basing, *Parish Fraternity Register: Fraternity of Holy Trinity and Saints Fabian and Sebastian in the Parish of St Botolph without Aldersgate*, London Record Society (1982), p. 5.

53 PRO C 47/46/453, 444, 450, 451, 449, 446, 448, C 47/40/116.

54 Lansdowne MS 403, fol. 18v.

55 Duffy, *The Stripping of the Altars*, p. 334.

56 MS Lansdowne 304, fols. 20r, 30v (Eston in 1429), fol. 29r (Adam Wyntryngham in 1421).

57 Skaife, *Corpus Christi*, p. v. It is not possible to be totally accurate as wives are not always named in the register and singly listed women in the obit list may not necessarily always be wives to men in the register with the same surname. The probable total of 'founders' is 209.

to have been chaplains. Only six vicars, two rectors and two monks are included in this total. One of the vicars was from Leeds and one of the rectors from Richmond. Additionally, there was a nun of Clementhorpe and at least six women who were the mothers of clerics or who were otherwise closely related to them.

Of the lay persons, twenty-five can be identified as being of mercantile families and twenty-two as craftsmen and their relatives. There were half a dozen county gentry, the best known being Lady Elizabeth Basy, widow of Richard Basy esquire, of York and Bilborough, who founded a chantry in St Mary Bishophill Senior in 1403.[58] The most significant lay group, however, was that connected with the civic government. The current Lord Mayor, Henry Wyman and his wife, Agnes, appear in the list which also includes John Northiby, a current chamberlain, and the wife of Peter Bucky, one of his colleagues. In all, the 'founders' list contains thirty-seven individuals who had held, or were to hold, civic office or who were members of their families.[59] It seems certain that, from its foundation, the Corpus Christi Gild, despite its ordinances, was already closely identified with the city's ruling families. At this early stage, however, the nucleus consisted of city chaplains, who formed the largest single group within the confraternity.

This point is strongly reinforced by the admissions to the gild recorded in its first year.[60] Excluding the six founding keepers, eighty out of the 110 names listed in the register were chaplains, although, strictly speaking, the group also included three rectors, three vicars and the master of Holy Trinity Hospital in Fossgate. It is the only admission list in which clerics outnumber lay people. This suggests that over 120 chaplains had been admitted between 1408 and 1409. This is almost half the number of parish chaplains calculated to have been present in the city in 1436.[61] The thirty lay persons in the 1408 list included four members of the mercantile Gare family, including Thomas Gare, junior, a future Lord Mayor, John Penreth, a former bailiff, and his wife, and Robert Lokton, a future sheriff, and his wife.[62] Also figuring in the list were Robert Sallay esquire of Saxton and his wife, Margaret, county gentry who, like the Basys, were connected with a chantry in the city.[63] It is not surprising that families maintaining chantries should be involved in a gild that had such a high membership of chantry priests.

The available evidence suggests that the Corpus Christi Gild arose out of an agreement between an existing Chantry Chaplains' Gild and the ruling group in the city, led by its Lord Mayor, Henry Wyman, to form a confraternity governed

---

58 MS Lansdowne 304, fol. 28r (1413). *Certificates*, I, p. 69.

59 MS Lansdowne 304, fol. 28r, Henry Wyman (1411), Agnes Wyman (1413), fol. 31v, John Northiby (1432), fol. 31r, Margaret Buccy (1430).

60 MS Lansdowne 304, fol. 20r–v.

61 According to Dobson, 'The Foundation of Perpetual Chantries', pp. 37–8. See Chapter 4, p. 154 note 176.

62 Dobson, *York City Chamberlains' Account Rolls*, p. 210. There is no bequest to the Corpus Christi Gild in his will, BIHR PR 3 610v.

63 MS Lansdowne 304 fol. 20v. Skaife *Corpus Christi*, p. 12. *Certificates*, I, p. 51.

by chaplains, but open to lay people, after the model of the gild in Beverley. This was based on a relationship between the two bodies that had already been established by the lawsuit of 1388. One effect of the agreement was to formalize the chaplains' ceremonial responsibilities towards the long-established Corpus Christi procession. It was, like all gilds, basically an expression of piety, as the ordinances and their preamble make clear. Whether, as Hughes suggests, the Minster clergy had a hand in composing these is not known.[64] If they did, they do not seem to have played any further part in the gild's genesis. Gentry involvement in the foundation was, in at least two cases, related to those who maintained chantries. Although the new gild subsequently attracted supporters of the cult of St Richard Scrope, including gentry and nobility, as Hughes has shown, out of all the individuals he names only the Wymans figured amongst the actual 'founders'.[65] Whatever hidden agendas there may have been, the promotion of Corpus Christi, which lay at the heart of orthodoxy, rebutting the Wycliffite challenge, attracted over 17,000 members to the gild during its life-span of 150 years.[66]

Gild Membership

After the entries recorded in its first year, the register shows little immediate sign of the gild's subsequent popularity, as Figures 5.1 and 5.2 demonstrate. This suggests either that most potential members had already been involved in its foundation, or that there was a desire on the part of the founders to keep the gild's membership exclusive. Thereafter, the patterns varied in a not dissimilar way to those of the city at large.[67] This is obviously because some of the factors affecting the fluctuations in the membership of this fraternity are the same as those which have already been discussed in the context of all York gilds.[68] It is, however, important to bear in mind that, whereas the evidence used in Chapter 4 was testamentary, in the case of the Corpus Christi Gild it is based on actual recorded admissions to the confraternity. Because Corpus Christi was such a large gild, accounting for a high proportion of bequests made to all gilds in York, correspondence between the two sets of data help to demonstrate how far the use of testamentary evidence is a reliable indicator of a gild's popularity.

There is little doubt that, almost from its foundation, the Corpus Christi Gild was the York gild that was most highly regarded by testators. It appears that this popularity was related, at various times, to the refurbishment of the shrine and to

---

[64] Hughes, *Pastors and Visionaries*, p. 234.

[65] *Ibid.*, pp. 313–14.

[66] Rubin, *Corpus Christi*, p. 350. Skaife, *Corpus Christi*, p. xii, estimates over 16,850, but this may not include 'founders'.

[67] See Figures 4.1 and 4.2.

[68] See Chapter 4, pp. 119–23.

Figure 5.1: Sample of Corpus Christi Gild Admissions

Year	Members		Year	Members		Year	Members
1408	106	(excluding 'founders')	1455	382		1505	148
1410	30		1460	56		1510	243
1415	22		1464/1465	40	(80 over 2 years)	1515	146
1420	22		1470	412		1520	175
1425	40		1475	219	(excluding Mount Grace)	1525	213
1430	81		1480	125		1530	124
1435	41		1485	229		1535	84
1440	148		1490	205		1540	39
1445	120		1495	227		1545	120
1450/1451	84	(167 over 2 years)	1500	163		1546	137

Figures are based on a count of the annual membership sampled one year in five, but also including the first and last years of the record. Joint membership by a married couple is counted as two persons. All the monks of Mount Grace Priory were admitted in 1475 but their numbers were not specified.

the provision of funerals.[69] However, these enthusiasms were indicative of the gild's popularity as a whole. Figure 5.3 shows that, once the gild was established, it never received less than thirty-five per cent of all bequests made to gilds in the city in each decade and that for most of its life the proportion was much greater than this, never falling below fifty per cent from the 1520s. During the thirty years from 1470 to the end of the fifteenth century, when admissions were generally high, bequests remained at about forty per cent or more of the York total. This shows a period of particular popularity in the gild's fortunes, when new members were joining it in large numbers at the same time as existing members were remembering it at the end of their lives. Although the numbers of bequests declined rapidly during the sixteenth century, the Corpus Christi Gild's share of the total continued to increase, indicating a continuing popularity in comparison with the rest.

There were, also, a number of specific events in the history of the gild itself which seem to have affected membership. Its growing popularity in the 1430s followed the official recognition by the city, implicit in the agreement relating to the new shrine.[70] The rise in membership in the 1450s might well have been stimulated by the archiepiscopal indulgence granted to it in 1446, offering a hundred days' remission for contributing to its maintenance.[71] By this time too

---

[69] See Chapter 4, pp. 145–6.
[70] YCA B/Y fols. 116Av–117v.
[71] BIHR Reg. Kemp fol. 104v.

Figure 5.2: Graph of Gild Admissions Sample

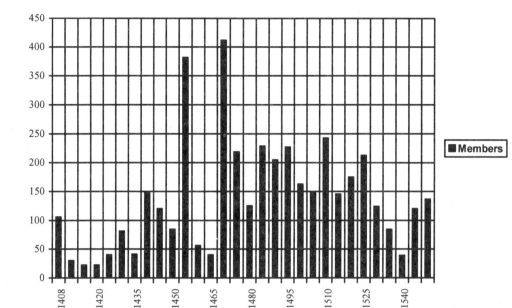

Figures are taken from MS Lansdowne 604 and based on a count of the annual membership sampled one year in five, from 1410–1545, but also include the first (1408) and last (1546) years of the register.

the gild was already performing the Creed Play, which is first mentioned in the account for 1449, and which must also have popularized it.[72]

Whilst these factors may help to explain the membership peak of the mid-1450s, they do not show why there was such a sharp decline thereafter. An examination of all the lists for the late 1450s and 1460s reveals that the returns for 1458 and 1459 are missing and that the recovery in membership did not really begin until 1467. It may be no coincidence that this gap, followed by much reduced admissions, took place at the same time as the most disruptive phase of the struggle between York and Lancaster. Although it has already been argued that this affected bequests to all York gilds, its effect on Corpus Christi member-ship may have been particularly deleterious.[73] In such battles as Wakefield and Towton, some of the more powerful lay members of the gild were involved on either side.[74] Fraternal feelings may have been much distorted by this situation.

---

[72] YCA G C99:3.

[73] See Chapter 4, p. 121.

[74] Pollard, *North-Eastern England During the Wars of the Roses*, pp. 189–90, gives a brief survey of the members of noble houses and their affinities who were also York Corpus Christi Gild members. He notes that the Percy family was unusual in not belonging to the gild.

**Figure 5.3: York Bequests to Corpus Christi Gild as a Proportion
of all York Gild Bequests**

Decade	All	Corpus Christi	Percentage
1401–1410	30	–	–
1411–1420	24	6	25.0
1421–1430	57	17	29.8
1431–1440	135	51	37.8
1441–1450	134	47	35.1
1451–1460	114	36	31.6
1461–1470	70	29	41.4
1471–1480	117	47	40.2
1481–1490	105	42	40.0
1491–1500	45	17	37.8
1501–1510	80	37	46.3
1511–1520	18	9	50.0
1521–1530	24	12	50.0
1531–1540	23	13	56.5
1541–1550	7	4	57.1
Totals	983	367	37.3

All: all recorded bequests to York gilds. This includes a few additional wills, not found by Eileen White, which were discovered from checking the Corpus Christi obituary and gild officers.
Corpus Christi: all recorded bequests to the Corpus Christi Gild by York residents.

The general political climate within the city, too, cannot have been unaffected. Even the incorporation of the fraternity in 1459 might have actually discouraged admissions. The gild already included a large number of members connected with power bases all over the north of England, who were undoubtedly politically aware. It was, even at this juncture, showing signs of becoming, in A. J. Pollard's words, 'something akin to a county club'.[75] The gild charter was granted by Henry VI in December 1458. By March 1461, after two and a half years of violence and confusion, he had been deposed. Potential members might have needed some reassurance before joining an organization that had been endorsed by a recently dethroned monarch.

Once the authority of the new king had been established, the rate of entries revived and the great and good of the realm were again admitted. In 1471, George Neville, archbishop of York, was entered, followed, in 1473, by Thomas Booth, the mitred abbot of St Mary's.[76] The final seal of approval was the enrol-

[75] *Ibid.*, p. 189.
[76] MS Lansdowne 304, fols. 63r (Neville), 67r (Booth).

ment of Richard, duke of Gloucester and future king, with his wife, in 1477.[77] This event, followed, in 1478, by the transfer of the St Thomas Hospital from Holy Trinity Priory to the gild, evidently attracted new members.[78]

Entries between the late 1470s and 1530 remained relatively stable in numbers, although there were changes in the quality of membership over this period, which will be discussed later. The register's response to the events of the 1530s was dramatic. A steady decline in admissions from a minor peak, in 1525, reached a low point of thirty-nine in 1540. Indeed the situation in the years surrounding 1540, not shown in the sample, is very confused. There were no entries for 1538 or 1539. The year 1541 was entered twice, showing four entries on the first occasion followed by a blank folio 149v. A second entry for the same year, with different officials listed, records thirty-three admissions. This crisis in record-keeping might have reflected difficulties within the gild in the wake of the suppression of Holy Trinity Priory, amongst all the other indirect attacks on the gilds' functions and infrastructure.[79] It was probably felt that the future of the gild was in doubt. However, this nadir was followed by a modest revival, probably related to the fall of Cromwell and the more conservative policy of Henry VIII's later years. The final entry in the register does not indicate an awareness of the impending dissolution.

The great importance of the register, as evidence of the gild's membership, lies in its completeness. A major disadvantage, however, is the absence, in many cases, of information beyond mere names. Detailed descriptions of individuals that include their occupations or parishes are only occasional. The sheer quantity of the listed names makes research into the backgrounds of a significant number of them a formidable task. Skaife's edition contains footnotes on particular individuals, usually county gentry or city dignitaries, but his information is not always entirely reliable and he admits that his index is highly selective. The York Freemen's Register offers information on members from the city but, as we shall see, many of the later members came from elsewhere and only a few of the many clerical members from York were recorded as freemen. Fortunately, details of the towns and, in the case of York, the parishes of members are, in some cases, available from the twenty-three surviving account rolls of the gild.[80] These vary greatly in quality. The first two are identical copies of the same account for 1415, which include a payment for a clerk to make a duplicate.[81] The next covers two years, from 1449 to 1451. The following one, for 1459, is so badly water-damaged

---

77 *Ibid.*, fol. 74v. Oddly, the scribes of the gild entered his wife as Elizabeth instead of Anne. They do not seem to have known her name, as it is left blank in the account roll (YCA G C99:5 m. 1). Furthermore, Duke Richard is entered there as George, duke of Gloucester. Richard's brother George, duke of Clarence, was imprisoned in the Tower in June 1477, to be murdered there in the following year. His wife was Isobel of Warwick. These factors indicate that the confusion is over Richard's first name rather than between Gloucester and Clarence.

78 YCA G13 and 14.

79 See Chapter 7, pp. 229–30.

80 YCA G C99:1–8, C100:1–6, C101:1–4, C102:1–3, C103:1–2.

81 YCA G C99:1 m. 2, 2 m. 2.

as to be almost completely illegible. That for 1476 is, by contrast, in excellent condition. That for the following year is atypical as it marks the acquisition by the gild of St Thomas' Hospital and much of the material within it relates to this. Twelve account rolls remain within the period from 1495 to 1520. Most of this group is in good condition, apart from C102:1, for 1519, which is imperfect. Three consecutive accounts from 1532 to 1534 survive, although only that for 1533 is in a reasonably good state of preservation. The series ends with C103:2, for 1540, which is water-damaged.

Basically these are records of account, through which the financial health of the gild can be charted and information gleaned about its property-holding, employees, feasts and ceremonial activities. The list of the gild's possessions, on the dorse of the earliest account, can be compared with similar lists set down in Lansdowne 304 and those noted by the commissioners in 1546. Whilst these records are an incomplete sequence and although some of them are in poor condition, it is fortunate that those that have survived represent a wide chronological spread from seven years after the gild's foundation to the decade of its suppression.

New members were listed in each year's accounts and their individual entry fees were recorded. These records were evidently the source for the membership register. Up to the 1530s, the names followed the same sequence as those in the introits of the rolls. After this point there seems to have been a new policy of promoting in the register the names of dignitaries, especially high clerics, to the head of the list of each introduction by a master or keeper. This may have led to some confusion, as there is an increase in the very few inconsistencies between the two lists from this period. Although the earlier account rolls yield little more information about the places of residence of new members, and their status, than the register, from the 1476 account onwards, most individuals have their parish recorded, if they lived in York, or their city, town, village or monastic house, if they came from elsewhere. This information permits analyses of the distribution of members to be made for the years where complete accounts are extant.

Initially, the chaplains who founded the gild and governed it during its early years continued to form a high proportion of its clerical membership. The large number that had been involved in the foundation, and in the initial year of the gild, meant that subsequent entries were on a more modest scale, but their numbers were probably sufficient at least to maintain their dominance. Until the gild's incorporation, the six keepers' posts were exclusively filled by them. Vicars and rectors did not achieve gild office until after that point. The sprinkling of beneficed clergy from York, and from neighbouring parishes during the early years, gradually increased however.[82] Higher clergy and brothers and, to a lesser extent, sisters of religious orders were also increasingly admitted to membership. Among the nine clerical admissions in 1409, the gild's second year, were two

---

[82] See above, pp. 168–9.

rectors and two vicars.[83] In 1441, a generation later, clerical admissions comprised five rectors, two vicars, three chaplains and the Archdeacon of Cleveland, with his entourage, consisting of a sixth rector, two deacons and two clerks.[84] Apart from considerations of piety, the popularity of the gild with vicars and rectors, both from the city and outside it, in these earlier years, does not appear to demonstrate a desire, on their part, to control the gild in any direct way. Their enthusiasm was more probably related to the contacts that it offered, with the possessors of advowsons and controllers of routes to promotion within the church, in the shape of noble laymen and, particularly, of higher clergy.

In 1411, William Styrkeland, the bishop of Carlisle, was the first high dignitary of the church to join.[85] He was followed in 1412 by no fewer than five higher clergy.[86] Thomas Spofford, then the abbot of St Mary's, was admitted along with his prior and sub-prior. Two canons of York Minster also joined in this year. In 1416, Stephen Scrope, archdeacon of Richmond, joined with members of his family.[87] The new gild's ability to recruit leading figures from both the Minster and the Abbey, York's two greatest ecclesiastical institutions, goes some way towards explaining the increasing numbers of clerics of all kinds who formed a substantial part of its membership, at all points in its life. Following the admission of Minster canons in 1412, four vicars choral appeared in the introit of 1415 and a further group of six was admitted in 1422.[88] Monks and friars from the city and from further afield were also frequent entrants.

Entries were the responsibility of the keepers. That of 1435 was the earliest example of what became the standard method of recording such gild admissions.[89] Each keeper was given the responsibility of recruiting new members. On this occasion William Marshall probably had a particular responsibility for recruiting Minster clergy, as the entrants he introduced included Richard Morton, succentor, John Brigg, parson of the Minster, and John Ely, rector of the nearby St John del Pyke, the advowson of which was held by the Minster Treasurer. The account of 1500 shows similar characteristics, when John Bekebane's entrants included the Chancellor of York Minster, one of the vicars choral, the sacristan, a deacon and three members of the Treasurer's staff.[90] One of the other keepers in this year was Robert Fern, who was the Corpus Christi Gild chaplain, at least between 1500 and 1502, when his salary is recorded in both account rolls. He introduced eight members from St Nicholas Micklegate, which confirms a continuing link between the gild and Holy Trinity Priory at this period.

83 MS Lansdowne 304, fol. 20v.
84 *Ibid.*, fols. 38r–39r.
85 *Ibid.*, fol. 21r–v.
86 *Ibid.*, fol. 21v.
87 *Ibid.*, fol. 24r.
88 YCA G C99:1 William Hunter, Richard Denton, Thomas Swanland and Thomas Northouse are identified as vicars choral in the account roll but not in MS Lansdowne 304, fol. 22v. See MS Lansdowne 304, fol. 24v for the extra six vicars choral.
89 MS Lansdowne 304, fol. 33r.
90 YCA G C100:3.

That recruitment was seen as a part of the gild officers' duties seems certain. The account rolls reveal that individual keepers often introduced large groups of lay persons from particular parishes or areas, suggesting that they used personal contacts to attract members.[91] Another feature of both the account rolls and membership register is that, once the custom had been fully established, the names of keepers who failed to recruit that year have 'nihil' entered after their names in the introit of the account and in the book.[92] This may be just good record-keeping but it also seems to convey a sense of reproach. Recruitment of members from outside York might also have been a matter of contacts, including, perhaps, family connections. However, the process might not always have been direct. As the keepers provided the only route to membership, aspirant members might well have approached existing members, who, in turn, would seek out the appropriate officer. Until incorporation, this control over membership stayed in the hands of chaplains.

The charter of 1459, however, changed the structure of the gild's government by allowing the election of a priest as supreme master and the appointment of six chaplains as keepers.[93] This had the effect of opening up gild office to beneficed clergy. In practice the post of keeper also became available to them. John Garnett, for example, became rector of St Mary, Castlegate, in 1464, prior to his first term as keeper of the gild in 1473.[94] Appendix 2, which lists all the masters of the gild in chronological order, shows that approximately half of them were rectors or vicars. The reason for this change is not apparent from the documents, but it is possible to speculate that it was related to the growing prestige of the gild. Perhaps the three members of the civic elite who were signatories to the charter, William Holbek, Richard Wartre and John Thrisk, felt that the fraternity was now too important to be left entirely in the hands of humble chaplains.[95] Alternatively, the group of chaplains might have been perceived as an increasingly powerful clique and the rectors and vicars as a restraining influence upon it. Another possibility is that it might have been thought that those chaplains who later acquired benefices should not lose their eligibility for office thereby.

Examination of the list of masters, however, suggests another possible reason for the choice of particular individuals.[96] They were most frequently supplied from the parishes of All Saints Pavement and St Saviour, whose clergy held office on eight occasions, followed by Holy Trinity King's Court whose clerics did so on

---

[91] See pp. 178, 180, 183 below.

[92] E.g. YC/G C103:2 and MS Lansdowne 304, fol. 150r.

[93] YCA AA 24, G11A.

[94] Skaife, *Corpus Christi*, p. 130n, MS Lansdowne 304, fol. 69v. He was master in 1482 and 1491. See Appendix 2.

[95] Holbeck, admitted to the gild in 1429 was Lord Mayor in 1449 and 1472. Wartre, admitted in 1423, was Lord Mayor in 1436 and 1451. Thrisk was possibly a 'founder' member and was Lord Mayor in 1442 and 1462. See Appendix 3.

[96] See Appendix 2.

seven. Some of the other wealthier parishes were, however, poorly represented.[97] The clergy of St Crux and St Helen Stonegate supplied only one master each over the period of eighty-five years and those of St Denys, St John Ousebridge, St Michael Spurriergate, St Martin Coneystreet and St Michael le Belfrey none at all. Minster clergy appeared only twice, represented by Thomas Norman, chantry chaplain, and John Hert, vicar choral, but the latter was also vicar of St Martin Micklegate and he was probably elected in the latter capacity. That the gild's highest office fell so often to clergy from the less wealthy, peripheral and suburban parishes, such as All Saints Peaseholme, St George Fishergate, St John Hungate, St Laurence in the Suburbs and St Margaret Walmgate, might have been because the post was particularly attractive to impoverished clerics. The post carried financial advantages, especially with regard to payment for funerals. This impression is reinforced by the fact that most of the masters drawn from rich parishes were chaplains, but that those from poorer ones were generally vicars and rectors. However, that they were elected to this post by others might also suggest a policy of promoting recruitment to the gild's membership in the less affluent parts of York, especially during the later part of this period, when the appointment of masters from poor parishes was most common.

Clearly, the officers of the gild had control of its recruitment policy. They also managed the day-to-day organization of its affairs.[98] However, at crucial points in its development, the city government was instrumental in making large scale decisions. It laid down regulations for the carrying of the newly-built shrine in 1432, and maintained control of it within the civic chapel of St William on Ouse Bridge, making provision that the Lord Mayor might retain a key, so that he could unlock its outer covering and show it to distinguished visitors, without question or delay.[99] The involvement of civic officials is also evident in the process of the gild's incorporation.[100] The strength of the influence brought to bear on the gild's affairs by laymen can be examined through an investigation of its lay membership. This is best done by concentrating on those years where information from the membership register can be supplemented by evidence from the account rolls.

Even if it is accepted that lay membership was principally driven by piety, and by a veneration of the eucharist in particular, it is clear that, from the foundation of the gild, commercial advantage and political ambition played a part in the motivation of at least some entrants. The presence of members of the victualling trades in the earlier years of the register, for example, is significant. The first extant account rolls, those of 1415, give a detailed account of the expenditure on the annual feast. That year the gild bought mutton to the total value of 9s.8d. from William Hovyngham, of 3s.4d. from William Brandesby and of 2s. from

---

[97] See Figure 4.8 above for the taxable wealth of York parishes.
[98] See pp. 184-9 below for discussion of the gild's income and expenditure.
[99] YCA BY fols. 116Av-117v.
[100] YCA AA24. The charter of incorporation names William Holbek, Richard Wartre and John Thrisk.

William Tankyrlay. These three butchers, with their wives, were all admitted to the gild during this period.[101] Their membership was clearly of commercial benefit to them, and probably to the gild too. There was, however, also a political dimension. Hovyngham, the largest meat supplier to the gild, became city chamberlain in 1416. This step took rather longer for William Brandesby, who gained the same office in 1423.[102] It was particularly difficult for butchers to attain civic office prior to 1500 and gild membership might well have been of material assistance to Brandesby and Hovyngham.[103]

Political advantage to gild members from these early years was not confined to its butchers. At least four of the entrants, in 1409, subsequently became city chamberlains: John Loftows merchant and vintner in 1411, John Waghen, chapman and mercer, in 1413, Robert Ebchestre, bower, in 1426 and Richard Crokelyn, fletcher, in 1431.[104] If, initially, the new gild attracted men of ambition who were likely to attain public office, it seems certain that membership soon became seen as a step to such office, or, at the very least, a means by which political contacts could easily be made. Although the gild was not admitting large numbers during these early years, it was increasingly attracting people of social standing and political weight. In 1415, for example, only twenty-two members were introduced, fourteen of whom were lay persons.[105] There were five single women, who may or may not have lived in York, and a widow who certainly did. Four married couples included two merchants, a tailor and a goldsmith, all from the city. Thomas Kyrkham, one of the merchants, who lived, with his wife, Joan, in the parish of St Crux, was city chamberlain in 1421. Richard Lowthe, mercer, who entered with his widowed mother, became city chamberlain in 1423.[106]

By the middle of the century, however, there had been a marked increase in lay admissions. The introit for the account for 1449–50 yields the names of 137 individuals over a period of two years.[107] Of these, eighty-two are identifiable as resident in York, although it is not possible to be more precise about the whereabouts within the city of more than a few. Amongst them was the female cook of St Andrew's Priory, a married couple from the parish of St Michael le Belfrey and a group of six persons from St Crux parish, including William Gyliott, mercer, who was city chamberlain in 1457, and his wife. A search of the Freemen's Register and the wills indices revealed the occupations of a further sixty-five persons, besides placing them as citizens of York. This group displayed a wider cross-section of trades than was found in earlier membership evidence. Besides

---

101 YCA G C99:1. MS Lansdowne 304, fol. 21r, Brandesby, 1409–10 Hovyngham and Tankyrlay, 1410–11.
102 Dobson, *York City Chamberlains' Account Rolls*, p. 209.
103 M. Wheeler, 'The Butchers of York, 1500–50' (unpublished MA dissertation, York 1989–90), p. 83.
104 MS Lansdowne 304, fol. 21.
105 YCA G C99:1/2.
106 Dobson, *York City Chamberlains' Account Rolls*, p. 209.
107 YCA G C99:3.

mercers, tailors and victuallers, the list included clerks, barbers, weavers, dyers, glovers, capmakers, cutlers, smiths, a pewterer and a female huckster. Two of the clerks were also described as gentlemen. The account shows that the increased numbers admitted by the gild had, by 1450, opened up membership to more of the master-craftsmen and artisans of the city. It also continued to attract merchants and aspirants to civic office, such as William Lamb and John Kent, both future Lord Mayors, and Robert Roos, gentleman, a future chamberlain. It was not, however, until after the reorganization of the gild, following its incorporation in 1458, that the account rolls began to record entrants' parishes, showing the territorial spread of membership within the city.

The first extant account to yield this information is that of 1477.[108] In this year all but three of the 107 new members from the city had their parishes noted after their names. Of these, there were seventeen persons from each of St Michael le Belfrey and St Olave, ten from All Saints Pavement, nine from St Peter the Little, six each from St Denys, St Margaret and St Helen Stonegate, five from St Crux, four each from St Mary Bishophill Senior, and St Sampson, three each from St John Hungate, St Laurence and St Michael Spurriergate, two from St Mary Castlegate and one each from All Saints Northstreet, St Edward, St Nicholas Micklegate, St Nicholas Walmgate, St Sampson and the House of St Katherine. There were also two entries from an unspecified parish of St Michael. There were no entries from Holy Trinity King's Court, St Martin Coneystreet, St John Ousebridge or St Martin Micklegate, all of which were comparatively wealthy and were sited, not only on principal thoroughfares of the city, where many of the civic elite owned houses, but also on the route of the Corpus Christi plays.[109] That some wealthy parishes provided members in this year and that others did not is related to the manner of recruitment that has been previously noted. As we have seen, members were introduced into the gild by the master or by individual keepers who often concentrated upon particular parishes and groups. For example, keeper Gawain Byrkheade introduced all but two of the new members from St Olave and a monk of St Mary's Abbey, John Digbe, introduced the majority of members from St Michael le Belfrey and all from St Michael Spurriergate and St Sampson. William Barton's introductions included a majority from All Saints Pavement and all from St Laurence and St Edward in the suburbs. Subsequent accounts show blocs of new members from different ranges of parishes.

The lay recruits from the city continued to include increased numbers of both merchants and craftsmen. A new phenomenon, in this account roll, was the introduction of the servants of prominent citizens. Two of the household of William Snawsell, who had been Lord Mayor in 1468, and four from that of William Chymney, who had been chamberlain in 1470 and would be Lord Mayor in 1486, were all introduced by keeper John Digbe. As these servants were admitted by the payment of a single entry fee for each group, the implication is that both

---

[108] YCA G C99:5.
[109] See Figure 4.8 above, and Crouch, 'Paying to see the Play', pp. 66–7.

Snawsell and Chymney paid for the membership of their people. Whilst this practice might have been regarded simply as a pious act on their part, it probably also had the effect of swelling their respective entourages, on gild occasions, to the enhancement of their social and political prestige. This year's list included five other servants who may have been similarly paid in by their masters and similar cases occur in later account rolls. The wider implications of this development point towards an extension of gild membership beyond the immediate families of wealthy citizens and illustrate lay influence being brought to bear on recruitment. The widening of membership, to include less affluent individuals, is further reflected in the steadily decreasing cost of admission that took place in the early sixteenth century.[110]

These extensions of the base of membership in no way diminished the regular flow of admissions from the city elite. Although it might not have been compulsory for civic office holders to belong to the gild, the vast majority of them appear to have done so. Of all the 640 individuals who held the three principal city offices of Lord Mayor, sheriff and chamberlain during the lifetime of the gild, almost seventy-three per cent were recorded as members either in the register, in the obituary or in both.[111] Of the 143 men who became Lord Mayor over this period, over eighty-eight per cent were members.[112] Six of the mayors that were not recorded held office during the early years of the gild, before the agreement with the city authorities of 1431.[113] It is, however, highly probable that at least some of these, as well as those non-members who held office in the years up to, say, 1455, were founder members who died after the closure of the obit list in 1437.[114] From 1466 until the gild's dissolution, only two mayors, Paul Gillow, mayor in 1522, and William Dodgeson, mayor in 1540, were not recorded as members, although Gillow's wife entered the gild in 1509.

The route to high civic office lay through the posts of bridgemasters of the Ouse and Foss Rivers. Recent research has shown a clear correlation between membership of the gild and appointments to these offices.[115] It may also have had some effect on an individual's progression to the post of chamberlain. It seems certain that entry to the gild was a useful step on the way to civic office, but that it did not represent a formal stage in the process. Although the vast majority were admitted before they became city chamberlains, six joined after that, but before they became sheriffs, and nineteen between holding the latter office but before becoming mayors. Six became members after or during the time they were mayors, including John Northeby, mayor in 1416, who was admitted

---

110 See Figure 5.6 below.
111 See Appendix 3. These figures are briefly discussed in D. J. F. Crouch, 'Religious Gilds in Late Medieval Yorkshire, 1400–1550: A Summary', *Medieval Life*, 9 (1998), 30–32 (p. 32).
112 A number of individuals held office more than once. See Appendix 3.
113 See p. 161 above.
114 See pp. 168–9 above.
115 C. E. Carpenter, 'The Office and Personnel of the Post of Bridgemaster in York 1450–1499 (unpublished MA dissertation, York 1995–96), pp. 56–61.

Figure 5.4: Provenance of Gild Members Derived from Selected Account Rolls

Year	Unknown	Outside Yorkshire	Yorkshire (ex-York)	York City	Total	York* Percent	Reference YCA G/
1415–16	8	0	0	14	22	100.0	C99:1/2
1449–51	43	0	13	82	137	87.2	C99:3
1476–77	7	4	54	107	165	67.7	C99:4
1500–01	2	9	123	80	212	38.7	C100:3
1501–02	0	0	84	90	179	50.3	C100:4
1533–34	4	15	148	114	277	41.1	C102:3
1540–41	5	0	1	28	34	96.6	C103:2

* York entries expressed as a percentage of all entries where the location of entrants is known.

posthumously in 1432. It seems certain that a really close analysis of the entire membership would reveal it to have been, in the eyes of York's civic elite, part of a complex route to political power within the city's government. By the latter half of the fifteenth century, however, its influence was spreading far beyond the ambit of the city.

After its incorporation, the gild progressed rapidly towards a situation where it became identifiable as an institution of national importance.[116] Once again, this phenomenon can be seen most clearly through the account rolls. In 1449–51, a mere handful of the members were noted as living outside the city.[117] Two lay persons were entered as being of Ackworth and Selby. There were also six members of the Ingleby family who were (and still are) lords of Ripley. Up to its incorporation the gild seems to have been similar in scale and character to the exclusive fraternity of Corpus Christi in Boston, Lincolnshire, although the balance between lay and clerical members was different, reflecting the clerical government of the York gild.[118] After incorporation it began to assume the characteristics of such nationally influential fraternities as the Holy Trinity gilds of Coventry, Warwickshire, and Luton, Bedfordshire, which attracted massive memberships from their respective towns, and from the surrounding areas, but also from much further afield, from noble and gentle families, prosperous merchants, religious houses and clerics.[119]

By 1477 the York Corpus Christi Gild was at the height of its popularity. It was in this year that the master, William Grundale, introduced, among others, the

---

[116] Swanson, *Church and Society*, p. 281.

[117] YCA G C99:3

[118] MS Harley 4795. Fenning, 'The Guild of Corpus Christi', pp. 37–8.

[119] Ed. M. D. Harris, *The Register of the Guild of the Holy Trinity, St Mary, St John the Baptist and St Katherine of Coventry* (London, 1935). Ed. J. Lunn, *The Register of the Fraternity or Guild of the Holy and Undivided Trinity and Blessed Virgin Mary in the Parish Church of Luton in the County of Bedford from a.d. Mcccclxxv. to Mvcxlvi* (Dunstable, 1984).

Duke and Duchess of Gloucester, with their entourage, that included groups from the Neville strongholds of Middleham and Sheriff Hutton.[120] In all, 32% of the new membership came from outside York. There were married couples from Beilby, Bristol, Bulmer, Howsom, Helmsley, Kendal, Riccall and Skelton. Among the single lay members were persons from Durham and Easingwold, John Roos, gentleman, of Ingmanthorpe, Ralph Beyston, esquire, of Leeds and Lady Elizabeth Scrope of Upsall, the wife of Lord Scrope. Clerical entries included the prior and four monks of Newburgh Abbey. Clearly, since 1449–51 the net of membership had become much wider geographically, and whilst the entry of both high and low clergy had continued unabated, there had been an increase in the admission of county gentry.

By the turn of the century, entries from outside York had overtaken those from within the city, as Figure 5.4 demonstrates. These patterns of recruitment continued into the next century as exemplified by the account of 1500.[121] John Jakson, chantry chaplain at the altar of St John the Baptist in the Hospital of Holy Trinity Fossgate and gild master in that year, introduced several blocks of entrants, including the prior, the rector, and ten canons of St Oswald, Nostell, ten persons from the Wakefield area, two from Bedale, three from Gryton in Swaledale, as well as a dozen from locations close to York including Fulford, Dringhouses and Hessay. He also introduced a married couple from St Michael Crooked Lane and a stockfishmonger from St Magnus, both London parishes.

Over thirty years later, in 1533, similar recruiting patterns persisted.[122] The gild master in this year was William Lyghtfuyt, chantry chaplain of the altar of St Thomas the Martyr in Holy Trinity King's Court. He admitted the abbot and fourteen monks of the Abbey of Cockersand in Lancashire. Furthermore, he also introduced no fewer than forty-four entrants from Bradford, representing sixteen per cent of all new members that year. He introduced groups from Doncaster, Hull, Harewood, Kirkby Overblow and from the York parishes of All Saints Pavement, St Nicholas and St Sampson. This year also saw the introduction, mainly by keepers Robert Herdyng and Gregory Woddall, of a dozen new members from places in Holderness, including Hornsea, Swine, Rise and Moortown. This area was not represented in earlier sampled rolls. Clearly, the recorded increase in local gilds in this part of the East Riding was mirrored by a new interest in gilds further afield, and particularly, perhaps, those with a national reputation that offered indulgences consequent on membership.[123]

Whilst some groups from a locality outside York might have been recruited at home, by gild officers with local contacts, there is every reason to suppose that others joined while visiting the city. The York Corpus Christi festivities were attended by many visitors to York who would have come to see both the plays

---

120 YCA G C99:5.
121 *Ibid.*
122 YCA G C102:3. This is the best preserved of the three surviving rolls from the 1530s.
123 See Chapter 2, pp. 66–71.

and the procession. This may very well have been used as an occasion for the recruitment of new members. Other groups came on pilgrimages to the shrine of St William and, particularly, to that of Richard Scrope.[124] Furthermore, the city, as an administrative, ecclesiastical and mercantile centre, was busy throughout the year. Official visitors to York who were persuaded to become members seem to have joined with their retinues. This was the case with the Duke of Gloucester in 1476–77 and also of ecclesiastical dignitaries such as Robert Myton, prior of Byland, who joined with four brothers of the abbey in 1469–70.[125]

By the late fifteenth century the gild contained large numbers of nobles and gentry from all over the north of England. The families of Bigod, Clifford, Constable, Conyers, Darcy, Fairfax, Lovell, Neville, Palmes, Plumpton, Roos, Scrope, Stapleton, Strangeways, Vavasour and Wentworth are represented in profusion. A. J. Pollard has made a brief survey of the members of noble houses, and their affinities, who were also York Corpus Christi Gild members during the struggle between York and Lancaster.[126] He notes that the Percy family was unusual in not belonging, which suggests that the gild might, at this time, have been identified with the Neville, Yorkist party. This view is supported by the Duke of Gloucester's admission and by the increase in membership during Edward IV's reign. Clearly, the gild had a political role of regional and national importance, running parallel to its civic function. The outward demonstration of its status as an important power base, within the political structures of the city, region and nation, was its ability to mount appropriately lavish ceremonial. Its political, social and devotional roles had, therefore, to be underpinned by sound finances.

Gild Finance

The membership patterns of the gild cannot adequately be considered in isolation from its prosperity. Its year-by-year financial health is a barometer of a material success that enabled it to discharge its obligations, thereby ensuring that it continued to attract new members. Its success can also be measured in terms of what its members paid to join it, of how they valued their membership in monetary terms at different points in its development. A third measure lies in its possessions, their kind, their value and their purposes.

There is little doubt that the gild was a successful institution in financial terms throughout its life, as Figure 5.5 demonstrates. The only extant roll to show a negative balance, that for 1478, is exceptional in that it deals almost exclusively with real estate, associated with the recent acquisition of St Thomas' Hospital from Holy Trinity Priory.[127] Although gild offerings are included in the 'receipts'

---

[124] B. Dobson, 'The Later Middle Ages, 1215–1500', in *A History of York Minster*, ed. G. E. Aylmer and R. Cant (Oxford, 1977), pp. 44–109 (p. 108).

[125] MS Lansdowne 304, fols. 74v, 59v.

[126] Pollard, *North Eastern England During the Wars of the Roses*, pp. 189–90.

[127] YCA G 13, 14.

Figure 5.5: Income and Expenditurs of the Gild

Year	Receipts	Expenses	Balance	Roll
1415–16	921	181	740	G C99:1/2
1449–51	1241	908	333	G C99:3
1459–60		indecipherable		G C99:4
1476–77	603	202	401	G C99:5
1478–79	873	896	–23	G C99:6
1489–90	818	542	276	G C99:7
1495–96	581	335	246	G C99:8
1497–98	563	334	229	G C100:1
1498–99	640	250	390	G C100:2
1500–01	624	386	238	G C100:3
1501–02	377	356	21	G C100:4
1504–05	533	326	207	G C100:5
1505–06	506	433	73	G C100:6
1507–08	492	289	203	G C101:1
1510–11	568	289	279	G C101:2
1511–12	598	309	289	G C101:3
1515–16	575	253	322	G C101:4
1519–20	614	449	165	G C102:1
1532–33	476	432	44	G C102:2
1533–34	648	402	246	G C102:3
1534–35	478	365	113	G C103:1
1540–41	446	361	85	G C103:2

Receipts: to the nearest shilling. Includes balance carried over from the previous year.

Expenses: to the nearest shilling.

Balance: annual balance of income over expenditure to the nearest shilling.

item of the account, there is no list of entries. The membership register shows that a substantial number of new members were introduced that year, including Henry Vavasour, high sheriff of Yorkshire, the Abbot of Meaux, the Prioress of Thicket and members of the city's mercantile elite, including Nicholas Lancaster and Bartram Dawson.[128] In terms of both the quantity and the quality of new members, the income from entries in 1478 must have been considerable. Despite the complete appearance of the roll, it seems certain that a second account relating to this year is missing.

The largest positive balances occurred in the earlier years of the gild's history. Thereafter, whilst the balance fluctuated from time to time, an average of approximately £10 was carried over each year. This pattern appears to be at vari-

---

[128] MS Lansdowne 304, fol. 76v–78r. Lancaster was Lord Mayor in 1485 and 1493, Dawson in 1511. See Appendix 3.

Figure 5.6: Gild Entry Fees Compared with Membership

Year	Receipts	Pence	Members	Average	Roll
1415–16	57s.4d.	688	22	31.3	G C99:1/2
1449–51	135s.0d.	1620	137	11.8	G C99:3
1459–60		indecipherable			G C99:4
1476–77	106s.2d.	1274	165	7.7	G C99:5
1478–79		no introit			G C99:6
1489–90	100s.8d.	1208	201	6.0	G C99:7
1495–96	63s.7d.	763	150	5.0	G C99:8
1497–98	59s.6d.	714	119	6.0	G C100:1
1498–99	116s.9d.	1401	240	5.8	G C100:2
1500–01	117s.10d.	1414	212	6.7	G C100:3
1501–02	118s.4d.	1420	179	7.9	G C100:4
1504–05	59s.9d.	717	149	4.8	G C100:5
1505–06	51s.4d.	616	133	4.6	G C100:6
1507–08	35s.4d.	424	111	3.8	G C101:1
1510–11	53s.4d.	640	185	3.5	G C101:2
1511–12	97s.11d.	1175	336	3.5	G C101:3
1515–16	60s.13d.	733	213	3.4	G C101:4
1519–20	43s.8d.	524	176	3.0	G C102:1
1532–33	22s.10d.	274	121	2.3	G C102:2
1533–34	47s.3d.	567	277	2.0	G C102:3
1534–35	10s.10d.	130	88	1.5	G C103:1
1540–41	6s.10d.	82	34	2.4	G C103:2

Year: the years for which accounts survive.

Receipts: total of receipts, in respect of membership, appearing in each of the account rolls under the item of Introit, given in shillings and pence. A small number of fees paid in kind are not taken into consideration.

Pence: the above totals converted to pence.

Members: the number of members for each year. Where the numbers shown in the introit of an account roll are uncertain because of the condition of the document, the Members' Register (BL Lansdowne 304) has been used. Husbands and wives are counted as two persons, although usually they paid only one membership fee.

Average: the average fee paid by a member in a given year, arrived at by dividing the total fees by the number of members. The amount is in pence, with fractions expressed in decimals to the nearest tenth of a penny.

Roll: the reference number of each account roll.

ance with that of the admissions to the gild. Generally speaking, it appears to have been at its richest when it had the smallest number of members. This illusion is created by several factors. The entry fee for members fluctuated, declining sharply in the sixteenth century. Parallel to this was a gradual accumulation of real estate, the income from which provided an increasingly large proportion of the gild's income, but which required a high level of expenditure in maintenance. Furthermore, much of its vast wealth was invested in its possessions, especially its treasure.

The gild's ordinances laid down that entrants should pay to the gild what their consciences dictated.[129] The account rolls show that this amount declined steadily throughout the gild's history, as Figure 5.6 shows. Thus, whilst the average payment was as much as 2s.7d. in 1415, it had declined, by 1500, to just over 6d. and, by 1540, to under 2d. Although the amount was theoretically a matter of conscience, there seems to have been a recommended rate for different groups of people at different times. Whether this was a matter of advice by the introducing gild officer, or simply a tacit understanding between entrants, is hard to establish. That all of the forty-four members from Bradford, in 1533–34, for example, paid 2d. each is surely no coincidence. A brief survey of the payments made in individual years, by different categories of member, supports the view that the amount paid was more a matter of policy than conscience.

Married couples almost invariably paid a single fee for both partners throughout all the accounts. In 1415–16, the lower clergy generally paid either 2s. or 20d. for entry, whilst lay people paid either 3s.4d. or 6s.8d. By 1449, the customary fee for most members varied between one and two shillings, although two entries were paid in kind: John Plumar and his wife contributed a torch worth 3s.4d. and Richard Bukler and his wife offered a silver crucifix worth 2s.[130] Some single women, however, paid only 6d. or 8d. and family memberships, where children were included, generally cost 3s.6d. Although the Duke and Duchess of Gloucester paid 6s.8d. in 1476, most entrance fees in that year were 12d. but servants and some single women, including widows, paid only 6d. By 1500 the introduction of a high proportion of outsiders had complicated the position. York chaplains generally paid 12d. but parochial clerics from elsewhere generally contributed 8d. or 6d. Lay people from the city paid sums varying from 12d. to 4d., with servants paying 4d. Most of those from outside York paid less than citizens, although three Londoners, in 1500, paid 2s. for a married couple and 12d. for a single man. By 1533 clerical fees were 4d., although some clerics from outside York paid only 2d., which was the most common fee for all lay persons, but some couples paid 4d. and some widows and single women paid only a penny. These levels were still maintained in 1540, in the legible portions of the roll. In every account in which they are represented, the higher clergy, and gentle and noble entrants usually paid rather more than the average rate.

---

[129] MS Lansdowne 304, fol. 18r: 'onerantes tamen conscientias eorundem sic intrare volentium'.

[130] YCA G C99:3.

These figures reflect two broad trends. One was the decline in the prosperity of the city's mercantile and textile groups, which has been discussed else-where.[131] Less affluent entrants became less generous to the gild as times became harder. Only the wealthiest paid more, according to conscience, than the general-ity. Even in these cases the actual sums were lower in the sixteenth century. In 1476 the Prior of Newburgh paid 2s.8d. and each monk 12d., but, in 1533, the Abbot of Cockersand himself contributed only 12d. and his monks paid only 4d. each. The other trend was a broadening of the membership that took place, after the gild's incorporation. The recruitment of more members clearly meant that a higher proportion of them were less able to afford a large entrance fee. The entry of a greater number of new members from outside York, after the gild's incorpo-ration, also seems to have affected the level of payments. A member who lived at some distance from the city might be less likely to benefit regularly from the social contacts that the gild provided and would find it more difficult to attend its feasts and festivals or to take advantage of its funeral arrangements. Such members generally seem to have considered that a lower entrance fee than that paid by York residents was appropriate.

Whilst the contributions of new members were a factor in ensuring a favour-able balance of income over expenditure during the whole life of the gild, an important part of its annual income was, from at least 1478, derived from real estate.[132] The account roll for that year is the first that mentions property transac-tions. It records the purchase and refurbishment of buildings associated with the hospital outside Micklegate Bar that had formerly belonged to Holy Trinity Priory. This involved the withdrawal of £40.3s.5½d. from the gild's stock, for the purchase of seven tenements in Baggergate, and expenditure on constructions, including a barn and a new house at the Bar. From this date onwards, building repairs became an important element in the gild's expenditure. It also shows a gross income of 18s.6d. from rents at Micklegate Bar, and in Monkgate and Bag-gergate. Figure 5.7 shows that from that date, receipts from the farm of tenements became an increasingly important element in the gild's income. By the 1530s they had become central to its financial success.

Although the actual receipts from property do not show such a dramatic rise as does their share of the gild's annual income, their values had almost doubled between 1489 and 1541, despite a general decline in rents in the city over this period.[133] If rents were falling at the same time as the gild's income from this source was growing, the gild must have continued to increase its real estate. In 1546, Henry VIII's commissioners identified substantial property holdings by the gild.[134] As well as the tenements in Baggergate, by Micklegate Bar and in Monk-

---

131 See Chapter 4, p. 120.

132 YCA G C99.6 onwards.

133 S. Rees Jones, 'Property Tenure and Rents: some Aspects of the Topography and Economy of Medieval York' (unpublished D.Phil. thesis York, 1987), p. 261. Bartlett, 'The Expansion and Decline of York', 17–33 (pp. 29–33).

134 *Certificates*, I, pp. 54–5, Skaife, *Corpus Christi*, pp. 285–7.

Figure 5.7: Income from the Farm of Tenements

Date	Tenements			Income			Percentage	Reference
	£	s	d	£	s	d		
1489–90	6	14	8	40	17	8½	17.1	G C99:7
1495–96	7	16	4	29	0	14	27.6	G C99:8
1497–98	9	4	8	28	2	6½	32.1	G C100:1
1498–99	8	18	10	31	19	10¼	28.1	G C100:2
1500–01	9	8	0	31	4	5¼	29.0	G C100:3
1501–02	9	8	0	30	17	2¾	29.0	G C100:4
1504–05	9	7	0	26	12	6¼	33.3	G C100:5
1505–06	9	7	0	25	6	0¾	36.0	G C100:6
1507–08	9	7	0	24	11	8¾	36.0	G C101:1
1510–11	9	6	10	28	8	3¾	32.1	G C101:2
1511–12	9	7	1	29	18	5¾	30.1	G C101:3
1515–16	9	8	1	28	15	0¼	31.0	G C101:4
1519–20	10	2	9	30	14	3¾	32.3	G C102:1
1532–33	12	16	1	23	16	(?)	54.2	G C102:2
1533–34	12	15	0	32	7	7¾	40.6	G C102:3
1534–35	12	14	4	23	17	9¼	54.2	G C103:1
1540–41	12	13	0	22	6	1¾	59.1	G C103:2

Tenements: gross income derived from the fee farm of tenements.
Income: total income from all sources.
Percentage: income from the fee farm of tenements as a proportion of total income to the nearest pound.

gate, that were previously noted, they recorded two in Thursday Market, two in Holgate, two in Buttercrambe, one in Naburn and one in Stamford Bridge, all to the annual value of £12.15s.4d. This sum tallies closely with the gild's income of £12.13s. from tenements in the account of 1540. These are, of course, rental, not capital values and they do not include any consideration of the actual value of gild houses and of the Hospital of St Thomas. They also reported on goods to the value of £11.10s.5d. and plate worth £219.13s.6d.

There is little doubt that much of the gild's real wealth lay in the goods that it accumulated and its growing prosperity can be charted through extant documentary evidence relating to them. An early list of its possessions was recorded on the dorse of the account for 1415.[135] This is an interesting collection of comparatively modest items, when compared with later lists. It includes pieces of equipment used in the Corpus Christi procession, such as torches, protective cloths, embroidered banners and, more mysteriously, ten painted castles (*castella*) with little canvas bags to cover them, and a set of three dozen wooden 'roundletts' that were to be placed on 'revetts', forty of which were newly bought

[135]   YCA G C99:1.

and forty of which were old. The inventory goes on to list large quantities of table-linen, cups, plates, bowls and cooking utensils, for use at the gild feast. Significantly, the salt cellars were of pewter. The silverware comprised one piece, two spoons and a mazer. Two books of ordinances were listed, perhaps the register and the obituary, and two letters of indulgence, one from the Archbishop of York and one from the Bishop of Carlisle. This record indicates that, despite the absence of a shrine, the early gild was more concerned with the proper equipping of the procession, and the holding of an elaborate feast, than with a display of wealth.

There is little direct indication that the first shrine was being planned as early as this first extant account. However, at this time the gild was keeping a large sum in its coffers.[136] £35.10s.7d. had been carried over from the previous year and £37.0s.13½d. was passed on to the new officials at the end of this account. It seems likely that a sum of such magnitude was being saved for some specific purpose. There is no extant account relating to the 1430s but the agreement with the city over the shrine makes it clear that it was built at the gild's expense and would continue to be embellished by it.[137]

The inventory of 1465 is a remarkable contrast to that of 1415.[138] An account of the silver-gilt Spofford shrine, worth £256, is followed by a long list of jewels associated with it.[139] Despite its value, however, it was not a very large object, as two men were able to carry it in procession.[140] Many, but not all, of the jewels are valued and, in some cases, the names of donors recorded. A few examples must suffice to give some impression of the range and value of this collection. A great monstrance of crystal, with silver angels, worth £40.6s.8d, was surmounted by an image of the Trinity. There were several tabernacles, including one of gold and pearls, with an image of the Virgin, a large number of crucifixes and crosses, in precious metals with jewels, and other images of the Virgin and of St Laurence, St Mary Magdalene, and Agnus Dei. Hung about the shrine were many rings, beads, girdles, spoons and cups, all of gold or silver, many set with stones. The gild's reliquaries contained a piece of the True Cross, relics of St Thomas of Canterbury, St Francis and St Thomas of Lancaster and two precious stones from the tomb of St Katherine. One of the chief treasures was the famous mazer that had either belonged to Archbishop Richard Scrope, or had been blessed by him, and which had reached the gild through Agnes, the widow of the former mayor, Henry Wyman.[141]

The account of the jewels is followed by an inventory of vestments and of a number of documents, including the charter, which was valued at £10, the membership book, copies of indulgences and the account rolls. The apparatus for carrying the shrine in the procession was embellished with images of the evangelists and of sixteen angels, with shields and scrolls in copper-gilt, a picture of the

136 See Figure 5.5.
137 YCA A:15.
138 MS Lansdowne 304, fols. 2r–5v.
139 See p. 161 above.
140 YCA G C100:1.
141 The mazer is now in the York Minster treasury. See p. 193 below.

Trinity and a four-piece blue valance, decorated with gold chalices and stars. The gild's copy of the Creed Play is recorded along with the banners and theatrical properties used in its performance, including a mitre, a crown, a key of St Peter and diadems for Christ and his apostles. Associated with the fourteen torches of the gild were the 'castles', banners, napkins, 'roundels' and 'revettes' that appeared in the 1415 account. The inventory ends with items of cooking equipment.

Many of the gild's jewels were donated by its members, presumably in their lifetimes, but some were bequeathed to it. The first, wooden, shrine received thirty-three bequests recorded in the probate registers between 1430 and 1449. Many of these were bequests of money, to pay for the shrine's construction, like that of Alice Upsall, the widow of a merchant in Coneystreet, who left 3s.4d. *ad fabricatorum feretri*.[142] Others left jewellery, to decorate it. Marion Marton, for example, the widow of a leatherworker of St Crux, in 1441, left a ring of gold that had a silver-gilt crucifix hanging from it.[143] Such bequests were also commonly made to the new shrine. As late as 1534 Janet Sparke bequeathed it her set of coral beads.[144]

The magnificence of its treasure, as an adjunct to its ceremonial, was a further public demonstration of the gild's wealth and power. Those members who added to the decoration of the shrine participated in this, as well as in the sanctity of a cult object. Such a donation enhanced the prestige of the donor's family within the social context of the gild. It ensured that the gift would be recorded in the fraternity's archive, to the lasting prestige of the giver, and that he or she would be especially remembered in the gild's prayers for ever. The gift itself would remain to proclaim, publicly, the gild's growing pre-eminence.

The importance of public demonstrations of the gild's status was further reflected in its paid servants. It was an employer of both permanent and temporary staff. It was already paying a salary to its beadle in 1449. In later accounts the beadles were named and this practice continued until the last extant account in 1540. His duties included the supervision of torches and torchbearers on gild occasions. His appearance was clearly important to the officers who provided him with a gown. When John Holme took over the post from John Dykson in 1496, the gild paid 13s. for a new one.[145] His badge of office was silver gilt and worth 41s.4d., enabling him to cut an impressive figure on ceremonial occasions.[146]

The 1476 account shows a salary of £4.13s.4d. paid to Gawain Byrkheade as gild chaplain. This post, too, continued to be sustained throughout the rest of the life of the gild, and the holders' names can be traced through the account rolls. It may be significant that the last named chaplain, William Watson, was recorded, uniquely, as being also chaplain of the gild hospital.[147] That a governing body of

---

142 BIHR PR 2 640r–v.
143 BIHR PR 2 27r–28r.
144 BIHR PR 11 85r.

145 YCA G C100:1.
146 MS Lansdowne 304, fols. 2r–3v.
147 YCA G C103:2.

chaplains needed to employ yet another chaplain to serve the gild might seem superfluous. It does not appear to have been necessary before the gild's incorporation. However, the increase in membership in the 1570s probably laid far too great a burden on the master and keepers, all of whom held other posts. The employment of the gild chaplain also might explain an inconsistency that surrounds Corpus Christi Gild funerals. If members were entitled to a funeral, why was it that so many testators made extra provision for one in their wills? The explanation might be that ordinary gild funerals were routinely conducted by the gild chaplain, but that the attendance of the master, keepers, beadle and torches was conditional on additional payment by those members who were sufficiently wealthy to demand this in their wills.

Payments for other duties seem to have been on the basis of occasional fees rather than a salary. The 1496 account, for example, shows fees for routine clerical tasks, such as maintaining the register and drawing up accounts.[148] It also details payments to clerics for duties in the annual procession. 2d. each was paid to the cross-bearer and to the four who carried the baldequin. The seven men who carried torches also received 2d. but the two who bore the shrine were each paid 3d. Such payments were also made in succeeding accounts. Gratuities were paid to officials employed by other bodies. The 1496 account records payments to the city bellman, for proclaiming obits, and those of 1505 and 1533 gratuities to the sacristan of Holy Trinity Priory and to the janitor of the Minster, *in rewardo*.[149]

Throughout the entire sequence of its accounts the gild never seems to have encountered any difficulties in meeting such obligations. It was clearly a successful institution in financial terms. Even in the difficult days of the early 1540s, it maintained a small balance of income over expenditure and continued to pay its chaplain's salary.[150] By this time, however, other pressures were being brought to bear on the gild's successful survival. Under these circumstances, lavish demonstrations of economic success were probably a positive disadvantage.

Dissolution

Although the dissolution of the religious gilds will be discussed in detail in a subsequent chapter, it is appropriate, in concluding this one, to look briefly at the demise of the York Corpus Christi Gild. The entry of 277 new members in 1533 suggests no diminution in its popularity, but, as figure 5.8 shows, admissions over the following twelve years demonstrate an interesting pattern, especially when it is related to political events.

A decline in membership can be seen to have followed the appointment of Cranmer to the see of Canterbury and the rise of Cromwell in 1533. This decline

---

[148] YCA G C100:1.
[149] YCA G C100:6, C102:3.

[150] YCA G C103:2.

Figure 5.8: Membership 1533–1546

Year	Members	Year	Members
1533–34	277	1540–41A	7
1534–35	89	1540–41B	39
1335–36	73	1541–42	80
1536–37	42	1542–43	80
1537–38	n/r	1543–44	178
1538–39	n/r	1544–45	119
1539–40	36	1545–46	137

accelerated during the suppression of the lesser monasteries in 1536, and no admissions at all were recorded between 1537 and 1539, in the aftermath of the Pilgrimage of Grace. Obviously the gild felt that its position was under threat, and not without cause. The forces of reform were already being felt within the city. The last recorded performance of the Creed Play took place in 1535. Although a performance was proposed in 1545, it seems not to have been approved by the civic authorities.[151] However, following the confusion of 1540, where two membership lists were compiled, with different officials recorded, there was a marked upturn in admissions. This coincided with the fall and execution of Cromwell and the beginning of a period of religious conservatism which continued until the death of Henry VIII.

The high number of entries during the gild's last years might not have been based entirely on a false sense of security. It seems possible that the act of joining the Corpus Christi Gild was seen as being, in some sense, a positive vote for the old order of society that was under attack by the forces of protestantism, which the king now rejected. It was felt, perhaps, that an organization of such size, wealth and prestige might, against all the odds, be able to withstand future assaults by the reformers. If this was their hope, it was to be disappointed.

There is no account or membership list for 1546. In that year, the king's commissioners visited the city and reported on the gild. The city government made no official move to preserve it, as they attempted in the case of the gild of St Christopher and St George.[152] The shrine and plate evidently disappeared into the royal coffers. There was, however, one notable exception to this. The mazer that had belonged to Archbishop Scrope found its way into the hands of the mistery of cordwainers, who later engraved it as belonging to them. This was clearly a way of concealing an object of great veneration from the commissioners. It was entrusted to the Dean and Chapter, when the cordwainers' company was dissolved, in the nineteenth century, and is now in the Minster treasury.[153]

Although the gild itself was dissolved, its hospital of St Thomas survived the

---

[151] Johnson, 'Plays of Religious Guilds', pp. 63–4.

[152] *YCR*, V, p. 8.

[153] Skaife, *Corpus Christi*, p. 291.

commissioners' depredations and succeeded in retaining the gild's lands and tenements. How this was achieved is not clear, but the commissioners' certificate lays great emphasis on the gild's role in running the hospital. It has already been noted that the last known gild chaplain was also described as being chaplain of the hospital.[154] This may well have all been part of a carefully prepared device to ensure that at least some of the gild's wealth remained within the city. At all events, it was being run, in 1551, by its then master, William Pindar, who invited the current mayor and aldermen to become brethren of the hospital.[155] The mayor was elected master ex officio. This was still the situation in 1557, when a Special Commission enquired into the links between the gild and the hospital, which was still in possession of its lands and rents, and was being officially run by each current Lord Mayor of the city as its master.[156] The hospital survived on its original site until 1862, and remained a civic responsibility.[157] That both the hospital and the precious mazer were preserved shows that, whilst the city's governing body was less vocal in its support of the Corpus Christi Gild than of St Christopher and St George, it was prepared to save what it could of the gild's assets in a more covert but, ultimately, a more effective way.

Conclusion

Despite the pious intentions of its founders, the gild, even in its relatively modest beginnings, seems to have had a political dimension. The early involvement of the city elite and the ability of some early members to gain commercial advantage from it prefigured later trends. The construction of the first shrine, and the city's involvement in its disposition, marked a point where the city and the gild drew even closer together. This identification was underpinned by the increasingly rich ceremonial that allowed its wealthier members to display themselves in their liveries, with their families and retinues, to the enhancement of their prestige and social standing.[158] At the same time, it allowed its poorer brothers and sisters to feel that they were part of a web of influence that might help their advancement. Basically the gild represented the established order in its doctrines, in its relationship with the city and, ultimately, with the national government. This was confirmed by its incorporation. This seminal event, however, altered both the constitution and, to some extent, the ethos of the gild. Its expansion during the 1470s transformed it into a quasi-national institution that extended its influence over the whole of the north of England and beyond. It pro-

---

154 See p. 191 above.
155 Skaife, *Corpus Christi*, p. 298.
156 *Ibid.*, pp. 313–16.
157 *Ibid.*, p. xiv.
158 Although its appearance is not known, lay members of the gild wore a livery. YML L2(4) fols. 200v–201v 1420 John Bouche apothecary of the parish of St Michael le Belfrey mentioned his livery of Corpus Christi in his will.

vided a web of contacts within which gentry and merchants might meet to talk finance or politics, where ambitious artisans might seek the social acceptance that could lead to public office, where clergy from all over the county could discuss benefices and career moves and where powerful figures could manipulate their affinities and make political manoeuvres. It provided a focus for many disparate groups and interests, offering them a common fraternal bond within a framework of traditional piety. Its dissolution was only possible when its devotional practices ceased to coincide with the policies of the central government.

In describing the national and regional importance of the Corpus Christi Gild it is, however, important not to lose sight of the fact that it was not the only great gild in York. At the height of its influence it was only part of a network of at least three gilds of, at the very least, regional significance, that were themselves just part of the city's complicated web of fraternities. Eileen White's work has made it clear that the St Christopher and St George Gild was even more intimately involved with the civic government than Corpus Christi.[159] Furthermore, her pamphlet, which draws heavily on York wills, tends to underestimate its influence beyond the city. We have seen that bequests to it from outside the city exceeded those of Corpus Christi, and White herself emphasizes the membership of Edward, prince of Wales, in 1483, and the gild's connections with the Scrope family.[160] Testators often made bequests to the fraternities of both Corpus Christi and St Christopher, as well as to the only slightly less popular St Anthony Gild.[161]

There is no doubt, however, that the Corpus Christi Gild possessed a special character, which is underlined by the manner in which it continued to attract new members during the 1540s. It commended itself widely throughout the population of the North, not merely through its political and commercial contacts, which other gilds could also offer. Its uniqueness lay in its sanctity, in its support of a popular cult that attracted, for most of its life, official encouragement and, above all, by its status as a holy confraternity led by the city's priests.

---

[159] White, *The St Christopher and St George Guild of York*, pp. 2–4, 18.

[160] *Ibid.*, p. 15. Figure 4.12 above.

[161] See Chapter 4, pp. 127–8.

CHAPTER SIX

Case Study Two:
The Gild of St Mary in Holy Trinity, Hull

The St Mary Gild of Holy Trinity parish was closely involved with the mercantile and civic elite of Hull.[1] Lacking the national dimension of great civic gilds, such as Corpus Christi, York, it was a relatively modest institution, sited in a borough of comparatively recent foundation. The records of its ceremonial and feasts suggest that its devotional and social functions followed patterns that have been examined elsewhere, giving us some insight into their practical organization.[2] Less typical, perhaps, was the gild's involvement in overseas trade.[3] This activity illuminates the relationship between the gild and the merchant community and between it and more overtly mercantile organizations. It is also clear that the gild had a close relationship with the town government. Most mayors of the borough also held office in the gild.[4] To what extent its disappearance from the record in 1536 was related to these factors will be examined.

The principal source of the gild's affairs is an account book, providing an unbroken record of its economic fortunes between 1463 and 1536.[5] Therefore, this case study will centre on the gild's financial fortunes, and its evolution will be seen largely in these terms. A note on the dorse of the rear endpaper of the account book claims, in a medieval hand, that it was begun in 1458 by John Eland of Hull. Eland was steward of the gild in the year ending 1464.[6] The first surviving account is for the year ending 1463, suggesting that some initial pages have been lost. The earlier entries are well written and carefully kept, containing much detailed information. They are penned in clerkly hands with some elaborate capitals. Both the calligraphy and the content deteriorate markedly, however, in the sixteenth century, when most of the entries are very untidy and contain little detail. The last entry is undated but probably belongs to the year ending 1536.

---

[1] Holy Trinity Church in Hull was technically a chapel of the parish of Hessle until 1661. *VCH ER*, I, pp. 287, 294.

[2] See Chapter 3, p. 105.

[3] See pp. 204–5 below.

[4] See Appendix 7.

[5] KHRO BRA 87/8 (previously M11).

[6] See Appendix 4.

The Evolution of the Gild

The St Mary Gild in the Chapel of Holy Trinity was already in existence in 1391, when William Wyllyngham, a Hull craftsman of Holy Trinity parish, bequeathed it the sum of 6s.8d.[7] It was an entirely separate fraternity from the gild of St Mary in St Mary's Chapel. Both gilds were individually left £1 by Joan Gregg in 1438, demonstrating that they were distinct entities.[8] The gild of St Mary in St Mary made a return in 1389, in which it claimed foundation in 1357 and where its connection with the Chapel of St Mary is clearly stated.[9] The two gilds are, however, confused in the Hull volume of the Victoria County History and this error has since been perpetuated elsewhere.[10] St Mary's Gild in St Mary was still active in 1451, but was not recorded subsequently.[11] The continued existence of the St Mary Gild in Holy Trinity is shown by two wills from the early 1450s, pre-dating the account book.[12] It seems likely that the extant book was a continuation of a previous one, now lost.

Unlike the documentation of the Corpus Christi Gild in York, the account book does not show us the pattern of a gild's history from its foundation to its dissolution.[13] It picks up the story in 1463, towards the middle of its recorded existence, and takes it through to a dozen years prior to the date of the national dissolution of religious gilds.[14] It provides an unbroken list of the principal officers of the gild, an alderman and two stewards each year, and a year-to-year account of the gild's cash-in-hand, as shown in Appendix 6. It does not, however, provide any indication of membership. The income for admissions, even in the most detailed of the accounts, is amalgamated with that from the gild's rental. William Haryngton was regularly paid a shilling every year for keeping the rental between 1475 and 1487, and admissions may well have been an item on it, but it has not survived.[15]

The information that the book provides, taken together with some other Hull sources, does, however, provide a picture of the changing fortunes and preoccupations of the gild. From relative affluence in 1463, partly based on commercial ventures, the gild descended into a period of financial crisis in the late 1470s,

---

7 BIHR PR 1 34r. He owned property in the town and bequeathed the tools of his unspecified trade.
8 BIHR PR 3 555v–556v.
9 PRO C 47/46/451.
10 *VCH ER*, I, p. 84. E.g. H. Calvert, *A History of Hull* (London and Chichester, 1978), p. 96.
11 BIHR PR 2 228v, will of Robert Birdsay.
12 BIHR PR 2 231r–v John Harpham. *Test. Ebor.* II, p. 171, 1454 William Clederhow merchant.
13 See Chapter 5 above.
14 All references to the year of individual entries are to the year in which the accounts are dated in the book. Thus, the account for 1463 is for the year ending 1463. The accounts were drawn up and dated on variable dates and days of the week in late April and early May, between Easter and Rogation Day.
15 KHRO BRA 87/8, pp. 31–71 *passim*.

probably brought about by a combination of bad debts and declining trade.[16] From then until 1500, its fortunes underwent a gradual up-turn. This was related to increased landholding, arising especially from the profits accruing from the farm of a large property that the gild had acquired from John Haynson and his wife to finance an obit.[17] Thereafter it maintained a healthy financial surplus, from year to year, until the end of the record. However, many of the sixteenth century accounts were not rendered in a full form, and detailed, itemized entries ceased altogether after 1512. This change in the gild's accounting practices suggests a change in the attitude of its members towards it and possibly in its entire ethos. From 1513, assumptions concerning the gild's functions are somewhat speculative.

Gild Functions

The largest item of expenditure in all the itemized accounts was the salary of the gild chaplain. In 1463, William Hundersley was paid £5 and this remained the standard rate until 1496, when it was increased, but this seems to have been a result of consolidating the obit fee into the total.[18] Entries after 1512 do not itemize the chaplain's salary. A bellman, possibly the town bellman, was paid 8d. for his services until 1467, when he received a sudden and unexplained cut in his remuneration. Thereafter he was paid 2d. until 1483 when the amount doubled.[19] By 1500 it had reverted to 8d., although in this account he is said be lighting candles, presumably additionally to his duties of advertising the obits and feasts.[20]

Also related to the gild's corporate devotional and ceremonial activities was the purchase of wax. The maintenance and renewal of torches and candlesticks and the carrying of lights were major items. The amounts were variable and were expressed in different ways from year to year. The totals for these payments in 1463 and in 1464 were under 10s. In 1465 the sum amounted to £1.4s.11½d., as two new torches and 11lbs. of wax, an unusually large supply, were bought.[21] This total was exceptional, however. The account for 1499 makes it clear that torches were carried on Corpus Christi Day and on the gild day.[22]

We can see, from payments made to bearers of the Rood, recorded in the first account in the book in 1463 and continuing up to 1505, that the fraternity carried it in an annual procession every Holy Cross or Rogation Day. There were also entries recording the purchase of cords for guiding the Rood on these occasions.[23] From 1507 references to the Rood ceased and the carrying of a banner (*vexilla*) was substituted.[24] Whether this was a banner representing the Rood,

16 See pp. 204–5 below.
17 See pp. 207–11 below.
18 KRHO BRA 87/8, pp. 2, 99.
19 *Ibid.*, p. 60.
20 *Ibid.*, pp. 44, 109.

21 *Ibid.*, pp. 2, 4–6.
22 *Ibid.*, pp. 107.
23 *Ibid.*, pp. 37, 99.
24 *Ibid.*, pp. 120, 124, 125.

whether the previous Rood was itself a banner, or whether this was a real change in practice is unclear. The cost of bearing it escalated from 1s. in 1464 to 2s. in 1477.

There were annual payments for an angel between 1463 and 1466.[25] It seems possible that the angel appeared in connection with the gild obit, because in 1476 the gild paid 7s. for painting an angel for this service.[26] It seems likely that the gild decided to substitute an image for a live actor, perhaps in the interests of economy. No further payments were made either to actors or angels. Although the scale of the gild's ceremonial life was relatively unspectacular, it was evidently an active one, involving at least three annual processions on Corpus Christi, Rogation Day and the gild day.

The gild's treasure was entirely concerned with its ceremonial and devotional practices and largely consisted of vestments and altarcloths. An inventory was added to the account of 1471. This was repeated in 1472, 1473, 1474, 1476, 1477, and 1479 and then annually up to 1482. On each occasion the list was substantially the same. It is not impressive, by comparison with that of Corpus Christi Gild, in York, for the same period. Its only plate was a chalice for use by the chaplain, its only book was his mass book. Its more valuable vestments included one of cloth-of-gold, with a matching corporax. One of its altar cloths was embroidered with the Coronation of the Virgin with St Katherine and St Margaret. Another was of damask with flowers of gold, with a matching frontal, and a third was white with crosses, for the lenten season. The gild also owned a privy chest that was bound with iron.[27]

There was a cloth-of-gold ' baldkyn' for the purchase of which the sum of 2s. was contributed, in 1470, by Henry Pacok, the master of the hospital attached to the Hull Charterhouse, as executor of the will of John Hedon, chaplain.[28] This cloth was to be placed on the tomb of the dead on the day of the gild obit. The account does not clarify whether the tomb in question was a symbolic one, to represent all gild members, or the tomb of John Hedon. It might also have figured in actual funerals. The St John the Baptist Gild of Dunstable owned a very valuable embroidered pall of cloth of gold and crimson velvet for use at the funerals of brothers and sisters.[29] The practice of covering coffins during individual anniversaries, which replicated funeral ceremonial, was common at this time.[30] Thomas Wodd, draper, who was mayor of Hull in 1480 and audited the accounts of the gild on three occasions, left his bed coverings, or hangings, to drape his grave

---

[25] *Ibid.*, pp. 2, 4, 6, 8.

[26] *Ibid.*, p. 10.

[27] *Ibid.*, p. 27.

[28] *Ibid.*, p. 15.

[29] It was donated to the gild by the Fayrey family, *circa* 1505, and is now housed in the Victoria and Albert Museum. I am indebted to J. Lunn for this information.

[30] Burgess, 'The Anniversary in Medieval Bristol', p. 87.

during his annual obit and to be hung up with all the others on the Feast of St George.[31]

Such possessions as these were intrinsically valuable but required maintenance. From time to time, expenditure on the washing and repair of gild vestments and altar furnishings was necessary. In 1464, 8d. was expended on washing albs, amices and towels, and Robert Tapy was paid 6d. for mending altarcloths.[32] Occasionally such items had to be renewed. In 1472, £1.16s.8d. was spent on a new set of white vestments for the use of the gild.[33] Such a large outlay must have been worrying at a time when annual income was steadily outstripping annual expenditure. Repetitions of the gild's inventory ceased after 1482, although Peter Lyne, goldsmith, received 8s.4d. for ornamenting the gild chalice in 1483.[34]

A particularly interesting outlay, in 1491, was 8d. for covering the copy of the gild's indulgence.[35] Unfortunately, no other record of this seems to have survived. The presence of an indulgence, whoever may have granted it, implied official ecclesiastical recognition of the gild and would be an important incentive for potential members. The indulgence might have been an old document at that time. If it were not, however, it might be related to other signs that the membership was increasing towards the end of the fifteenth century.

Once the gild's affluence was clearly established, in the 1490s, it made occasional large payments to devotional and worthy causes within its parish and, subsequently, the town at large. In 1490, it contributed £5.7s.6½d. towards building a new organ in Holy Trinity Church.[36] In 1498, £10 was paid towards the construction of the tower and, in 1500, a further £10 was given to make a shrine to carry the Corpus Christi.[37] It is not possible to say whether the shrine was intended for general use in the church or was in response to an unrecorded initiative by the parish Corpus Christi Gild, although the latter is the more likely explanation. During the early sixteenth century, the St Mary Gild put its surplus funds to the service of the town on at least three occasions, in 1517, 1518 and 1520, when it consented to contribute substantial sums to the repair of the town walls.[38] Between 1520 and 1522 there were three payments, totalling £11.16s.8d., towards the purchase of a 'pare of organs' for the gild chapel of St Mary in Holy Trinity church, for use in Our Lady's mass.[39] In 1529, a further £2.16s.8d. was

---

[31] BIHR PR 5 402v–403v 1490. Throughout this chapter the years of office of Hull mayors and sheriffs have been taken from the lists in J. J. Sheahan, *History of the Town and Port of Kingston-upon-Hull* (Beverley, 1866), pp. 296–7, 303–4.

[32] KHRO BRA 87/8, p. 4.

[33] *Ibid.*, p. 21.

[34] *Ibid.*, p. 60.

[35] *Ibid.*, p. 84.

[36] *Ibid.*, p. 82.

[37] *Ibid.*, pp. 82, 105, 110.

[38] *Ibid.*, pp. 127, 128, 130.

[39] *Ibid.*, pp. 130–2.

paid to Barnard, the organmaker, for repairs.[40] During this period two payments were also made to the church of St Mary in Hull. In 1507, the gild contributed 9s.7d. to the church bell tower and, in 1531, 26s.8d. to the St Mary altar there.[41] In the latter case the payment was 'agreyd concluyd and Decideyd by Mr mayr his Bredys and the holl Brederyn off our lady gylt', indicating that the mayor and town aldermen were present at the meeting and led the decision-making process.

These payments were made to the 'increase of Divine Service', like those made by the chantries in Bristol, as described by Burgess.[42] They also reveal a close relationship with the town government, whose needs and requests it was able to fulfil through its reliable yearly income. Despite its healthy finances, however, the gild's accounts ended in 1536. Prior to this, signs of actual neglect of the gild's devotional obligations by its officers occurred. In 1533, they were enjoined to ensure that the torches and other gild lights be properly maintained.[43] Despite this, it was further agreed, probably in 1534, that every alderman and steward should henceforth keep the four lights of the gild 'sufficiently' and leave them 'whole made' when they demitted office.[44] These strictures must have been ignored, for the following entry, for 1535, includes an instruction that the torches should be made in wax by the previous year's alderman and stewards. Such problems might indicate a decline in enthusiasm for the fraternity's pious role.

The social functions that emerge most clearly from the account were the gild feasts. These events were held following the annual obit for the souls of former brothers and sisters and on gild election day, when the new officers were chosen and the accounts delivered.[45] The total for bread and other expenses, in 1463, was 6s.8d. By 1469, although there was no recorded purchase of bread, 11s.3d. was spent on 'seven and a half dozen of beer' and 3s.10d. on cheese. In 1475, 11s.2d. was spent on bread, 3s.6d. on cheese and 16s.6d. on 'eleven dozen of beer'.[46] The price of beer, at 18d. a dozen, was the same in 1469 and 1475. These expenses suggest that the membership of the gild was increasing over this period, as more people were clearly attending the feasts to consume the bread and beer. Cheese was quantified only once in this period. In 1466, six stones were bought at 8d. the stone.[47]

A need to economize, during the financial crisis of the 1470s, might have led to the early disappearance of professional entertainment at these functions. 8d. was paid to players (*histrionibus*), for their services, in 1463, 1464 and 1466.[48] Whether this indicates that there was a play or a musical entertainment is unsure. Payments for performers were not made again until 1485, when a minstrel received 4d.[49] From 1464, there was an annual purchase of a garland, costing 8d. up to 1468, and 1s. thereafter, possibly to adorn the feast. As the gild grew wealthier,

40 *Ibid.*, p. 137.
41 *Ibid.*, pp. 120, 139.
42 C. Burgess, ' "For the Increase of Divine Service" ', p. 65.
43 KHRO BRA 87/8, p. 140.
44 *Ibid.*, p. 141.

45 *Ibid.*, p. 32.
46 *Ibid.*, pp. 2, 14, 32.
47 *Ibid.*, p. 8.
48 *Ibid.*, pp. 2, 4, 8.
49 *Ibid.*, p. 65.

towards the end of the fifteenth century, its feasts and meetings seem to have become grander occasions. The 1491 account records payment to a cook.[50] This was to become a regular annual outlay, although there is no record of any expenditure on meat or any food that was to be cooked. Payments were still made just for bread, beer and cheese. Meat certainly was cooked, however, as the 1500 account includes a fee to the spit-turners.[51] It seems likely that meat was donated by members. In 1492, a regular amount of 8d. began to be paid to minstrels.[52] These were probably the town waits, who provided the music in 1503.[53] By that date, too, it had become necessary to employ a doorkeeper, indicating a large attendance, requiring professional control, and a possible increase in ceremonial.

The gild did not own its own premises for these meetings and feasts and where they were held originally is not known. In 1491, however, a payment of a shilling was first made as an easement, or hire charge, for the Hall Garth. This was the local name for the manor that had been confiscated from Michael de la Pole, earl of Suffolk, in 1388.[54] It was within the town walls, occupying a large plot to the north-west. The building contained a great hall, sixty feet long by forty feet wide. Next to it was a great chamber with adjoining privies. At the other end of the hall was a buttery, a pantry and a large kitchen. It was obviously a highly suitable venue for gild feasts. Subsequently, this payment became a regular one. It is, of course, entirely possible that the gild had met there regularly in previous years, on a grace and favour basis, but that now it was regarded as wealthy enough to pay for its accommodation. A more likely explanation may lie in an expanding membership.

In 1507, the easement for the Hall Garth was still being paid.[55] The next full account, in 1511, recorded an easement paid simply for a hall, and the last full account, in the following year, recorded one made for the brothers' hall.[56] No further easements were recorded. The account of 1528 includes the cryptic note, 'Item pyd to the frers of y's xxs'.[57] The undated account, that seems to belong to 1534, records a payment of 13s.4d. to the Austin Friars.[58] The evidence is very slim, but might indicate that the friars were, by the second decade of the sixteenth century, providing accommodation for gild functions. A connection with the friary, shortly before the latter's dissolution, could well have been a factor in the gild's disappearance from the record in 1536.[59]

In its employment of a full-time chaplain, in its devotional practices and its feasts and meetings, the gild had much in common with other parish gilds in the county. Indeed, its practices seem to have been similar to many of those fraternities that responded to the gild survey of 1389.[60] Compared with the rituals described in the returns from Beverley, its ceremonial was apparently on a

[50] *Ibid.*, p. 84.

[51] *Ibid.*, p. 109.

[52] *Ibid.*, p. 87.

[53] *Ibid.*, p. 113.

[54] R. E. Horrox, *The Changing Plan of Hull, 1290–1620* (Hull, 1978), pp. 62–3.

[55] KHRO BRA 87/8, p. 119.

[56] *Ibid.*, pp. 124, 126.

[57] *Ibid.*, p. 137.

[58] *Ibid.*, p. 140.

[59] *VCH ER*, I, p. 334.

[60] See Chapter 1, pp. 30–5.

modest scale, but this was typical of Hull gilds.[61] The St Mary Gild was, however, unusual in one important respect: it was involved in international commerce.

Commerce

It is evident that, throughout the life of the gild, the vast majority of its officers with identifiable occupations were merchants.[62] Some of them, Robert Alcok and Robert Fyssher, for example, officers in 1466, are shown to have been merchants from their wills.[63] Most of them, however, including Alcok and Fyssher, are more readily identified from the Hull customs accounts of the period.[64] Roger Bussell, for instance, steward in 1463 and alderman in 1464, appeared many times in these lists, importing and exporting a wide range of commodities between the 1450s and the 1480s, including cloth, stockfish, dried fruit, dyestuffs, oil, iron, lead, felt hats and kettles.[65] He became mayor in 1476. Thomas Calthorne, who held gild office in 1467 and 1469, was also an international trader on a large scale, whose cargoes included armour and cutlery as well as cloth, grain and metals.[66] Ralph Langton, alderman in 1472, a merchant on a similar scale, also leased a salthouse from the town and was mayor three times.[67] Most of the gild officers of the late fifteenth century shipped many cargoes through the port. There were a few exceptions. John Grene was less active in international trade but was the king's collector of customs in 1461 and 1463.[68] John Tyttelot had imported wine and stockfish in 1453, but died in 1484 describing himself as a draper, and John Typpyng, who invested in a single import of wine, was a mariner when he made his will in 1472.[69] Richard Burdon, steward in 1464, who does not appear in the customs accounts, gave 'Bower' as his alias, which might suggest that that was his craft.[70] He is probably the Richard Bower who was alderman in 1474. This occupation, however, like that of drapers and mariners, often involved its practitioners in international trade, and he certainly died a wealthy man.[71]

This group of rich entrepreneurs was united not only by bonds of common interest, but, in some cases, by ties of family and friendship, as their surviving wills demonstrate. The Alcoks were brothers. The Fysshers and Swattoks were related by marriage. A common obit was instituted for both Robert Fyssher and

---

61 This point is pursued in greater detail in Chapter 3, p. 105.

62 See Appendix 4.

63 BIHR PR 5 8 (Fyssher), 229 (Alcok).

64 Ed. W. R. Childs, *The Customs Accounts of Hull 1453–1490*, YAS 144 (1986).

65 *Ibid.*, pp. 13–179 *passim*.

66 *Ibid.*, pp. 32–124 *passim*.

67 *Ibid.*, pp. 33–218 *passim*. Ed. R. Horrox, *Selected Rentals and Accounts of Medieval Hull 1293–1528* YAS 140 (1983), pp. 122, 181.

68 Childs, *Hull Customs Accounts*, appendix.

69 *Ibid.*, pp. 7, 14 (Tyttelot), 98 (Typpyng). BIHR PR 5 246v–247r (Tyttelot), 4 182v (Typpyng).

70 BIHR PR 5 357r.

71 Swanson, *Medieval Artisans*, 101–2.

John Whitfeld by the latter's foster son, Thomas Dalton.[72] Many of these men witnessed, supervised or executed each other's wills. Richard Myrwyn witnessed that of Roger Bussell. Bussell himself, with Thomas Phelip, supervised the will of John Ryddesdale, of which Robert Pellet (or Pylate) was executor.[73]

The mercantile nature of the gild at this time is emphasized by the accounts themselves. The first account in the book, for 1463, shows loans being made to members for trading ventures: to Christopher Alenson and Robert Peton for Icelandic stockfish, to Robert Pellet for an import of wine and to others for unspecified purposes.[74] The gild received interest or profits on these loans. In the following year the fraternity itself bought a pipe of wine through Robert Pellet.[75] The wine alone cost 4s., but the freight and the ' lewage and stowage' added a further 3s.11d. to the cost. It is not clear whether the wine was purchased as an investment or for use at the gild feast, as no profit from it was recorded, but beer was the usual drink for that occasion. The 1472 account gives details of further loans and payments to the gild.[76] In this year the fraternity invested a total of £14.18s.7d. in the ventures of various individuals. John Typpyng made a profit for the gild of 14s.9d. on an outlay of 11s.1d. from trading in Iceland, John Buller made 2s. from 14s.6d. trading in Zealand and John Nelesune made two profits trading wine in Bordeaux, both of 11s.1d., on two separate loans of 15s. Most other accounts do not give so much specific detail but simply provide a total of interest, or profit. Some investment seems to have been made in shipping as well as cargoes. In 1465, the gild received £1 from Robert Spofforth and the four masters of a ship called 'The Lord Duvvys Barge', although there is no record of any outlay on the vessel.[77]

Loans to some members proved difficult to recover. John Tyttelot repaid £2.2s.4d. in 1463, part of a previous loan from the gild, and made a further part payment in 1464, but an outstanding 3s.4d. was carried in the accounts until the debt was finally discharged in 1470.[78] Thomas Alcok owed the gild the large sum of £8 in 1470 and paid only £1 of this in the following year. By 1472 the outstanding £7 loan appears to have been transferred to Henry Acclom.[79] This seems to have been a disastrous move for the gild. In 1472, Acclom was instructed to pay the sum within seven days. In the following year he was told to pay it by the Feast of the Nativity of St John the Baptist. In 1474 he was given until Pentecost. Finally, in 1475, he was ordered to repay within twenty days or forfeit his (unspecified) pledge.[80] This note of desperation was understandable: the gild's

---

[72] BIHR PR 5 229v–230r (Alcok), PR 5 410r–v (Swattok), PR 6 51r–v (Dalton).

[73] BIHR PR 5 87v–88r (Bussell), PR 5 167v (Ryddesdale).

[74] KHRO BRA 87/8, pp. 1–2.

[75] *Ibid.*, p. 4.

[76] *Ibid.*, p. 20.

[77] *Ibid.*, p. 5.

[78] *Ibid.*, p. 15.

[79] *Ibid.*, pp. 18, 20.

[80] *Ibid.*, pp. 22, 26, 29, 32, 33.

cash balance that year was only 7s.4d., the rest of its assets being in the form of unpaid debts. Acclom paid up, as was recorded in the 1476 account, and financial crisis was averted for a couple of years.

Although mercantile profits never represented a large proportion of the gild's income, they seem to have provided the vital difference between an annual profit and loss. From over £6 in 1463, this source of income had fallen to £2.16s.8d. by 1474 and to 1s.8d. in 1478. These figures mirror a general decline in Hull's trading activities between 1467 and 1487, as compared with activity earlier in the century, and is related to a fall in wool exports and in imports of wine, following the loss of Gascony.[81] The drop in the value of profits from trade was probably a more serious problem to the gild than Henry Acclom's bad debt, which was, after all, eventually repaid. Gild profits began to recover in the late 1480s and continued to be recorded in the accounts until 1512, although at this period they were seldom ascribed to individuals and no details of ventures were given.[82]

Even in the sixteenth century, most of the gild's office-bearers are identifiable as merchants. Whilst the Hull Customs Accounts do not cover the working lives of many of the later officials, listed in Figure 6.1, a higher proportion of them had wills recorded in the probate registers. Of the gild aldermen holding office over this period, most can be identified as merchants but there a few of other professions: mariners, a goldsmith, a spicer, a cordwainer and a yeoman.[83] In addition, those stewards who did not rise to the rank of alderman included a few who were not merchants.[84] Merchants, however, still represented by far the largest single group, especially amongst those who became gild aldermen. A few of these individuals were even of the stature of the wealthy merchants who had held office in the 1460s. James Johnson, who uniquely served as steward twice, in 1519 and 1523, and alderman twice, in 1524 and 1526, was not only a merchant but was a substantial property owner in the town and was elected mayor in the

---

[81] Kermode, 'Merchants, Overseas Trade, and Urban Decline', p. 57.

[82] BIHR PR 13B 572r–v.

[83] BIHR PR 6 128 1504 Henry Paty bower, PR 6 214 1505 William Bank merchant and mariner, PR 6 173 1506 Thomas Warne, PR 9 24 1515 William Johnson merchant and capper, PR 9 144 1520 John Wardell goldsmith, PR 9 213 1521 John Rogerson spicer, PR 9 268 1523 William Rand mariner, PR 9 382 1527 Thomas Huntington merchant, PR 9 440 1528 Thomas Smyth occupation unknown, PR 10 67 1530 Robert Vergus occupation unknown, PR 10 62 Adm. 1530 William Browne mariner, PR 11 108 1534 Edmund Sheffeld merchant of the Staple of Calais, PR 11A 352 1538 Roger Busshelle merchant, PR 11A 381 and 383 1539 Robert Walker merchant, PR 11B 418 John Care, PR 11B 455 1540 Henry Holdernes cordwainer, PR 11B 483 1540 Richard Meyklay merchant, PR 13B 1549 James Johnson merchant, PR 13B 614 1549 William Thow yeoman.

[84] BIHR PR 8 13 1509 John Shipley, PR 8 62 1510 William Drax occupation unknown, PR 9 240 1520 Geoffrey Thrusscross merchant, PR 9 220 1522 Allan Armstrong mariner, PR 9 187 1522 Robert Hapsham merchant, PR 9 163 William Roclyff occupation unknown, PR 9 448 1529 John Baxter merchant, PR 11A 51 Robert Parker occupation unknown, PR 11B 430 1539 Henry Dynlaye merchant, PR 11B 456 1540 Thomas Thomson merchant, PR 11B 487 1540 John Thornton, merchant, PR 11B 611 1541 William Robinson shipwright, PR 13A 103 1545 James Roger merchant, PR 15C 145 1558 George Hull merchant.

years ending 1534 and 1546.[85] The same might be said of Roger Bussell, junior, who also died wealthy, having been mayor twice, in 1509 and 1517.[86]

Its heavy involvement in overseas trade, and the high incidence of merchants amongst its officers, begs the question as to whether the fraternity was, in reality, an occupational gild. There is, however, no indication in any of its documentation that it was in any way exclusive, or any suggestion of mercantile regulations being enforced by it. It must be borne in mind that the only members that can be identified were the officers, who were among the wealthiest inhabitants of a busy seaport, in which wealth and trade were almost synonymous. Other factors also suggest that, whilst this gild was a fraternity dominated by merchants, it was not a merchant gild.[87]

Real Estate

Important as the income from commercial ventures was to the gild's prosperity, the rents from its properties were probably a more reliable source of funds. The amounts derived from its landholdings in Hull fluctuated from just over £4 to just over £5 each year. It seems likely that the variations were caused by the amalgamation of the rental with income from admissions. We have seen that the St Mary Gild rental accounts were made but have not survived. However, it is possible to estimate the extent of the gild's holdings by extrapolation from another Hull source.

A book containing the rental of the Corpus Christi Gild of Hull from Martinmas 1523 to Martinmas 1525 is in existence.[88] The annual income from its properties in Corpus Christi Lane, Blackfriargate, Mytongate, Whitefriargate and Vicar Lane amounted to £4.17s.6d., and approximately this amount was collected in half-yearly instalments. The last recorded annual total for the St Mary Gild was £4.4s.6d. in 1512. This does not include income from the Haynson tenement. These figures suggest that, excluding large farmed properties, the two gilds may have held real estate of a similar value.[89]

The four lists of rental receipts, in the Corpus Christi document, are followed by four pages of itemized expenditure. It is not clear whether these pages cover one year or four. The first page is headed 1522 but subsequent pages are undated. Embedded in lists of expenditures on building materials and labour, are a few items that one might expect to find in a different kind of account. The first page

[85] KHRO BRA 87/8, p. 125.

[86] BIHR PR 11A 352r–v.

[87] See below pp. 215–16.

[88] KHRO BRA 88. A stitched paper book with leaves folded vertically, it is unpaginated. The rental receipts cover four pages and the payments a further four.

[89] R. Horrox, *Changing Plan*, p. 7, suggests that Corpus Christi was 'the major landowner' among Hull gilds. The reason for this impression may be the loss of the St Mary rental accounts.

includes two payments for the bearing of torches at Easter, two for the purchase of wax, one for the making of torches and one for the bearing of the shrine, a major item of 6s.2d. On the third page appears a payment of 23s.4d. to the priest. The fourth page records payments of 3s.4d. to John Cowtham for mending the shrine, 2d. for bearing torches at Easter, 6s.2d. for bearing the shrine, and other costs, and 6d 'for makyng of xij Wex'. It seems reasonable to suppose that the lost St Mary rental might have taken a similar form.

The inclusion of statements of expenditure in rental books is not unique to Hull at this time. The rental book of the Trinity Gild in Coventry, of 1532–33, includes much more detailed accounts of expenditure on specific occasions.[90] It has been suggested that these are rough jottings which might have later been incorporated into the accounts. If this were the case with the St Mary Gild, it may be that a more detailed account of expenditures was also made in the lost rental book and that, when the book-keeping deteriorated in the sixteenth century, it ceased to be transcribed into the account book by the officials, who now took less interest in the gild's affairs.

In 1476, during the gild's period of financial crisis, it received a windfall, partly at the hands of the mayor and aldermen of the borough, which ultimately contributed to its economic stability. When John Haynson died in 1458, he left a messuage near the King's Staithe in Hull, with the income from the property's own staithe, to his wife, Margaret, for the rest of her life, under certain conditions.[91] The messuage was at that time held by Thomas Etton for the duration of his life. The will provided that, after the death of Margaret, it should be held in trust by the mayor and burgesses of the town in order that they might provide an honest chaplain to say mass perpetually for the souls of John and Margaret Haynson, in the Chapel of St Anne in Holy Trinity, in return for an annual salary of £5. They were also to ensure that an annual obit was held. It was to be announced by the bellman and be attended by the vicar of the church, and by twelve Priests of the Table, with due ceremony and the burning of candles.[92] This kind of arrangement was not uncommon at this time. Roger Bussell senior, merchant, former mayor and gild alderman in 1476, also left a tenement in trust to the mayor and burgesses, to found an obit, in 1483, and Thomas Dalton left a house in trust jointly to the commons of Hull and the Priests of the Table to found an obit for the souls of Robert Fyssher and his grandfather Whitfeld, in 1502.[93]

The Haynson property may not have been in a particularly good condition. The town had told John to repair it in 1456, and, as we shall see, it was in a poor state ten years later, but it was clearly extremely valuable in the light of its

---

[90] Phythian Adams, *Desolation of a City*, pp. 118–27.

[91] BIHR PR 2 393r–v.

[92] The chantry chaplains of Holy Trinity were collectively known as the Priests of the Table and had a corporate identity. They owned property in the town. Documents referring them can be found in KHRO box BRA 87.

[93] BIHR PR 5 87v–88r (Bussell), 51r–v (Dalton).

position.[94] It was a long, narrow plot on a corner site. It ran from Hull Street to the river, where it had its own staithe, and a room above the staithe. To the south, along one of the long sides of the plot, ran Kirk Lane, that connected Marketgate and Hull Street to the River Hull and the staithes. To the north was a complex of tenements, which included town land, a salthouse that was held by Ralph Langton in 1472, and buildings that had belonged to the de la Poles.[95] Valuable as the property was, however, it did not yield enough income to carry out Haynson's wishes.

In 1476 an indenture was drawn up, 'to fulfill the godly purpose of the said John Haynson', between the mayor and burgesses of the town, Margaret Haynson and Robert Stavelay, a chaplain, who was one of the witnesses of John's will, and the gild of St Mary in Holy Trinity.[96] The document acknowledges that the income from the property assigned to the chantry was insufficient to pay the priest's salary. It was agreed that half of the income from the messuage should be paid to the aldermen and stewards of the gild during Margaret's lifetime. Thereafter the gild officers should receive the whole profit and, in return, the gild priest and his successors would pray for the souls of John and Margaret Haynson, their parents, their relatives and for all Christian souls. They undertook to see that an annual obit was conducted on St Vincent's Day (22 January). The property was to be administered by the gild officers and kept in good repair, under the supervision of the mayor and his successors.

Clearly, John Haynson himself had not intended that the St Mary Gild should be responsible for his obit. He did not mention the fraternity in his will. All charitable donations had been left to the discretion of his wife. This solution to the problems posed by the Haynson bequest may well have been an initiative on the part of the town government, who were aware of the state of the gild's finances at this time. Roger Bussell, as that year's mayor, was also an auditor of the gild's accounts.[97] The appointment of the current mayor to this post had been common practice since 1471, indicating close financial supervision of the gild by the government of the borough. Similar arrangements for the administration of chantries by the mayor and commonalty were also common in York at this period.[98]

The immediate effect of this acquisition on the gild's finances was, however, disastrous. It was a major contributor to the negative balance of 1479. The account for 1477 shows no income from the new property and an expenditure of £3.16s.1d. for repairs to it.[99] In 1478, the tenement was farmed out to William White, who was gild steward in the following year. He paid repair bills to the

---

94 Horrox, *The Changing Plan of Hull*, pp. 45–6, 185.

95 *Ibid.*, pp. 43–5.

96 KHRO BRA 8/4.

97 KHRO BRA 87/8, pp. 34–5.

98 *Ibid.*, p.18. Rees Jones, 'Property, Tenure and Rents', pp. 194–7.

99 KHRO BRA 87/8, p. 37.

amount of £3.12s.1½d.[100] Further repairs relating to the previous year cost an additional 5s.10d. The tenement was subject to tax and a regular sum of £1 per annum was, thereafter, paid to the sheriff of Hull, by the gild. The obit of John Haynson was celebrated at a cost of 4s., and Margaret Haynson was paid 13s.4d. The only income, in 1478, seems to have been a half-year's rent of 7s. from William Haddeson, a cordwainer, who lived in a cottage on the property. However, in 1479, when the gild received no monies carried over from the previous year, White contributed a modest profit of 2s.3d. and, after this date, the tenement yielded the gild a regular income of £5.13s.4d. until 1495.[101] This amount was reduced by the regular outgoings, of the tax and the obit fee, and by frequent repair bills. By 1495, these had become so onerous that the farm was reduced to £4.[102] Major repairs were undertaken at the gild's expense in 1496.[103] Although the current holder of the farm, Richard Gybson, paid 2s. for glazing, the gild itself contributed £5.16s.4d. to what was clearly ongoing work. Building materials still remained at the site.

> iij Bawes A panne A lode of lyme And Sande A pere of Webbe leede And a dogge of yerenne And alle the glasse in every wyndow belongeth to the hows That is to saye . . . [unfinished]

Similar materials were still there in 1501 and 1502, in the possession of Robert Vergus, the new farmer, and the account for 1502 records gild expenditure of over £9.3s.1½d. on repairing the tenement.[104] Clearly, by this time, the decaying property was becoming a declining asset. In 1504, the current mayor of Hull, Robert Garner, took over the farm, for a yearly fee of 66s.8d., from which he undertook to pay the tax, and to repair the building at his own cost, handing it over in good condition after seven years.[105] The situation remained stable until the tenure of John Car, which began in 1530.[106] The final entry relating to the tenement is for 1531, when the deeds of the property and an inventory were produced before the masters and brethren.[107] It also records the payment of arrears of £6 in tax. This suggests some difficulty with the tenure of the farm during the last few years of the gild's recorded life.

The Haynson tenement was evidently very important to the gild. The net income from it was roughly similar to that from the rest of the rental, combined with entry fees. It is also clear that the responsibilities connected with it were taken very seriously. The Haynson obit appears as an expense in all the fully itemized accounts from 1478.[108] The care taken over its administration is evident from its history. Such responsibilities were, however, overseen by the town government, rendering even closer a relationship which was already in

---

100 *Ibid.*, pp. 39–41.
101 *Ibid.*, pp. 45–94 *passim.*
102 *Ibid.*, p. 97.
103 *Ibid.*, p. 100.
104 *Ibid.*, pp. 101, 110–11.

105 *Ibid.*, p. 116.
106 *Ibid.*, p. 138.
107 *Ibid.*, p. 139.
108 *Ibid.*, p. 40 *et seq.*

Figure 6.1: Hull Mayors who were Officers of the St Mary Gild in Holy Trinity

The table is based on KHRO BRA 87/8, and on the list of mayors and sheriffs in J. J. Sheahan, *History of the Town and Port of Kingston-upon-Hull* (Beverley, 1866) p. 328.

Name	Mayor	Steward	Alderman	Auditor
Nicholas Elys	1456 1465	–	–	1473 1474 1475
John Barker	1463	–	–	–
John Grene	1464	–	1463	–
John Swanne	1466 1475	–	–	1464 1465
John Day	1467 1470	–	1470	1466 1467
John Hadilsey	1471	–	–	1471 1472
Robert Benyngton	1472	–	–	1465 1467 1472
John Whytfeld	1473	–	1465	1470 1473
William Brampton	1474	–	–	1474 1479 1480 1485
Roger Bussell	1476	1463	1464	1465 1466 1467 1468 1470 1471 1473 1474 1477 1478 1479 1480 1482
John Ricard	1477	–	–	1468 1470
Thomas Alcok	1479	1465	1466	1472 1477 1478
Thomas Wadd	1480	–	–	1473 1482 1486
Robert Alcok	1481	–	1468	1479 1480
Henry Swattok	1481	1474	–	–
Ralph Langton	1482 1486 1495	–	1472	1468 1474 1480 1482 1483–4 1485 1487 1489 1491 1492 1494 1495 1496 1498
William Baron	1483	–	–	1483–4
Thomas Phelip	1484 1492	1471	–	1481 1482 1485 1486 1487 1489 1490 1491 1492 1493 1494 1495 1496
Richard Burdon	1485	1464	–	1475 1483–4 1486 1487
John Chapman	1487	–	–	–
John Dalton	1488	–	–	1486 1489 1490 1492
Thomas Elton	1489	–	–	1486 1487
Laurence Swattok	1490	–	–	1489 1490 1491
Thomas Dalton	1491 1500	–	–	1490 1491 1492 1493 1494 1497 1498
Robert Chapman	1493	–	–	1481 1483–4 1485 1487 1489 1490 1491 1592 1493 1494 1495
William Welesmee	1494	1492	1494	1495 1498
Henry Myndram	1497 1507	–	–	1497 1505
William Gudnape	1498	–	–	1497 1498
Robert Howle	1499	1477	1487	1494 1496 1497 1498
Thomas Guseman	1501	1478	1482	–
Edward Baron	1502 1510	–	–	1497 1498 1505 1509

Name	Mayor	Steward	Alderman	Auditor
Robert Garner	1504	–	–	1504
John Gylle	1505	1490	1496	1505
Thomas Wilkynson	1508 1521 1528	–	–	1509 1519 1520 1521
Roger Bussell Jr.	1509 1517	1496	1501	1509 1519 1520 1525 1527
Sir John Eland	1511 1518 1525	1464	–	1518 1519 1520 1525 1527
Robert Haryson	1512	1502	–	1509 1519
George Matthewson	1514 1529	–	–	1518 1519 1520
Thomas Huntington	1516	–	–	1518 1519 1520 1521 1525 1527
Robert Hapsham	1519	–	–	1518 1519
Edward Madeson	1520	–	–	1520 1525 1527
John Langton	1522	1503 1510	–	1518 1519 1521 1525
Thomas Thomson	1524 1532	1515	–	1525 1527
William Knowll	1526 1535	1515	–	1527
Robert Parker	1527	1516	–	1527
Stephen Clare	1531	1514	–	1525
James Johnson	1534 1546	1519 1523	1524 1526	–
John Harryson	1538 1549	1526	–	–
William Caterall	1540	1533	–	–
Henry Thruscross	1541 1554	1534	–	–

existence. Indeed, without a close connection between town and gild, the tenement would not have been placed in the latter's hands in the first place.

The Gild Accounts and the Town Government

Even before the agreement over the Haynson obit, there were close links between the officers of the gild and the mayor and burgesses of the town, which can be seen throughout the account. Not only did thirteen future mayors of the town hold the office of gild alderman, and twenty-two that of steward, almost all of the rest were involved with it as auditors, as the Figure 6.1 shows. Auditors were not listed in every account, and not at all after 1527, but it seems likely that they were all gild members. After 1489 the mayor appears to have audited the accounts almost ex-officio, during his year of office. The frequency with which some of them performed this duty links them with the fraternity, even when they had not held executive office in it. Service in the administration of the gild may well have been regarded as suitable preparation for civic office at this time, although there was clearly no connection as formal as that which obtained in late medieval Coventry.[109]

In such circumstances it is not surprising that the mayor and burgesses were quick to act when the gild encountered financial difficulty. The account for 1479,

[109] Phythian Adams, *Desolation of a City*, pp. 118–27.

when the alderman received no sum carried over from the preceding year, shows a rallying of the members to assist the gild.[110] Foremost amongst them were former mayor Roger Bussell who lent 10s. and future mayor Ralph Langton, who had been town sheriff in 1474, and who lent 6s 8d. As we have seen, the mayor and burgesses had already taken steps to place the gild on a sounder financial footing by drawing up the agreement over the Haynson obit.[111]

This crisis was followed by a period of stability when the gild, controlled by officials, most of whom are identifiable as merchants, and audited by the current mayor and other Hull dignitaries, was financially secure. Despite this growth in the gild's fortunes, the smooth annual recording of accounts and the succession of officials was interrupted twice during this period. Alderman Thomas Butteler and his stewards, Richard Myrwyn and John Oseller, exceptionally held office for two successive years and rendered an account for both years together in spring 1485.[112] The double account is followed by a blank page, perhaps for an inventory that was not recorded.[113] This hiatus may well have been a result of political uncertainty in the town, covering as it did the minority of Edward V and the brief, turbulent reign of Richard III. It is, of course, also possible that the reasons were internal to the workings of the gild and are unknown. The account for 1488 is missing and was never recorded. Blank pages were left to supply the information at a later date.[114] The account for 1489 is in a new hand and William Haryngton, who had been steward in 1474, was no longer being paid for writing the account and the rental, as he had been from 1475. Perhaps he died unexpectedly and could not be easily replaced as record-keeper. No will is extant. The name of Thomas Karre, who was alderman in 1488, is known from the 1487 account, and the amount he handed over to his successor was recorded in 1489. The names of the two stewards for 1488 are not known.

Although it was able to finance more lavish feasts and was prepared to make donations to pious causes in the late fifteenth century, the gild does not seem to have numbered as many future mayors amongst its major office holders as it had in 1460s. Most of these were, however, still members of the merchant community and several figured in the customs' accounts.[115] An exception was Thomas Guseman, who was probably a relative of the John Guseman who had supplied wax to the gild from 1467 to 1471 and of William Guseman who was steward in 1581.[116] Thomas Guseman does not appear as a gild auditor, but he almost cer-

---

110 KHRO BRA 87/8, pp. 43–6.

111 See p. 208 above.

112 KHRO BRA 87/8, p. 60.

113 *Ibid.*, pp. 59–61.

114 *Ibid.*, pp. 73–6 are blank.

115 E.g. Childs, *Customs Accounts*, p. 214 (Welesmee), p. 209 (Howle *alias* Oule etc.), 46, 140, 142. BIHR PR 6 175 (Gylle).

116 KHRO BRA 87/8, pp. 10, 11, 13, 16 (John), 51 (William).

tainly served as such during his mayoral year of 1501. Auditors were not listed in that particular account.[117]

Although fewer future mayors held high office in the gild, during the six-teenth century, there was no decrease in the town's involvement in the gild's affairs in respect of financial supervision. Even after the accounts ceased to be itemized, the mayor continued to head the list of auditors in most years. The apparent decrease in mayoral auditors at the very end of the period, seen in Figure 6.1, is caused by the gild's failure to record auditors at all, as the quality of the account continued to deteriorate. The custom of the mayor's auditing the accounts, as a matter of course, probably continued: the gaps in the mayoral list coincide generally with years when auditors were not recorded.

Mayors who were never gild officials also continued to serve as auditors after their mayoral year, including George Matthewson, Robert Hapsham, Edward Madeson and Thomas Wilkynson, three times mayor, who was wealthy enough to found his own perpetual obit.[118] There is no doubt that many of the gild office-holders and auditors were still members of a group that was intimately connected with the town government. Their wills, extant in greater numbers in the sixteenth century, show family and friendship connections even more clearly than was the case in earlier periods. James Johnson, for example, supervised or witnessed the wills of Robert Parker, John Thornton and James Roger.[119] Thomas Wilkynson's daughters were married to William Knowll and Thomas Dalton.[120] Roger Bussell bequeathed jewelled rings to his friends, Masters Johnson and Langton.[121]

It is, however, noteworthy that several merchants, whose wills display consid-erable wealth, held office as stewards but not aldermen. These included Thomas Thomson (1520), James Roger (1530), Henry Dynlaye (1535) and John Thornton (1535).[122] It may have been that whilst some involvement in the St Mary Gild was a desirable step, or even a duty, for men at the brink of a mercantile or a political career, the post of alderman was no longer a necessary one. This can be seen in Figure 6.1. Only two gild aldermen became mayors of Hull between 1501 and 1536, but ten of the stewards rose to that rank. These included such luminaries as Sir John Eland, who was mayor three times, and Thomas Thomson, William Knowll, John Harryson and Henry Thruscross, who held the office twice.

The relationship between the gild and the town government was so close that it provokes the question as to whether the former was simply a creature of the latter; whether the gild was simply an arm of the town council. This suggestion, however, might be to lend the gild more prominence than it actually enjoyed. The

---

117 *Ibid.*, p. 110.
118 BIHR PR 11A 259–2r.
119 BIHR PR 11A 51, PR 11B 487v, PR 13A 130v.
120 BIHR PR 11A 359–2r, Dalton was a gild auditor. See Figure 6.1.
121 BIHR PR 11A 352r–v.
122 BIHR PR 11B 456r (Thomson), PR 13B 572r–v (Roger), PR 11B 430v–431r (Dynlaye), PR 11B 487v (Thornton).

St Mary Gild in Holy Trinity was only one of at least seventeen Hull gilds, and there are indications that members of the ruling group in the borough were equally involved with some of the others. Bequests by former mayors suggest this. John Swanne, in 1476, left 6s.8d. to every gild in Hull that had a priest and John Whytfeld, in 1479, bequeathed 2s. to each gild in the town.[123] Roger Bussell, despite being gild alderman in 1476, left nothing to the St Mary Gild, but bequeathed 6s. to the St John the Baptist Gild and £8 to buy a canopy for the Corpus Christi shrine.[124] It seems more likely that the St Mary Gild was part of a web of fraternities, many of which enjoyed a relationship with the mayor and burgesses. Interconnections between gilds can be shown through wills such as that of John Nicholson, alderman of St Mary's Gild, who bequeathed a shilling each to Corpus Christi, Resurrection, St Mary, St George, and all the other gilds in Holy Trinity Church.[125] We have also seen that the gild made contributions to the Corpus Christi shrine and to the St Mary altar in St Mary's Church.[126] Furthermore, Robert Spofford, gild steward in 1466, was also, between 1465 and 1469, supervising the accounts of Trinity House, as alderman of Holy Trinity Gild.[127] If the religious gilds of Hull formed such a web of interlocking pious institutions, representing the commercial and political interests of the ruling elite, there are signs that this role was at least modified during the 1490s. The deterioration in the St Mary Gild accounts in the early sixteenth century might well have been a symptom of a shift in interest on the part of the mercantile and, by extension, the governing group to a gild of a newer kind.

St Mary Gild and Other Fraternities in Hull

In the 1490s a series of new ordinances governing crafts and occupations in Hull were drawn up.[128] The weavers' ordinances of 1490 included a provision that a proportion of the fines levied on members should finance a light of St Peter. In 1498, the walkers and shearmen similarly provided for a light before the image of St Christopher in Holy Trinity and for bearing torches at members' funerals. This was to be carried out without charge if the member died in poverty. Similar provisions were laid down by the glovers in 1499 who were to maintain a light before Our Lady of Pylo in Holy Trinity. All three fraternities were clearly intended to be craft gilds, but also to fulfil pious purposes. This might suggest that the usurpation of the function of religious fraternities by craft gilds, that

---

[123] BIHR PR 5 7r–v (Swanne), PR 5 148v–149r (Whytfeld).
[124] BIHR PR 5 87v–88r 1483.
[125] BIHR PR 9 51 1517.
[126] See pp. 200–1.
[127] Woodward, 'The Accounts of the Building of Trinity House, Hull, 1465–1476', pp. 157–61.
[128] KHRO BRE 5/1 (weavers), BRE 5/2 (walkers and shearmen), BRE 5/3 (glovers).

David Lamburn suggests might have taken place in Beverley, was occurring in Hull at a later date.[129]

In 1499, a new merchant gild was established in Hull.[130] Its organization and purposes seem to have had much in common with those of the St Mary Gild, and it seems probable that it was set up in direct competition to it. The gild regulations were agreed at a meeting in the gild hall of Hull, before Mayor Robert Houll, who was himself a merchant, and who had served the St Mary Gild as steward in 1477 and as alderman in 1487.[131] The meeting was held 'principally for the lawde honour and worship of allmyghty god and of the holy martyr Seynt George'. The new gild was to meet annually, on the Thursday following St George's Day, to elect an alderman and two stewards and collect a levy of 12d. from 'every man merchant of the same town and brother of the sayd gild'. A levy of 3s.4d. was also sought from each member, as an initial payment,

> With the which contynowelly an able and a vertuous preste and oon of the prestes of the table shall be founden dayly to say or cause to be sayd at the Altar of Seynt John Baptist and of Seynt George betwixt v and vj of the clokke in the mornyng a masse called the mary masse . . .

This ' new' gild of St George, in employing its own chaplain, evidently saw itself as a religious fraternity. Whether it was really new is, however, doubtful. There had been a gild of St George in Holy Trinity in Hull since at least 1398, when it received 3s.4d. in the will of John Hornsee, burgess and merchant. Thereafter it received further bequests in 1438, 1451, 1480 and 1493.[132] It is likely that this was either the re-foundation of a gild, that can only have failed within the previous six years, or that the existing gild of St George had been taken over by a group of influential merchants for their own purposes. There were precedents in Hull for such a take-over. The shipmen had annexed the Holy Trinity Gild to their craft, in 1456, in much the same way.[133] The ordinances of 1499 make it clear that St George's Gild was, thenceforth, to be no ordinary religious fraternity. There was provision for the employment of a priest. Following this was a complaint that the merchants of Hull had been 'hyndered and preiudicially wronged' by men of other crafts and occupations, including tailors and shoemakers, who bought, sold and displayed goods that were not appropriate to their crafts. The ordinance laid down regulations designed to ensure that only merchants should engage in mercantile activities and that foreigners and persons of other occupations be excluded from doing so. The new gild of St George was to be an exclusive asso-

---

129 Lamburn, 'Politics and Religion in Sixteenth Century Beverley', pp. 295–6, 305–6. See Chapter 3 pp. 106–7 above.

130 KHRO BRE5/4

131 Childs, *Customs Accounts*, p. 209. Robert Owll [*sic*] imported madder, oil and brushes in 1489.

132 BIHR PR 3 11r (John Hornsee), PR 3 555v–556v (Joan Gregg), PR 2 233r–v (Richard Bille), PR 5 402v–403v (Thomas Wodd), PR 436v (Thomas Tateham).

133 *VCH ER*, I, p. 398.

ciation of merchants. Every Hull merchant was expected to be a member. This kind of movement was not unique to Hull, or even Yorkshire. The international merchants of Bristol, for example, also attempted to found a gild at about this time that was distinct from other occupations.[134]

From this action it can be inferred that the St Mary Gild in Holy Trinity no longer served the commercial needs of the Hull merchants. Too many of its members were evidently not only not merchants, some of them were even encroaching on what the mercantile community regarded as its own legitimate business territory. It cannot be assumed that the St Mary Gild was the only fraternity in the town that was dominated by a mercantile group. There is little hard evidence for the occupations of the office-bearers of other gilds. The refoundation of the St George Gild may have been in competition with other fraternities too. The new one seems to have survived. It was incorporated in 1523 and was probably dissolved in 1547.[135] It seems likely that the controlling merchant group of the St Mary Gild had, to some extent, lost interest in it, no longer insisting on detailed accounting, and had turned its attention to the new gild of St George, which both fulfilled its devotional needs and supported its commercial advantage.

If some of the energies of this mercantile clique had been diverted into the organization and maintenance of the St George Gild, which now represented their commercial interests more exclusively, and at the same time fulfilled their devotional needs, it is not surprising that less time and money was expended on the accounts of the St Mary Gild, which represented the kind of ethos which the former gild had been established to combat. The increasing presence of mariners and craftsmen among the office-holders suggests that the threat they represented to the merchant interest, in the St Mary Gild, was a real one. Continued involvement with the gild was, however, essential to this ruling group. The Haynson tenement, and the obit which it financed, were in the hands of the gild but were also under the supervision of the town, under the terms of the agreement of 1476. The continuity of the account, even in an unsatisfactory form, shows the borough's ruling group protecting its investment.

The End of the Gild

The final entry in the account shows a cash balance of £32.6s.8d. to be handed on to the next group of office-holders, although there was some doubt in the scribe's mind as to who was to hold which office.[136] Robert Thorpe's name was deleted, as alderman, and that of James Huchison substituted. Instead, Thorpe took over Huchison's original post as steward. This page, and those that precede it, are ill-

---

[134] D. H. Sacks, 'The Demise of the Martyrs: the Feasts of St Clement and St Katherine in Bristol, 1400–1600', *Social History* 2 (Hull, 1986), 141–69 (pp. 157–8).

[135] *VCH ER*, I, pp. 90, 145.

[136] KHRO BRA 87/8, p. 142.

written and untidy, in stark contrast to the elegant calligraphy and careful accounting of earlier entries. It can be argued that these signs show a lack of interest in a moribund institution. However, by this date (1535) other, exterior, forces were already at work. News of attacks on images, in the early 1530s, in East Anglia for example, must have been heard in Hull, and although the Ten Articles agreed at Convocation in 1536 did not abolish lights and images, they were clearly under attack by radical elements within the Church.[137] The reluctance of the gild's officers to maintain its lights between 1533 and 1535 might suggest doctrinal objection on the part of individuals, rather than simple neglect, although this did not reflect the position of the majority who censured them.[138] Furthermore, the dissolution of the lesser monasteries signalled a threat, to the astute merchants of Hull, that the funds of their fraternities were not safe from royal sequestration. It was rumoured in Grimsby, in 1536, that the people of Hull had sold their church plate and jewels and paved the town with the proceeds, to keep them out of the king's hands.[139] Even though it was probably untrue, this story suggests an atmosphere in which the concealment of gild funds, or their covert annexation by the town, was a likely strategy. An official gild account book had become an unsafe document in which to record a current balance.

The episode of the Pilgrimage of Grace, and its aftermath, was a highly confused one in Hull.[140] Two former gild stewards, John Eland and William Knowll, personally treated with the pilgrims on behalf of the town and Eland was later thanked by the king for his hand in capturing the rebel captain John Hallam.[141] It is not surprising that, following these traumatic events, the account ceased to be kept. The end of the gild is, however, shrouded in mystery. It does not appear in the commissioners' certificates in 1546 or 1548, but, as late as the fiscal year 1540–41, the gild aldermen [*sic*] were still paying 20s. tax to the town for the Haynson tenement.[142] It seems certain that the gild disappeared at some point between these dates, along with the images in the church and the lights that burned before them.

Conclusion

The gild of St Mary in Holy Trinity, Hull, was a major gild in an important commercial centre. This is evident from the nature of the men who held office and controlled its affairs. From its possessions and activities, however, it was poor and relatively inactive when compared with fraternities in other towns of com-

---

[137] Duffy, *The Stripping of the Altars*, pp. 381–4.

[138] See p. 325 above.

[139] M. H. and R. Dodds, *The Pilgrimage of Grace and the Exeter Conspiracy*, 2 vols. (London, 1915) I, p. 79.

[140] *VCH ER*, I, pp. 91–2. See Chapter 7 below pp. 233–4.

[141] A. G. Dickens, 'New Records of the Pilgrimage of Grace', *YAJ* 33 (1936–38), pp. 305–6.

[142] Horrox, *Changing Plan*, p. 46.

parable size. Any comparison with gilds such as St Christopher and Corpus Christi, in York, or with the major gilds of Norwich or Lincoln is not valid. These were all fraternities in established cities. It is fairer, perhaps, to measure it against those in seaport towns such as Boston or country towns such as Louth. The gild of St Mary in Boston was employing ten chaplains and a choir by the end of the fifteenth century. The Corpus Christi Gild in the same town had nine chaplains and even the St Mary and Holy Trinity Gilds in Louth had two each.[143] These figures put the Hull St Mary Gild's efforts to maintain the salary of a single chaplain into perspective. Both the St Mary and Corpus Christi Gilds of Boston commissioned plays, employed jewel-keepers and sacrists to look after their treasure and provided education for their choristers.[144]

The Hull gild's wealth and activities were not on this scale. It possessed property for rent, but did not own its own premises, having to hire accommodation for its meetings and feasts. The accounts suggest that its ceremonials were both modest and orthodox. Its pious obligations to the Haynsons seem to have been conscientiously discharged. The inventory shows decent but not spectacular provision. The annual procession, when the Rood was carried, and the bearing of torches at Easter and Corpus Christi, appears to have been their limit, at least after the financial crisis in the 1470s. If there was more, then money was not expended on it. The feasts do not seem to have been lavish. Only bread, cheese and beer were paid for by the gild, although meat was also being consumed by the last quarter of the fifteenth century. Entertainment was, at this time, confined to music by the town waits. Its charitable donations showed some generosity, but they were clearly made at the instance of the borough officials.

The status of many of its officers suggests that it was closely connected with the governing group of the borough, and it is clear that it was closely supervised, in its financial affairs, through its auditors, who usually included the current mayor. It was also linked, in various ways, to other gilds in the town. Unfortunately, beyond its ruling body, we know almost nothing of the quality of its general membership, although we can guess that it included numbers of merchants as well as members of other occupations. Its principal worldly preoccupations were mercantile. It was in receipt of a low level of trading profits at least until 1512. The lack of full accounts, after that date, might indicate that the mercantile element had become less important. If, from that time onwards, the purely devotional activities of the gild became its principal preoccupation, then it would be particularly vulnerable to official attacks on 'superstitious' practices. In the politico-religious climate of the 1530s and early 1540s, a gild that had lost the full support of a craft or merchant organization, in a town dominated by mercantile concerns, might find it difficult to survive. It is hardly surprising that it was allowed to disappear quietly by a town government that was beset by far more urgent problems.

---

143 Owen, *Church and Society in Medieval Lincolnshire*, p. 129.
144 *Ibid.*, pp. 130–1.

CHAPTER SEVEN

The Reformation and the Dissolution of the Gilds

William Page, writing in 1894, in the preface to his edition of the 1546 commissioners' certificates, for the County of York, expressed surprise that they reported on only five gilds in the whole of Yorkshire.[1] This implies a cataclysmic decline in gild numbers prior to the survey. There are, of course, factors which conspire to make this a particularly low figure. Neither of the surveys, which Page edited, have survived complete, the most obvious omission being the entire rural East Riding. Furthermore, he did not recognise that many of the West Riding services were, in effect, gilds and, as we shall see, he may have failed to identify a number of other fraternities which had not been recorded in the certificates in a straightforward way.[2] Even so, it appears that, by 1546, the vast majority of Yorkshire gilds, known to us through testamentary and other evidence, had either disappeared or not been recorded by the commissioners. It is the purpose of this chapter to investigate the reasons for this apparent decline.

The dissolution of the gilds was simply one strand in the complex web of the Reformation. Various debates about the causes and nature of the Reformation itself may be relevant to their disappearance and a number of pertinent questions must be addressed. For example, how far was the lay population dissatisfied with the late medieval church in terms of its rituals, its beliefs and the conduct of its hierarchy? To what extent did the doctrines of the continental reformers represent a groundswell of latent Lollardy? How far did political events drive religious changes and what was the extent of public support for them?[3] The following study of the disappearance of the county's religious gilds will allow these problems to be addressed in the context of the large and highly diverse county of Yorkshire, where local events and regional attitudes had their own particular flavour and emphasis.

---

[1] *Certificates*, I, p. ix.

[2] See Chapter 2, pp. 74–6 and pp. 240–2 below.

[3] Tanner, 'The Reformation and Regionalism', pp. 130–41, provides a useful brief approach to these questions in general terms.

The Decline of the Gilds

That the religious gilds were doomed long before their dissolution in 1547 is clear. Where and when the process of decline began is more contentious, but there is some unanimity concerning urban centres in the country at large. In London, recruitment to fraternities waned after the 1520s.[4] Large urban gilds in Boston, Coventry and Sleaford showed signs of decline at the same time.[5] We have seen that, in York, the testamentary evidence shows peaks, where the numbers of bequests to gilds exceeded fifty per decade, between 1421 and 1490, and again in the decade 1501–10, but that there was a dramatic decline thereafter.[6] In Pontefract and Doncaster there was a particularly sharp downturn, after 1530, in bequests made to gilds recorded in the county will sample, although a similar decline began considerably earlier in Hull, after the 1490s, and earlier still in Beverley and Scarborough, in the 1470s.[7]

In Beverley, and perhaps in Hull, this decline in bequests to religious gilds was coupled with an increase in the devotional activities offered by occupational gilds, and it has been suggested that the latter, to some extent, replaced the functions of the former in these towns.[8] There is evidence to suggest that this process was also taking place, to some degree, in York itself.[9] That pious laypersons in these places were encouraging this change does not, however, indicate a decline in their support for traditional religion. The ordinances of the occupational gilds in Hull in the 1490s, for example, show an enthusiasm for lights, images, processions and funerals.[10] Rather, it indicates a need to economize, to combine the commercial protection offered by the occupational gild with the spiritual advantages of the religious fraternity under one head of expenditure. This phenomenon was, apparently, just one further aspect of the link between the decline of gilds and commercial decay, in particular urban areas, that has previously been discussed.[11] There is little indication, in Yorkshire, of the attitudes which led the Bristol authorities, in 1530, to compel gilds to take part in religious processions, although it has been argued that, in York itself, the craft associations were, to some degree, unwilling participants in the annual Corpus Christi play cycle.[12] This particular lack of enthusiasm, however, seems to have been on economic rather than doctrinal grounds.

Outside the major centres of population there was every indication that gilds

---

4   Haigh, *English Reformations*, p. 172.
5   Scarisbrick, *The Reformation and the English People*, pp. 34–5.
6   See Figure 4.1.
7   See Figure 2.5.
8   See Chapter 3, pp. 106–7.
9   See Chapter 4, pp. 133–40.
10   KHRO BRE5/1–4. See Chapter 6, pp. 214–16.
11   See Chapter 2, pp. 78–9, Chapter 4, p. 120.
12   D. H. Sacks, 'The Demise of the Martyrs', p. 168. Swanson, 'The Illusion of Economic Structure', pp. 29–48, especially p. 44.

were flourishing in the country at large. Whilst few fraternities were recorded in Exeter on the eve of the Reformation, they were found in profusion in the rural West Country.[13] Somerset gilds, for example, continued to receive bequests right up to the dissolution, and a gild in Cornwall was still attracting recruits as late as 1547.[14] In Lincolnshire, the major centres of Lincoln and Boston had accounted for 83.3% of all bequests to gilds in the county between 1506 and 1510.[15] By the period 1526–30 their share had fallen to 25.4% of a much higher total of bequests. The following two years saw a further drop to 10.4%. There was a corresponding rise in the number of bequests to rural gilds. We have seen that there was a similar increase in bequests to gilds and services in the rural areas of Yorkshire, over the same period, especially in the increasingly prosperous area of Holderness and in the dales of the West Riding.[16] Whilst it seems likely that this increase in bequests was due more to a change in the status and occupation of testators than an actual proliferation of gilds, it shows that a large number of religious fraternities was present in the county in the first half of the sixteenth century.[17] Even in the countryside, however, the proportion of wills containing bequests to gilds declined after 1530, although a few were still being made as late as 1547.[18]

It seems likely that a major indicator of the fluctuating fortunes of recorded gilds prior to the 1530s was the wealth of the communities in which they operated, as reflected in the numbers of members who were affluent enough to make bequests to them. Subsequently, whatever the local effects of economic factors might have been, however intimately the gilds were bound up with urban governing elites or with the power-bases of local magnates, no matter how central they were to the ceremonial and social activities of their members, by the 1530s events and movements on a national scale were beginning to affect gild activity. These factors were doctrinal, liturgical and, ultimately, political. The gilds became enmeshed in the English Reformation.

Lollards and Conservatives

Before examining the actual process of the Reformation and its effects upon the gilds, it is essential to look at its intellectual background. As the gilds themselves were closely involved in governmental structures, especially at a local level, it is important to judge how far local opinion had been conditioned to accept the ideas of the reformers. One important aspect of this is the possibility that reform-

---

[13] R. Whiting, *The Blind Devotion of the People* (Cambridge, 1989), p. 107.

[14] Haigh, *English Reformations*, p. 36.

[15] Based on statistics derived from Foster, *Lincoln Wills*.

[16] See Chapter 2, p. 66.

[17] See Map 3.

[18] See Figures 2.1 and 2.2. E.g. BIHR PR 13A 359v Thomas Beverley of Hornsea: 12d. to every gild in the town 'over and beside there wagies', PR 13A 344r–v Hugh Anderson of Swine, 12d. to St Mary Gild.

ist ideas had been fermenting throughout the county since the Lancastrian perse-
cution of the Lollards in the early years of the fifteenth century. How far the influence of Wycliff and his followers remained in the social consciousness, providing
a seed-bed for reformist ideas, that were eventually translated into protestantism, is a matter of debate.

The Lollard threat to gilds, in the early fifteenth century, can be seen as an
indirect one, attacking their spiritual assumptions rather than their fraternal purposes. There is little doubt that a number of Wycliff's ideas were hostile to some
of the basic premises that underlay gild membership. For example, he attacked,
as idolatry, the veneration of images, including that version of the Trinity which
was symbolic of Corpus Christi.[19]

> And thus laymen depict the Trinity unfaithfully, as if God the Father was an
> aged paterfamilias, having God the Son crucified on his knees and God the
> Holy Spirit descending on both as a dove.[20]

He held that images represented an error in faith on the part of both lay persons
and the ecclesiastical authorities who might think the 'Father or Holy Spirit or
angels to be corporeal'.[21] Such attitudes were developed by his followers. The
Lollard 'Twelve Conclusions' of 1395 also attacked images and transubstantiation, and, from a gild point view, even more sinisterly, prayers for the dead.[22]

It is a matter of debate how far, and where, the heresy survived to lend an
impetus to the Reformation. It has been suggested that the movement created an
intellectual climate for the reception of reformist ideas and, at the same time,
caused a reaction in the church hierarchy, which became increasingly hostile to
all criticism.[23] This view has since been both modified and attacked. Lollard influence has been described as being principally literary, providing the reformers
with a series of works which they could re-interpret in the light of continental
ideas and experiences.[24] It has also been argued that fifteenth century Lollards
represented not so much a movement as a number of small, self-sufficient
kinship groupings, coming largely from the lower orders of society, geographically separated, but sited principally in southern counties, and holding a variety
of views.[25] The few, notable individuals who suffered publicly for their heresies
were often atypical.[26] Even in Essex, where Lollardy was particularly rife, its
beliefs were confined to particular communities and did not affect those of most

---

[19] See Chapter 3, p. 98.

[20] *De Mandatis Divinis*, quoted in M. Aston, *Lollards and Reformers: Images and Literacy in Late Medieval Religion* (London, 1984), p. 139.

[21] *Ibid.*

[22] A. G. Dickens, *The English Reformation* (London, 1964), p. 24.

[23] *Ibid.*, pp. 36–7.

[24] Aston, *Lollards and Reformers*, *passim*.

[25] R. G. Davies, 'Lollardy and Locality', *Transactions of the Royal Historical Society*, 6th series 1 (1991), 191–212 (p. 200).

[26] *Ibid.*, p. 211.

ordinary people.[27] Further north, Lollard influence was even weaker. There is, for example, little evidence of any tradition linking medieval heretical views with the Reformation in Lancashire.[28] The view, that the importance of Lollardy has been given undue emphasis by reformation historians, is particularly apposite in the context of the North.[29]

The question of continuity between Lollardy and the Reformation in York-shire has been studied in great detail by A. G. Dickens but all his examples are drawn from the sixteenth century, and only the case of Roger Garfield of Wake-field, who, in 1512, admitted repeating heresies he had heard from a Lincolnshire cleric, pre-dated Luther's influence.[30] The 'Dutchmen', whose careers, in the late 1520s and 1530s, that he outlines, were all subject to continental influences.[31] The later Yorkshire Lollards he examines, including those involved in the Pilgrimage of Grace, such as Francis Bigod, seem to have been influenced more by literary Wycliffite sources and by continental ideas than by any vast groundswell of public opinion.[32]

The general view of many commentators is that Yorkshire was, on the whole, pious in a conservative rather than a reformist manner.[33] York itself remained predominantly traditionalist throughout the whole process of the Reformation.[34] Indeed, extreme Puritanism had little influence in the city before 1603.[35] Pallis-er's analysis of 'will formulae' in the city, despite its admitted shortcomings, shows that York testators still bequeathed their souls in traditional form in over-whelming numbers between 1538 and 1547.[36] A similar exercise, conducted within the two last sample periods in testamentary evidence for the county, excluding York, yields very similar results. It shows that, in the period March 1537 to March 1541, 98.6% of all testators bequeathed their souls in traditional form, but that this number had fallen to 76.2% by the period from March 1547 to March 1548. Even this latter percentage is high, considering the religio-political climate of the first year of Edward VI's reign. Whether the employment of these formulae in wills was related to the wishes of the testator or to the predilections of the scribe, it is, nevertheless, indicative of a climate of opinion.

The actual contents of wills indicate no diminution of traditional piety. The general impression given, both by the York wills containing gild bequests and the county will sample, is similar. Even in the minority of cases where a testator

---

27 L. R. Poos, *A Rural Society after the Black Death: Essex 1350–1525* (Cambridge, 1991), p. 279.

28 C. Haigh, *Reformation and Resistance in Tudor Lancashire* (Cambridge, 1975), p. 76.

29 Duffy, *The Stripping of the Altars*, p. 6.

30 A. G. Dickens, *Lollards and Protestants in the Diocese of York, 1509–1555* (Oxford, 1959), pp. 16–17.

31 *Ibid.*, pp. 17–29.

32 *Ibid.*, pp. 29–137, *passim*.

33 Heath, 'Urban Piety', p. 228, Cross, 'Parochial Structure and the Dissemination of Protestant-ism', p. 272.

34 Palliser, *The Reformation in York*, pp. 30–32.

35 *VCH York*, p. 151.

36 Palliser, *The Reformation in York*, pp. 18–21, table on p. 32 and note to reprint.

bequeathed his or her soul to God alone, suggesting an awareness of reformist doctrines, some testators, in a contradictory fashion, proceeded to make traditional pious bequests. In 1540, Jennet Etherington of Holme in Spaldingmoor, left money for torches for the parish church, William Barker of Wistow, made a bequest to the rood light there, and Christopher Nayler, of Chidwell, in Dewsbury parish, wished to found an obit.[37] Even as late as 1547, testators continued to leave money for such forbidden purposes as the purchase or maintenance of church lights, suggesting that they were still in use.[38] Also in 1547, Henry Wedall of Nafferton asked for a priest to 'sing for his soul' and expected the churchwardens to arrange his obit.[39] In the same year, however, Richard Royse, a gentleman of Knottingley, who left a substantial sum for the curate of St Giles Chapel in Pontefract to sing for the repose of his soul, was clearly more aware of the political realities of the time: 'Item yf the lawe wyll not suffre a preste to syng for me then I wyll that the sayd viij li shall be gyven to poor folkes . . .'[40] This clause indicates clear support for traditional religious practices on the part of a well-informed member of the gentry with urban connections.

Even the Lollards' economic attitudes, shown in their attacks upon an overwealthy church, do not seem to have been a major factor in forming public opinion. In the population at large, there was clearly the same resentment over such traditional church levies as tithes and mortuaries as over any form of taxation.[41] However, this did not give rise to armed revolt. Indeed, the Pilgrimage of Grace was, at least in part, an indignant response to royal depredations practised upon the Church.[42] It was believed by the rebels that the new parish registers were being introduced to enable the government to levy taxes on baptisms, weddings and funerals.[43] Such economic factors as there were seem to have been anti-government rather than anti-clerical.

If the ideas of the old Lollard heresies had little effect on the religious conservatism of sixteenth century Yorkshire, those of the new reformers undoubtedly did. Their influence, however, seems to have been a matter of imposition rather than persuasion.

---

[37] BIHR PR 13 343, 338, 364.

[38] BIHR PR 11 552 1547 George Wallas for a rood lamp at Brandesburton, PR 11 556 1547 William Gedney to the Sepulchre light at Welwick, PR 11 496 1547 Robert Mayson to the Lady Light at Guisborough.

[39] BIHR PR 13 356.

[40] BIHR PR 12A 18.

[41] Swanson, *Church and Society*, pp. 212–17.

[42] See below, p. 233.

[43] Dodds, *The Pilgrimage of Grace*, I, p. 77. Haigh, *English Reformations*, p. 151.

Purgatory, Intercession and the Eucharist

Like the Lollards, the reformers do not seem to have regarded the gilds, initially, as a target for their attacks. Here again, the danger to fraternities was, at least to begin with, an indirect one. Even Henry VIII's move against them, in the Act of 1545, was motivated by a need to raise funds for his wars in France and Scotland.[44] This was, of course, the same excuse that had prompted the legislation that had instituted the 1389 gild returns. It was not until 1547 that they were fatally attacked by Somerset's regime on doctrinal grounds.[45] Even then the assault was not aimed at all fraternities. Occupational gilds were exempt. Thus, it was not the principle of fraternity to which the reformers objected so strongly, it was to certain of their practices and their doctrinal and liturgical bases.

Theologically, the continental reformers were attacking the assumptions of the medieval church over the means of salvation and, in particular, they denied the elaborate structure of the penitential 'cycle' on which so much of the medieval church's practices and beliefs depended.[46] This inevitably affected many of the devotional activities of the gilds. The images of the saints, the lights that burned before them and the rituals and processions performed in their names were useless. The dedications and many of the ceremonials of the gilds were not merely ineffectual, they were idolatrous, and contrary to the tenets of the second commandment, prohibiting the worship of graven images. Symbolic of such worship were not only the images that the fraternities maintained with such care, but also the votive lights that figured so large in the 1389 gild returns and in the accounts of gilds such as St Mary in Holy Trinity, Hull.[47] Even the Virgin Mary, the most popular of all gild saints, was not regarded as capable of intercession, and the apocryphal events surrounding her life and death, such as her dormition, assumption and coronation, were denied.

As crucial to gild survival as the attack on saints and their images was the whole question of intercession for the dead. In denying the efficacy of the clerically controlled rites of penance and absolution and in their rejection of the concept of a state of grace in this world, the reformers called into question the importance of the deathbed confession, extreme unction and the whole panoply of the medieval way of death. Indeed, if the soul of the departed proceeded directly to God alone for judgement, then the whole concept of purgatory, for which there was no biblical authority, was challenged. If there were no purgatory, then gild obits, funerals and most bequests to gilds, which were made in the expectation of fraternal prayers, no longer had any function. We have seen that both of these elements, especially obits, were major elements, not only in gild devotional practices, but also in their economic health.[48] The chantries, which

---

[44] *The Statutes of the Realm*, III, pp. 988–93.

[45] *Ibid.*, pp. 24–33.

[46] Cameron, *The European Reformation*, pp. 80 (Fig. 1), 111–35 *passim*, 154, 192.

[47] See Chapters 1, p. 31, and 6, p. 198 above.

[48] See Chapters 5 and 6 above.

many gilds, including some of the largest, maintained, were also vulnerable for similar reasons. Papal and episcopal indulgences, too, Luther's first target, which played a part in recruitment to some of the larger gilds, would no longer have been regarded as valid. Here the denial of purgatory, coupled with a repudiation of the powers of the Church to offer absolution, especially in return for payments, such as entrance fees, formed a potent threat to gild survival.

The new theories also affected the charitable functions of fraternities. If salvation were to be granted, by faith, to those whom God had selected, then it could not be earned by those who discharged the Acts of Corporal Mercy in the hope of turning away God's wrath. To maintain a maisondieu, for example, would not ease the way to heaven. An individual act of charity might be a sign that the giver was one of the righteous, but this was a matter between him, or her, and the deity. Such corporate charity could ultimately be of little spiritual value and might merely display pride. Justification was by faith, not works.[49]

Another debate that threatened a number of gilds concerned the nature of the eucharist. Individual reformers might disagree as to the nature of Christ's presence at the mass but, ultimately, belief in transubstantiation was generally rejected in favour of a communion that was basically commemorative or symbolic. Such a belief reinforced the view that an ordained priest could no longer be regarded as possessing special powers that enabled him to perform the miracle of the eucharist. This called into question the purpose of employing a gild or service priest especially to serve the intercessory needs of a fraternity. Furthermore, the host itself was no longer to be regarded as a holy substance to be worshipped and glorified. Latimer, in a sermon in 1548, claimed that all the rituals of the mass were a diminution of the Passion and an insult to Christ.[50] In the light of such attitudes to eucharistic ritual, the cult of Corpus Christi, and the processions and ceremonials that were connected with it, were unacceptable and the gilds that promoted them were clearly open to attack.[51]

Neither the average gild member nor the average Yorkshire man or woman subscribed to these reformist beliefs. As we have seen, they attracted little support within the county, even in 1547. Those ordinary people who were not directly exposed to reformist preaching would be aware of disturbing rumours but would be little affected, in their daily lives, by the intellectual arguments of reformation. It is hard to say how far most people were even aware of them. Far more potent must have been the physical effects of the new ideas: the changes that took place in the furnishings of their churches, in the conduct of once-familiar rituals and in the disappearance of local institutions. The denial of purgatory might have destroyed a major intellectual justification for gild membership, but the gradual removal of its ritual focus was probably even more destructive. The impetus for this process was imposed by reformers and influ-

---

[49] Cameron, *The European Reformation*, pp. 121–5.

[50] *Ibid.*, p. 120 and note.

[51] Rubin, *Corpus Christi*, pp. 354–5.

ences in both state and church hierarchies and seems to have been a combination of reformist zeal and political expediency.

Images, Lights and Ceremonial

In 1532, four Suffolk men entered the church of Dovercourt, in Essex, at night, and burned the miracle-working rood there, perhaps with the connivance of a local curate of reformist views.[52] How far this particular action was an echo of Lollard tendencies and how far a response to recent continental events it is hard to say, but there is little doubt that the latter were a major factor. The violent outbreak of iconoclasm in Wittenberg led by Gabriel Zwilling in 1521–22, the breaking of images in Zurich in 1523, followed by their wholesale removal by the city authorities in 1524, and subsequent similar events in numbers of cities, in Switzerland and Germany, throughout the 1520s, could not have passed unnoticed in England.[53] Nearer home, the mutilation of a statue of the Virgin in Paris, in 1528, was drawn to the attention of an indignant Henry VIII.[54] The Dovercourt incident was simply one of the more widely-recorded of a number of such happenings in England. Whilst most of these seem to have taken place in Essex, Suffolk and London, images were defaced in Worcester and altar-furnishings broken in Louth.[55] Iconoclasm, at this point, was an extremist gesture against the established church and contrary to law. The three Dovercourt offenders who were captured were executed. Luther's writings were already being exported to England by 1519 and were, reportedly, being widely read.[56] Reformist ideas, however, were not encouraged by the establishment prior to the fall of Wolsey. In 1520, the Cambridge authorities held a public burning of Lutheran books and, in 1521, the Cardinal presided over a larger, similar ceremony at St Paul's in London.[57] A few months later the king himself published his *Assertio Septem Sacramentorum*, an anti-Lutheran treatise, which earned him the title *Fidei Defensor* from Leo X, who granted an indulgence to all who read it.[58] It was not until the matter of the royal divorce and the consequent collapse of his foreign policy that it became clear that Henry's matrimonial difficulties could be solved only by removing the English church from papal authority.[59] This provoked an abrupt change in royal policy. The clergy were rendered submissive to the crown by a revival of the Act of Praemunire, and to Parliament, through the Supplication against the Ordinaries,

---

52 Aston, *England's Iconoclasts*, p. 133.

53 Cameron, *The European Reformation*, pp. 249–51.

54 Aston, *England's Iconoclasts*, pp. 210–11.

55 *Ibid.*, p. 212. Duffy, *The Stripping of the Altars*, p. 381.

56 Dickens, *The English Reformation*, p. 68.

57 *Ibid.*

58 E. Doernberg, *Henry VIII and Luther: an Account of their Personal Relations* (London, 1961), pp. 16–20.

59 W. J. Sheils, *The English Reformation 1530–1570* (London, 1989), p. 17.

making it impossible for them to mount concerted opposition to change.[60] Henry's appointment of Thomas Cromwell as his principal adviser, in 1530, and Cranmer's elevation to the province of Canterbury, in 1533, ensured the presence of reformers in positions of power and influence, opening the way to the introduction of measures that would undermine the devotional functions of gilds.

In June 1536, Hugh Latimer, recently promoted to the diocese of Worcester, preached a sermon before Convocation, in which he attacked images, relics, indulgences and 'purgatory pick-purse', all of which were papal devices to take money.[61] Images should not be dressed or lit, and the ceremonies surrounding them should be suppressed: '. . . if ye purpose to do anything, what should ye sooner do, than to take utterly away these deceitful and juggling images . . .?'[62] This sermon was the prelude to the adoption by Convocation of the Act of Ten Articles. Although the articles did not go as far as Latimer in seeking the abolition of images, they represented the first steps of authority against them. Images might still stand in the churches, to inspire the faith of the laity, but they might not be worshipped with kneeling or incense, nor should people believe that 'any saint doth serve for one thing more than another, or is patron of the same'.[63] The latter provision, although this was not its overt intention, in effect removed the whole point of the dedication of gilds to specific saints.

It was followed eight days later by the removal of the occasion for many gilds to celebrate their patron saints at all. In an act 'for the abrogation of certain holydays', Convocation ruled that the feasts of the patronal saints of churches and all feasts falling in harvest-time and during Westminster term-times, should be celebrated with a simple mass only, and that they should be ordinary workdays.[64] Only a few major festivals, including those of the Virgin Mary and the Apostles, were excepted. Among those abolished were a number of feasts of the more popular gild dedications. Examples are those of St Katherine, St Mary Magdalene, Holy Cross, The Holy Name of Jesus, St Anne, St Martin, St Margaret, St Laurence, St John of Beverley and the Translation of St Thomas of Canterbury. Effectively, the act prohibited ceremonial gild masses on these days, and rendered processions impossible. Trouble in Beverley, over a priest's failure to announce St Wilfrid's Day, was subsumed in the general chaos surrounding the Pilgrimage of Grace but the Act was also unpopular elsewhere.[65]

Meanwhile, in August 1536, Cromwell had issued injunctions to beneficed clergy, reinforcing the Ten Articles and forbidding them to 'set forth or extol any images'.[66] In the following year the Bishops' Book took the reformist cause against images a stage further, forbidding the making or possession of them with

---

[60] Haigh, *English Reformations*, pp. 106–16.

[61] Aston, *English Iconoclasts*, I, p. 222. Duffy, *The Stripping of the Altars*, pp. 390–1.

[62] Quoted in Duffy, *The Stripping of the Altars*, pp. 390–1.

[63] *Ibid.*, p. 393.

[64] *Ibid.*, pp. 394–5.

[65] *Ibid.*, pp. 395–8.

[66] Quoted more fully in Aston, *English Iconoclasts*, I, p. 224.

the intent to worship them. By this time, words were being translated into actions and iconoclasm was occurring on an official basis. Cromwell's officials were already dismantling pilgrimage shrines and stripping or removing miracle-working images in some parish churches, as well as in the dissolved religious houses.[67] A further set of injunctions, in 1538, instructed parish clergy to assist in the process.

> That such feigned images as ye know of in any of your cures to be so abused with pilgrimages or offerings of anything made thereunto, ye shall, for avoiding that most detestable sin of idolatry, forthwith take down and delay, and shall suffer from henceforth no candles, tapers, or images of wax to be set before any image or picture . . .[68]

The instruction goes on to except the lights on the altar, rood-screen and Easter sepulchre. This was a further savage blow to gild practice. The maintenance of lights was, as we have seen, an important function of many gilds, and was a major item of expenditure in their accounts.[69]

A clue as to how some gilds reacted to this measure may be found in one of the very rare examples of pre-reformation Yorkshire parish records.[70] A light of St Sitha was maintained in St Michael Spurriergate in York. The records do not indicate whether there was an actual gild of St Sitha but there was, at least, an organization that was referred to as 'the kepers of saynt Syth lyght'.[71] In the year ending 1537, the keepers were clearly trying to reduce the size of the stock. There are two entries in that year of the church paying substantial sums to the city chamberlain's office 'to helpe to bryng ytt owt of det'. In both cases the money was taken out of the St Sitha stock.[72] These payments were made prior to the 1538 injunctions, but it seems likely that the parochial authorities feared that the light was in danger of abolition and that the fund that financed it might be liable to sequestration. What better way could there have been of using the money than by purchasing the good will of the city authorities? In the following year the parish decided not to renew the stock's supply of wax, although the light might still have been burning at this date. Under the heading 'legaseys' is the following item.

> Rasayved of Saynt Sythe Stok what tyme that we shuld have bowght wax wyth itt to have mayd Seynt Sythe lyght & fyve dossen wax compleyt: xiijs iiijd.[73]

However, under 'the expences a bowytt the Churche' is the entry, 'Item for ij dore bandes wher Seynt Syths torches doyth stand: jd ob.'[74] Once the parish had made

---

[67] Aston, *English Iconoclasts*, I, p. 225. Duffy, *The Stripping of the Altars*, pp. 402–3.
[68] Quoted in Aston, *English Iconoclasts*, I, p. 227.
[69] See above p. 225.
[70] BIHR PRY/MS4.
[71] *Ibid.*, fol. 134v.
[72] *Ibid.*, fols. 134v, 137r.
[73] *Ibid.*, fol. 142v.
[74] *Ibid.*, fol. 143v.

provision for securing the funds and purchases of the St Sitha light, the records show that, in the year ending 1539, the light itself was removed in accordance with the injunctions and at parochial expense: 'Item for takyng downe of seynt sythe candylstyke and other candylstyks mo: iiijd.'[75] Some of the reasons for this apparently tame surrender will be examined later, but it may well have been typical of the attitude of many of the gilds and services in York at this time.[76]

Cromwell's 1538 injunctions contained other provisions that affected the gilds less directly but which further diminished the reverence for the saints, which underpinned so much of their ceremonial, such as the removal of supplications to the saints in the litany.[77] The abolition of the angelus bell and of the use of the rosary, too, were both aimed at the cult of the Virgin Mary, by reducing the occasions when the recitation of the Ave Maria was obligatory. Cromwell's commissioners continued to remove and destroy shrines and images from monastic institutions, including those of Our Lady at Walsingham (Norfolk), of the Rood at Boxley (Kent) and of St Thomas of Canterbury.[78] However, the injunctions still permitted the retention of images that were not worshipped or 'abused with offerings'. In the diocese of York, the moderate Archbishop Lee, in a series of injunctions, interpreting those of Cromwell, whilst forbidding lights before saints, allowed that, 'images be suffered only as books, by which our hearts may be kindled to follow the holy steps and examples of the saints represented by the same'.[79] Thus, whilst the St Sitha light in St Michael Spurriergate was removed, there is no record, at this stage, of the image itself being taken down.

Henry VIII's proclamation of 16 November 1538, a prelude to the Act of Six Articles in the following year, has been seen as the beginning of a period of official reaction to the process of reformation.[80] It was becoming clear that the Vicar General and his supporters were taking reform beyond the point that his master, as Supreme Head of the Church in England, would accept. However, the Six Articles contained no provision to halt the dismantling of shrines or the destruction of images and the dissolution of the greater monasteries proceeded apace. Indeed, the 1538 proclamation officially suppressed the cult of St Thomas of Canterbury, denying his sainthood, expunging his name from the liturgy and commanding the destruction of all his images.[81] Thus, another popular gild dedication lost its validity, this time for overtly political reasons, the saint having been a rebel against his king. At Ashburton (Devon) the gild of St Thomas Becket responded by becoming the gild of St Thomas Apostle.[82] After Cromwell's fall in

---

75 *Ibid.*, fol. 154v.
76 See below pp. 234–5.
77 Duffy, *The Stripping of the Altars*, p. 408.
78 Aston, *English Iconoclasts*, I, p. 234.
79 Duffy, *The Stripping of the Altars*, p. 413.
80 Haigh, *English Reformations*, p. 152.
81 P. L. Hughes and J. F. Larkin, *Tudor Royal Proclamations* (New Haven and London, 1964–69), I, pp. 275–6.
82 Haigh, *English Reformations*, p. 158.

1540, the progress of reform was, in most respects, halted. It was not, however, reversed as regards those matters that indirectly affected gilds. As we shall see, Henry personally initiated measures to enforce the policy towards images, enshrined in the 1538 injunctions, during his visit to Yorkshire in 1541.[83] In the same year, although he restored three saints' days, he abolished others, including the boy-bishops' and misrule festivities connected with such feasts as St Nicholas and Holy Innocents.[84] On the other hand, the King's Book of 1543 represented a slight softening of the official view on images, whereas the King's Primer of 1545 omitted traditional prayers for the dead, to the Virgin, to saints and to the eucharist.[85] Despite these ambiguous statements, at least one Yorkshire gild showed signs of revival during this period. We have seen how the recruitment of new members to the Corpus Christi Gild in York recovered from no new members, in 1537–39, to an annual figure of 178, in 1543–4, a higher total than had been achieved in any year since 1534.[86]

It was not until after Henry's death that the final blow fell. The injunctions of 1547, issued by the Edwardian government, abolished all religious processions and required the removal of all lights, except those at the altar, and the destruction of all shrines and 'misused' images, including paintings and stained glass.[87] The parish of St Michael Spurriergate complied:

> Item to two smythes for takyng done of candylstykes in the churche: ijd.
> . . . Item to a laborar ffor beryng moke owt of þe church and þe churche yerd what tyme the seyntes was takyn Down: ijd.[88]

The statue of St Sitha was not specified, but was probably a part of the destruction. That the account refers to them as 'seyntes' and not as images, or idols, suggests that they were still regarded with reverence and that their removal was a matter of regret. There does not seem to have been a wholesale destruction of glass. Medieval windows still survive in the church and in York generally.[89] Even despite the 1538 injunction attacking St Thomas of Canterbury, some of a series of windows celebrating his cult, probably connected with the gild, survive in St Michael le Belfrey.[90] Whilst an image could be relatively cheaply removed, the replacement of windows would be both expensive and essential. With the loss of the images the ceremonial focus of the gilds had disappeared.

By 1547, of course, they were already under direct attack. Before the actual cir-

[83] Aston, *English Iconoclasts*, I, p. 238. Duffy, *The Stripping of the Altars*, pp. 431–2. See below, p. 235.

[84] Duffy, *The Stripping of the Altars*, pp. 430–1.

[85] *Ibid.*, pp. 429, 446–7.

[86] See Figure 5.8.

[87] Aston, *English Iconoclasts*, pp. 256–7. Duffy, *The Stripping of the Altars*, p. 451.

[88] BIHR PRY/MS4 fol. 213v.

[89] *RCHM York*, V, pp. 3, 8–9, 17–19, 21–2, 28–9, 38–9.

[90] Window nV. Part of the sequence of Becket panels is now in the Minster Chapter House, window CH1. See Toy, *A Guide and Index to the Windows of York Minster*, p. 41.

cumstances of their dissolution are discussed, however, another question needs to be addressed. If gilds were as popular and vital, in early sixteenth century Yorkshire, as most of the evidence seems to suggest they were, why was there so little protest at their demise? One answer to this question lies not in the events of 1547 but in those of a decade earlier, in 1536–7.

The Pilgrimage of Grace and its Aftermath 1536–41

There has been considerable debate over the causes of the Pilgrimage of Grace. That there were economic and political dimensions to the struggle is apparent. It has been seen as a protest against taxation and enclosure by agricultural workers, as a plot hatched by the local gentry, as a bid for power by the Percy family and as an attempt by the religious to stave off dissolution.[91] Other commentators have, however, emphasized its basically religious nature.[92] It has been pointed out that when the commons took action during the uprising, what they did was related to their religious, not their economic, grievances.[93] There seems little doubt that, whatever the motives of their leaders, and whether or not they manipulated the actions and emotions of their followers, the majority of the pilgrims acted as they did for reasons which included piety. They were opposed to the religious changes, of which the dissolution of the lesser monasteries was the latest unpopular manifestation. They pinned on their badges of the Five Wounds of Christ and followed their leaders in the hope of persuading their king to halt the process, dismiss his advisers and allow them to return to the religious practices of their forefathers. Robert Aske's message to the mayor and council of York, when he called for 'the preservacyon of crystes church' and 'the punnyshement of herytykes and subverters of the lawes', probably represented the feeling of the vast majority of the pilgrims.[94] His entry into York, on 16 October 1536, was to popular acclaim.[95] The common people had already declared their support for the pilgrims on 11 October, and there seems to have been little opposition from the mayor and council. Mayor Harrington endorsed the rebels' articles in his own hand, although there was a prudent failure to minute any of the incidents of the rebellion in the House Book.[96] The atmosphere in the city seems to have been

[91] Both A. G. Dickens, 'Secular and Religious Motivation in the Pilgrimage of Grace', *The Province of York*, Studies in Church History 4 (Leiden, 1967), pp. 39–64 and G. R. Elton, *Reform and Reformation: England 1509–1558* (London, 1977), pp. 264–9, emphasize the secular causes of the Pilgrimage. Haigh, *Reformation and Resistance in Tudor Lancashire*, p. 135, implies that monks, at least in Lancashire, were implicated in fomenting the rebellion.

[92] C. S. L. Davies, 'The Pilgrimage of Grace Reconsidered', *Past and Present* 41 (December 1968), 54–76 (pp. 72–4). M. L. Bush, 'The Richmondshire Uprising of October 1536 and the Pilgrimage of Grace', *Northern History* 29 (Leeds, 1993), 64–98 (p. 95).

[93] C. Haigh, *English Reformations*, p. 148.

[94] Quoted in Dodds, *The Pilgrimage of Grace*, I, p. 176.

[95] *Ibid.*

[96] *Ibid.*, Palliser, *The Reformation in York*, pp. 7–8. YCR, IV, p. v.

euphoric. The nuns of Clementhorpe and the monks of Holy Trinity were reinstated in their dissolved houses.[97] Gentry in the countryside around took the rebels' oath, albeit under some duress, and there was some plundering of the houses of those opposed to the rising.[98] The main body of rebels stayed in York for only a few days, but other elements of the force, including Sir Thomas Percy and his entourage, rode through later, to the delight of the populace.[99] Later still, from 21 to 25 November, York was chosen by the rebels as the venue for its Great Council.[100] Its citizens appear to have given the pilgrims widespread support.

In Beverley, before the failure of the Lincolnshire rising was fully known, the town held a public meeting, followed by an armed muster, on 8 October.[101] Beverley and Howden were early focuses of the rebellion, before the forces from both areas combined to march on York. Hull, however, was reluctant to become involved and, after a parley with a detachment of the rebels, the mayor and alderman would only agree to allow those of the town who wished to join the rebels to do so without equipment or provisions.[102] The pilgrims besieged the town, which surrendered to them on 20 October.[103] Before Lord Darcy's open involvement with the rebellion, he was besieged by the townsfolk of Pontefract who had risen and declared for the pilgrims on 17 October.[104] Although the Doncaster men also sympathized with the pilgrims, the rebel army avoided the town because of plague, but camped nearby. [105] At the northern end of the county, Scarborough Castle withstood a rebel siege throughout the rising. There is no doubt that all the major population centres of the county were closely involved in the Pilgrimage. Everyday life was widely disrupted and, with the possible exception of those of Hull, the inhabitants generally supported the pilgrims.

The immediate religious impetus for the rising was twofold. The dissolution of the lesser monasteries had begun in May and the commissioners' actions were unpopular.[106] The Act of Ten Articles and the injunctions that supported them were also being promulgated. The suppression of feast days led, as we have seen, to trouble in Beverley.[107] It seems certain that it caused protest elsewhere in the county. Outrage was magnified by rumour. In October 1536, at the height of the rebellion, the king issued a proclamation against the spreaders of malicious rumour, complaining that:

> . . . divers devilish and slanderous persons have sown, bruited and spread abroad that we should pretend to have . . . brought to our tower to be touched . . . the chalices, goods and ornaments of parish churches, and fines for christen-

---

97 Palliser, *The Reformation in York*, pp. 8–9.

98 Dodds, *The Pilgrimage of Grace*, p. 183.

99 *VCH York*, p. 145.

100 Dodds, *The Pilgrimage of Grace*, pp. 311–18.

101 *Ibid.*, pp. 144–6.

102 *Ibid.*, p. 159.

103 *Ibid.*, p. 166.

104 *Ibid.*, p. 184.

105 *Ibid.*, p. 251.

106 *Ibid.*, p. 74.

107 See p. 228 above.

ing, wedding and burying; and for license to eat wheat, bread, pig, goose or capon with many other slanderous, false, and detestable rumours, tales and lies . . .[108]

Such rumours were rife throughout the country and, whether they were deliberate political propaganda, as the king believed and as some historians agree, or whether they were simply the product of panic is, when assessing the state of mind of the majority of the pilgrims, largely immaterial.[109] The story that the burgers of Hull had sold their church treasures and used the money for paving the town, so that the king's commissioners should not take them, has no known foundation in truth, but the people of Grimsby gave it credence.[110] Such tales simply served to deepen the anger of the people at what was seen as the oppression of the king's bad advisers, 'the herytykes and subverters of the lawes' of Aske's letter to York. Recent research suggests that the central core of the uprising was the fear that there would be a wholesale attack on the ceremonials and trappings of parish worship.[111] The pilgrims were concerned about their investment, in the sense of a local pride in their churches and of their roles within them, rather than in purely financial terms. Furthermore, their parochial activities, as churchwardens and as gildsmen, gave them a particular stake in their parish churches, which led them to protest, in this extreme fashion, at the threatened spoliation.

The end of the pilgrimage, in frustration and confusion, produced by Norfolk's mendacious promises and the king's masterly inaction, saw the rebel army disperse, in the belief that the protest would lead to a favourable review of its grievances by the promised parliament. The king's pardon in December 1436, however, offered no concessions and ascribed the rebellion to ignorance and false rumours 'most craftily, untruly and spitefully set abroad . . . by certain malicious and seditious persons'.[112] The later rising, of January 1537, headed by Francis Bigod and John Hallam, which involved unsuccessful attempts to take Scarborough and Hull, offered the king an opportunity to take revenge for both risings from what was now a position of strength. Norfolk was dispatched to Yorkshire to administer oaths of loyalty and pacify the North. There were hangings in York, Hull, Scarborough, Watton, on Yersley Moor and on Richmond Moor.[113] The subsequent north-western insurrection led to Norfolk's assize in Carlisle where seventy-four Cumberland insurgents were executed.[114] On his return to Yorkshire, several of the original leaders of the pilgrimage were sent to London where they were arraigned for high treason.

---

[108] Hughes and Larkin, *Tudor Royal Proclamations*, I, p. 244.

[109] Dodds, p. 76.

[110] *Ibid.*, p. 79.

[111] C. S. L. Davies, 'Popular Religion and the Pilgrimage of Grace', in *Order and Disorder in Early Modern England*, eds. A. Fletcher and J. Stevenson (Cambridge 1985), pp. 79–80.

[112] Hughes and Larkin, *Tudor Royal Proclamations*, I, p. 246.

[113] Dodds, *The Pilgrimage of Grace*, II, pp. 82, 110.

[114] *Ibid.*, p. 226.

The total number of executions resulting from the Pilgrimage has been calculated at 216.[115] Of these, 185 took place in the North and two of these, in particular, were carried out to maximum effect in Yorkshire. Sir Robert Constable was executed in Hull and his body hanged on Beverley Gate.[116] Robert Aske was hanged in York, from Clifford's Tower.[117] Most of the rebels of noble birth, or high ecclesiastical status, including Lord Darcy, Sir Thomas Percy, Sir Francis Bigod, the Priors of Guisborough and Bridlington and the Abbots of Fountains and Jervaulx were executed in London.[118] The effect on the morale of the population of the county must have been devastating. Although the numbers of the dead were not spectacular, they included men of respected family and of high status.

An atmosphere of fear and guilt still pervaded York as late as 1541, when Henry VIII made a state visit to the city in October. From July the House Book entries were dominated by the preparations.[119] It is hardly surprising that a royal entry should be planned with such care, the city cleaned, festivities planned, pageants brought forth and gifts prepared. What is striking is the Recorder's address to the monarch, delivered kneeling, on behalf of the Lord Mayor, aldermen and commons, also kneeling, at Fulford Cross.

> . . . we your humble subjects . . . have agaynst our naturall allegyaunce disobedyently and contrary your Grace ys lawes for the common welth provyded grevously and traitoryously offendyd your high invyncible and moste royall majesty . . . in the most odyous offence of traterous rebellyon, whereby your Grace . . . graunttid to us wretches, beyng desparat of any maner hope or releyff, your most gracyous and charytable remissyon, frank and free pardon, whos bountyfull hart and liberall graunte we of our selfs ar in no wise able to recompence or satisfye but contynually have been from the bothoms of our stomaks repentaunt, wo and sorrowfull for our said unnaturall and haynous offencs . . . we promyse and vow . . . frome thys time forwards . . . to serve, obey, love and dreyd your Majestie Royall . . .[120]

This fulsome effusion demonstrates the anxieties of the city authorities. They had obviously been badly frightened by the executions. Perhaps they also feared the withdrawal of their charter. A few days after the visit, on the King's orders, the shrine of St William in the Minster was despoiled, part of the profits being used to buy Bibles for local parish churches.[121] There appears to have been no protest.

The whole region seems to have been cowed by the events of four years earlier. The king's visit simply reinforced its lessons. In the light of the failure of the rebellion and its bloody aftermath, it is scarcely surprising that later reformist measures were accepted, and largely complied with, without overt opposition. The slow erosion of the spiritual and ceremonial functions of the gilds was

---

115 *Ibid.*, p. 82.
116 *Ibid.*, p. 220.
117 *Ibid.*, pp. 223–5.
118 Elton, *Reform and Reformation*, p. 262.

119 YCR, IV, pp. 54–70.
120 *Ibid.*, p. 69.
121 Aston, *English Iconoclasts*, I, p. 239.

allowed to continue and, by the time they were attacked directly, as part of the process for dissolving the chantries and colleges, the capacity for resistance, from within the county, had already been destroyed.

The Process of Dissolution

The dissolution of the chantries, gilds and colleges was not a swift and tidy process. Begun by Henry VIII, with the Act of 1545 and the survey of 1546, it was not completed until after his death, by the regime of Protector Somerset, through a further Act in 1547 and two more surveys in 1548.[122] The commissioners in the 1546 survey were instructed to search out and identify all the 'chauntries hospitalls colleges free chappells fraternyties brotherheadds guyldes and stypendarye prestes' in the county and to investigate:

> to what intentes purposes and dedes of charity . . . [they] were founded . . . in what manner the revenews and profitts . . . be used expended and imployed . . . to thintent we may know whiche shallbe mete to stond and remayne as they nowe be or to be dissolvyd altered or reformyd making to us a perfyte certyficatt of every particuler poynte therof accordinglie.[123]

They were to make inventories of all lands, goods and possessions and were given powers to examine all the king's subjects to complete their enquiries. All local officials were ordered to cooperate with them. In Yorkshire, the commission was headed by Robert Holgate, the archbishop of York, but the other commissioners were all gentry, comprising Sir Michael Stanhope, Sir Leonard Beckwith, four esquires and three gentlemen. This survey was organized by deaneries. Unfortunately, it does not survive complete. The four deaneries of Buckrose, Dickering, Harthill and Holderness, in the archdeaconry of the East Riding, are missing. So too is the portion of the deanery of Lonsdale that lay within the county, although the other Yorkshire deaneries of the archdeaconry of Richmond are extant. Alone of the East Riding certificates, that from Hull has survived, although it has become separated from the other Yorkshire material.[124]

In accordance with the king's detailed instructions, the information in the certificates was presented in columns, generally under a number of headings.[125] The first comprised the name and number of the institution. The next contained the name of the incumbent, the foundation of the institution, its purpose and the quality, degree and function of the incumbent. The distance of the institution from its parish church and its function were then required, in order to assess whether it contributed usefully to the parish. The last three columns were

---

[122] *Statutes of the Realm*, III, pp. 988–93, IV, pp. 24–33. PRO E 301 63–72, 102–3, 105–6, 119, DL 38 11–13.

[123] PRO E 301 66.

[124] KHRO BRA 87/8.

[125] PRO E 301 66.

devoted to an examination of the institution's assets. An enquiry as to any lands sold or acquired by it since 2 February 1536 usually elicited a negative response. Finally there was an inventory of its goods, plate and jewels and a survey of its lands, tenements and revenues. This set of certificates presents a valuable account of the various institutions they assessed.

The record of the commission set up by Edward VI's government, as a result of the 1547 Act, and making its return in February 1548, is much less informa-tive.[126] The new commissioners were again headed by the Archbishop of York and contained two names that survived from the preceding one, William Babthorpe, now a knight, and Robert Chaloner esquire. It also contained John Bellow, a Lincolnshire lawyer and businessman, who, as Sir Michael Stanhope's 'solicitor', later figured in the purchase of gild lands in the East Riding.[127] The purpose of this survey was not to examine what institutions might be dissolved, it was to assess the property that used to belong to them and which was now, under the Act, the property of the crown. In effect, these commissioners were implementing the sequestration of the assets of the chantries, gilds, colleges and hospitals. Although the instructions given to the commissioners were less explicit than those of 1546, the same format was used for the certificates and they are penned in a similar hand. Most of the individual returns are, however, much briefer. This time the survey was made not by deaneries but by ridings and wap-entakes. It is a clear signal that the property was no longer in church hands. Once again the certificates for the East Riding are missing, with the exception of the City of Hull, Hullshire and the Bailiwick of Beverley.

An additional survey was set up in July 1548 to assess the pensions of those priests whose chantries had been dissolved. Once again the same format was employed, but this time the numbers of commissioners were fewer and the infor-mation given was even more terse. Like the commission in February, the survey was conducted by ridings and wapentakes. This survey is important in that it does include a certificate for most of the East Riding, although Holderness is rep-resented only by its middle bailiwick. The East Riding certificate was drawn up by John Bellow alone.[128] It has been analysed, although not transcribed, along with other relevant material, in a most useful article by C. J. Kitching.[129]

Although the response to this phase of the Reformation was somewhat muted in most of the county, there was at least one incident of extreme violence. On 25 July 1549, the parish clerk of Seamer, Thomas Dale, and a local yeoman, William Ambler, led an armed revolt which culminated in the death of Matthew White, one of the Yorkshire commissioners in February of the previous year, his wife, a servant of Walter Mildmay, who was one of the July 1548 commissioners, and Richard Savage, former Lord Mayor of York, at the hands of the mob.[130] The

---

126 *Certificates*, II, pp. 371–2.
127 PRO E 315/67 Part II fol. 612. Bellow is described as Stanhope's 'solicitor' in *YCR* V, p. 18.
128 PRO E 301/119 m. 1.
129 Kitching, 'The Chantries of the East Riding', pp. 178–94.
130 Duffy, *The Stripping of the Altars*, p. 459.

reasons given for the riot were related to the religious changes and the support of local gentry for them. That three of the victims were directly connected with the dissolution can have been no coincidence.

Elsewhere in Yorkshire argument and concealment were more usual responses. The corporation of the City of York, for instance, was still making representations to the central government 'for the preservacon of the guyldes of Seynt George and Seynt Crystofer in York' as late as 1549.[131] In the light of the events of the previous twelve years, it seems certain that any politically-aware gild official in the whole country would have understood the intention, and have anticipated the consequences, of the establishment of the first survey in 1546. Those gilds that persisted, despite the undermining of their doctrinal and ceremonial purposes, must have been concerned to salvage what they could of their economic assets.

Those urban gilds with occupational connections survived as craft gilds, shedding their devotional trappings. Occupational gilds had been exempted from the Act of 1547 due to the parliamentary influence of the London livery companies.[132] Thus the tailors' gild of St John the Baptist and the mercers' Holy Trinity Gild, in York, and the shipmen's Holy Trinity Gild, in Hull, all survived as secular institutions. Others preserved elements of their identity, such as the Corpus Christi Gild of York, which continued in the guise of St Thomas' Hospital.[133] Most, however, seem to have disappeared, as gilds, before the dissolution process was complete. A case in point was the St Anthony Gild of York, the third largest, in terms of testamentary evidence, in the city. The corporation, far from seeking its preservation, as it had with the St Christopher and St George Gild, chose to deny its existence.

> Item Maister White beyng one of the King's resayvours in thes Northe parties dyd dyrecte his lettres unto John Wylson of the Citie of York, baker, the coppy whereof the said Henry Mason haith up with hym to shewe for somuche as ther is no gylde of Saynt Antony founded within the said Citie as is supposed by the said lettres.[134]

Despite this protestation, the gild's hall was in the possession of the mayor and aldermen, in 1551, and was already being used, in 1554, to house the meetings of those trade gilds in the city that had no building of their own.[135]

The seizure and subsequent concealment of gild and chantry property by town authorities was by no means confined to York. In Richmond the bailiffs and burgesses anticipated the visit of the commissioners by taking over and selling, to private individuals, most of the chantries and obits in the borough.[136] The only

---

[131] White, *The St Christopher and St George Guild of York*, p. 20.

[132] Scarisbrick, *The Reformation and the English People*, p. 36.

[133] See Chapter 5, pp. 193–4.

[134] *YCR*, V, p. 4.

[135] *Ibid.*, pp. 64, 106.

[136] L. P. Wenham, 'The Chantries, Guilds, Obits and Lights of Richmond, Yorkshire', *YAJ* 38 (1952–55), 97–111, 110–11, 185–214, 310–22 (pp. 96–8).

exceptions were two chantries, previously held by now dissolved monasteries, and a hospital that was administered by the crown. These institutions would be well known to the commissioners. The concealed property included the endowment of an obit for Thomas Stevinson and the brethren of St John the Baptist's Gild in the town. Chantries dedicated to St Mary, St Thomas the Apostle and St John the Baptist also figured amongst the property sold.[137] The three gilds in Richmond, identified from testamentary sources, also had these dedications.[138] The case for concealment was not pressed home until Elizabeth's reign and, even then, was resolved in favour of the town.[139] Similar concealment took place in Ripon, where the property of the Holy Cross Gild was used by the town to found a school and where the town government's actions were investigated by the crown in 1577.[140] If the authorities in a remote township like Richmond could receive prior warning of the commission and successfully conceal so much property, it seems certain that more southerly parts of the county were in an even better position to do so.

Concealment may also have been aided by the way in which the commission was appointed, and the manner in which it carried out its duties. The 1389 gild survey had been discharged by obliging gilds to make returns themselves, supervised by sheriff's officers, local men, who, presumably, were each familiar with the area in which they proclaimed the writ.[141] The certificates of 1546–48 were produced by royal commissioners, directly appointed by the king, who, although they were mostly northerners and knew the county, might have been unfamiliar with many of the individual locations in the wide areas that they covered. They were sequestering local assets to the crown in the name of new beliefs which were not widely accepted. Furthermore, it may well have been noticed that at least some of the commissioners, like Stanhope and Bellow, were in the process of making personal fortunes by buying and re-selling confiscated lands.[142] It is hardly surprising that when they began their survey they found very few gilds in the county.

It seems certain that the majority of fraternities took measures to ensure that their physical assets were hidden from the commissioners. Most of their devotional functions had already been stripped away. Gild officials, in the face of the new threat, clearly decided that the best course was to dissolve their fraternities before the commissioners arrived and return all the liquid assets to the membership. Most gild possessions were easier to dispose of in this way than those of institutions such as colleges, hospitals and chantries. Profits from commercial undertakings, entrance fees and livestock could be readily concealed. The mysterious 'decay' of four-score sheep of the stock of Pockley Chapel was noted by the

---

137 *Ibid.*, p. 101.
138 BIHR PR 5 248r–v 1484, William and Margaret Walker.
139 Wenham, 'The Chantries, Guilds, Obits and Lights of Richmond', pp. 110–11, 185.
140 Ed. A. F. Leach, *Early Yorkshire Schools*, YAS 27, 2 vols. (1898), II, pp. 201–15.
141 See Chapter 1, p. 22.
142 PRO E 315/67 Part II fol. 612. *Cal. Pat. 1548–1549*, pp. 27–9.

commissioners, but it seems likely that in many unrecorded cases both gild money and chattels disappeared into the community.[143] Income from real estate, used to pay for priestly stipends, obits and chantries, could not be so readily hidden, although towns such as Richmond and Ripon evidently succeeded in doing so. Where such lands had been willed, certificates in mortmain had to be purchased and tax paid to the crown, as was the case with the Haynson obit of the St Mary Gild in Holy Trinity, Hull.[144] In York, the city government had itself been administering a number of chantries subsequent to a charter of 1393.[145] This probably aided concealment. Where there was a recent crown record of assets, however, they were more easily detectable. These factors, especially with regard to chantries, might lead us to view the survival of gilds in the county, at a point just prior to their formal dissolution, in a new light.

Gild Survival

In assessing how many fraternities survived to the eve of the dissolution, it is necessary to examine all the gilds and services that have been identified and to quantify those that were mentioned in the documents relating to the process. By far the largest body of evidence for gilds in Yorkshire prior to the dissolution is, of course, testamentary. Appendix 5 lists all gilds that appear to have survived up to the eve of the dissolution. Of the total of 376 gilds and services identified in the county from all sources, 71 (18.9%) are directly mentioned in the certificates. Of these, 16 (4.6%) were referred to, at least once during or just after the process, as gilds and 55 (14.6%) as services. That more services were found by the commissioners than gilds was probably due to the nature of the service as an institution.[146] As its primary function was to maintain a priest, and as he was frequently funded by revenue from lands, services were difficult for their members to conceal. There is, however, evidence to suggest that this argument can be taken a stage further.

The commissioners were far from consistent in their terminology. For example, Appendix 5 shows that the Holy Trinity Gild in Bawtry, called a gild in the testamentary evidence, was referred to in February 1548 as a chantry or gild, and in July 1548 as a chantry or service.[147] The St Mary Gild of Rotherham was called a service in 1546, a gild or service in February 1548 and a chantry in July 1548. Such confusions may provide a clue to the small number of gilds recorded as such by the commissioners. When the dedications of previously identified gilds and services are compared with those of the chantries found in the survey in the same locations, there is a high correlation between the two. Among the

---

143 See Chapter 3, p. 114, above.
144 See Chapter 6, p. 209, above.
145 S. Rees Jones, 'Property, Tenure and Rents', pp. 193–6.
146 See Chapter 2, pp. 72–5.
147 Bawtry Holy Trinity Gild: BIHR PR 3 553v 1438, PR 2 29r–v 1441. See Appendix 5.

most famous gilds missing from the certificates was the Corpus Christi Gild in Pontefract, where a chantry with the same dedication was described as being 'put in by the mayr and his bretherne'. There is no entry for the St Christopher and St George Gild of York either, yet the two St Christopher chantries in York Minster are entered as being of the foundation of the gild in the 1546 certificates. In a large number of cases the commissioners found a chantry in a location where a former gild or service of the same dedication was identified by other evidence. It is reasonable to suppose that the existence of these chantries in 1546, or in 1548, or later, indicates that the gild in question was probably still active shortly before the dissolution process began. Whilst a gild might have dissolved itself, distributing the assets that were not easily traceable by the crown, the chantry belonging to it would remain. It seems certain that many of the chantries noted by the commissioners, especially, but not exclusively, those that they described as being 'without foundation', were gild chantries. In all, of 376 previously identified gilds and services, 78 (20.7%) appear to be referred to as chantries at least at one point in the dissolution evidence.

It also seems highly probable that a large number of chantries, again especially those without recorded founders, that were noted by the commissioners, might well have been maintained by gilds that cannot be otherwise identified. In the absence of corroborative evidence, however, their number cannot be quantified with any accuracy and they have not been included in any of the statistics used in this study.

The commissioners' certificates do not yield the only gild evidence relating to dissolution. Twenty-nine (07.7%) gilds were identified from post-dissolution land records taken from a number of primary sources including an Office of Augmentations account book, the *Calendar of Patent Rolls*, and a variety of secondary sources.[148] It seems probable that all the gilds found in these sources were also active shortly prior to dissolution. To these has been added, in Appendix 5, a handful of gilds with bequests, or other references, in wills of 1546 and 1547.[149] All these groups of gilds and services overlap one another but, taken together, they total some 160 that probably survived until the eve of the dissolution process and that were sufficiently wealthy to maintain a gild chantry, or to own lands, or were too prominent to conceal their assets. They represent 42.6% of all identified Yorkshire gilds and services. This is a remarkably high percentage, taking into consideration that the list of all identified gilds includes a number

---

[148] PRO E 315/67/ Part II, fols. 612v, 613r, 657r. Secondary sources include Kitching, 'The Chantries of the East Riding', Wenham, 'The Chantries, Guilds, Obits and Lights of Richmond' and *VCH ER*.

[149] YML L2(5)b 16r–v 1546 Agnes Thomson to St John (Baptist?) Gild York, BIHR PR 13A 304v 1546 Jennet Brery to Corpus Christi Gild York, PR 13A 313r 1547 Edmund Kendall to St Nicholas Gild Guisborough, PR 13A 352v 1547 Thomas Beverlay to the gilds of Hornsea, PR 13A 401v–402r 1547 Thomas Hodgeson to Corpus Christi Gild Hornsea, PR 13A 389v–380r 1547 Edward Saltmarshe to the gild of Thorganby, PR 13A 344r–v 1547 Hugh Andersone to St Mary Gild Swine.

that were absorbed into others in the previous century, especially in York, or that may have disappeared for other reasons before the 1530s.[150]

Conclusion

That at least 160 Yorkshire fraternities survived the pressures of the Cromwellian stage of the Reformation and persisted, despite the disruption and bloodshed of the Pilgrimage of Grace and its aftermath, is undoubted proof of their continuing popularity. That they chose to dissolve themselves in face of inevitable government action was simply an act of economic common sense. The events of the previous twenty-five years had shown that resistance to religious change was not merely ineffective, it was extremely dangerous. All the evidence suggests that the concealment of their assets was undertaken with the collusion and, in some cases, with the active assistance of local authority. This highlights the growing identification of interest between religious fraternities and local secular powers that had become increasingly evident throughout the previous century. Whilst the national government and the powerful local figures that often controlled gilds, through membership and influence, both supported the orthodox beliefs and structures which the gilds represented, the religious fraternities were a conduit of secular power, as well as a focus for public piety.

When national and local government opinion diverged on doctrinal questions, force majeure was triumphant. If the early tribulations of the gilds were an indirect result of theological ideas and liturgical reform, their final downfall was also due to governmental cupidity and, perhaps, to a realization that they might become focuses for local unrest. Indeed, it has recently been argued that gilds were local power bases that were seen by Tudor administrations as a threat to their drive towards centralized government control.[151] Thus, Protector Somerset carried out the abortive initiative of the Cambridge Parliament, possibly for parallel reasons. The result was permanent. Had the gilds been abolished in 1389, there is little doubt that, like the frequently suppressed confraternities of contemporary Florence, they would have reappeared almost at once.[152] The early stages of the English Reformation, however, had destroyed the context within which they could operate so completely that attempts to resurrect them, during the brief period of Mary's regime, such as the revival of the St George's Day pageant in York and the appointment there of a 'Maister of St Anthonys', were ultimately doomed to failure.[153]

There is nothing to suggest that the suppression of the gilds was, in any sense, a popular measure in Yorkshire but it had become inevitable. Whatever their personal beliefs, and there is every reason to suppose that the majority of gildsmen

---

[150] See Chapter 4 above.

[151] Bainbridge, *Gilds in the Medieval Countryside*, p. 149.

[152] Weissman, *Ritual Brotherhood in Renaissance Florence*, pp. 164–9.

[153] Palliser, *Tudor York*, p. 242. YCR V, p. 182.

and women were opposed to the new doctrines and their ritual and physical consequences, the religious ethos of their fraternities had been so far eroded as to be no longer worth preserving. The 1547 injunctions stripped away the last of their devotional and ceremonial functions. They had been reduced to economic entities. Whilst those fraternities with a vital economic function, the craft and trade gilds, survived and metamorphosed, most religious gilds were left with no alternative but to salvage what assets they could from the wreckage. Their efficiency in carrying out this operation rendered it difficult for the commissioners to record their number accurately and has presented problems to historians ever since. William Page's assertion that only five gilds were recorded in the first volume of his edition of the certificates is a measure of their success.[154]

---

[154] See p. 219, above.

GENERAL CONCLUSION

These gilds after the Reformation, were defam'd for having been Structures of Superstition, and Places where the State then thought that Conspiracies were, or might be, form'd against them: and Tradition informs us, there were two sorts of Gilds, viz. Religious, and Civil: The former, for settling Matters spiritual; the latter, temporal: The first consisted of both Clergy and Laity, whose intent was to see Religion, and the Rules of the Church perform'd more strictly; for which End, they contributed to erect a Chapel, and Hall, wherewith to pray and keep an Agapæ, or Love-Feast, by which Revenues accrued to them, as tho' they might be reckoned a kind of Lay-Monasteries. But those Gilds, that were purely for particular Trades, were managed by the Professors of such Occupations, who often built Hospitals to maintain their Poor.[1]

Thomas Gent's assessment of gilds was expressed less than two hundred years after their dissolution. His views on how they were perceived by their contemporaries accord, in some respects, not only with those of Somerset's regime in 1547, but also with those of the petitioners to the Cambridge Parliament in 1388. Whilst gilds were clearly seen by the Protestants as 'Structures of Superstition', the fear that they might form focuses for conspiracy was expressed by the fourteenth century petition.[2] Both groups made distinction between 'Religious' and 'Civil' gilds, although they did not use those terms, and excepted the latter from their attacks. Furthermore, they both intended to confiscate the sources of the gilds' 'Revenues'.[3] The period between these two assaults, the first ineffective and desultory, the second persistent and ultimately decisive, saw the gilds attain the height of their power and influence.

Their importance has, however, often been underestimated. This is the direct result of the nature of the surviving evidence. The 1389 returns, which historians have, perforce, relied upon for much of their material, were compiled under conditions which led gilds to maximize their devotional, and minimize their processional, fraternal and economic activities. The commissioners' certificates of 1546 and 1548 were drawn up at a time when gilds were attempting to conceal their assets and, in some cases, denying their existence.[4] This has influenced many commentators, from Westlake onwards. Testamentary evidence tends unduly to emphasize their funereal role. For example, Scarisbrick's view, that, 'In their most modest form . . . fraternities were simply poor men's chantries',[5] does not bear

---

1   T. Gent, *History of Hull* (York, 1735), p. 80.
2   Chapter 1, p. 14.
3   Chapters 1, pp. 13–14; 7, 238–40.
4   See Chapter 7, pp. 238–40.
5   Scarisbrick, *The Reformation and the English People*, p. 20.

close examination in the context of Yorkshire. Their functions were far more complex than this. It has been shown that even in places of low population gilds were landowners.[6] In rural areas we have seen that they were connected with powerful local and, in some cases, national political figures.[7] Their activities in urban areas were closely bound up with both the personalities and the mechanisms of borough and civic government.[8]

A principal reason for their success as institutions lies in the politico-religious policies of the fifteenth and early sixteenth century monarchy. It was national government that wished to see 'Religion, and the Rules of the Church perform'd more strictly', in terms of orthodox piety.[9] In this they had gained the support of the church hierarchy and of the lay political establishment. The crusade against heresy was pursued through strategies that reinforced the importance of the sacrament of confession, the doctrine of purgatory, the value of intercession and the validity of transubstantiation, all of which had been challenged by Lollards.[10] The gilds proved to be allies in this initiative. Individual examples of Lollardy within gild memberships generally pre-date Henry V's initiatives of 1414.[11] The Act of 1436 ensured their future compliance with royal policy. Gilds became public manifestations of orthodox lay piety, contrasting with the contemporary increase in private devotion which, associated with a growth in literacy and the invention of printing, might lead to dissent. Gild membership was an open statement of devotion to a particular cult that was demonstrated publicly by ritual and display. The cult figures adopted by gilds as dedications were overwhelmingly Christo-centric and traditional.[12]

The ceremonial and social activities of the religious gilds were organized on a fraternal, and usually sororal, basis. They required a strong sense of loyalty, discipline and honour from their members, as many of the returns they made in 1389 make clear.[13] Encouragement by the crown, symbolized by the participation in the membership of gilds, including at least two in York, by members of the blood royal and by other establishment figures from the nobility and the Church, helped the fraternities to flourish throughout the fifteenth and into the sixteenth century.[14] The ecclesiastical authorities further boosted memberships by granting indulgences to those who supported favoured fraternities.[15] The success of the gilds was manifest in that the largest of them continued to increase in size

---

6   E.g. Bessingby, Burstwick, Fraisthorpe, Winestead. See Figure 2.3.
7   E.g. Sheriff Hutton, Spofforth, Swine, pp. 62–3.
8   See Chapters 3, pp. 86–7; 4, pp. 149–53; 6, 211–14.
9   Chapters 1, p. 44; 2, pp. 50–51.
10   Chapter 7, p. 222.
11   Rubin, *Corpus Christi*, p. 243. Catto, 'Religious Change under Henry V', p. 106.
12   Chapter 3, pp. 98–102.
13   Chapter 1, pp. 32–3.
14   Chapter 5, pp. 173–4; White, *St Christopher and St George Guild*, p. 15.
15   E.g. St Mary Gild, Guisborough: Brown, *Cartularium Prioratus de Gyseburne*, II, pp. 409–10: indulgence of forty days granted by Archbishop Lawrence Booth to all contributing to the gild of the Blessed Virgin Mary at Guisborough in 1498. Corpus Christi Gild, York: MS Lans-

and smaller fraternities proliferated throughout the land to the extent that they were present in most parishes.

In fifteenth century Yorkshire they were most frequently identified in wealthy, commercially active communities, favourably placed on the county's communications network.[16] Whilst affluent towns and villages stimulated the foundation of successful gilds and created conditions in which it was likely that they would receive bequests, it is equally the case that the gilds themselves produced wealth within the communities they served. In order to fulfil their pious, ceremonial, social and charitable functions, it was necessary that they were financially stable. Wealth was accrued through subscription and bequest and was typically invested in real estate which provided an income.[17] Many gilds also raised funds through other commercial means, including corporate trading ventures and agricultural projects.[18] As landowners, traders, employers and consumers, the more successful fraternities became important economic entities within their communities.

Inevitably a proportion of a gild's income was spent on administering its possessions, including the repair and development of its real estate, on record keeping and on the expenses of its officers. Where chaplains were employed, their salaries were generally a major item.[19] Many gilds also invested heavily in the ceremonial associated with their cults, or to aid their rituals and liturgies. Payments to torchbearers, beadles and bellmen were common and the maintenance and the renewal of vestments was a continuing expense.[20] Both accounts and bequests show that the provision of wax for candles and torches was another major item. A gild's wealth was further displayed in the intrinsic value of its ceremonial objects. The massive treasure revealed in the inventories of the Corpus Christi Gild of York was exceptional, in both its quantity and quality, but it has been shown that other gilds constructed shrines and received rich gifts from testators.[21]

If a gild's public piety was demonstrated through its rituals, its sense of fraternity was cemented by its feasting. Gent's definition of an 'Agapæ, or Love-Feast', is substantially accurate. Rules for the regulation of feasts were usually designed to prevent quarrels and arguments, emphasizing accord and harmony.[22] Fraternal meals differed in scale from gild to gild, from the provision of simple bread, beer and cheese to the elaborate collations of the York Corpus Christi Gild, but they all not only symbolized the function of the gild as a kind of extended family

---

downe 304, fols. 104v, 154r: indulgence of a hundred days granted by Archbishop Kempe in 1446 and of forty days by Archbishop Booth in 1489.

16 Chapter 2, pp. 58–9.

17 Chapters 5, p. 188; 6, pp. 206–9.

18 Chapters 3, pp. 113–15; 6, pp. 203–5.

19 E.g. Chapter 6, p. 198.

20 *Ibid.*, pp. 198–99.

21 Chapters 5, pp. 189–91; 6, pp. 199–200; 3, p. 108.

22 Chapter 1, pp. 32–3.

but also reminded members of the sacred meals of Christ's ministry: of the Feeding of the Five Thousand and, above all, of the Last Supper and the miracle of the eucharist. Whilst the gild's pious rituals were conducted fraternally, it is also true to say that its fraternal celebrations were, in essence, pious.[23]

This applies equally to their funeral practices and their role as intercessors for their brothers and sisters who, although dead, were still members of the fraternity. Clearly a gild funeral was special. The wills commissioning them, especially in York, show that they were distinguished by a high level of ceremony.[24] Attendance at gild obsequies was the duty of all members, whose fraternal prayers would ease the passage of the deceased through Purgatory. The annual general obit further displayed the concept that the complete fraternity was a communion of the living and the dead. Both enjoyed the succour of the gild. Whilst impoverished members might accept charitable assistance from the fraternity when alive, the dead received prayers from the gild priest, whether salaried or feed for the occasion, and from the living membership. Public piety was, in some cases, extended into the community at large. Some of the larger religious gilds supported hospitals and maisonsdieu (*pace* Gent) whilst others ran schools.[25] Parish gilds contributed to the maintenance of the parish church, of a chapel or in answer to an appeal by other institutions or by the community at large.[26] There is little evidence, in Yorkshire, of Rosser's contention that there was inherent conflict between parish and gild.[27]

The activity that defined the relationship of the fraternity with the community at large was the procession. In their examinations of Corpus Christi festivities, James sees an event that symbolizes the creation of a central harmony within the social body but Rubin argues that it combined a whole range of, spiritual, doctrinal and symbolic values, in which disparate groups sought to establish their identities.[28] I find Rubin's argument the more persuasive, but believe that underlying most gild ceremonial, by the latter half of the fifteenth century, was a political agenda laid down by local government. It was inevitable that successful, wealthy institutions, based on a piety that coincided with the thrust of national government, should be attractive to local authorities. We have seen that, in Yorkshire, gilds were associated with local government at all levels. In rural areas,

---

[23] Chapters 4, p. 145; 6, pp. 201–2; 2, p. 115.

[24] Chapter 4, p. 146.

[25] In York, the gilds of Corpus Christi, St Anthony and Holy Trinity Fossgate all ran hospitals. See Chapters 5, p. 167; 4, pp. 139, 142. Schools were run by gilds in Topcliffe (Chapter 2, p. 59) and possibly Sedburgh: *Cal. Pat. 1549–1551*, pp. 97–8: Grant of a Grammar School to Sedburgh: '. . . the messuage called Depmyre in tenure of Brian Huddelston within the parish of Mellyng Lancashire which belonged to the late gild called the Rood Gild in Sedburgh and all other possessions of that gild . . .' may record the re-foundation of a gild school.

[26] Chapter 6, pp. 200–1.

[27] Rosser, 'Communities of Parish and Gild', pp. 4–5. See Chapter 3, pp. 93–5.

[28] James, 'Ritual, Drama and the Social Body', pp. 8–12. Rubin, *Corpus Christi*, pp. 237–43, 269–71.

relationships between gilds and local lords can be discerned.[29] In towns and in York itself the connection is much more obvious.[30] Bequests to gilds are common from members of the ruling elites of all the larger towns, and we have observed that the St Mary Gild in Holy Trinity, Hull, was closely supervised by the mayors of the borough.[31] The material from the Corpus Christi Gild of York shows us a gild that threw its net even wider, and covered in its membership lay and ecclesiastical powers throughout the north of England and beyond.[32]

Most of those gilds that were rich enough to be recorded were those that were of use to the establishment in its drive against heresy. The religious orthodoxy of the larger gilds appears through all the extant evidence. There are, however, hints that some of the less powerful gilds took a slightly different line. The Plough gilds in Holderness were a manifestation of pre-Christian popular superstition which might also have been present in the fraternities of the Young Men in Beverley and the Children in Seamer.[33] Perhaps more significant is the impression that some parish fraternities accorded women a special place in their ceremonies. However, whilst we might speculate that a host of unrecorded gilds did not follow orthodox practices, it is clear that most of those that can be identified did and that this was a major reason for their success.

This assessment, however, does not take into account the ways in which Yorkshire gilds changed between 1389 and 1547. Nor does it explain their decline in the latter part of the period. There are strong indications that rural gilds continued to proliferate at least until the 1530s and the local trauma of the Pilgrimage of Grace. This was particularly so in the south of the county. In East Dickering, Holderness and the Humberhead Levels it seems to have been related to a growing agrarian prosperity consequent on the marsh drainage of the previous century.[34] In the West Riding the foundation of services was probably associated with the success of the growing local textile trade.[35] The basis of this impression is partly derived from testamentary evidence. It can be argued that, because these areas were becoming wealthier, more wills were made and there is, therefore, a higher probability of bequests to gilds and services emerging from the sample. However, it seems certain that the richer the area, the greater was the likelihood of successful gilds being maintained, and it is the successful gilds that attracted bequests. That they did so in large numbers suggests proliferation and is an indicator of their growing popularity. This argument is reinforced by the evidence of the commissioners' certificates and of post-reformation land transactions, which show the survival of large numbers of gilds that were wealthy enough to employ priests or own land, on the eve of their dissolution.[36]

The larger urban areas of the county show similar patterns of testamentary evidence to those in rural areas, in that they were related to fluctuations in pros-

---

[29] Chapter 1, pp. 61–3.

[30] Chapter 4, pp. 152–3.

[31] Chapter 6, p. 211.

[32] Chapter 5, pp. 182–4.

[33] Chapter 3, p. 103.

[34] Chapter 2, pp. 65–71.

[35] Chapter 2, pp. 71–2.

[36] Chapter 7, pp. 240–1.

perity, but the timing of peaks and troughs was different in each case.[37] The recording of bequests to gilds declined as prosperity decreased at different times and at different rates in Beverley, Scarborough and Hull. Increasing affluence in Pontefract and Doncaster led to a larger number of bequests being made there at later dates. In York, where the evidence is more plentiful, the general trend also followed that of the city's economic decline, although here it is possible to see that lesser variations in the general rate of decline were related to other factors, including political events, both local and national, and demography.[38]

The general decline in bequests, especially to urban gilds, prior to the government intervention of the 1530s that began the long process of dissolution, was also affected by changes within the gilds themselves. In some respects the great urban fraternities were victims of their own success. They became larger in size and fewer in numbers through amalgamations and take-overs, as exemplified by the expansion of the St Anthony Gild of York.[39] As their ceremonial and social events became more lavish, they became massively involved in economic activity. They became landlords on a large scale and involved themselves in a variety of commercial ventures. They were becoming more worldly.

At the same time, merchant and craft associations were involving themselves directly in gild affairs. In York, there are examples of particular trades taking over and sustaining gilds that already existed, as well as founding new fraternities for the members of their misteries, throughout the fifteenth century.[40] The occupation and the gild, however, generally remained separate organizations. The gild was not necessarily exclusive to members of the craft. This led, in the early sixteenth century, to the foundation of other craft gilds that probably were exclusive. This was the case in Hull, where there are indications that the success of the St Mary Gild in Holy Trinity was compromised by the re-foundation of the St George Gild as an exclusively merchant fraternity in 1499.[41] In Beverley, trade gilds probably fulfilled most of the functions of the religious gilds during the fifteenth century.[42] The blurring of the distinction between religious gilds and occupational organizations probably brought gilds closer to the urban secular authorities in terms of political control, but might have made members less likely to make bequests to them. It may be significant that Hull testators in the sixteenth century tended to make bequests to the maisonsdieu of the town's gilds rather than the gilds themselves.[43]

That the Corpus Christi Gild of York was, to some extent, an exception to the general decline in bequests to gilds reinforces arguments that the county remained doctrinally conservative throughout the upheavals of the Reformation. Large numbers of the sixteenth century bequests made to it asked for gild funerals and the ceremonial associated with them.[44] In particular, the presence and the prayers of the gild's clerical officers were specified. These testators were clearly

---

[37] Chapter 2, pp. 77–83.
[38] Chapter 4, pp. 118–24.
[39] Chapter 4, pp. 140–2.
[40] Chapter 4, pp. 134–40.

[41] Chapter 6, pp. 215–16.
[42] Chapters 2, p. 80; 3, pp. 106–7.
[43] Chapter 2, p. 79.
[44] Chapter 4, pp. 145–6.

still convinced of the validity of the doctrine of purgatory and the efficacy of intercession.

That the gilds were dissolved in 1547 with apparently little local protest was due to three factors, none of which was directly connected with a wholesale, willing acceptance of the new beliefs adopted by the regimes of Thomas Cromwell and Protector Somerset. In the first place, the earlier interventions of government were gradual, piecemeal and indirect. Attacks on images, lights and processions and the suppression of saints' feasts whittled away the ritual basis of the gilds' public demonstrations of piety.[45] Their intercessory role was abolished with the denial of purgatory and their ceremonials further diminished by the substitution of commemoration for transubstantiation.[46] Although not attacked directly by the government until the late 1540s, their traditional practices, and the doctrines that underpinned them, no longer reflected the policies of central government. Whilst this process applied to all the gilds in the country, the second factor was more particularly northern. The failure of the Pilgrimage of Grace and its bloody aftermath had shown the futility of protest.[47] All the large urban centres of the county had been involved, and York had, in many ways, been its epicentre. Overt opposition was impossible from a cowed society. The third factor was, in some respects, a protest but a very muted one. The concealment of gild possessions and what seems to have been a wholesale and covert self-dissolution of fraternities, in advance of the arrival of the commissioners, was largely an attempt to ensure that their assets disappeared into the community, rather than into the king's coffers.[48] This seems to have been aided by the exception made of craft gilds. Local authorities were often able, sometimes at a price, to retain gild properties for communal use.

Concealment, however, was not entirely a matter of lands and assets. When the Corpus Christi Gild of York chose to preserve, by subtle subterfuge, St Richard Scrope's mazer, rather than any of its more spectacular treasures, it was not a valuable cup but a pious object that was entrusted to the cordwainers.[49] Old attitudes to piety and fraternity lingered when all power had been stripped away. In 1550, Christopher Paynter, formerly chantry chaplain of the gild altar of St Mary, in All Saints Pavement, York, and master of the Corpus Christi Gild in 1543, made the following bequest: 'Item I gif to euere on of my brother of Corpus Christi hospital viij d. and they to be at my beriall . . .'.[50] Aware that a full gild funeral was no longer possible, Paynter was attempting to reconstruct something approximate to it under the new rules.

In dismantling the gilds as 'Structures of Superstition', the Tudor governments of the mid-sixteenth century swept away one of the pillars of late medieval traditional lay piety. The new Church in England demanded less ceremony and simpler rituals. The splendid processions and fraternal feasts were no more. The

---

45 Chapter 7, pp. 227–31.
46 Chapter 7, pp. 225–6.
47 Chapter 7, pp. 232–6.

48 Chapter 7, pp. 238–40.
49 Chapter 5, p. 193.
50 BIHR PR 13 703r.

prayers and perpetual obits that transcended the grave were discontinued. The relationships between parishes and their gilds, between town governments and the fraternities they controlled, between members of different callings and classes within and between gilds, all disappeared. The complex webs of influence vanished as economic assets were hastily concealed or lost to the government. Their unique mixture of pious unanimity, fraternal concord, economic success and political interdependence was irreplaceable. The power of the religious gilds had departed, leaving a vacuum which could never be completely filled. Laymen would seek other ways of expressing piety and fraternity. They had to do so within a society that was embarking on a process of fragmentation that would end, within a century, in a civil war, involving the abolition of the monarchy itself.

APPENDIX 1: Identified Yorkshire Gilds

This list does not assemble all the data available on each gild and its location. It is intended only as a brief summary. Full references to all the gilds and services listed, including details of all testators, bequests and information on each location, can be found in the gazetteer section of D. J. F. Crouch, 'Piety, Fraternity and Power' (unpublished D.Phil. thesis, York, 1995).

Location: name of the place where the gild was found.
Gild: name of the gild or service where known.
Evidence: description of the type of evidence found.
No: number of bequests made to the gild or service.
1st: date of the first reference to the gild or service from any source.
Last: date of the last reference to the gild or service from any source.

Certificates Commissioners' certificates at dissolution. Most of these can be found in Page's edition of *Certificates*.
Cal Pat Reference to be found in the appropriate volume of the *Calendar of Patent Rolls*.
VCH Reference to be found in the appropriate volume of *The Victoria County History (Yorkshire, East Riding, North Riding* or *City of York)*.
Town Docs Reference to be found in Leach, *Beverley Town Documents*.

Location	Gild	Evidence	No	1st	Last
Aldborough WR	St Lazarus Gild	testamentary	1	1474	–
	St Robert Gild	testamentary	1	1474	–
Aldbrough ER	St Mary Gild	testamentary	8	1504	1529
	St Peter Gild:	testamentary	8	1504	1529
Almondbury WR	St Mary Service	testamentary	2	1527	1538
	St Nicholas Service	testamentary	1	1538	–
Alne NR	St Mary Gild	testamentary	3	1487	1540
Badsworth WR	Holy Trinity Service	*Certificates*	–	1546	1546
Barmby on the Marsh ER	Holy Trinity & St Mary Gild	*Cal Pat*	–	1459	1459
Bawtry WR	Holy Trinity Gild	testamentary	2	1438	1441
Bedale NR	Holy Trinity Gild	PRO C 47/46/444	–	1389	–
	Jesus Gild	testamentary	1	1506	–
	St Mary Gild:	testamentary / *Certificates*	3	1506	1548
Bempton ER	Corpus Christi Gild	*VCH/Cal Pat*	–	1569	–
	St Mary & St Helen Gild	*VCH/Cal Pat*	–	1569	–
	St Michael Gild		2	–	1569

Location	Gild	Evidence	No	1st	Last
Bempton ER	Unnamed Gild:	testamentary	1	1528	–
Bessingby ER	St Mary Magdalene Gild:	*VCH/Cal Pat*	3	1549	1570
Beswick ER	Unnamed Gild	testamentary	1	1505	–
Beverley ER	Corpus Christi Gild	PRO C 47/46/445 *VCH/Town Docs/* testamentary	6	1352	1408
	Holy Trinity Gild in St Mary	*VCH*/testamentary	1	1452	–
	Paternoster Gild	*VCH/Town Docs*	–	1431	–
	St Helen (and St Mary) Gild	PRO C 47/46/446 1389/*Town Docs/VCH*	–	1389	–
	St John in May Gild	*Town Docs/VCH*	–	–	–
	St John of Beverley, Great Gild Hansehouse	PRO C 47/46/447/ *Town Docs/VCH/* testamentary	5	1389	1506
	St John the Baptist Gild	*Town Docs/VCH*	–	–	1440
	St Mary of the Red Ark Gild	testamentary	1	1538	–
	St Mary Gild in St Mary	PRO C 47/46/448/ *Town Docs/* testamentary	3	1355	1484
	St Mary Gild in St Nicholas Holmkirk	testamentary/	1	1396	–
	St Peter of Milan Gild	*Town Docs/VCH*	–	–	–
	Youngmen's Gild Called the Four Yeomen in St Mary Parish	*Town Docs/VCH*	–	1503	–
	Youngmen's Gild Called the Four Yeomen in the Minster Parish	*Town Docs/VCH*	–	1508	–
Bingley WR	St Laurence Gild	testamentary	1	1427	–
Birstall WR	Jesus Service	*Certificates*	–	1546	–
	St Mary Service	*Certificates*	–	1546	–
Bishopthorpe WR	Unnamed Service	*Certificates*	–	1546	–
Bolton Percy WR	St Mary Gild	testamentary	1	1471	–
Bossall NR	St Botolph Gild	testamentary	4	1527	1529
Bramham WR	Unnamed Gild	*Certificates*	–	1548	1548
Brandesburton ER	Plough Gild	testamentary	1	1517	–
Bridlington ER	General Gild References	testamentary/*Cal Pat*	1	1464	1548
	Holy Trinity Gild	testamentary	6	1473	1507
	St John the Baptist Gild:	testamentary	1	1473	–
	St Mary Gild	testamentary	6	1473	1507
Broughton in Craven WR	Unnamed Service	*Certificates*	–	1548	1548

Location	Gild	Evidence	No	1st	Last
Burn WR	St Katherine Gild	testamentary	3	1482	1483
Burneston NR	St Mary Gild	*Certificates*	–	1548	–
Burnsall WR	St Anthony Gild	testamentary	1	1472	–
	St Robert Gild	testamentary	1	1472	–
Burstwick ER	St Mary Gild	*VCH*	–	–	–
Burton Agnes ER	St Mary Gild	testamentary/*VCH*	1	1505	–
Campsall WR	St Mary Service	*Certificates*	–	1546	1546
Carnaby ER	St John Baptist	testamentary/*VCH*	1	1526	1569
Cottingham ER	General Gild Bequests	testamentary	3	1506	1538
	Corpus Christi Gild	testamentary	3	1504	1517
	Plough Gild	testamentary	1	1517	1517
	St George, Corpus Christi and Saviour Gild	testamentary/*VCH*	1	1517	1552
	St Mary Gild	testamentary	1	1517	1517
Coxwold NR	St Mary Gild	testamentary	4	1537	1539
Danby NR	St Mary Gild	testamentary	1	1438	1438
Darton WR	St Mary Service	*Certificates*	–	1548	1548
Doncaster WR	General Gild Bequests	testamentary	6	1505	1506
	Cordwainers' Gild	testamentary	1	1505	1505
	Corpus Christi Gild	testamentary	4	1398	1505
	Holy Cross Gild or Service	testamentary/*Certificates/Cal Pat*	2	1482	1548
	Holy Trinity Gild	testamentary	2	1471	1482
	Paternoster Gild	testamentary	1	1398	1398
	St Anne Gild	testamentary	1	1371	1471
	St Anthony and St Sitha	testamentary	1	1480	1480
	St Barbara Gild	testamentary	1	1467	1467
	St Bega Gild	testamentary	1	1467	1467
	St Christopher Gild	testamentary	5	1482	1518
	St Erasmus	glass	–	15C	–
	St George Gild	testamentary	14	1471	1529
	St Giles Gild	testamentary	1	1501	–
	St James & St Sitha Gild	testamentary	1	1482	1482
	St John Baptist Gild in the Chapel of St Mary Magdalene	testamentary	1	1498	–
	St Katherine Gild	testamentary	2	1398	1482
	St Laurence Gild	testamentary	1	1505	1505
	St Leonard Gild	testamentary	1	1471	1471
	St Mary Gild	testamentary	1	1482	1482
	St Mary Coronation Gild	testamentary	1	1505	1505
	St Mary Magdalene Gild	testamentary	2	1471	1482
	St Sebastian Gild	testamentary	1	1505	1505
	St Sonday Gild	testamentary	1	1507	1507

Location	Gild	Evidence	No	1st	Last
	St Thomas of Canterbury Gild	testamentary/ *Certificates*	2	1505	1546
Drax WR	Holy Sepulchre Gild	testamentary	2	1464	1474
Easington ER	Apostles Gild	testamentary	3	1504	1528
	St Mary Gild	*VCH*	–	–	–
Easingwold NR	St Mary Gild	testamentary	8	1430	1540
Ecclesfield WR	St Mary Service	*Certificates*	–	1548	1548
	St John Baptist Service	*Certificates*	–	1548	1548
Egton NR	Unnamed Gild	testamentary	1	1463	1463
Elland WR	St Mary Service	testamentary	1	1505	1505
Ellerby NR	St Mary Gild	testamentary	1	1540	1540
Featherstone WR	St Mary Service	testamentary	4	1528	1539
Felkirk West WR	St Peter Service	*Certificates*	–	1546	1546
Fishlake WR	Holy Trinity Service	testamentary/ *Certificates*	2	1505	1548
Flamborough ER	Holy Trinity Gild	testamentary	1	1504	1504
	St Margaret Gild	*VCH*	–	1566	1633
Folkton ER	St John Baptist Gild	testamentary	1	1527	1527
Foston NR	Holy Trinity Gild	testamentary	1	1437	1437
Foston on the Wolds ER	Holy Trinity Gild	testamentary/ *VCH*	1	1438	1566
Fraisthorpe ER	Unnamed Gild	*VCH*	1	1566	1566
Garton ER	Holy Trinity Gild	testamentary	1	1566	1566
Garton on the Wolds ER	St Mary Gild	testamentary	1	1430	1430
Giggleswick WR	St Mary Gild	testamentary	2	1527	1528
	St Mary Service	testamentary	1	1538	1538
Goathland NR	Unnamed Gild	testamentary	1	1429	1429
Great Driffield ER	Holy Trinity Gild	testamentary	2	1463	1528
	St Mary Gild	testamentary	3	1463	1528
	Unnamed Gild	*Cal Pat*	–	1548	1548
Grimston by York ER	St Helen Gild	testamentary	6	1451	1494
Guisborough NR	St Mary Gild	*Cart. Prior. de Gyseburne* testamentary/ *Cal Pat*	1	1498	1558
Hackness NR	St Hilda Gild	testamentary	4	1440	1539
Halifax WR	Holy Cross Service		–	1546	1548
	Morrow Mass Service	testamentary/ *Certificates*	1	1526	1546
	St George Service	testamentary	1	1526	–
	St Mary Service	testamentary	2	1526	1538
Halsham ER	Unnamed Gild	*VCH*	–	–	–
Hampsthwaite WR	Unnamed Gild	*Certificates*	–	1546	–

Location	Gild	Evidence	No	1st	Last
Hatfield WR	St Katherine Service	*Certificates*	–	1546	1548
	St Mary Service	*Certificates*	–	1546	1548
	St Mary Service in the Chapel of Stanford	*Certificates*	–	1546	–
Hawnby NR	St Mary Gild	testamentary	1	1538	–
Hedon ER	Holy Cross Gild	*VCH/Cal Pat/* testamentary	12	1392	1572
Helmsley NR	Holy Trinity Gild	testamentary	1	1506	–
	St Mary Gild	testamentary	2	1461	1506
Hemsworth WR	St Mary Service	testamentary	1	1540	–
Heptonstall WR	St Mary Service	*Certificates*	–	1546	1548
Hollym ER	St Mary Gild	testamentary/ *Cal Pat*	2	1529	1548
Hornsea ER	General Bequests to the Four Gilds	testamentary	11	1505	1547
	Corpus Christi Gild	testamentary	6	1526	1547
	Holy Trinity Gild	testamentary	9	1504	1539
	St Katherine Gild	testamentary	6	1504	1539
	St Mary Gild	testamentary	4	1504	1539
Howden ER	Holy Trinity Gild	*Cal Pat*	–	1549	1551
Huddersfield WR	St Mary Service	*Certificates*	–	1546	–
	St Nicholas Service	testamentary	1	1537	–
Hull, Kingston-upon ER	General Gild Bequests	testamentary	4	1451	1517
	Corpus Christi Gild in Holy Trinity Parish	PRO C 47/46/449 KHRO BRA81 testamentary/ *Certificates*	12	1349	1548
	Holy Trinity Gild in Holy Trinity Parish	*VCH*/testamentary	6	1408	1540
	Jesus Gild in St Mary Parish	*VCH*	–	–	–
	Resurrection Gild in Holy Trinity Parish	*VCR*/ testamentary	5	1389	1517
	St Anne Gild in Holy Trinity Parish	*VCH* testamentary/ *Certificates*	2	1418	1548
	St Anne Service in St Mary Parish	*Certificates*	–	1548	–
	St Christopher Gild in Holy Trinity Parish	testamentary	1	1398	–
	St George Gild in Holy Trinity Parish	*VCH*/testamentary	5	1398	1517
	St Gregory Gild in Holy Trinity Parish	*VCH*/testamentary	1	1461	–

Location	Gild	Evidence	No	1st	Last
	St Helen Gild in St Mary Parish	*VCH*	–	–	–
	St James Service in Holy Trinity Parish	*Certificates*	–	1548	–
	St James Gild in St Mary Parish	*VCH*/testamentary	1	1418	–
	St John Baptist Gild in Holy Trinity Parish	PRO C 47/46/450/ *VCH*/testamentary	5	1389	1538
	St Katherine Gild in Holy Trinity Parish	*VCH*/testamentary	4	1405	1451
	St Loy Gild in Holy Trinity Parish	*VCH*/testamentary	2	1399	1438
	St Mary Gild in Holy Trinity Parish	KRHO BRA87/ testamentary/*VCH*	4	1391	1539
	St Mary Gild in St Mary Parish	PRO C 47/46/451/ *VCH* /testamentary	4	1357	1451
	St Nicholas Bishop Gild in Holy Trinity Parish	testamentary	1	1485	–
	St Ninian Gild in the Carmelite Friary	testamentary	1	1502	–
	St Saviour Gild in St Mary Parish	*VCH*	–	–	–
	Unnamed Service in Holy Trinity Parish	*Certificates*	–	1548	–
Humbleton ER	St Mary Gild	testamentary	8	1486	1517
Hunmanby ER	Jesus Gild	testamentary	1	1519	–
	St Mary Gild	testamentary	15	1462	1539
Ingleby Greenhow NR	Jesus Gild	testamentary	1	1506	–
Keighley WR	Unnamed Service	*Certificates*	–	1548	–
Keyingham ER	St Mary Gild	*VCH*	–	–	–
Kildwick in Craven WR	St Mary Service	*Certificates*	–	1548	–
Kilham ER	St Laurence Gild	testamentary/*Cal Pat*	1	1493	1563
Kilnsea ER	All Saints Gild	testamentary	1	1504	–
Kirby Grindalyth ER	St Mary Gild	testamentary	1	1484	–
Kirby Misperton NR	St Katherine Gild	testamentary	1	1484	–
	St Mary Gild	testamentary	1	1517	–
Kirkburn ER	St Katherine Gild	testamentary	1	1483	–
Kirkburton WR	St Nicholas Service	*Certificates*	–	1548	–
	St Mary Service	*Certificates*	–	1546	–

Location	Gild	Evidence	No	1st	Last
Kirkby Malzeard WR	St Mary Gild	testamentary	1	1482	1482
Kirkby Overblow WR	St Mary Service	testamentary	1	1540	–
Kirkheaton WR	St Mary Service	testamentary / *Certificates*	2	1495	1546
Knaresborough WR	St Robert Gild	testamentary	2	1480	1531
Langtoft ER	St Katherine Gild	testamentary / *VCH*	1	1528	–
Lastingham NR	Holy Trinity Gild	testamentary	2	1475	1485
	St Mary Gild	testamentary	1	1485	–
Leconfield ER	Unnamed Gild	*Cal Pat*	–	1548	–
Leeds WR	Jesus Gild	testamentary	6	1515	1537
	St George Gild	testamentary	1	1517	–
Levisham NR	Holy Trinity Gild	testamentary	2	1475	1483
	St Mary Gild	testamentary	2	1475	1483
Loversall WR	Unnamed Service	*Certificates*	–	1548	–
Malton, New NR	St John the Baptist Gild	testamentary / licence	1	1444	1450
	St Mary Gild in the Chapel of St Michael	testamentary	1	1407	1407
Malton, Old NR	St Mary Gild	testamentary	1	1399	–
	Unnamed Service in the Chapel of St Leonard	*Certificates*	–	1548	–
	Unnamed Service in the Chapel of St Michael	*Certificates*	–	1548	–
Middlesborough NR	St Thomas of Canterbury Gild	testamentary	1	1439	–
Middleton by Pickering NR	St Mary Gild	testamentary	2	1516	1528
Newton upon Ouse NR	St Mary Gild	testamentary	1	1540	–
Normanton WR	St Mary Service	*Certificates*	–	1548	–
Northallerton NR	Holy Trinity Gild	testamentary	1	1485	–
	St Mary Gild	testamentary	1	1485	–
North Cave ER	St Mary Gild	*VCH*	–	1468	–
North Frodingham ER	St Helen Gild	testamentary	1	1537	–
	St Thomas Gild	testamentary	1	1537	–
Otley WR	St Katherine Gild or Service	testamentary / *Certificates*	1	1518	1548
Ottringham ER	Corpus Christi Gild	*VCH* / testamentary	2	1499	1540
	St Mary Gild	testamentary / *VCH Cal Pat*	6	1452	1548
Owthorne ER	St Mary Gild	testamentary	1	1529	–

Location	Gild	Evidence	No	1st	Last
Patrington ER	Corpus Christi Gild	*VCH*	–	1544	1545
	Holy Trinity Gild	testamentary/*VCH*	2	1518	1548
	St Christopher Gild	testamentary	1	1518	–
	St Mary Gild	testamentary/*VCH*	2	1518	1548
Paull ER	Holy Cross Gild	*VCH*	–	–	–
	St Andrew Gild	testamentary	1	1537	–
	St Mary Gild	testamentary/*VCH*	2	1493	1537
Penistone WR	St Erasmus Service	testamentary	1	1529	–
	St Mary Service	testamentary	1	1529	–
Pickering NR	St Mary Gild	testamentary	1	1496	–
Pocklington ER	Apostles Gild	testamentary	1	1494	–
	Holy Cross Gild	testamentary	2	1396	1397
	St Mary Gild	testamentary	3	1396	1494
Pontefract WR	Corpus Christi Gild	testamentary	52	1387	1540
	Jesus Gild	testamentary	4	1507	1529
	Jesus and St Roch Gild	testamentary	1	1515	–
	St Mary Service	testamentary	11	1437	1540
	St Mary Gild or Service in St Giles Chapel	testamentary	5	1462	1540
	St Roch Gild	testamentary	1	1507	–
	St Thomas of Lancaster Gild	testamentary	3	1428	1529
Preston ER	Plough Gild	testamentary	2	1485	1507
	St Katherine Gild	testamentary	2	1429	1537
	St Mary the Virgin Gild	testamentary/*VCH*	10	1472	1537
	St Mary of Pity Gild	testamentary/*VCH*	5	1472	1507
Richmond NR	General Gild Bequest	testamentary	1	1541	–
	St John the Baptist Gild	testamentary	1	1484	–
	St Mary Gild	testamentary	3	1446	1484
	St Thomas Gild	testamentary	1	1484	–
Ripley WR	St John Baptist Service	*Certificates*	–	1546	–
	St Mary Gild or Service	*Certificates* /*Cal Pat*	–	1546	1548
Ripon WR	Holy Cross Gild	testamentary	9	1452	1529
	St Mary, St Wilfrid and All Saints Gild	PRO C 47/46/452 testamentary	1	1379	–
Roos ER	Unnamed Gild	glass	–	–	–
Rossington WR	Holy Cross and St Mary Gild	testamentary	1	1493	–
Rotherham WR	Holy Cross Gild	PRO C 47/46/453	–	1356	1389
	St Katherine Gild or Service	testamentary/ *Certificates*	2	1391	1548
	St Mary Gild or Service	testamentary/ *Certificates*	1	1472	1548

Location	Gild	Evidence	No	1st	Last
	St Laurence Service in the Chapel of Tymslake	*Certificates*	–	1546	–
Rudston ER	Holy Trinity Gild	testamentary/*Cal Pat*	2	1540	1548
	St Mary Gild	testamentary/*Cal Pat*	2	1540	1548
Sandall Magna WR	St Mary Service	*Certificates*	–	1548	–
Sandall Parva WR	St Nicholas Service	*Certificates*	–	1548	–
Scarborough NR	All Saints Gild	*VCH*	–	1426	–
	Corpus Christi Gild	*VCH*	–	1426	–
	Holy Trinity Gild	*VCH*	–	1426	–
	St Clement Gild	testamentary/*VCH*	3	1400	1518
	St George Gild	testamentary/*VCH*	1	1349	1426
	St James Gild	*VCH*	–	1426	–
	St John Baptist Gild	*VCH*/testamentary	–	1425	1451
	St John Baptist Gild in St Sepulchre Chapel	testamentary	1	1462	–
	St Katherine Gild	testamentary	1	1400	–
	St Mary Assumption Gild	*VCH*	–	1426	–
	St Mary in Jerusalem Gild	testamentary	1	1390	–
	St Nicholas Gild	testamentary/*VCH*	1	1408	1426
	St Sitha Gild	*VCH*/testamentary	1	1426	1462
Seamer NR	Puerorum Gild	testamentary	1	1473	–
	Unnamed Gild	testamentary	2	1539	–
Sedburgh WR	Holy Cross Gild	*Cal Pat*	–	1551	–
Selby WR	St Mary Assumption Gild	testamentary	1	1441	–
Sheffield WR	St Crux Service	testamentary/*Certificates*	1	1441	1548
	St Mary Service	testamentary/*Certificates*	1	1474	1548
Sherburn in Hartford Lye ER	Holy Trinity Gild	testamentary	1	1505	–
Sherburn-in-Elmet ER	St Christopher Gild	testamentary	1	1484	–
Sheriff Hutton NR	Holy Cross Gild	testamentary	3	1472	1529
Silkeston WR	St Mary Service	testamentary	2	1427	1428
Skeffling ER	Unnamed Gild	*Cal Pat*	–	1558	–
Skelton NR	St Mary Gild	testamentary	1	1527	–
Skipsea ER	Unnamed Gild	testamentary	2	1537	1538
Skipton WR	St Mary Service	*Certificates*	–	1548	–
Snaith WR	Holy Trinity Gild or Service	*Certificates*	–	1546	–
	St Mary Service	*Certificates*	–	1546	–
Spofforth WR	Holy Cross Gild	testamentary	2	1408	1428
	St Mary Gild	testamentary	2	1408	1428
	St Mary Magdalene Gild	testamentary	2	1408	1428

Location	Gild	Evidence	No	1st	Last
Stainburn WR	Unnamed Service	*Certificates*	–	1548	–
Stainforth WR	St Mary Service	*Certificates*	–	1548	–
Staveley WR	St Mary Gild	testamentary	1	1408	–
Stirton WR	St Mary Gild	testamentary	1	1505	–
Sutton on the Forest	St Mary Gild	testamentary	12	1438	1529
Swine ER	St Mary Gild	testamentary	17	1480	1547
	St Peter Gild	testamentary	1	1520	–
Swinefleet WR	St John Gild	testamentary	1	1452	–
	St Mary Gild	testamentary	1	1452	–
Tadcaster WR	St Christopher Gild	testamentary	1	1418	–
	St Katherine Gild	testamentary	4	1408	1438
Thirsk NR	St Mary Gild	testamentary / *Certificates*	2	1431	1546
Thorganby ER	St Helen Gild	testamentary / *VCH*	1	1547	1566
Thorne WR	St Mary Service	*Certificates*	–	1546	–
	St Michael Service	*Certificates*	–	1546	–
Thwing ER	Holy Trinity Gild				
Tickhill WR	Holy Cross Gild	testamentary / *Certificates*	2	1429	1546
	St Christopher Gild	testamentary	1	1429	–
	St Mary Assumption Gild	testamentary	2	1395	1405
Tollerton NR	St Michael Gild	testamentary	1	1482	–
Topcliffe NR	St Mary Gild	testamentary / *Certificates*	8	1483	1548
Waddington WR	St Mary Service	*Certificates*	–	1548	–
Wakefield WR	Corpus Christi Gild	testamentary	1	1521	–
	Holy Cross Service	testamentary	1	1452	–
	Holy Trinity Gild	testamentary	1	1521	–
	Morrow Mass Service	*Certificates*	–	1548	–
	St Christopher Gild	court rolls	–	1529	–
	St George Gild	testamentary	1	1521	–
	St John's Chapel Service	*Certificates*	–	1548	–
	St Mary Service	testamentary	1	1452	–
Walkingham WR	General Gild Bequest	testamentary	1	1528	–
Wath upon Dearne WR	St Mary Service	testamentary	1	1538	–
	St Nicholas Service	testamentary	1	1538	–
Wawne ER	Plough Gild	testamentary	2	1504	1505
	St Mary Gild	testamentary	10	1440	1537
Weaverthorpe ER	Corpus Christi Gild	testamentary	1	1378	–
	St Mary Gild	testamentary	2	1516	1529
	Unnamed Gild	testamentary	2	1539	1540
Welwick ER	St Mary Gild	testamentary / *Certificates / Cal Pat*	1	1504	1548

Location	Gild	Evidence	No	1st	Last
Wheatley WR	Unnamed Gild	testamentary	1	1517	–
Whitby NR	Holy Cross Gild	testamentary	1	1397	–
	Holy Trinity Gild	testamentary	1	1396	–
	St Christopher Gild	testamentary	2	1429	–
Whitgift WR	Holy Trinity Gild	testamentary/ *Certificates*	4	1407	1546
Wilberfoss ER	St Mary Gild	*VCH*	–	–	–
Willerby ER	St Lazarus Gild	testamentary	1	1484	–
Winestead ER	Unnamed Gild	*Cal Pat/VCH*	–	1548	1571
Wintringham ER	St Mary Gild	testamentary	1	1515	–
Worsbrough WR	St Mary Service	*Certificates*	–	1546	–
Wragby WR	St Mary Service	testamentary/ *Certificates*	4	1471	1546
York, City of	General Gild Bequest	testamentary	1	1473	–
	Chantry Chaplains' Gild	testamentary	2	1399	1407
	Cordwainers' Corpus Christi Light	testamentary	1	1391	–
	Corpus Christi Gild	testamentary/ MS Lansdowne 304/ *Certificates et al.*	367	1408	1548
	Corpus Christi Light in St Saviour	testamentary	1	1416	–
	Holy Cross Gild in St Crux	testamentary	2	1440	1458
	Holy Ghost Gild of the Weavers	testamentary	1	1428	–
	Holy Trinity Gild (illegal)	Assize Roll 1107	–	1306	–
	Holy Trinity Gild Fossgate of the Mercers	MA Archive/ testamentary	20	1410	1525
	Holy Trinity Gild of the Augustine Friars	testamentary testamentary	3	1438	1471
	Holy Trinity Gild of the Dominican Friars	YMB2 70 2	–	1418	–
	Paternoster Gild	PRO C 47/46/454 testamentary/*et al.*	22	1389	1439
	Paternoster and St Anthony Gild	testamentary	5	1444	1480
	Resurrection Gild of the Austin Friars	YMB3 254–55	–	1482	–
	St Anne Gild in St Laurence in the Suburbs	testamentary/ *Certificates*	9	1404	1548
	St Anne Gild in St Margaret	BIHR Y/Marg. 36	–	1397	–
	St Anne Gild in St Saviour	testamentary	1	1537	–

Location	Gild	Evidence	No	1st	Last
York, City of *cont.*	St Anthony Gild	YMB II p70–2 testamentary/*et al.*	77	1415	1558
	St Augustine Gild of the Cordwainers	testamentary	2	1506	1520
	St Christopher and St Andrew Gild [?in St Helen Stonegate]	testamentary	1	1399	–
	St Christopher and St George Gild	testamentary/*et al.*	36	1466	1551
	St Christopher Gild	testamentary/*Cal Pat*/ *Certificates/et al.*	230	1396	1543
	St Francis Gild	testamentary	6	1428	1453
	St George Gild	testamentary *Cal Pat*/ *Certificates*	29	1394	1546
	St John the Baptist Gild in St Denys	testamentary	1	1390	–
	St John the Baptist Gild in St John Hungate	testamentary	1	1449	–
	St John the Baptist Gild (of the Tailors)	PRO C 47/46/455 testamentary/*Cal Pat*	44	1399	1546
	St Katherine Gild in St Denys	testamentary	2	1503	1506
	St Katherine Gild of the Austin Friars	testamentary	10	1414	1537
	St Martin and St Anthony Gild	testamentary	2	1449	1475
	St Martin Gild	testamentary/ *Cal Pat*	1	1446	1451
	St Mary and St Anthony Gild	testamentary	1	1473	–
	St Mary and St Austin Gild	testamentary	1	1509	–
	St Mary and St Francis Gild	testamentary	1	1429	–
	St Mary and St Martin Gild	testamentary	20	1450	1494
	St Mary Gild (unspecified)	testamentary	1	1471	–
	St Mary Gild at the Abbey	testamentary	43	1420	1487
	St Mary Gild in All Saints Pavement	testamentary	2	1485	1512
	St Mary Gild in Fossgate (also known as Jesus and St Mary)	testamentary/*Cal Pat*	1	1357	1365

Location	Gild	Evidence	No	1st	Last
York, City of *cont.*	St Mary Gild in St Andrew Fishergate	testamentary	1	1428	–
	St Mary Gild in St Helen Stonegate	testamentary	1	1478	–
	St Mary Gild in St Laurence	testamentary	1	1404	–
	St Mary Gild in St Mary Bishophill Senior	testamentary	1	1453	–
	St Mary Gild in St Michael le Belfrey	testamentary	4	1486	1509
	St Mary Gild in St Nicholas Micklegate	testamentary	1	1486	–
	St Mary Gild in St Olave	testamentary	1	1434	–
	St Mary Gild in the Carmelite Friary sustained by the Cordwainers	testamentary	30	1402	1527
	St Mary Gild of the Friars Minor	testamentary	1	1420	–
	St Mary Gild of the Skinners in St Giles	testamentary	5	1435	1445
	St Mary Gild of the Weavers	testamentary	12	1406	1528
	St Mary Magdalene Gild	testamentary	5	1480	1537
	St Mary, St Martin and St Anthony Gild	testamentary	2	1460	1467
	St Nicholas Gild	testamentary	3	1491	1509
	St Nicholas Gild in St Thomas Chapel	testamentary	1	1430	–
	St Sitha Light in St Michael Spurriergate	BIHR PRY/MS4	–	–	–
	St Thomas of Canterbury Gild in St Michael le Belfrey	testamentary	2	1398	1399
	St Thomas the Martyr Gild in St Martin Micklegate	testamentary	1	1454	–

APPENDIX 2: Masters of the Corpus Christi Gild in York 1461–1546

Derived from gild register, accounts and testamentary evidence. Page references are to Skaife, *Corpus Christi*. Benefices of rectors and vicars are usually recorded in the register and accounts. It has been assumed that clerics who are not otherwise ascribed posts were chaplains. There are 84 records.

Date: date that the Master assumed office.
Master: name of the Master.
Status: the Master's ranking and employment.
Post: the parish and, where appropriate, the chantry of the Master.
Page: page reference in Skaife, *Corpus Christi*.

Date	Master	Status	Post	Page
1460	William Outhwaite	chaplain	–	61
1461	John Burton	rector	St Martin Micklegate	62
1462	William Laverok	rector	Holy Trinity	63
1463	William Laverok	rector	Holy Trinity	64
1464	William Caber	chaplain	–	64
1465	William Caber	chaplain	–	64
1466	Thomas Ouren	rector	–	66
1467	John Burton	rector	St Martin Micklegate	66
1468	John Hert	vicar	St Martin Micklegate and Vicar Choral	68
1469	John Burton	rector	St Martin Micklegate	70
1470	John Wyntryngham	chantry chaplain	Wartre chantry in St Saviour	74
1471	John Fox	chaplain and master	Holy Trinity Gild Hospital in Holy Trinity Fossgate	79
1472	John Giliot	chaplain	–	82
1473	John Wyntryngham	chantry chaplain	Wartre chantry in St Saviour	84
1474	John Bykker	vicar	Holy Trinity King's Court	84
1475	Thomas Symson	rector	St John Baptist Hungate	96
1476	Roger Barton	rector	St Saviour	99
1477	William Grundale	rector	St Mary Bishophill Senior	101
1478	John Wynton	rector	St Gregory	103
1479	Thomas Hornby	chantry chaplain	Catton chantry in All Saints North Street	104
1480	Roger Barton	rector	St Saviour	107
1481	William Barton	vicar	St Laurence in the Suburbs	109
1482	John Garnett	rector	St Mary Castlegate	111

Date	Master	Status	Post	Page
1483	Henry Hudson	rector	All Saints North Street	113
1484	William Eure	rector	All Saints Peaseholme	115
1485	John Rudby	parochial chaplain	St Olave	118
1486	John Rudby	parochial chaplain	St Olave	118
1487	John Rudby	parochial chaplain	St Olave	120
1488	William Setton	chantry chaplain	St Thomas Martyr in All Saints Pavement	121
1489	William Gillyng	chantry chaplain	SS Katherine and John Baptist in All Saints Pavement	124
1490	John Rypley	vicar	St Mary Bishophill	128
1491	John Garnet	rector	St Mary Castlegate	130
1492	John Bollyng	chantry chaplain	St Thomas Martyr in St Saviour	132
1493	Thomas Metcalf	vicar	Holy Trinity King's Court	135
1494	William Brygham	gild chaplain	SS Christopher and George Coney Street	137
1495	Thomas Hannegeman	chantry chaplain	St John Baptist St Mary Castlegate	138
1496	John Rypley	vicar	St Mary Bishophill	141
1497	Christopher Wardman	chaplain	–	143
1498	Thomas Topham	rector	St Gregory	144
1499	Thomas Topham	rector	St Gregory	146
1500	William Gudwyn	chantry chaplain	St William Chapel Ouse Bridge	149
1501	John Jakson	chantry chaplain	St John Baptist in Holy Trinity Hospital Fossgate	149
1502	John Ranar	vicar	St Helen Stonegate	154
1503	William Clarkson	vicar	St Laurence	157
1504	William Seton (Setton)	chantry chaplain	St Thomas Martyr in All Saints Pavement	159
1505	Thomas Smyth	rector	Holy Trinity Goodramgate	161
1506	Stephen Canon	chantry chaplain	St Nicholas in St Sampson	162
1507	John Newton	chantry chaplain	St Thomas Martyr in St Saviour	164
1508	William Snar	vicar	St George	167
1509	William Cokaa	chantry chaplain	St Thomas Martyr in Holy Trinity Micklegate	168
1510	John Kettlywell	rector	St Wilfrid Blake St	170
1511	Henry Rayncok	rector	St Peter the Little	173

Masters of the Corpus Christi Gild

Date	Master	Status	Post	Page
1512	William Folnetby	chantry chaplain	SS Peter and Paul in Holy Trinity King's Court	175
1513	William Sherburne	rector	St Saviour	179
1514	Robert Lelegrave	chaplain	–	182
1515	William Cokaa	chantry chaplain	St Thomas Martyr in Holy Trinity Micklegate	184
1516	William Wyle	chaplain	–	186
1517	John Hart	chaplain	–	189
1518	John Newton	chantry chaplain	St Thomas Martyr in St Saviour	191
1519	Robert Gomersal	chaplain	–	193
1520	William Symson	chaplain	–	195
1521	Thomas Smyth	rector	Holy Trinity Goodramgate	198
1522	Thomas Orynton	chaplain	–	198
1523	Thomas Orynton	chaplain	–	200
1524	George Rychardson	rector	All Saints Pavement	204
1525	Henry Cukson	chantry chaplain	St William's Chapel Ouse Bridge	204
1526	John Chatburne	chantry chaplain	St Thomas Martyr in St Peter the Little	206
1527	Thomas Marschall	chantry chaplain	St Thomas Martyr in All Saints Pavement	208
1528	Thomas Norman	chantry chaplain	St Stephen Protomartyr in York Minster	208
1529	Christopher Bossall	chantry chaplain	St Peter in All Saints Pavement	213
1530	James Symson	chantry chaplain	St Mary in St Sampson	215
1531	William Phylypson	rector	St Wilfrid	217
1532	James Barker	rector	St Margaret	218
1533	John Johnson	chantry chaplain	Holy Trinity King's Court	219
1534	William Lyghtfuyt	chantry chaplain	St Thomas Martyr in Holy Trinity King's Court	221
1535	William Marton	rector	St Crux	224
1536	John Barnard	rector	All Saints Peaseholme	225
1537	William Pynder	chantry chaplain	St Mary in St John Baptist Hungate	226
1540?	Robert Jakson	rector	St Martin Micklegate	226
1540?	John Beyn	rector	St Mary Bishophill Senior	227
1541	George Cooke	rector	St Margaret	227
1542	John Sympson	chantry chaplain	St Peter in All Saints Pavement	228

Date	Master	Status	Post	Page
1543	Christopher Paynter	chantry chaplain	St Mary in All Saints Pavement	229
1544	John Stapleton	vicar	Holy Trinity King's Court	230
1545	John Wallcar	rector	St Margaret	233
1546	John Wyllson	chantry chaplain	SS Peter and Paul in Holy Trinity King's Court	235

APPENDIX 3: York City Officials Index 1397–1550 Showing Corpus Christi Gild Membership

This index comprises an alphabetical list of the Lord Mayors of York, holding office from 1397 to 1550, and the principal officials who served under them. The principal sources include *FR*, Dobson, *York City Chamberlains' Account Rolls*, Drake, *Eboracum*, the Probate Registers housed in the BIHR and YML, MS Lansdowne 403, and Skaife, *Corpus Christi*. I am grateful to Philip Stell for the use of his unpublished index to this work. My index has been thoroughly checked against the Appendix to A. Kulukunis, 'The *Cursus Honorem* in fifteenth century York' (unpublished MA dissertation, York, 1990–91). I have also made use of other unpublished lists supplied by Philip Stell, the Appendix to C. E. Carpenter, 'The office and personnel of the post of Bridgemaster in York 1450–1499' (unpublished MA dissertation, York, 1995–96) and Skaife, 'York City Officials'. The **surnames** retain the original spellings but do not necessarily include all the known variations of them. Where discrepancies are particularly wide, alternative spellings are given. **Forenames** are given in modern spelling. Where possible, the titles of **occupations** have been standardized. For example 'tanners' include 'barkers', 'cordwainers' include 'shoemakers'. Multiple occupations divided by '/' show that different crafts have been recorded against an individual's name in different places in the sources. Those divided by '&' show that they were so recorded in the same place. Years are given in modern reckoning. **Free** shows the corrected date of entry into the city franchise. **Cham, Sher**, and **Mayor** show the dates on which individuals took up office as Chamberlain, Sheriff and Lord Mayor respectively. Those listed as 'Sheriffs' for dates prior to 1397 were, in fact, Bailiffs. **CC** shows the date of entry into the Corpus Christi Gild. 'Founder' indicates an individual's presence in the gild obit but not elsewhere in the register.

Forename	Name	Free	Occupation	Cham	Sher	Mayor	CC
William	Aberford	1427	merchant	1438	1440	–	–
Thomas	Abney	1509	merchant	1519	–	–	1509
Thomas	Alan	1447	baker	1467	1470	–	1473
Henry	Albone	1441	skinner	1484	–	–	1446
John	Aldestanemor	1412	merchant	1418	1421	1427	1416
Thomas	Aldestanemor	1412	merchant	1432	–	–	1424
Richard de	Allerton	–	tanner	1401	–	–	–
William	Alne	–	merchant	1394	1396	1415	founder
Robert	Amyas	1463	merchant	1468	1469	1481	1473
Robert	Appilby	1449	mariner	1472	–	–	–
Roger	Appilby	1456	tanner	1480	1485	–	–
Thomas	Apylyerd	1529	merchant	1536	1542	–	1542
Miles	Arwhom (Harom)	1464	vestmntmker	1488	1496	–	1473
Adam	Atkinson	1463	tanner	1485	–	–	1457
Adam	Atkynson	1509	tanner	1527	–	–	1515
John	Atkynson	1538	tanner	1547	–	–	1541

Forename	Name	Free	Occupation	Cham	Sher	Mayor	CC
Anthony	Atkyrk	1527	merchant	1540	–	–	1527
Thomas del	Aton	1401	mercer	1410	1421	–	–
John	Bacheler	1504	cordwainer	1534	–	–	–
William	Bacheler	1511	butcher	1532	1548	–	–
Thomas	Bailley	1497	butcher	1521	1522	–	1497
Richard	Baitman	1512	mariner	1534	–	–	1530
Adam del	Banke	1371	dyer	1384	1387	1405	–
Thomas	Bankhouse	1476	draper/tailor	1494	1500	1521	1506
Richard	Bargeman	1535	goldsmith	1548	–	–	–
William	Barker	1465	baker	1482	1483	1525	1497
William	Barker	–	cornchapmn	1515	–	–	1508
William	Barker	1482	merchant	1486	1489	1532	1472
William	Barker	1465	baker	1482	1516	–	1489
William	Barlay	1432	mercer	1448	1450	–	1437
John	Barnardcastell	–	mariner	1392	1400	–	–
William de	Barneby	1389	wright/smith	1396	–	–	1414
John	Barns	1526	butcher	1537	–	–	1534
Thomas	Barton	1436	grocer/spicer	1439	1443	1450	1442
William	Barton	1409	skinner	1432	–	–	1433
John	Bateman	1482	tailor	1506	1508	–	1487
John	Bateman	1493	horsemarshl	1511	–	–	1498
Reginald	Bawtre	1414	merchant	1429	–	–	1428
John	Baynbryg	1386	potter	1415	1418	–	–
Robert	Baynes	1475	tiler	1497	–	–	1482
John	Bean	–	innholder	1535	1538	1545	1525
Robert	Bean	1503	walker	1544	–	–	–
John	Bedale	1386	mercer	1401	1405	1419	1430
William	Bedale	1403	merchant	1415	1423	1437	1423
William	Bekwith	–	merchant	1540	1543	–	1530
William	Belford	1413	merchant	1428	1429	–	1441 wife
John	Beseby Sr	1467	merchant	1484	1486	–	1475
John	Beseby Jr	1490	merchant	1491	1507	–	1489
John	Besyngby	1393	mercer	1410	–	–	–
Henry	Bettes	1477	waxchandler	1500	–	–	1495
John	Beverley	1478	merchant	1483	1485	–	1475
Thomas	Beverley	1440	merchant sta	1447	1450	1460	1453
Henry	Bewn	–	tailor	1532	–	–	–
Henry	Bielby	–	–	–	1530	–	–
John	Birdsall	1463	merchant	1473	–	–	1468
John	Birkhed	1480	merchant	1492	1498	1507	1480
Nicholas	Blackburn Sr	1397	merchant	–	–	1412	1414
Nicholas	Blackburn	1422	merchant	1433	1438	–	–
John	Blackburn Jr	1401	merchant	1424	1427	1429	1412

Forename	Name	Free	Occupation	Cham	Sher	Mayor	CC
Ralph	Blades	1518	pewterer	1546	–	–	1490
James	Bladez	1507	haber/draper	1515	1523	–	1509
Robert	Bold	–	cardmaker	1544	–	–	1518
William	Bolton	1410	tailor/merch	1426	–	–	–
John	Bolton Jr	1410	merc/merch	1417	1419	1431	1430
John	Bolton Sr	1374	merchant	1384	1387	1410	–
Christopher	Both	1432	merchant	1454	1459	–	–
John	Boure (Voure)	–	merchant	1451	1452	–	1452
William	Bowes Jr	1417	merchant	1425	1431	1443	1428
William	Bowes Sr	1390	merchant	1399	1402	1417 1428	1414
Thomas	Bracbryg	1392	weavr/merch	1412	1415	1424	1430
William	Bracebrig	1449	merchant	1450	1454	–	–
Patrick	Bradlay	1415	butcher	1435	–	–	–
William	Bradlay	1435	butcher	1448	1458	–	1453
Brian	Bradley	1510	waxchandler	1522	–	–	1510
Thomas	Brakke (Braxez)	1485	baker	1498	1503	–	1503
William	Brandesby	1397	butcher	1423	–	–	1426
Richard	Breray	1535	goldsmith	1539	1555	–	1556
John	Brereton	1430	merchant	1450	1564	–	1453
Thomas	Brereton	1397	mercer/merch	1420	–	–	1455
Adam del	Brigg	1364	mercer	1398	1403	–	–
Robert	Broddes	1516	tailor	1537	1546	–	–
William	Brokden	1506	cooper/yeoman	1549	–	–	1545
Thomas	Bromflete (Brounflete)	1400	merchant	–	1426	–	–
John	Brounflete	1389	apothecary	1420	1427	–	1423
Thomas	Brounflete	1430	merchant	1456	1457	–	1423
William	Brounflete	1434	clerk/merchant	1464	–	–	1489
Cuthbert	Brownles	1486	dyer	1496	–	–	–
Richard	Buckden	1415	merchant	1430	1435	1444	1414
Peter	Bucky (Buksy)	1392	grocr/merch	1408	1411	1426	1430
Thomas	Bugwith (Bubwith)	1476	grocer	1497	–	–	–
Henry	Bulmer	1477	merchant	1503	–	–	–
Hugh	Buntyng	1479	fletcher	1528	–	–	–
Richard	Burdon	1547	tailor	1550	–	–	–
Richard	Burland	–	innholder	1546	–	–	–
Robert	Burton	1409	merchant	1413	1415	–	–
Roger	Burton	1392	skinner	1417	1420	–	–
Thomas	Burton	1437	walker	–	1442	–	–
Thomas	Burton	1485	miller/merch	1517	1518	1522	1507
William	Burton	1430	–	1433	1437	–	1453
Thomas	Bussy	1392	draper	1403	–	–	1422
Adam	Bynkes	1542	merchant	1550	–	–	–

Forename	Name	Free	Occupation	Cham	Sher	Mayor	CC
Michael	Bynkes	1524	mariner	1535	1544	–	–
William	Bynkes	1523	baker	1543	–	–	1525
Richard	Calom	1534	tailor	1546	–	–	–
John	Carre	1434	merchant	1438	1440	1448 1456	1423
Thomas	Carre	1406	draper	1422	1427	–	1423
John	Carter	1477	merch/tailor	1500	–	–	1519
John	Catour	1477	merchant	1487	–	–	1480
John	Catryk	1425	merc/merch	1440	1443	1453	–
Thomas	Catryk	1401	mercer	1429	1430	–	–
Thomas	Caytour	1441	mercer	1462	1465	–	1446
John	Chapman	1487	saddler	1507	1512	–	1489
Thomas	Chapman	1472	saddler	1487	–	–	1506
Richard	Charlesby	1487	merchant	1503	–	–	1527
John	Chellowe	1435	merchant	1459	–	–	1446 wife
William	Chymney	1455	draper	1470	1474	1486	1457
Richard	Claybruke Sr	1402	baker	1439	1444	–	–
Richard	Claybruke Jr	1438	baker	1457	1460	–	1451
Richard	Clerk	1452	hosier/draper/ tailor	1478	1479	–	1474
William	Clerk	1517	potter	1540	–	–	1457
Christopher	Clerke	1501	dyer	1543	–	–	1543
John	Clerke	1495	innholder	1536	–	–	1493
William	Cleveland	1425	draper	1453	1455	–	1439
Richard	Clidero	1525	tailor	1541	–	–	–
Edward	Clifford	–	gentleman	1507	–	–	1507
Thomas del	Clogh	1369	bower	1397	–	–	–
Richard	Clowbek	1432	–	1550	–	–	1526
William	Clyff	1427	merchant	1442	1444	–	1442
Richard	Cokrell	1428	woolman	1446	–	–	–
Laurence	Collynson	1533	innholder	1547	–	–	1535
William	Colton	1539	waxchandler	1548	–	–	–
Christopher	Colyer	1524	pewterer	1541	–	–	–
John	Colyer	|–	pewterer	1524	1528	–	1513
Robert	Colynson	1426	merc/merch	1442	1445	1457	1429
Brian	Conyers	1457	merchant	1475	–	–	1473
Christopher	Conyers	–	merchant	1536	–	–	1520
Miles	Cook	1531	merchant	1538	–	–	1527
William	Copland	1522	tailor	1537	1543	–	–
Robert	Cornot	–	–	–	1525	–	–
John	Cotes	1436	butcher	1461	1463	–	1457
Edward	Cottsbrook	1375	glover	–	1401	–	–
Peter	Couke	1454	yeomn/barkr	1488	1492	–	–

Forename	Name	Free	Occupation	Cham	Sher	Mayor	CC
Robert	Couke	1517	waxchandler	1531	1534	–	–
John	Coupeland	1426	tanner	1454	1458	–	1441
William	Couper	1423	tanner	1455	–	–	1421
William	Cowper	1540	merchant	1546	–	–	1535
Thomas	Crathorne	1422	merchant	1440	1441	1445	1440
William	Crathorne	1432	merchant	1447	–	–	1440
John de	Craven	1369	glovr/merch	1390	1392	1411	–
William	Craven	1418	merchant	1419	1422	–	–
Thomas	Cravyn	1526	innholder	1538	–	–	1526
Percival	Crawfurth	1534	moneyer	1549	1550	–	–
William	Croft	1442	clerk	1456	–	–	1469
Richard	Croglyn	1418	fletcher	1431	–	–	1437
John	Croser	1429	dyer	1437	1438	1447	–
William	Crosseby	1440	dyer	1461	1464	–	1453
Robert	Cryplyng	1539	bower	1542	–	–	–
Thomas	Cundall	1452	barber	1494	–	–	–
William	Curre	1504	haberdasher/ lawyer	1510	1511	–	1484
Thomas	Curtays	1421	mercer	1444	1449	–	1422
John	Custance	1462	baker	1487	1493	–	1471
John	Custance	1487	merchant	1493	–	–	1501
Robert	Dale	1463	shipman	1493	–	–	1472
Thomas	Danby	1424	merch/merc	1438	1439	1452	–
Richard	Danyell	1527	tapiter	1549	1558	–	1545
Thomas	Danyell	1424	tailor	1449	1451	–	1446
Thomas	Darby	1482	merchant	1490	1493	–	1480
Alexander	Dauson	1467	merchant	1485	1489	–	–
Thomas	Davy	1401	draper	1416	1419	–	1433/5 widow
Bertram	Dawson	1476	merch/tailor	1491	1496	1511	1439
Thomas	Dawson	1540	mercer	1516	1517	–	1506
William	Dawson	1519	butcher	1550	–	–	1455
William	Dekyn	1437	weaver	1477	–	–	1464
Henry	Deyson	1504	dyer	1522	1524	1531	1506
John	Dobson	1522	butcher	1539	–	–	1493
John	Dodyngton	1402	vintn/merch	1419	1425	–	–
John	Dogeson	1482	merchant	1490	1497	1517	1489
William	Dogeson	1515	mercer	1526	1532	1540	–
Thomas de	Doncastre	1377	mercer	1397	1400	–	1426
Thomas	Drawswerd	1496	carver	1501	1505	1515 1523	1500
William	Drewe	1536	butcher	1548	1556	–	1544
Roger	Drury	1534	saddler	1541	–	–	1534
John	Dryng	1452	mercer	1465	–	–	1455

Forename	Name	Free	Occupation	Cham	Sher	Mayor	CC
Ralph	Duffeld	–	innholder	1542	–	–	–
Richard	Dyatson	1521	baker	1533	–	–	–
George	Dycconson	1538	draper	1549	–	–	–
Robert	Dyconson	1501	merchant	1510	–	–	–
Robert	Ebchestre	1409	bower	1426	1434	–	1409
Robert	Ecop	1426	brewer	1444	–	–	1437
Anthony	Eden	–	merchant	1541	–	–	–
Robert	Elden	–	tanner	1539	1536	–	1518
John	Ellys	1475	waxchandler	1491	1503	–	1495
John	Elwald	1471	merchant	1486	1490	1499	1471
Robert	Elwald	1506	merchant	1530	1532	1539	1517
Ralph	Elwyk	1513	hosier/tailor	1535	1545	–	1527
George	Essex	1475	apoth/grocer	1494	1500	1509	1479
Peter	Esshe	1519	fisher	1544	1546	–	1527
John	Esyngwald	1414	mercer	1422	1431	–	–
Richard	Esyngwald	1369	merchant	1408	–	–	–
Thomas	Esyngwald	1384	merchant	1407	1411	1423	–
Robert	Fauconer	1415	merchant	1434	–	–	1431
Richard	Fell	1542	tanner	1546	–	–	–
John	Fereby	1447	merchant	1462	1471	1478 1491	1469
Wilfrid	Foddergyll	1530	locksmith	1546	–	–	–
Robert	Fons	1499	innholder	1513	1521	–	–
Edward	Forster	1467	draper	1490	1492	–	1473
William	Foster	–	roper	1538	–	–	1533
Thomas	Foulne(t)by	1479	merchant	1483	1488	–	–
Simon	Foxgill	–	butcher	1544	1545	–	1533
Richard	Foxgyll	1518	butcher	1534	1545	–	1418
Thomas	Freman	1483	tanner	1499	1501	–	1495
Sir William	Frost	–	–	–	–	1396–7 1400–4 1406–7	–
Thomas	Fynch	1469	merc/merch	1480	1484	–	1470
Robert	Gare	–	merchant	–	1408 1409	–	–
Thomas del	Gare	1385	mercer	–	1394	1420	1408
Thomas	Gare Jr	1418	merchant	1427	1428	1434	1408
Richard	Garnet	1470	parish clerk	1493	–	–	1490
William	Garnet	1499	merchant	1509	1510	–	1511
Edward	Garneter	1441	draper/dyer	1467	–	–	1469
John	Gascoigne	1388	woolman/ merchant	1418	1420	–	–
William	Gatesheud	1396	goldsmith	1412	1423	–	–
Robert	Gaunt	1396	mercer	1404	–	–	1408

Forename	Name	Free	Occupation	Cham	Sher	Mayor	CC
William	Gaunt	1427	merchant	1454	–	–	1416
John	Gaunte	1557	merchant	1488	–	–	1457
George	Gayle	1513	goldsmith	–	1530	1534 1549	1511
John	Geggez	1486	bower	1498	1509	–	1497
Roger	Geggez	1490	bower	1504	–	–	1511
John	Geldert	1486	shipwright	1512	1515	–	1494
John	Gelstrop	1535	tanner	1541	–	–	1473
Thomas	Gilbank	1490	armourer	1514	1517	–	–
Sir John	Gilliot Sr	1439	merc/merch	1451	1453	1464 1474	1455
Sir John	Gilliot Jr	1482	merchant	1482	1484	1490 1503	1480
William	Gilliot	1444	chapman/ mercer	1457	–	–	1449
Paul	Gillow	1495	merchant	1509	1514	1522	1509 (wife)
Peter	Gillyot	–	merchant	1523	–	–	–
William	Girlyngton	1405	draper	1421	1426	1440	–
John	Glasyn	1436	mercer	1452	1453	–	1451
Thomas	Glasyn	1452	mercer	1468	1469	–	1468
John	Goodale	1417	mercer	1441	1443	–	–
Thomas	Goodyere	1537	pewterer	1546	1548	–	1546
Thomas	Gookeman	1493	tanner	1527	–	–	–
Conan	Gossep	–	merch/merc	1487	–	–	1489
Thomas	Graa	–	–	–	1395	1398	–
Peter	Gray	1518	butcher	1539	–	–	1425
Robert	Gray	1415	draper	1431	1437	–	1423
Thomas	Gray	1469	goldsmith/ grocer	1482	1488	1497	1471
Henry	Grayve	1532	tapiter	1539	–	–	–
Thomas	Gregge	–	–	–	1521	–	1527
Robert	Grenbank	1483	tailor	1499	–	–	1498
Miles	Grenebank	1455	tailor	1481	1482	–	1471
Edmund	Grenebury	1546	draper	1549	1550	–	1546
William	Grysdale	1527	capper	1537	–	–	1544
Richard	Gurnard	1499	tapiter	1508	–	–	–
John	Gurnerd	1471	walker	1497	–	–	1474
William	Gutterswyk (Guttersworth)	1459	mercer	1465	–	–	–
Richard	Gybson	1484	cordwainer	1537	–	–	1526
Robert	Gyll	1458	pewterer	1471	1478	–	–
John	Hag	1471	merchant	1477	1480	–	1474
John	Hall	1481	tanner	1501	1504	1516	1483

Forename	Name	Free	Occupation	Cham	Sher	Mayor	CC
Ralph	Hall	1532	merchant	1538	–	–	–
Robert	Hall	1517	merchant	1532	1533	1541	1518
Robert del	Hall	1447	cordwainer	1449	–	–	1440
William	Halle	1508	tailor	1523	–	–	1514
Alan	Hamerton	1375	chapman/ merchant	1405	–	–	–
Robert	Hancok	1462	grocer	1471	1477	1488	1461
William	Hancok	1471	apothecary	1484	–	–	1475
Richard	Harbottel	–	merchant	1518	–	–	1512
Richard	Hardesang	1456	fishmonger	1478	1483	–	–
Thomas	Hardsang	1480	fishmonger	1492	–	–	–
John	Hargill	–	cornmerch	1541	–	–	1541
John	Harper	1471	merch/merc	1478	1481	1489	1473
William	Harper	1512	tailor/draper	1536	1541	–	1529
James	Harrygton	1523	merchant	1541	1549	1560	1533
William	Harryngton	1500	grocer/ merchant	–	1531	1536	1508
Robert	Harwod	1426	fletcher	1469	1472	–	1445
Thomas	Hassle (Hesill)	1395	–	–	1407	–	–
Thomas	Haukesworth	–	–	1405	–	–	–
William	Haxby	1431	tanner	1460	–	–	1445
Robert	Hekkylton	1509	fishmonger	1533	1535	1543	1530
John	Helmesly	1397	mercer	1405	–	–	–
Thomas	Hemylsay	1432	clerk	1453	1456	–	?1488
William	Henlake	1519	cornmerch	1543	–	–	–
William	Herryson	1533	wiredrawer	1541	–	–	1523
Matthew	Hertley	–	tailor	1536	–	–	–
William	Hewbank	1494	tanner	1530	–	–	1511
George	Hewetson	–	baker	1543	–	–	–
John	Hewetson	1527	glover	1537	–	–	1544
Thomas	Hewetson	1530	glover	1548	–	–	1543
Hugh	Hewley	–	vintner	1534	1525	–	1506
John de	Hewyk	1384	mercer	1396	1398	–	–
John	Hodlowe	1465	mercer	1479	–	–	1470
Robert	Hog	1529	girdler	1538	–	–	1530
John	Hogesson	1517	merchant	1524	1527	1533	1514
Thomas	Hoggeson	–	glover & innholder	1504	–	–	1489
William	Holbeck	1425	merchant sta	1437	1439	1449 1458 1470–2	1429
Nicholas	Holgate	1430	merchant	1445	1448	1459	1448
Henry	Holme	1489	draper	1516	1519	–	1501
Robert de	Holme	1395	vintnr/merch	1400	–	–	–

Forename	Name	Free	Occupation	Cham	Sher	Mayor	CC
William	Holme	–	barber	1529	–	1546	1506
Robert	Holme Jr	1390	merchant	–	1399	1413	–
John	Hoode	–	–	1520	–	–	–
Christopher	Horner	1490	mason	1511	1512	–	1482
William	Hoveden	1403	merchant	1423	–	–	1429
William	Hovyngham	1385	butcher	1416	–	–	founder
Thomas	Howden	1392	tanner	–	1397	–	–
Richard	Howe	1386	dyer	1399	1404	–	–
William	Hubank Sr	1465	tanner	1505	–	–	1486
William	Huby	–	horner	1495	1507	–	1500
Thomas	Hunter	1529	tanner	1543	–	–	?1489
George	Hutchonson	1537	baker	–	1549	–	1497
Richard	Hutchonson	1495	butcher	1520	1523	–	1508
Robert	Hutchonson	1479	goldsmith	1498	–	–	–
James	Huton	1537	tapiter	1545	–	–	–
John	Huton	1457	cook	1485	–	–	1477
John	Huton	1456	potter	1486	1491	–	1467
Richard	Huton	1535	tapiter	1546	–	–	–
John	Hydwyn	1519	merchant	1535	1536	–	1520
Alan	Hyll	1427	merchant	1436	–	–	1429
John	Ince	1436	merchant	1448	1455	–	–
Peter	Jakson	1510	merchant	1517	1520	1526	1510
Thomas	Jakson	1535	tanner	1537	–	–	1527
Robert	Jakson	1476	waxchandler	1489	–	–	1476
Thomas	Jameson	1486	merchant	1492	1497	1504	1489
Thomas	Jameson	1508	merchant	1519	–	–	1500
John de	Jarum	1385	mercer	1402	–	–	–
John	Johnson	1527	merchant	1542	–	–	1530
Robert	Johnson	1465	grocer	1484	1487	1496	1468
Robert	Johnson	1504	armourer	1537	–	–	1522
Thomas	Kendall	1466	marshal	1492	–	–	1478
John	Kendell	1440	weaver/draper	1452	–	–	1455
John	Kent	1438	merchant	1456	1460	1466	1450
Robert	Kirkby	1399	merchant	–	1406	–	
Sir George	Kirke	1475	merchant	1485	1487	1495	1483
						1512	
Thomas	Kirke	1411	mercer	1430	1432	1441	1427
Thomas	Kirkham	1402	merch/merc	1421	1422	1435	1415
Thomas	Knaton	–	–	1510	–	–	1470
Thomas	Knolles	1469	draper	1489	–	–	1480
William	Knolles	1453	draper	1465	1471	–	1455
Richard	Knyght	1408	chandler	1429	–	–	?1476
John	Kyrkeby	1399	dyer	1415	–	–	1421

Forename	Name	Free	Occupation	Cham	Sher	Mayor	CC
William	Lambe	1442	ironmonger/ merchant	1464	1468	1475	1449
George	Lampton	1532	merchant	1534	–	–	–
John	Lamyman	1491	literatus	1526	–	–	–
Nicholas	Lancaster	1472	clerk/lawyer/ merchant	–	–	1485 1493	1479
Ralph	Langley	–	merchant	1522	–	–	1490
John	Langton	1486	draper	1499	1509	– 1537	1486
Sir George	Lawson	1527	merchant	–	–	1530	1516
Peter	Ledaile	1517	baker	1533	1537	–	1535
Christopher	Ledale	1535	baker	1545	–	–	1528
John	Ledale	1530	merchant	1547	–	–	1534
William del	Lee	1366	bower	–	1402	–	1414
Richard	Lematon	1440	merchant	1446	1447	1455	1452
John	Leng	1518	potter	1538	–	–	1521
Christopher	Leremouth	1537	victualler/ innholder	1548	–	–	–
John	Lethelay	1441	butcher	1464	1467	–	–
William	Letwyn	1442	tailor	1477	–	–	1446
John	Lewes	1517	tailor/draper	1532	1537	1550	1520
John	Lightloupe	1463	mercer	1467	1470	–	1470
John	Lister	1507	draper	–	1526	–	1516
Laurence	Littester	–	–	1396	–	–	–
John	Lofthous	1396	vintnr/merch	1411	1417	–	1409
Robert de	Lokton	1387	draper	1404	1410	–	1408
John	Long	1467	miller	1488	–	–	1479
Thomas	Lounde	1489	saddler	1517	–	–	1491
James	Lounesdale	1459	tailor	1489	–	–	1495
William	Lourance Sr	1517	tilemaker	1533	–	–	1524
John de	Louth	1407	merc/merch	1414	1424	–	–
Richard	Louthe	1415	mercer	1423	1425	–	1415
William	Louthe	1415	mercer	1420	–	–	–
John	Lund	1542	goldsmith	1549	–	–	1545
William	Lund	1484	tanner	1506	–	–	1485
John	Lyllyng	1394	merc/merch	1418	1420	–	1439
John	Lyncoln	1483	merchant	1491	1502	–	1482
William	Lyons	1395	merchant	1407	–	–	–
Tristram	Lytster	1539	draper	1547	–	–	1546
Richard	Makblith	1482	clerk	1508	–	–	1489
Laurence	Mallom	1505	pewterer	1529	1531	–	1503
Robert	Man	1519	merchant	1536	–	–	1526
William	Man	1515	merchant	1528	–	–	–
Henry	Market	1412	merchant	1437	1442	–	1428

Forename	Name	Free	Occupation	Cham	Sher	Mayor	CC
Christopher	Marshall	1452	merchant/ gent	1460	1461	1473	1470
Henry	Marshall	1495	grocer	1501	–	–	1494
John	Marshall	1445	merchant sta	1455	1457	1467 1480	1470
John	Marshall	1438	draper	1455	1459	–	1470
John	Marshall		merchant	1521	1522	–	1515
William	Marshall	1432	tilemaker	1436	–	–	1449
William	Marshall	1478	smith	1490	–	–	1470
William	Marston	–	–	–	1407	–	–
John	Marton	1428	merchant	1447	1449	–	1432
Thomas	Maryot	1461	mercer	1466	1473	–	1470
Henry	Mason	1522	haberdasher/ innholder	1545	–	–	1530
John	Mason	–	innholder	1530	–	–	1512
Thomas	Mason	1510	hosier	1514	1518	1528	1513
Thomas	Mason	1522	parchmentmaker	1543	–	–	1530
William	Mason	1473	hosier	1493	–	–	1479
Richard	Merston	1459	cardmaker	1476	1479	–	–
John	Metcalfe	1482	merchant	1491	1494	1498	1482
Oliver	Middelton	1497	merchant	1502	1504	–	1500
Robert de	Middilton	1396	vintnr/merch	1405	1418	–	–
Anthony	Middylton	1509	merchant	1518	–	–	1507
Thomas del	More	1398	mercer	1406	1410	–	1510
John de	Moreton	1398	mercer	–	1408	1418	1432
William	Mowbray	–	tiler	1544	–	–	1498
William de	Muston	1378	fishmonger	1404	1407	–	1417
Thomas	Neleson	1433	merchant	1442	1447	1454	1465
William	Neleson	1488	merch/gent	1489	1495	1500	1483
John	Newton	1469	dyer	1473	1474	1483	1469
John	Norman	1469	merchant	1487	1490	–	1470
John	Norman	1503	merchant	1512	1514	1524	1512
John	North	1515	tanner	1527	1529	1538	1507
Richard	North	1491	tanner	1512	1513	–	1495
William	North	–	tilemaker	1497	–	–	1482
John	Northeby	1402	merchant	1408	1409	1416	1432 per exec
William	Northeby	1432	merchant	1435	1438	–	1455
Roger	Nyecolson	1532	pewterer	1548	–	–	1545
William	Ormesheued	1404	merchant	1411	1414	1425 1433	1414
Nicholas	Parant	1382	draper	1397	–	–	–
Thomas	Parkour	1487	tailor/draper	1500	1502	1520	1497
Gregory	Paycok	1547	merchant	1548	–	–	–
Robert	Paycok	1532	merchant	1537	1540	1548	–

Forename	Name	Free	Occupation	Cham	Sher	Mayor	CC
John	Peghen	1478	merchant	1540	–	–	–
William	Pennyngton	1535	merchant	1544	–	–	1534
John	Pereson	–	cooper	1545	–	–	?1516
William	Pereson	1532	tailor	1545	–	–	1513
Robert	Perte	1429	dyer	1443	1448	–	1439
Sir John	Petty	1471	glazier	1488	1494	1508	1474
Robert	Pety	1480	tapiter	1496	1499	–	1505
John	Pettyclerk	1399	vintnr/merch	1409	1412	–	1426 wife
Nicholas	Pierson	1457	dyer/yeoman	1474	1476	–	1459
Thomas	Pierson	1464	pewterer	1481	1482	–	1486
Richard	Plaskett	1437	merchant	1542	–	–	–
John	Plewman	1514	miller	1532	1533	–	1519
Robert	Plompton	1459	yeoman	1470	–	–	1489
William	Plumber	1466	plumber	1486	–	–	1470
John	Pollerd	1531	victualler/ moneyer	1550	–	–	1511
Otwell (Hetwell)	Portyngton	1483	merchant	1491	–	–	1482
Henry	Preston	1381	mercer	1400	1404	1422	–
John	Preston	1427	bower	1444	–	–	1431
Robert	Preston	1466	glazier	1496	–	–	1467
George	Pulley (Pulleyn)	1532	merchant	1535	–	–	1530
William	Pulley	1506	tailor	1544	–	–	1516
Ralph	Pulleyn	1502	goldsmith	1521	1526	1537	1506
Wilfrid	Pynder	1515	tapiter	1545	–	–	1519
John	Radcliff	1411	merchant	1425	1430	–	1414
John	Raghton	1422	clerk/merch	1424	1428	–	1423
William	Rakshawe	–	spicer/ apothecary	1466	–	–	–
John	Rasyn	1499	merchant	1513	1515	–	1500
Robert	Rede	1466	girdler	1495	–	–	1486
Thomas	Rideley	1424	merchant	1432	1434	1439	–
Thomas de	Rillyngton	1391	merc/merch	1402	–	–	–
Robert de	Ripon	1387	merchant	1398	–	–	1427
Peter	Roberdes	1433	fishmonger	1469	–	–	1473
William	Robinson	1478	weaver	1503	–	–	1426
John	Robynson	1486	tailor	1488 1489	–	–	1474
John	Robynson	1491	tailor	1492	–	–	1495
John	Robynson	1539	miller	1547	1561	–	1531
Peter	Robynson	1520	merc/merch	1533	1538	1544	1518
Richard	Robynson	1472	butcher	1493	–	–	1480
William	Roche	1485	waxchandler	1497	–	–	1481

Forename	Name	Free	Occupation	Cham	Sher	Mayor	CC
Thomas	Roderham	1397	–	1424	1432	–	–
William	Rodes	1414	dyer	1421	–	–	–
John	Roger	1488	baker	1508	1524	–	–
Thomas	Roger	1530	baker	1545	–	–	1535
Robert	Roos	1444	gentleman	1457	–	–	1464
John	Roston	–	–	1445	–	–	–
John	Rukeby	1502	draper	1428	1432	–	–
John	Russell	1429	merchant	1443	–	–	1437
Richard	Russell	1396	merc/merch	1409	1412	1421 1430	1426
Richard	Russell	–	vintner	1427	–	–	–
John	Rychardson	1507	painter & haberdasher	1525	1527	–	1517
Edward	Rycherdson	1541	pewterer	1547	–	–	–
Anthony	Sandwith	1517	bower	1542	–	–	1529
Thomas	Santon	1370	mercer	1399	1403	1414	–
Geoffrey (Godfrey)	Sauvage	1386	skinner	1411	1413	–	–
Richard	Savaige	1513	parish clerk	1537	1540	–	1511
Richard	Sawer	1446	mercer	1470	–	–	1484
Roger	Sawer	1479	tapiter	1495	1506	–	1476
John	Saxton	1486	innholder	1498	–	–	1487
Thomas	Scauceby	1429	mercer	1443	1446	1463	1439
William	Scauceby	1463	merchant/ gent	1473	–	–	1461
William de	Scawsby	1382	draper	1394	1399	–	–
Richard	Scotton	1437	merchant	1449	–	–	–
Thomas	Scotton	1458	merchant	1472	1476	1492	1457
Robert	Seirle	1447	fletcher	1479	–	–	1455
Roger	Selby	1402	spicer	1422	–	–	1416
William	Selby	–	–	–	1398	–	–
John	Semper	1445	dyer	1458	1462	–	1470
John	Shadloke	1525	merchant	1531	1534	1542	1519
John	Shawe	1469	merchant	1483	1486	1510	1467
John	Shawe	1524	merchant	1525	1528	1538	1519
Leonard	Shawe	1522	merchant	1529	–	–	1519
William	Sheffeld	1417	skinner	1452	1456	–	1427
Thomas	Shereburn	1517	cooper/ brewer	1535	–	–	1517
Richard	Sherwod	1416	–	1430	1436	–	1442
William	Shirburn	1426	bower	1453	–	–	1432
John	Shirwood	1411	fletcher	1425	–	–	1430
William	Shirwood	1430	–	1445	1454	–	1433
Thomas	Shoreswod	1442	skinner	1459	–	–	1445
John	Shylito	1536	notary & merchant	1548	–	–	–

Forename	Name	Free	Occupation	Cham	Sher	Mayor	CC
Stephen	Skelton	1538	cook	1550	–	–	1544
John	Skipwith	1441	merc/merch	1466	–	–	1476
John	Skryvnere als Fletcher	1510	tapiter	1534	–	–	?1502
William	Skynner	1445	vintner	1458	1461	–	1470
William	Skypton	1477	tailor/draper	1495	1501	–	1479
Thomas	Skyroo (Skirrow)	1508	armourer	1540	–	–	–
Henry	Smith	–	yeoman	1549	–	–	1425
John	Smyth	1506	tanner	1518	1526	–	1507
Robert	Smyth	1537	merchant	1547	–	–	1517
Thomas	Smyth	1533	merchant	1537	–	–	1526
Thomas	Snawden	1396	pewterer	1414	1416	1432	–
William	Snawsell	1437	goldsmith	1459	1464	1468	1455
John	Somerby	1396	dyer	1417	–	–	–
Richard	Sourby	1366	mercer	1416	–	–	–
John	South	–	–	–	1424	–	–
Martin	Soza	1530	goldsmith	1535	1545	–	–
William	Spence	1448	armourer	1475	1477	–	1455
Richard	Spencer	1398	mercer/dyer	1410	1414	–	1413
Ralph	Sproxton	1422	dyer	1436	–	–	–
Tristram	Stalleworth	1398	merchant	1419	–	–	–
Thomas	Standevyn	1538	innholder/ vintnr/notary	1539	1547	1559	1544
Richard	Standiche	1464	parish clerk	1499	–	–	–
William	Stanes	1426	mariner	1441	1445	–	1442
Alan	Stavelay	1489	merc/merch	1494	1499	1506 1519	1488
William	Stavelay	1487	merchant	1498	–	–	1481
John	Stillyngflete	1376	marshal	1409	–	–	–
William	Stockton	1420	merchant	1434	1437	1446 1461	1432
John	Stokdall	1476	merchant	1487	1491	1501	1477
Henry	Stokton	1441	fisherman	1469	1472	–	1457
John	Strensall	1420	barker	1446	1451	–	1452
Robert	Sumpter	1530	cook	1544	–	–	1526
John	Sutton	1472	mason	1500	–	–	1482
Robert	Swan	1526	cornmerch	1531	1536	–	1481
Richard	Sydes	–	–	1537	–	–	1526
Anthony	Symson	–	barber	1542	–	–	1534
James	Symson	1535	pewterer	1543	1547	–	–
Ralph	Symson	1511	pewterer	1525	1529	–	1534
Richard	Symson	1478	dyer	1490	–	–	1473
Robert	Symson	1458	fuller/walker	1502	1504	–	1489
Thomas	Taillour	1491	merchant	1496	–	–	1470

Forename	Name	Free	Occupation	Cham	Sher	Mayor	CC
Robert de	Talkan	–	–	1377	1380	1399	–
William	Tayte	1453	tailor/hosier	1476	1478	–	1453
Richard	Tebbe	1476	butcher	1494	–	–	1481
Leonard	Temple	1538	merchant	1549	–	–	–
Thomas	Temple	1524	glover	1543	–	–	1453
John	Tesedale	1457	baker	1474	–	–	1470
Brian	Tesymon	1516	cordwainer	1537	–	–	–
Richard	Tew	–	–	–	1506	–	–
William	Thikpenny	–	fishmonger	1537	–	–	1500
Richard	Thomlyngson	1516	tanner	1537	1539	–	1524
John	Thomson	1471	wiredrawer	1496	–	–	1494
Richard	Thomson	1513	butcher	1537	–	–	1524
William	Thomson	1497	glazier	1526	–	–	1515
Richard	Thoresby	1391	ironmonger	1406	–	–	1410
John	Thornton	–	grocr/merch	1505	1508	1514	1514
John	Thornton	1523	shipwright	1543		–	1534
Richard	Thornton	1414	walker	1441	1446	–	1441
Richard	Thornton	1481	grocer/spicer	1492	1495	1502	1486
Thomas	Thornton	1509	merchant	1531	–	–	1524
William	Thorp	1442	merchant	1458	1462	–	1470
Thomas	Thrisk	1460	tailor	1481	–	–	1470
John	Thriske	1427	merchant sta	1433	1435	1442 1462	founder
Peter	Thuresby	1391	spicer	1412	–	–	1411
John	Tirell	1447	weaver	1476	–	–	–
Sir William	Todd	1462	merchant	1471	1476	1487	1464–5
John	Tonge	1456	mercer	1462	1468	1477	1460
Thomas	Toone	1503	butcher	1519	–	–	1508
John	Touthorp	1438	butcher	1463	1466	–	1441
William	Touthorp	1415	butcher	1434	–	–	1443
John	Tramell	–	–	1507	–	–	1516
John de	Trepland	1383	vintner	1403	–	–	1409
Robert	Tubbac	1471	merchant	1489	–	–	1469
Thomas	Tubbac	1430	merchant	1454	–	–	1440
Robert	Turnour	1586	cook	1516	–	–	1489
John	Turpyn	1424	dyer	1435	1441	–	–
William	Undroune	1479	pardoner	1497	–	–	1475
John	Unkethorpe	1402	dyer	1414	–	–	–
John de	Useburn	1390	dyer	1402	1406	–	founder
Nicholas	Usflete	1412	merchant	1427	1433	1438	1430
Nicholas	Vicars	1471	grocer	–	1485	–	1473
Simon	Vycars	1500	chapman & haberdasher	1511	1513	1521	1513
John	Wady	1427	–	1440	–	–	–

Forename	Name	Free	Occupation	Cham	Sher	Mayor	CC
John	Waghen	1394	merchant	1413	1416	–	1409
Robert	Walker	1456	merchant	1468	–	–	1464
Robert	Walton	1433	fishmonger	1463	–	–	1445
John	Warde	1403	mercer	1413	1424	–	1423
Thomas	Warde	1498	barber	1537	–	–	1510
William	Warde	1462	draper	1475	–	–	1472
Richard	Wartre	1416	goldsmith/ merchant	1426	1429	1436 1451	1423
Edward/ Edm	Warwyk	1495	merchant	1506	–	–	1493
John	Wath	1520	merchant	1542	–	–	1520
John	Watson	1517	butcher	1536	–	–	1519
John	Watson	1518	tiler	1545	–	–	1521
Thomas	Watson	1451	tanner	1490	–	–	1475
William	Watson	1482	spicer	1495	–	–	1487
William	Watson	1533	merchant	1536	1541	1547	1530
John	Weddell	1514	merchant	1515	1516	–	1496
Charles	Wedderall	1522	cordwainer	1537	–	–	–
Anthony	Welburn	1489	baker	1496	–	–	1491
Thomas	Welles	1460	goldsmith	1489	–	–	1461
William	Welles	1453	vintnr/merch	1461	1468	1479	1473
John	Wetelay	1426	glover	1439	–	–	–
William	Wharton	1537	tanner	1547	–	–	–
John	White	1492	grocer	1505	1510	–	1494
Michael	White	1467	dyer	1479	1480	1494 1505	1469
William	White	1472	dyer	1480	1481	1491	1472
Richard	Whyte	1529	tailor	1537	1544	–	–
John	Whyte(eyron)	–	ironmonger	1494	–	–	1494
Robert	Whytfeld	1512	merchant	–	1519	1529	1521
Alan	Wilberfoss	1473	gent/merch	1474	1475	–	1470
Richard	Wilde	1532	tapiter	1540	–	–	–
Robert	Wilde	1501	merchant	1514	1520	1527	1490
Henry	Williamson	1456	merchant	1472	1473	–	1470
Richard	Williamson	1480	merchant	1493	–	–	1517
Wilfrid	Williamson	1517	tailor	1541	–	–	1530
William	Wilson	1487	fishmonger	1498	–	–	1492
William	Wilson	1491	goldsmith	1504	1505	1513	1492
Henry	Wodde	1507	waxchandler	1523	–	–	1509
William de	Wortlay	1379	skinner/tailr	1406	–	–	–
Thomas	Wrangwish	1458	merchant	1463	1466	1476 1484	1461
John de	Wrawby	1388	merchant	1399	1401	–	–
William	Wrawby	1411	vintner	1428	–	–	–

Forename	Name	Free	Occupation	Cham	Sher	Mayor	CC
Henry	Wright	1494	plumber	1520	–	–	1496
John	Wright	–	cooper	1527	–	–	1510
Richard	Wright	1519	baker	1542	–	–	1524
William	Wright	1449	notary	1451	1453	–	1441
William	Wright	–	merchant	1509	1511	1518 1535	1503
Edward	Wylkok	1535	glover	1550	–	–	–
Thomas	Wylkok	1535	glover	1550	–	–	–
Robert	Wyllie	1547	merchant	1550	–	–	–
Henry	Wyman	1387	merchant	–	–	1407–9	founder
Richard	Wynder	1474	pewterer	1495	1498	–	1483
William	Wynkburn	1397	–	1407	1413	–	–
Nicholas	Wyspyngton	1425	merchant	1431	1433	–	1431
William de	Wystowe	1361	potter	1398	–	–	–
John de	Wyton	1391	spicer	1401	1405	–	–
Robert de	Yarum	1389	mercer	1403	1417	–	1425
Sir Richard	York	1457	merchant sta	1460	1465	1469	1469 1482
Thomas	York	1498	merchant & gentleman	1502	–	–	1495
Bartholo-mew	Yorke	1527	merchant	1534	–	–	1525

APPENDIX 4: Officers and Financial State of the St Mary Gild in Holy Trinity, Hull, 1463–1537

This summary is based on KHRO BRA 87/8. Additional information has been derived from testamentary evidence, from Childs, *The Customs Accounts of Hull* and from Sheahan, *History of the Town and Port of Kingston-upon-Hull*.

* Undated account.
‡ Occupation unknown.
† Account not fully itemized.

Date	Alderman	Stewards	Balance		
			£	s	d
1463	John Grene merchant	John Tyttelot merchant/draper	8	6	1
		Roger Bussell merchant			
1464	Roger Bussell merchant	John Eland merchant	16	16	0
		Richard Burdon als Bowe			
1465	John Whytfeld merchant	Thomas Alcok merchant	19	19	10½
		Peter Herryson merchant			
1466	Thomas Alcok merchant	Robert Spofford merchant	19	0	7½
		Robert Fyssher merchant			
1467	Robert Fyssher merchant	Thomas Calthorne merchant	16	15	3½
		John Hoggeson merchant			
1468	Robert Alcok merchant	William Goldyng merchant	18	8	10½
		Robert Pellet merchant			
1469	Thomas Calthorn merchant	William Ratclyff merchant	18	11	4
		Thomas Knaresburgh ‡			
1470	John Day merchant	Thomas Berrige merchant	17	2	4
		John Ryddsdale merchant			
1471	Robert Marschall merchant	Thomas Phelip merchant	14	18	7
		Thomas Butteler merchant			
1472	Ralph Langton merchant	Burtyn Gilliot merchant	5	2	4
		John Typpyng merchant/mariner			
1473	Richard Buller ‡	William Davyll ‡	2	6	8
		John Karler ‡			
1474	Richard Bower [als Burdon]	Henry Swattok ‡	2	0	10
		William Haryngton ‡			
1475	Peter Herryson merchant	John Hardy merchant	0	7	4
		Hugh Narham ‡			

Date	Alderman	Stewards	Balance		
			£	s	d
1476	John Rydesale merchant	John Wylson merchant	7	5	7
		Thomas Wynflet ‡			
1477	John Hoggeson merchant	Robert Howlle merchant	4	5	1½
		John Grynder ‡			
1478	Bartram Gilliot merchant	Thomas Guseman ‡		NIL	
		Alexander Cardewell ‡			
1479	William Davyll ‡	William White merchant	–	6	9
		John Hapsham merchant			
1480	William White merchant	William Fyssher merchant	3	3	9
		William Doncaster ‡			
1481	John Hardy merchant	William Guseman barber/ waxchandler	3	15	3
		William Goldsmyth merchant			
1482	Thomas Guseman ‡	Thomas Andrew merchant	17	13	8
		John Shipman ‡			
1483	Thomas Butteler merchant	Richard Myrwyn merchant	12	1	2½
		John Oseller merchant			
1484	(No account. The 1485 account covers two years)		–	–	–
1485	Thomas Berrige merchant	Henry Hobson ‡	–	–	–
		Thomas Karre ‡			
1486	William Fyssher merchant	William Palframan merchant	7	17	4½
		John Baxter merchant			
1487	Robert Howle merchant	John Bulle merchant	22	5	6 ½
		Adam Milner ‡			
1488	Thomas Karre ‡ (No account – 4 blank pages)		24	15	7
1489	John Richardson merchant	John Nycholson ‡	26	10	7
		John Lawraunce ‡			
1490	Thomas Andrewe merchant	John Gylle merchant	24	0	0
		Walter Nicholson merchant			
1491	John Catham ‡	John Jespere merchant	26	0	0
		Richard Gybson merchant			
1492	Adam Androwson ‡	William Welesmee merchant	28	12	7
		John Staveley ‡			
1493	Henry Hobson ‡	Thomas Jenkson ‡	30	4	10½
		Robert Richman ‡			
1494	William Welesmee merchant	Thomas Burnette merchant	32	4	3½
		Thomas Smetheley ‡			
1495	Thomas Jenkynson ‡	Harman Wabyll ‡	36	4	8½
		Henry Paty bower			
1496	John Gylle merchant	Roger Busshell‡	34	19	7½
		Thomas Warner merchant			
1497	John Nicholson ‡	Edmund Stephenson merchant	49	16	8½
		Thomas Felton merchant			

Date	Alderman	Stewards	Balance		
			£	s	d
1498	Harman Wable ‡	Thomas Gunere ‡	29	6	8½
		Thomas Brompton merchant			
1499	Thomas Burnett merchant	Robert Somerby ‡	29	11	9
		Robert Hapsham merchant			
1500	Edmund Stephenson	William Tudenham ‡	22	12	0½
	merchant	John Gyles merchant			
1501*	Roger Bussell Jr. merchant	William Talyere ‡	26	1	1 †
		not known			
1502*	William Bank merchant	William Johnson merchant	21	12	4½ †
		Robert Haryson ‡			
1503	Thomas Powysse ‡	John Langton merchant	25	0	9
		Robert Cowling bower			
1504	Henry Pate bower	John Shipley ‡	26	13	4
		William Brice ‡			
1505	Thomas Warne merchant	Richard Doughty merchant	27	13	4
		John Harman ‡			
1506	Thomas Felton merchant	Anthony Potter merchant	20	9	7 †
		William Garnar ‡			
1507	John Gyles merchant	John Herryson goldsmith	20	0	0
		John Taverner ‡			
1508	John Stavelays ‡	Robert Vergus ‡	20	0	1 †
		William Drax ‡			
1509	William Johnson merchant	John Metson ‡	21	0	2 †
		John Crouche ‡			
1510	Richard Doughty merchant	John Langton merchant	23	6	11 †
		Robert Ethefeld ‡			
1511	Richard Doughty merchant	John Langton merchant	20	6	8
		Robert Ethefeld ‡			
1512	John Harman ‡	John Wardell goldsmith	26	6	8
		John Enderby ‡			
1513	John Herryson goldsmith	John Dubbyng ‡	22	6	8 †
		John Rogerson spicer			
1514	John Vergos ‡	Stephen Clare ‡	23	16	8 †
		Thomas Necolson ‡			
1515	John Wardall goldsmith	Thomas Thomson ‡	24	10	0 †
		William Knowll ‡			
1516	John Metson ‡	Robert Parker ‡	26	3	4 †
		Richard Deane ‡			
1517	John Enderby ‡	William Rand mariner	26	0	0 †
		Henry Holdernes cordwainer			
1518	John Rogerson spicer	Alan Armstrang mariner	25	14	4 †
		Richard Haburn ‡			

Date	Alderman	Stewards	Balance		
			£	s	d
1519	Richard Deyne ‡	William Roclyff ‡	27	7	8 †
		James Johnson merchant			
1520	William Thow yeoman and John Garden ‡ joint officers		23	0	0 †
1521*	Henry Holdernes	Richard Millet ‡	21	0	0 †
	cordwainer	William Sevyer ‡			
1522	William Rande mariner	William Browne mariner	23	0	0 †
		Thomas Smyth ‡			
1523*	Thomas Necolsone ‡	Richard Meyklay merchant	22	0	0 †
		James Johnson merchant			
1524*	James Johnson merchant	John Danyell ‡	24	3	4 †
		William Thruscross ‡			
1525	Richard Meyklay merchant	Aird Juryanson ‡	27	3	4 †
		Leonard Yngylsone ‡			
1526	James Johnson merchant	Richard Oversall ‡	29	0	0 †
		John Harryson Jr oil miller			
1527	Thomas Daniell ‡	Hugh Oversall ‡	31	0	0 †
		Edward Sheffeld merchant			
1528	Thomas Smythe ‡	Robert Walker merchant	32	6	8 †
		Ellis Stokdayll barber			
1529	William Browyn mariner	William Robinson shipwright	30	13	4 †
		Thomas Wharton ‡			
1530	John Hereson goldsmith	William Yong mariner	32	6	8 †
		James Roger merchant			
1531	William Thruscross ‡	Robert Car ‡	31	6	0 †
		Thomas Care ‡			
1532	William Clark ‡	Thomas Halwyke ‡	33	13	4 †
		Richard Colle ‡			
1533*	Edward Scheffeld merchant	William Caterall ‡	39	11	0 †
		George Hull merchant			
1534*	Robert Walker merchant	Henry Thruscross ‡	29	13	4 †
		Thomas Wylliamson ‡			
1535	Hugh Oversall ‡	John Thornton merchant	31	1	10 †
		Adam Huchonson ‡			
1536*	John Care ‡	George Calland ‡	32	6	8 †
		Henry Dynlaye ‡			
[1537]	James Huchison ‡	Robert Thorpe ‡	–	–	–
		James Clarke ‡			

APPENDIX 5: Yorkshire Gilds and Services Surviving to the Dissolution

Table based on testamentary evidence, *Certificates* I and II, PRO E 301, PRO E 315/67 II, *Calendar of Patent Rolls*, *VCR*, *VCR ER*, Kitching, 'The Chantries of the East Riding of Yorkshire', pp. 178–94.

Location: name of location. Second name is of chapel or, in large towns, of parish or religious house.

Gild: name of gild or service.

Beq: date of last known bequest.

1546: reference following PRO E 301 (except in the case of Hull) and nomenclature of institution in 1546 commissioners' certificates.

Feb 1548: reference following PRO E 301 and nomenclature of institution in February 1548.

Jul 1548: reference following PRO E 301 and nomenclature of institution in July 1548 commissioners' certificates (Pensions). Also includes information from Kitching 'The Chantries of the East Riding of Yorkshire' , from PRO E 315/67 II, from *Cal. Pat.*, *VCH* and some other sources.

Abbreviations: G = Gild, Ch = Chantry, Sv = Service, Sp = Stipend, Sa = Salary, Sch = School, Md = Maisondieu, K = Kitching. CP = Calendar of Patent Rolls, *VCH* = Victoria County History.

N.B. References other than testamentary and dissolution records are not included.

Location	Gild	Beq	1546	Feb 1548	Jul 1548 etc.
Badsworth WR	Trinity Sv	–	67/26 Sv	–	–
Bawtry WR	Trinity	1441	–	64/71 Ch/G	103m4d Ch/Sv
Bedale NR	St Mary	1506	66/130 Ch	63/88 Ch	–
Bempton ER	Corpus Christi	–	–	–	–
Bempton ER	St Mary & St Helen	–	–	–	119m6d Ch
Bempton ER	St Michael	–	–	–	Ch K185
Bessingby ER	St Mary Magdalene	–	–	–	CP EdVI 148 1549
Beverley Blakfrs ER	St Peter of Milan	–	–	72/Bev Ch HT	119m3 Ch HT
Beverley Holmkirk ER	St Mary	1396	–	72/Bev Ch	119m3 Ch
Beverley St John ER	Corpus Christi	1463	–	72/Bev Ch	119m3 Ch
Beverley St John ER	St John Beverley	1506	–	72/Bev Ch	119m3 Ch
Beverley St John ER	St John Baptist	–	–	72/Bev Ch/ Md	119m3 Ch/Md
Beverley St Mary ER	St Mary	1484	–	–	–
Birstall WR	Jesus Sv	–	E65/41 Sv	–	–
Birstall WR	St Mary Sv	–	E65/41 Sv	–	–

Location	Gild	Beq	1546	Feb 1548	Jul 1548 etc.
Bramham WR	unnamed	–	–	64/33 G/Sv	103m2d G/Sv
Bridlington ER	Trinity	1507	–	–	E315/67/II
					612v G
Broughton Craven ER	unnamed Sv	–	–	–	103m3
Burneston NR	St Mary	–	–	63/121 G	–
Burstwick ER	St Mary	–	–	–	VCH V 19
Burton Agnes ER	St Mary	1505	–	–	119m7d Ch
Campsall	St Mary Sv	–	67/66 Ch/Sv	–	
Carnaby ER	St John Baptist	1526	–	–	CP Eliz 237 1569
Catterick Bolton NR	St Mary Sv	–	66/129 Ch/Sv	63/95 Ch/Sv	–
Cottingham ER	Holy Trinity	–	–	–	119m6 Ch
Cottingham ER	St Saviour	–	–	–	119m6 Ch
Crofton WR	St Mary Sv	1529	E65/72 Ch/Sv	–	–
Danby NR	St Mary	1538	–	–	–
Darfield WR	St Mary Sv	–	67/55 Ch/Sv	–	–
Darton WR	St Mary Sv	–	67/17 Sv	–	–
Doncaster WR	Holy Cross	1505	–	64/25–6 Ch	103m2 Ch
				/Sv	
Doncaster WR	Trinity	1482	67/39 Ch	64/25–6 Ch	103m2 Ch
Doncaster WR	St James & St Sitha	1482	–	64/25–6 Cpl	103m2 Chpl
Doncaster WR	St Katherine	1482	67/37 Ch	64/25–6 Ch	103m2 Ch
Doncaster WR	St Mary	1482	67/38 Ch	64/25–6 Ch	103m2 Ch
Doncaster WR	St Mary Magdalene	1482	67/41 Chapel	64/25–6 Ch	103m2 Ch
Doncaster WR	St Thomas Cant	1505	–	–	–
Easington ER	St Mary	–	–	–	VCH 5 29
Fishlake WR	Trinity Sv	1528	67/65 Ch	64/20 Sv	103m1d Sv
Fishlake WR	St Mary Sv	1529	67/63 Ch	64/20 Sv/Sp	103m1d Sv
Flamborough ER	Trinity	1504	–	–	E310/32/192 54
Foston Wolds ER	Trinity	1538	–	–	119m7d Ch
Fraisthorpe ER	unnamed	–	–	–	VCH II 207 1556
Garton Wolds ER	St Mary	1430	–	–	–
Giggleswick WR	St Mary	1528	–	64/50 Ch	103m3 Ch
Great Driffield ER	Trinity	1528	–	–	Gild K185
Great Driffield ER	St Mary	1528	–	–	119m6 Ch
Guisborough NR	St Mary	1547	–	–	–
Hackness NR	St Hilda	1539	–	–	Whitby
					Cartulary
Halifax WR	Holy Cross Sv	–	65/31 Sp/Sv	64/66–8 Sv	103m4 Sv
				/Sp	
Halifax WR	Morrow Mass Sv	1526	65/36 Sv	–	–
Halifax WR	St Nicholas Sv	–	–	–	103m4 Sv
Halifax WR	St Mary Sv	1538	–	64/66–8 Ch	103m4 Sv/Ch
				/Sv	
Halifax Hep'stall WR	unnamed	–	65/34 Sv	64/66–8 Sp	–

Location	Gild	Beq	1546	Feb 1548	Jul 1548 etc.
Halsham ER	unnamed	–	–	–	*VCH* V 38
Hampsthwaite WR	unnamed	–	69/35 Ch/G	–	–
Hatfield WR	St Katherine Sv	–	67/4 Sv	64/22 Ch/Sv	103m2 Ch/Sv
Hatfield WR	St Mary Sv	–	67/3 Sv	64/22 Sv	103m2 Sv
Hatfield Stanford WR	St Mary Sv	–	67/5 Sv	64/22 Sv	103m2 Sv
Hatfield Thorne WR	St Mary Sv	–	67/6 Sv	64/18 Ch	–
Helmsley NR	Trinity	1506	66/143 Ch	–	–
Helmsley NR	St Mary	1506	–	63/122 Ch	–
Hollym ER	St Mary	1529	–	–	E315/67/II 613r G
Hornsea ER	Corpus Christi	1547	–	–	K187 G
Hornsea ER	Trinity	1539	–	–	K187 G
Howden ER	Trinity	–	–	–	CP 3&7 Ed VI
Huddersfield WR	St Mary Sv	–	65/14 Sp/Sv	64/62 Ch	103m4 Ch
Hull Trinity ER	Corpus Christi	1517	BRA87 Sp/Sv	63/Hull Sp /Sv	119m4 Sp
Hull Trinity ER	St Anne	1418	BRA87 Sa/Sv	63/Hull Sp /Sv	119m4 Sp
Hull Trinity ER	St James Sv	–	BRA87 Sv/Sa	63/Hull Sp	119m4 Ch
Hull Trinity ER	St Laurence	–	BRA87 Sa/Sp	–	–
Hull St Mary ER	St James	1418	BRA87 Sp/Sa	63/Hull Sp /Sv	–
Hull St Mary ER	St Anne	–	BRA87 Sp/Sa	–	119m4 Sp
Keighley WR	unnamed Sv	–	–	64/56 Ch/Sv	103m3d Ch/Sv
Keyningham ER	St Mary	–	–	–	*VCH* V 63
Kilham ER	St Laurence	1493	66/156 Ch	–	119m8 Ch
Kilnsea ER	All Saints	1504	–	–	E315/67/II 613r G
Kirkburton WR	St Mary Sv	–	65/43 Sv/Sp	64/69 Sp/Sv	–
Kirkburton WR	St Nicholas Sv	–	65/44 Sp	64/69 Sv	–
Kirkby Overblow WR	St Mary Sv	1540	–	64/34 Sv/Sp	103m2d Sv/Sp
Kirkheaton WR	St Mary Sv	1537	65/58 Sv	–	–
Leconfield ER	unnamed	–	–	–	E315/67/II 613r G
Loversall WR	unnamed Sv	–	–	64/24 Ch /Sv	103m2 Ch/Sv
Malton NR	St John Baptist	1450	66/149 Ch	–	–
Malton St Michl NR	St Mary	1407	66/150 Sp/Sv	63/134 Sp/Sv	–
Middleton Pick'g NR	St Mary	1528	66/117 Ch	–	–
Normanton WR	St Mary Sv	–	65/62–4 Ch	64/63 Ch/Sv	103m4 Ch/Sch
Northallerton NR	unnamed Sv	–	–	63/61 Sv	–
Otley WR	St Katherine	1518	–	64/32 Dn/Sv	103m2 Dn/Sv
Otley Fernley WR	unnamed Sv	–	–	64/32 Sv	–
Ottringham ER	St Mary	1529	–	–	119m5d G

Location	Gild	Beq	1546	Feb 1548	Jul 1548 etc.
Patrington ER	Holy Trinity	1540	–	–	Gild K188
Patrington ER	St Mary	1486	–	–	119m5 G
Pickering NR	St Mary	1496	66/68 Sv	–	–
Pocklington ER	St Mary	1494	66/108 Ch	–	119m6 Ch/Sch
Pontefract WR	Corpus Christi	1529	65/2 Ch	–	–
Pontefract WR	St Roch	1507	65/4 Ch	–	–
Pontefract WR	St Mary Sv	1540	65/3 Sv	–	–
Pontefract St Gil WR	St Mary	1529	65/5 Ch	–	–
Preston ER	St Mary Virgin	1537	–	–	119m5 Ch/Sp
Richmond NR	St John Baptist	1484	–	–	Wenham
Richmond NR	St Mary	1484	–	–	Wenham
Richmond NR	St Thomas	1484	–	–	Wenham
Ripley WR	St John Baptist Sv	–	71/7 Sv	–	–
Ripley WR	St Mary	–	71/6 Sv	–	E315/67/II 613r G
Ripon WR	Holy Cross	1529	–	–	Leach – Sch
Ripon WR	St Mary	1529	68/4 Ch	–	–
Ripon WR	SS Mary Wilfrid AS	–	68/9 Ch	–	–
Rotherham WR	Holy Cross Sv	–	67/69 Ch	–	–
Rotherham WR	St Katherine	1391	67/71 Sv	64/8–9 Sv/G	103m1d Sv/G
Rotherham WR	St Mary	–	67/70 Sv	64/8–9 Sv/G	103m1d Ch
Rudston ER	Trinity	1540	–	–	E315/67/II 613r G
Sandall Magna WR	St Mary Sv	–	65/62 Ch	64/64 Ch/Sv	103m4 Ch
Sandall Parva WR	St Nicholas Sv	–	67/33 Ch	64/23 Sv	103m2 Sv
Scarborough NR	St James	–	66/154 Ch	63/140 Ch	–
Scarborough NR	St Mary Assumption	–	66/153 Ch	63/138 Ch	–
Sedburgh WR	Holy Cross	–	–	64/59 Ch /Sch	103m3d Ch/Sch
Selby WR	St Mary Assumption	1441	–	–	103m2d Sv/Ch
Sheffield WR	Sv of 3 Priests	–	–	64/37 Sv/Sp	103m2d Sv/Sp
Sheriff Hutton NR	Holy Cross	1540	66/114 Ch	–	–
Silkeston WR	St Mary Sv	1528	6/58 Ch	–	–
Skeffling ER	unnamed	–	–	–	CP Ph&M 1558
Snaith WR	Trinity	–	65/17 Sv/G	–	–
Snaith WR	St Mary	–	65/16 Sp/Sv	–	–
Spennythorne NR	unnamed Sv	–	–	63/111 Sv/Sp	–
Spofforth WR	St Mary	1428	69/34 Ch	64/35 Ch	103m2d Ch
Spofforth WR	St Mary Magdalene	1428	–	–	–
Sutton-Forest NR	St Mary	1529	–	64/35 Money	–
Swine ER	St Mary	1547	–	–	119m5 G
Tadcaster WR	St Katherine	1438	69/19 Ch	64/1 Ch	–
Thirsk NR	St Mary	1485	66/111 Ch/Sv	63/51 Ch/Sv	–

Location	Gild	Beq	1546	Feb 1548	Jul 1548 etc.
Thorganby ER	St Helen	1547	–	–	*VCH* III 119 1566
Thorne WR	St Mary	–	67/6	–	–
Thorne WR	St Michael	–	67/7	–	–
Tickhill WR	Holy Cross	1430	67/47 G/Sv	–	–
Topcliffe NR	St Mary	1540	66/107 Sv/G	63/40 Ch/G	102/m4 G
Wakefield WR	Trinity	–	–	64/61 Ch	103m3d Ch
Wakefield WR	Morrow Mass Sv	–	65/62 Sv	64/61 Sv	103m3d Sv
Wakefield WR	St Mary	–	65/51 Ch	64/61 Ch/Sv	103m3d Ch
Wakefield St Jn WR	St Mary	–	65/55 Ch	64/61 Ch/Sv	103m3d Ch
Wath-u-Dearne WR	St Mary Sv	1538	67/19 Ch	–	–
Wath-u-Dearne WR	St Nicholas Sv	1538	67/20 Ch	–	–
Welwick ER	St Mary	1504	–	–	E315/67/II 613r G
Whitgift WR	Trinity	1474	65/21 G/Sv	–	–
Winestead ER	unnamed	–	–	–	CP EdVI 1548
Worsbrough WR	St Mary Sv	–	67/58 Ch/Sv	–	–
Wragby WR	St Katherine Sv	–	65/45 Perp Sp	–	–
Wragby WR	St Mary Sv	1527	65/46 Ch/Sv	–	–
York	Corpus Christi	1550	66/64 G	–	–
York	H Trinity Fossgate	1525	–	63/2 Sp	–
York	SS Chris & George	1543	66/20 Ch	63/1 Ch	–
York	St John Bapt Tailors	1546	–	–	–
York All Saints Pvt	St Mary	1512	66/72 Ch	63/7 Ch	–
York Trinity Priory	Trinity	1459	–	63/15 Ch–	–
York St Denys	St John the Baptist	1390	66/73 Ch	–	–
York St Denys	St Katherine	1503	66/73 Ch	–	–
York St Helen Stgt	SS Chris & Andrew	1399	–	–	–
York St Helen Stgt	St Mary	1478	66/86 Ch	63/3 Ch	–
York St Laurence	St Agnes	–	–	63/11 G Stock	–
York St Laurence	St Mary	1404	66/49 Ch	–	–
York St Michael Belfr	St Mary	1486	66/84 Ch	–	–
York St Saviour	St Anne	1527	66/80 Ch	63/25 Ch	–

BIBLIOGRAPHY

Primary Manuscript Sources

Beverley, Humberside County Record Office:
  BC II 3
  DD HE 31
Kingston upon Hull Record Office:
  BRA 8/4, 87, 87/8, 87/39, 87/45, 87/54, 87/53, 87/55, 87/52, 88
  BRE 5/1, 5/2, 5/3, 5/4
  D 142, 149, 15, 452A
  M 39
London, British Library:
  MS Lansdowne 403
  MS Harley 4795
London, Public Record Office: C 47/46/444–55, /116, /482:28–30
  E 301 63–73, 102–119, 131
  E 315/67/part II
  DL 38 11–13
York, Borthwick Institute of Historical Research:
  Probate Registers of Wills: PR 1–13
  Archbishops' Registers: Reg 10–29
  D&C5
  Y/Marg 36
  PRY/MS4
York, City Archive:
  A15
  AA24
  A/Y, B/Y Memorandum Books
  E 20, E 20A
  G C99:1–8, C100:1–6, C101:1–4, C102:1–3, C:103:1–2
  G 11A, G 13, G 14, G 70 33
York, Merchant Adventurers' Archive:
  Administration 1/1A–B, /2A–B, /2C, /3
  Guild of St Mary: Account Book 1358–69
York, Minster Library:
  MS Add. 2. The Bolton Book of Hours
  YML L2(4), L2(5)a, L2(5)b
  Wills vol. 4

Primary Printed Sources

Atkinson, J. C., ed., *The Whitby Cartulary*, 2 vols. Surtees Society 62 and 72 (1879–78).

Attreed, L. C., ed., *York House Books*, 2 vols. (Stroud, 1991).

Baildon, W. ed., *Select Cases in Chancery*, Selden Society 10 (1972).

Basing, P., ed., *Parish Fraternity Register: Fraternity of the Holy Trinity – Fraternity of Holy Trinity and Saints Fabian and Sebastian in the Parish of St Botolph without Aldersgate*, London Record Society (1982).

Brown, W., ed., *Cartularium Priorius de Gyseburne*, 2 vols., Surtees Society 86 and 89 d (1889–94).

Brucker, R., ed., *The Society of Renaissance Florence: A Documentary Study* (New York, 1971).

Caley J., ed., *Valor Ecclesiasticus Temp. Henry VIII Auctoritate Regia Institutus* (London, 1825).

Calendar of Charter Rolls.

Calendar of Close Rolls.

Calendar of Papal Registers: Letters.

Calendar of Patent Rolls.

Cawley, A. C., ed., *The Wakefield Pageants in the Towneley Cycle* (Manchester, 1958).

Childs, W. R., ed., *The Customs Accounts of Hull 1453–1490*, Yorkshire Archaeological Society 144 (1986).

Collins, F., ed., *Register of the Freemen of the City of York*, 2 vols., Surtees Society 96 and 102 (1897–99).

———, ed., *Wills and Administrations from the Knaresborough Court Rolls*, Surtees Society 104 (1902).

Cox, J. C., ed., 'Poll Tax of the East Riding', *Transactions of the East Riding Antiquarian Society*, 15 (1908).

Davies, R., ed., *Extracts from the Municipal Records of the City of York* (London, 1843).

Dobson, R. B., ed., *York City Chamberlains' Account Rolls 1396–1500*, Surtees Society 192 (1980).

Foster, C. W., ed., *Lincoln Wills*, 3 vols., The Lincoln Record Society (1914–30).

Gairdner, J., ed., *Letters and Papers, Foreign and Domestic, of the Reign of Henry VIII* (London, 1892).

Glasscock, R. E., ed., *The Lay Subsidy of 1334*, British Academy, Records of Social and Economic History NS 2 (Oxford, 1975).

Harris, M. D., ed., *The Register of the Gild of the Holy Trinity, St Mary, St John the Baptist and St Katherine of Coventry*, Dugdale Society 13 (1935).

Harrison, B., ed., 'The 1377 Poll Tax Returns for the North Riding', *Cleveland and Teeside Local History Society Bulletin* 10 (1970).

Horrox, R. E., ed., *Selected Rentals and Accounts of Medieval Hull 1293–1528*, Yorkshire Archaeological Society Record Series 140 (1983).

Hoskin, P., ed., 'Some late fourteenth-century Gild Accounts and Fabric Wardens' Accounts from the Church of St Margaret's, Walmgate, York', in *The Church in*

Medieval York, records edited in honour of Professor Barrie Dobson, gen. ed. D. M. Smith (York, 1999), pp. 75–86.

Hudson, W., ed., *Leet Jurisdiction in the City of Norwich during the Thirteenth and Fourteenth Centuries*, Selden Society 5 (1822).

Hughes, P. L. and J. F. Larkin, eds., *Tudor Royal Proclamations*, 3 vols. (New Haven and London, 1964–69).

Johnston, A. F., and M. Rogerson, eds., *Records of Early English Drama: York*, 2 vols. (Manchester, 1979).

Leach, A. F., ed., *Early Yorkshire Schools*, 2 vols., Yorkshire Archaeological Society Record Series 27 and 33 (1899–1903).

———, ed., *Beverley Town Documents*, Selden Society 14 (1900).

Lunn, J., ed., *The Register of the Fraternity or Guild of the Holy and Undivided Trinity and Blessed Virgin Mary in the Parish Church of Luton in the County of Bedford from 1475 to 1546* (Dunstable, 1984).

Northeast P., ed., *Boxford Churchwarden's Accounts 1530–1531*, Suffolk Records Society 23 (1982).

Owen D. M., ed., *The Making of King's Lynn: a Documentary Survey*, British Academy, Records of Social and Economic History NS 9 (1984).

Page W., ed., *The Certificates of the Commissioners Appointed to Survey the Chantries, Guilds, Hospitals, etc. in the County of York,* 2 vols., Surtees Society 91 and 92 (1894–5).

Peacock, E., ed., 'Subsidy Roll for York and Ainsty', *Yorkshire Archaeological Journal* 4 (1877), 170–201.

Percy, J. W., ed., *York Memorandum Book B/Y 1371–1596*, Surtees Society 186 (1969).

Raine, A., ed., *York Civic Records*, 5 vols., Yorkshire Archaeological Society Record Series 98, 103, 106, 108 and 110 (1939–46).

Raine, E. J., ed., *Wills and Administrations from the Knaresborough Court Rolls*, Surtees Society 104 (1902).

———, ed., *Wills and Inventories for the Registry of the Archdeaconry of Richmond*, Surtees Society 26 (1853).

Robinson, F. N., ed., *The Poetical Works of Chaucer* (London, undated).

'Rolls of the Collectors in the West Riding of the Lay Subsidy (Poll Tax) 2Richard II', *Yorkshire Archaeological Journal,* 5, 6 and 7 (1879–1883) 5: 1–51, 241–66, 417–32, 6: 1–44, 129–71, 306–42, 7: 1–31, 143–86.

Ryan, W. G., ed., *Jacobus de Voragine, The Golden Legend*, 2 vols. (Princeton, 1993).

Salter, H., ed., *Munimenta Civitatis Oxoniae*, Oxford Historical Society 71 (1917).

Sellers, M., ed., *York Memorandum Book A/Y*, 2 vols., Surtees Society 120 and 125 (1912–15).

———, ed., *The York Mercers and Merchant Adventurers 1356–1917*, Surtees Society 129 (1918).

Skaife, R. H., ed., *The Register of the Guild of Corpus Christi in the City of York*, Surtees Society 57 (1872).

Smith, T., ed., *English Gilds*, Early English Texts OS 40 (Oxford, 1870).

Smith, L. T., ed., *York Plays : The Plays Performed by the Crafts or Mysteries of York on the day of Corpus Christi in the 14th, 15th and 16th Centuries* (Oxford, 1885).

——, ed., *The Itinerary of John Leland in or about the Years 1535–1543*, 5 vols. (London, 1964).

Statutes of the Realm, 11 vols. (London, 1810–24).

Templeman, G., ed., *The Records of the guild of Holy Trinity, St Mary, St John the Baptist and St Katherine of Coventry*, Dugdale Society 19 (1944).

Testamenta Eboracensia, 6 vols., Surtees Society 4, 30, 45, 53, 79 and 106 (1836–1906).

Windeatt, B. A., ed., *The Book of Margery Kempe* (Penguin, London, 1985).

Secondary Printed Sources

Allison, K. J., ed., *The Victoria History of the County of York: East Riding*, 6 vols. (Oxford, 1969–89).

Aston, M., *Lollards and Reformers: Images and Literacy in Late Medieval Religion* (London, 1984).

——, ' "Caim's Castles": Poverty, Politics and Disendowment', in *The Church, Politics and Patronage in the Fifteenth Century*, ed. B. Dobson (Gloucester, 1984), pp. 45–81.

——, *England's Iconoclasts* (Oxford, 1988).

——, 'Corpus Christi and *Corpus Regni*: Heresy and the Peasants' Revolt', *Past and Present* 143 (May, 1994), 4–47.

Bainbridge, V. R., *Gilds in the Medieval Countryside: Social and Religious Change in Cambridgeshire c.1350–1558*, Studies in the History of Medieval Religion 10 (Woodbridge, 1996).

Baker, A. R. H., 'Changes in the later Middle Ages', in *A New Historical Geography of England*, ed. H. C. Darby (Cambridge, 1973), pp. 186–247.

Barron, C., 'The Parish Fraternities of Medieval London', in *The Church in Pre-Reformation Society*, ed. C. M. Barron and C. Harper-Bill (Woodbridge, 1985), pp. 13–37.

Bartlett, J. N., 'The Expansion and Decline of York in the Later Middle Ages', *Economic History Review*, 2nd Series, 12 (1959), 17–33.

Beadle R., 'The York Cycle', in *The Cambridge Companion to Medieval English Theatre*, ed. R. Beadle (Cambridge, 1994), pp. 85–108.

Beresford, M., *The Lost Villages of England* (London, 1954).

——, and J. G. Hurst, *Deserted Medieval Villages* (Guildford and London, 1971).

Bolton, J. L., *The Medieval English Economy 1150–1500* (London, 1980).

Bossy J., *Christianity in the West* (Oxford, 1985).

Bowden, P. J., 'Economic change: wages, profits and rents 1500–1750', in *Chapters from The Agrarian History of England and Wales*, gen. ed. J. Thirsk, 5 vols. (Cambridge, 1990), I, pp. 13–187.

Brigden, S., 'Religion and Social Obligation in Early Sixteenth-Century London', *Past and Present* 103 (1984), 67–112.

Britnell, R. H., 'The Proliferation of Markets in England, 1200–1349', *Economic History Review* 2nd Series 24 (1981), 209–21.

——, *The Commercialisation of English Society 1000–1500* (Cambridge, 1993).

Burgess C., ' "For the Increase of Divine Service": Chantries in the Parish in Late Medieval Bristol', *Journal of Ecclesiastical History* 36 (January, 1985), 46–65.

——, ' "By Quick and by Dead": wills and pious provision in medieval Bristol', *English Historical Review* 102 (1987), 837–58.

——, 'A Service for the Dead: The Form and Function of the Anniversary in Late Medieval Bristol', *Transactions of the Bristol and Gloucestershire Archaeological Society* 105 (1987), 183–211.

——, ' "A fond thing vainly invented": an essay on Purgatory and pious motive in later medieval England', in *Parish, Church and People: Local Studies in Lay Religion 1350–1750*, ed. S. J. Wright (London, 1988), pp. 56–84.

——, 'Late Medieval Wills and Pious Convention: Testamentary Evidence Reconsidered', in *Profit, Piety and the Professions in Later Medieval England*, ed. M. Hicks (Gloucester, 1990), pp. 14–33.

——, 'The Benefactions of Mortality: The Lay Response in the Late Medieval Urban Parish', *Studies in Clergy and Ministry in Medieval England*, ed. D. Smith, Borthwick Studies in History 1 (York, 1991).

——, and B. Kümin, 'Penitential Bequests and Parish Regimes in Late Medieval England', *Journal of Ecclesiastical History* 44 (Cambridge, 1993), 610–30.

Burton, J. E., *The Yorkshire Nunneries in the Twelfth and Thirteenth Centuries*, Borthwick Paper 56 (York, 1979).

Bush, M. L., 'The Richmondshire Uprising of October 1536 and the Pilgrimage of Grace', *Northern History* 29 (1993), 64–98.

Calvert, H., *A History of Hull* (London and Chichester, 1978).

Cameron, E., *The European Reformation* (Oxford, 1991).

Catto, J., 'Religious Change under Henry V', in *Henry V: The Practice of Kingship*, ed. G. L. Harriss (Oxford, 1985), pp. 97–115.

Charlesworth J., and A. V. Hudson, *Index of Wills and Administrations entered in the Registers of the Archbishops at York: The Archbishops' Wills*, Yorkshire Archaeological Society Record Series 93 (1937).

Childs W., *The Trade and Shipping of Hull 1300–1500*, East Yorkshire Local History Series 20 (1990).

Clarkson, C., *The History and Antiquities of Richmond in the County of York* (Richmond, 1821).

Collins, F., *Index of Wills in the York Registry*, 2 vols. Yorkshire Archaeological Society Record Series 6 and 11 (1889–91).

——, *Index of Wills etc. from the Dean and Chapter's Court at York 1321–1636*, Yorkshire Archaeological Society Record Series 38 (1907).

Cross, M. C., 'The Economic Problems of the See of York: Decline and Recovery in the Sixteenth Century', *Land Church and People*, ed. J. Thirsk, British Agricultural History Society 18 Supplement (Reading, 1970), pp. 64–81.

——, *Church and People 1450–1660: The Triumph of the Laity in the English Church* (London, 1976).

——, 'Parochial Structure and the Dissemination of Protestantism in Sixteenth Century England: A Tale of Two Cities', in *The Church in Town and Countryside*, ed. D. Baker, Studies in Church History 16 (Oxford, 1979), pp. 269–78.

———, 'Priests into Ministers: the establishment of Protestant Practices in the City of York 1530–1630', in *Reformation Principle and Practice: essays in honour of Arthur Geoffrey Dickens*, ed. P. N. Brooks (London, 1980), pp. 203–25.

Crouch, D. J. F., 'Paying to See the Play: The Stationholders on the Route of the York Corpus Christi Play in the Fifteenth Century', *Medieval English Theatre* 13 (1991), 64–111.

———, 'Religious Gilds in Late Medieval Yorkshire, 1400–1550: A Summary', *Medieval Life* 9 (York, Summer 1998), 30–2.

Cullum, P. H., *Cremetts and Corrodies: Care of the Poor and Sick at St Leonard's Hospital, York, in the Middle Ages*, Borthwick Paper 79 (York, 1991).

Cullum, P. H., and P. J. P. Goldberg, 'Charitable Provision in Late Medieval York: "To the Praise of God and the Use of the Poor" ', *Northern History* 29 (1993), 24–39.

Darby, H. C., *The Medieval Fenland* (Cambridge, 1940).

Davies, C. S. L., 'The Pilgrimage of Grace Reconsidered', *Past and Present* 41 (Dec. 1968), 54–76.

———, 'Popular Religion and the Pilgrimage of Grace', in *Order and Disorder in Early Modern England*, ed. A. Fletcher and J. Stevenson (Cambridge 1985), pp. 58–91.

Davis, R., *The Trade and Shipping of Hull 1500–1700*, East Yorkshire Local History Series 8 (1964).

Davies, R. G., 'Lollardy and Locality', *Transactions of the Royal Historical Society*, 6th series 1 (1991), 191–212.

Dickens, A. G., 'New Records of the Pilgrimage of Grace', *Yorkshire Archaeological Journal* 33 (1936), 305–6.

———, *The English Reformation* (London, 1964).

———, 'Secular and Religious Motivation in the Pilgrimage of Grace', in *The Province of York*, Studies in Church History 4 (Leiden, 1967), pp. 39–64.

———, *Lollards and Protestants in the Diocese of York, 1509–1555* (London, 1982).

Dobson, R. B., 'The Foundation of Perpetual Chantries by the Citizens of Medieval York', *The Province of York*, Studies in Church History 4 (Leiden, 1967), pp. 22–38.

———, *The Peasants' Revolt of 1381* (London, 1970, 2nd Edition 1983).

———, 'Admissions to the Freedom of the City of York in the Later Middle Ages', *Economic History Review*, Second Series 26 (1973), 1–21.

———, 'The Later Middle Ages, 1215–1500', in *A History of York Minster*, ed. G. E. Aylmer and R. Cant (Oxford, 1977), pp. 44–109.

———, 'Yorkshire Towns in the Late Fourteenth Century', *Miscellany* 18, Thoresby Society 129 (1983), 1–21.

———, 'Citizens and Chantries in Late Medieval York', in *Church and City 1000–1500: Essays in honour of Christopher Brooke*, ed. D. Abulafia, M. Franklin, M. Rubin (Cambridge, 1992), pp. 3–22.

Dodds, M. H. and R., *The Pilgrimage of Grace and the Exeter Conspiracy*, 2 vols. (London, 1915).

Doernberg, E., *Henry VIII and Luther: an Account of their Personal Relations* (London, 1961).

Drake, F., *Eboracum* (London, 1736).

Duffy, E., *The Stripping of the Altars* (Yale, 1992).

Edwards, J. F., and B. P. Hindle, 'The transportation system of medieval England and Wales', *Journal of Historical Geography* 17 (April 1991), 123–34.

Elton, G. R., *Reform and Reformation: England 1509–1558* (London, 1977).

English, B., *The Great Landowners of East Yorkshire 1530–1910* (Hemel Hempstead, 1990).

Everitt, A., 'The Marketing of Agricultural Produce, 1500–1640', in *Chapters from The Agrarian History of England and Wales*, gen. ed. J. Thirsk, 5 vols. (Cambridge, 1990), IV, pp. 15–156.

Farmer, D. H., *The Oxford Dictionary of Saints* (Oxford, 1978).

Fenning, H., 'The Guild of Corpus Christi', *The Guilds in Boston*, ed. W. M. Ormrod (Boston, 1993), pp. 35–9.

Fieldhouse, R., and B. Jennings, *A History of Richmond and Swaledale* (London, 1978).

Fisher, J. L., *A Medieval Farming Glossary* (London, 1968).

Fox, L., 'The Administration of Gild Property in Coventry in the Fifteenth Century', *English Historical Review* 55 (1940), 634–47.

Fryde, N., 'Gilds in England Before the Black Death', *Vorträge und Forschungen* 29 (1985), 215–29.

Ganderton, E. W., and J. Lafond, *Ludlow Stained and Painted Glass* (Ludlow, 1961).

Gent, T., *History of Hull* (York, 1735).

Given-Wilson, C., *The English Nobility in the Later Middle Ages: The Fourteenth Century Political Community* (London and New York, 1987).

Glasscock, R. E., 'England *circa* 1334', in *A New Historical Geography of England*, ed. H. C. Darby (Cambridge, 1973), pp. 136–85.

Goldberg, P. J. P., 'Female Labour, Service and Marriage in the Late Medieval Urban North', *Northern History* 23 (1986), 18–38.

———, 'Mortality and Economic Change in the Diocese of York, 1390–1514', *Northern History* 24 (1988), 38–55.

———, 'Women in Fifteenth-Century Town Life', in *Towns and People in the Fifteenth Century*, ed. J. A. F. Thomson (Gloucester, 1988), pp. 107–28.

———, 'Urban Identity and the Poll Taxes of 1377, 1379 and 1381', *Economic History Review*, 2nd Series 43 (1990), 194–216.

———, *Women, Work and Life Cycle in a Medieval Economy: Women in York and Yorkshire c1300–1520* (Oxford, 1992).

———, 'From Conquest to Corporation', in *Doncaster: A Borough and its Charters*, ed. B. J. Barber (Doncaster, 1994), pp. 47–121.

Gross, C., *The Gild Merchant*, 2 vols. (Oxford, 1890).

Haigh, C., *Reformation and Resistance in Tudor Lancashire* (Cambridge, 1975).

———, *English Reformations* (Oxford, 1993).

Hanawalt, B. A., and B. R. McRee, 'The guilds of *homo prudens* in late medieval England', *Continuity and Change* 7 (1992), 163–79.

Harrison, G. V., 'Agricultural Weights and Measures', in *Chapters from The Agrarian History of England and Wales*, gen. ed. J. Thirsk, 5 vols. (Cambridge, 1990), I, pp. 307–413.

Hatcher, J., *Plague, Population and the English Economy, 1348–1530* (Macmillan, 1977).

————, 'Mortality in the Fifteenth Century: Some New Evidence', *Economic History Review* 39 (1986), 19–38.

Heath, P., 'North Sea Fishing in the Fifteenth Century: the Scarborough Fleet', *Northern History* 3 (1968), 53–69.

————, *The English Parish Clergy on the Eve of the Reformation* (London and Toronto, 1969).

————, 'Urban Piety in the later Middle Ages: the Evidence of Hull Wills', in *The Church, Politics and Patronage in the Fifteenth Century*, ed. B. Dobson (Gloucester, 1984), pp. 209–34.

Henderson, J., 'Confraternities and the Church in Late Medieval Florence', in *Voluntary Religion: Studies in Church History* 23, ed. W. J. Shiels and D. Wood (Oxford, 1986), 69–83.

————, 'Religious Confraternities and Death in Early Renaissance Florence', in *Florence and Italy: Renaissance Studies in Honour of Nicholai Rubinstein*, eds. P. Denley and C. Elam (London, 1988), pp. 383–94.

Hey, D., *Yorkshire from AD 1000* (London, 1986).

Hill, Sir F., *Medieval Lincoln* (Cambridge, 1948).

Hill, R. M. T., 'Town Mice and Country Mice in the Province of York 1317–40', in *The Church in Town and Countryside*, Studies in Church History 16 (Oxford, 1979), pp. 201–5.

Hilton, R. H., *Peasants, Knights and Heretics*, Studies in Medieval English Social History (Cambridge 1976).

————, and Ashton, T. H., *The English Rising of 1381* (Cambridge 1984).

Hindle, B. P., 'The Road Network of Medieval England and Wales', *Journal of Historical Geography* 2 (1976), 207–21.

————, *Medieval Roads* (Aylesbury, 1982).

Horrox, R. E., *The Changing Plan of Hull, 1290–1620* (Hull, 1978).

————, *Richard III and the North* (Hull, 1986).

Huddleston, N. A., *A History of Malton and Norton* (Scarborough, 1962).

Hughes, J., *Pastors and Visionaries: Religion and Secular Life in Late Medieval Yorkshire* (Woodbridge, 1988).

————, 'The Administration of Confession in the Diocese of York in the Fourteenth Century', in *Studies in Clergy and Ministry in Medieval England*, ed. D. M. Smith (York, 1991), pp. 87–163.

James, M., 'Ritual, Drama and Social Body in the Late Medieval English Town' *Past and Present* 98 (1983), 3–29.

Jewell, H. M., *English Local Administration in the Middle Ages* (Newton Abbot, 1972).

————, 'The Cultural Interests and Achievements of the Secular Personnel of the Local Administration', in *Profession, Vocation and Culture in Later Medieval England*, ed. C. H. Clough (Liverpool, 1982), pp. 7–50.

Johnson, B., *The Acts and Ordinances of the Company of Merchant Taylors in the City of York* (York, 1949).

Johnston, A. F., 'The Plays of the Religious Guilds of York: The Creed Play and the Pater Noster Play', *Speculum* 50 (1975), 55–90.

Kermode, J. I., 'Urban Decline? The Flight from Office in Late Medieval York', *Economic History Review*, 2nd series 35 (1982), pp. 179–98.

———, 'Merchants, Overseas Trade, and Urban Decline: York, Beverley, and Hull *c.* 1380–1500', *Northern History* 13 (1987), 51–73.

———, 'Obvious Observations on the Formation of Oligarchies in Late Medieval English Towns', in *Towns and People in the Fifteenth Century*, ed. J. A. F. Thomson (Gloucester, 1988), pp. 87–106.

Kitching, C. J., 'The Chantries of the East Riding of Yorkshire at the Dissolution in 1548', *Yorkshire Archaeological Journal* 44 (1972), 178–94.

Knowles, J. A., *Essays in the History of the York School of Glass-Painting* (London, 1936).

Kolve, V. A., *The Play Called Corpus Christi* (Stanford, 1966).

Kümin, B. A., *The Shaping of a Community: The Rise and Reformation of the English Parish c. 1400–1560* (Aldershot, 1996).

Langdale, T., *A Topographical Dictionary of Yorkshire* (Northallerton, 1822).

Leggett, J. I., 'The 1377 Poll Tax Return for the City of York', *Yorkshire Archaeological Journal* 43 (Wakefield, 1971), 128–46.

Lund, J., 'Medieval Figures in Dunstable Priory Church', *Bedfordshire Magazine* 24 reprinted in pamphlet form (1993).

Mackie, P., 'Chaplains in the Diocese of York, 1480–1530: The Testamentary Evidence', *Yorkshire Archaeological Journal* 58 (1986), 123–33.

McCutcheon, K. L., *Yorkshire Fairs and Markets to the End of the Eighteenth Century*, Thoresby Society 39 (1940).

McHardy, A. K., 'Careers and Disappointments in the Late-Medieval Church', in *The Ministry: Clerical and Lay*, Studies in Church History 26, eds. D. Wood, W. J. Sheils and D. B. Foss (Oxford, 1989), pp. 111–30.

McKenna, J. W., 'Popular Canonisation as Political Propaganda: the Cult of Archbishop Scrope', *Speculum* 45 (1970), 608–23.

McRee, B. R., 'Religious Gilds and Regulation of Behaviour in Late Medieval Towns', in *People, Politics and Community in the Later Middle Ages*, eds. J. Rosenthal and C. Richmond (Gloucester, 1987), pp. 108–22.

———, 'Peacemaking and its Limits in Late Medieval Norwich', *English Historical Review* 109 (1994), 831–66.

———, 'Unity or Division? The Social Meaning of Guild Ceremony in Urban Communities', in *City and Spectacle in Medieval Europe*, eds. B. A. Hanawalt and K. L. Reyerson (Minneapolis, 1994), pp. 189–207.

Mill, A. J., 'The Hull Noah Play', *Modern Language Review* 33 (October 1938), 489–505.

Moran, J. H., *Education and Learning in the City of York*, Borthwick Paper 55 (York, 1979).

Morris, W. A., *The Medieval English Sheriff to 1300* (Manchester, 1927).

Muggleston, J., 'Some Aspects of the Two Late Medieval Chamberlains' Account Books of York', *Yorkshire Archaeological Journal* 67 (1995), 133–46.

Northeast, P., 'Parish Gilds', in *An Historical Atlas of Suffolk*, eds. D. Dymond and E. Martin (Bury St Edmunds, 1988).

Owen, D. M., *Church and Society in Medieval Lincolnshire*, History of Lincolnshire 5 (Lincoln, 1971).

Page, W., ed., *The Victoria History of the County of York*, 3 vols. (London, 1907–13).

——, ed., *The Victoria History of the County of York: North Riding*, 2 vols. (London, 1914–23).

Palliser, D. M., *The Reformation in York 1534–1553*, Borthwick Paper 40 (York, 1971).

——, *Tudor York* (Oxford, 1979).

——, 'Introduction: the parish in perspective', in *Parish, Church and People*, ed. S. Wright (London, 1988), pp. 6–27.

——, 'Urban Decay Revisited', in *Towns and People in the Fifteenth Century*, ed. J. A. F. Thomson (Gloucester, 1988), pp. 1–21.

Pevsner, N., *The Buildings of England: Yorkshire: The West Riding* (Harmondsworth, 1959).

——, *The Buildings of England: Yorkshire: York and the East Riding* (Harmondsworth, 1972, repr. 1992).

——, *The Buildings of England: Yorkshire: The North Riding* (Harmondsworth, 1966, repr. 1989).

Phythian-Adams, C., 'Ceremony and the Citizen: The Communal Year at Coventry 1450–1550', in *Crisis and Order in English Towns*, ed. P. Clark and P. Slack (London, 1972), pp. 57–85.

——, *Desolation of a City: Coventry and the Urban Crisis of the Late Middle Ages* (Cambridge, 1979).

Platt, C., *The English Medieval Town* (London, 1976).

——, *The Parish Churches of Medieval England* (London, 1981).

Pollard, A. J., *North-Eastern England During the Wars of the Roses 1450–1500* (Oxford, 1990).

Pollock, F., and F. W. Maitland, *The History of English Law before the time of Edward I*, 2 vols. (Cambridge, 1898).

Poos, L. R., *A Rural Society after the Black Death: Essex 1350–1525* (Cambridge, 1991).

Postan, M. M., *The Medieval Economy and Society: an Economic History of Britain in the Middle Ages* (London, 1972).

Poulson, G., *The History and Antiquities of the Seigniory of Holderness*, 2 vols. (Hull, 1841).

Raine, A., *Mediaeval York* (London, 1955).

Razi, Z., *Life, Marriage and Death in a Medieval Parish: Economy, Society and Demography in Halesowen 1270–1400* (Cambridge, 1980).

Rees Jones, S., ed., *The Government of Medieval York: Essays in commemoration of the 1396 Royal Charter*, Borthwick Studies in History 3 (York, 1997).

Reynolds, S., *Kingdoms and Communities in Western Europe 900–1300* (Oxford, 1984).

Rigby, S. H., ' "Sore Decay" and "Fair Dwellings": Boston and Urban Decline in the Later Middle Ages', *Midland History* 10 (1985), 47–61.

——, 'Urban "Oligarchy" in Late Medieval England', in *Towns and People in the Fifteenth Century*, ed. J. A. F. Thomson (Gloucester, 1988), pp. 62–86.

Rose, R. K., 'Priests and Patrons in the Fourteenth-century Diocese of Carlisle', in *The Church in Town and Countryside*, Studies in Church History 16 (Oxford, 1979), pp. 207–18.

Rosenthal, J. T., *The Purchase of Paradise – Gift Giving and the Aristocracy 1307–1495* (London, 1972).

———, 'The Yorkshire Chantry Certificates of 1546: An Analysis', *Northern History* 9 (1974), 26–47.

Rosser, G., 'Communities of Parish and Guild in the Late Middle Ages', in *Parish, Church and People: Local Studies in Lay Religion 1350–1750*, ed. S. J. Wright (London, 1988), pp. 29–55.

———, *Medieval Westminster 1200–1540* (Oxford 1989).

———, 'Parochial Conformity and Voluntary Religion in Late-Medieval England', *Transactions of the Royal Historical Society*, 6th Series 1 (London, 1991), 173–89.

———, 'Going to the Fraternity Feast: Commensiality and Social Relations in Late Medieval England', *Journal of British Studies* 33 (October 1994), 430–46.

Rowntree, A., *The History of Scarborough* (Dent, 1931).

Royal Commission on Historical Monuments (England), *An Inventory of the Historical Monuments in the City of York*, 5 vols. (London, 1962–81).

Rubin, M., 'Corpus Christi Fraternities and Late Medieval Piety', in *Voluntary Religion*, eds. W. J. Shiels and D. Wood, Studies in Church History 23 (Oxford, 1986), pp. 97–109.

———, *Charity and Community in Medieval Cambridge* (Cambridge, 1987).

———, *Corpus Christi: The Eucharist in Late Medieval Culture* (Cambridge, 1991).

———, 'Small Groups: Identity and Solidarity in the Late Middle Ages', in *Enterprise and Individuals in Fifteenth-Century England*, ed. J. Kermode (Stroud, 1991), pp. 132–48.

———, 'Religious Culture in Town and Country: Reflections on a Great Divide', in *Church and City 1000–1500 Essays in honour of Christopher Brooke*, eds. D. Abulafia, M. Franklin and M. Rubin (Cambridge, 1992), pp. 3–22.

Russell, J. C., *British Medieval Population* (Albuquerque, 1948).

Sacks, D. H., 'The Demise of the Martyrs: the Feasts of St Clement and St Katherine in Bristol, 1400–1600', *Social History* 2 (Hull, 1986), 141–69.

Sayles, G. O., 'The Dissolution of a Gild at York in 1306', *English Historical Review* 55 (1940), 83–97.

Scarisbrick, J. J., *The Reformation and the English People* (Oxford, 1984).

Schiller, G., *Iconography of Christian Art*, II, transl. J. Seligman (London, 1972).

Sheahan, J. J., *History of the Town and Port of Kingston-upon-Hull* (Beverley, 1866).

Sheail, J., 'Distribution of taxable population and Wealth in England during the Early Sixteenth Century', *Transactions of the Institute of British Geographers* 55 (1972), 111–26.

Sheppard, J. A., *The Draining of the Hull Valley*, East Yorkshire Local History Series 8 (1958).

———, *The Draining of the Marshlands of South Holderness and the Vale of York*, East Yorkshire Local History Series 20 (1966).

Sheppard Routh, P. E., 'A Gift and its Giver: John Walker and the East Window of Holy Trinity, Goodramgate, York', *Yorkshire Archaeological Journal* 58 (1986), 109–21.

Shiels, W. J., *The English Reformation 1530–1570* (London and New York, 1989).

Smith, D. M., *A Guide to the Archives of the Company of Merchant Adventurers of York*, Borthwick Texts and Calendars 16 (York, 1990).

Smith, R. M., ed., *Land, Kinship and Life-Cycle* (Cambridge, 1984).

Solloway, L., *The Alien Benedictines of York* (Leeds, 1910).

Southern, R., *Western Society and the Church in The Middle Ages* (London, 1970).

Stacpole, A., ed., *The Noble City of York* (York, 1972).

Swanson, H., *Building Craftsmen in Late Medieval York*, Borthwick Paper 63 (York, 1983).

———, 'The Illusion of Economic Structure: Craft Guilds in Late Medieval English Towns', *Past and Present* 121 (November 1988), 29–48.

———, *Medieval Artisans* (Oxford, 1989).

Swanson, R. N., *Church and Society in Late Medieval England* (Oxford, 1989).

Tanner, N. P., 'The Reformation and Regionalism: Further Reflections on the Church in Late Medieval Norwich', in *Towns and Townspeople in the Fifteenth Century*, ed. J. A. F. Thomson (Gloucester, 1988), pp. 129–47.

Thirsk, J., ed., *The Agrarian History of England and Wales*, IV, *1500–1640*, gen. ed. H. P. R. Finberg (Cambridge, 1967).

Thrupp, S., 'Social Control in the Medieval Town', *Journal of Economic History*, 1, Supplement (1941), 39–52.

Tillot, P. M., ed., *The Victoria History of the County of York: The City of York* (Oxford, 1961).

Toy, J., *A Guide and Index to the Windows of York Minster* (York, 1985).

Tuck, J. A., 'The Cambridge Parliament, 1388', *The English Historical Review* 331 (April, 1969), 237–38.

Tudor-Craig, P., 'Richard III's Triumphant Entry into York, August 29th, 1483', in *Richard III and the North*, ed. R. Horrox (Hull, 1986), pp. 108–20.

Vickers, N., 'The Social Class of Yorkshire Medieval Nuns', *Yorkshire Archaeological Journal* 67 (1995), 127–32.

Walker, J. W., *Wakefield: Its History and People* (Wakefield, 1939).

Weissman, R. F. E., *Ritual Brotherhood in Renaissance Florence* (New York, 1982).

Wenham, L. P., 'The Chantries, Guilds, Obits and Lights of Richmond, Yorkshire', *Yorkshire Archaeological Journal* 38 (1952–55), 96–111.

Westlake, H. F., *The Parish Gilds of Mediæval England* (London, 1919).

White, E., *The St Christopher and St George Guild of York*, Borthwick Paper 72 (York, 1987).

Whiting, R., *The Blind Devotion of the People* (Cambridge, 1989).

Woodward, D., 'The Accounts of the Building of Trinity House, Hull, 1465–1476', *Yorkshire Archaeological Journal* 62 (1990), 153–70.

Unpublished Works

Carpenter, C. E., 'The Office and Personnel of the Post of Bridgemaster in York, 1450–1499' (unpublished MA dissertation, York, 1995–96).

Crouch, D. J. F., 'A Medieval Paying Audience: The Stationholders on the Route of the

York Corpus Christi Play in the Fifteenth Century' (unpublished MA dissertation, York, 1989–90).

——, 'Piety, Fraternity and Power: Religious Gilds in Late Medieval Yorkshire 1389–1447' (DPhil. thesis, York, 1995).

Glass, S. L. T., ' "*Pro Anima Mea*": Aspects of Pious Devise in Fifteenth Century Scarborough' (unpublished MA dissertation, York, 1989).

Kulukundis, A., 'The *Cursus Honorem* in Fifteenth Century York' (unpublished MA dissertation, York, 1990–91).

Lamburn, A. D. J., 'Politics and Religion in Sixteenth Century Beverley' (unpublished DPhil. thesis, York, 1991).

Rees-Jones, S., 'Property, Tenure and Rents : Some Aspects of the Topography and Economy of Medieval York' (unpublished DPhil. thesis, York, 1987).

Skaife, R. L., 'City Officials of York', 3 volumes, unpublished MSS in York City Reference Library.

Smith, R. M., 1377 poll tax returns for Yorkshire (unpublished).

Wheatley, L. R., 'The York Mercers' Guild, 1420–1502 – Origins and Ordinances' (unpublished MA dissertation, York, 1993).

Wheeler, M., 'The Butchers of York, 1500–50' (unpublished MA dissertation, York, 1989–90).

White, E., 'Bequests to Religious Gilds in York', MS in BIHR.

Wyatt, D. K. J., 'Performance and Ceremonial in Beverley before 1642: an annotated edition of local archive sources' (unpublished D.Phil. thesis, York, 1983).

INDEX

Abson, Richard, of Swinton, 72 n.103
Acclom, Henry, merchant of Hull, 204–5
Ackworth (WR), 182
Addyson, Thomas, husbandman of
    Heworth by York, 159, n.190
Affordeby, John, master of hospital in
    Stillingfleet, 154 n.178, 156 n.187
Agnus Dei, 190
Alcock,
    family of, 203
    Robert, merchant and mayor of
        Hull, 203, 210 (Fig. 6.1)
    Thomas, merchant and mayor of
        Hull, 204, 210 (Fig. 6.1)
Aldborough (WR), 59, 157 n.188
    gilds in
    St Robert, 102
Aldbrough (ER), 67 (Fig. 2.4)
    gilds in
    St Mary, 69, 110–11
    St Peter, 69, 88
Aldestanmor, family of, 167
Aleby, Helen of Guisborough, 157 n.188
Aleby, Thomas of Broughton, 157 n.188
Alenson, Christopher, merchant of Hull,
    204
Allerton, see Northallerton
Almondbury (WR), 53 n.25
Alne (NR), 53 n.25, 98 n.71
    gilds in
    St Mary, 108
Ambler, Richard, of Halifax, 53 n.27, 72,
    76 n.128
Ambler, William yeoman of Seamer, 237
Andersone, Hugh, of Swine, 69 n.85, 221
    n.18, 241 n.149
Anstan, John, vicar of York, 155 n.180
Appleby (Apulbie etc.), Robert, cleric of
    Hull, 74
Armstrong, Alan, mariner of Hull, 205
    n.84
Armstrong, John, mariner of Hull, 88 n.8
Arthure, William of Heslington, 127
    n.49, 156 n.185
Arundel, Thomas, archbishop of York
    and Canterbury, 165

Ashburton (Devon), 230
Aske, Robert, 232, 234–5
Asshe, Robert, of Pocklington, 70 n.95
Asy, Peter, husbandman of Preston, 89
Athelstan, king, 39
Atkynson, Janet, of Sherburn, 102 n.103
Atkynson, John, of Sherburn, 102 n.103
Atkynson, Thomas, gild priest of Hull,
    74
Atkynson, William, butcher of Leeds, 71
    n.99
Austen, Thomas, sheriff of London, 17
Austwyk, Hugh, mercer of Pontefract,
    82 n.157, 86 n.5, 112
Auty, Simon, of Tickhill, 74 n.112
Avery, William, clerk of London, 17

Babthorpe, Sir William, king's
    commissioner, 237
Badsworth (WR),
    gilds in
    Holy Trinity Service, 76 n.124
Bainbridge (WR), 65
Bakehouse, William, of Doncaster, 82
Balderstone, Edmund de, chaplain of
    York, 166
Bank, William, merchant and mariner of
    Hull, 205 n.83
Barchard, William, of Patrington, 50 n.18
Barker, John, mayor of Hull, 210 (Fig.
    6.1)
Barker, John, of Catwick, 64
Barker, William, barker of Whitby, 88
Barker, William of Wistow, 224
Barnby (ER), 46 n.5
Baron, Edward, mayor of Hull, 210 (Fig.
    6.1)
Baron, William, mayor of Hull, 210 (Fig.
    6.1)
Barron, William, draper of Hull, 86 n.4
Barton, Thomas, spicer and alderman of
    York, 121 n.13
Barton, William, chaplain of York, 180
Barton, William, skinner of York, 126
    n.44, 135 n.88
Barwick in Elmet (WR), 157 n.188